PAGAN VIRTUE IN A CHRISTIAN WORLD

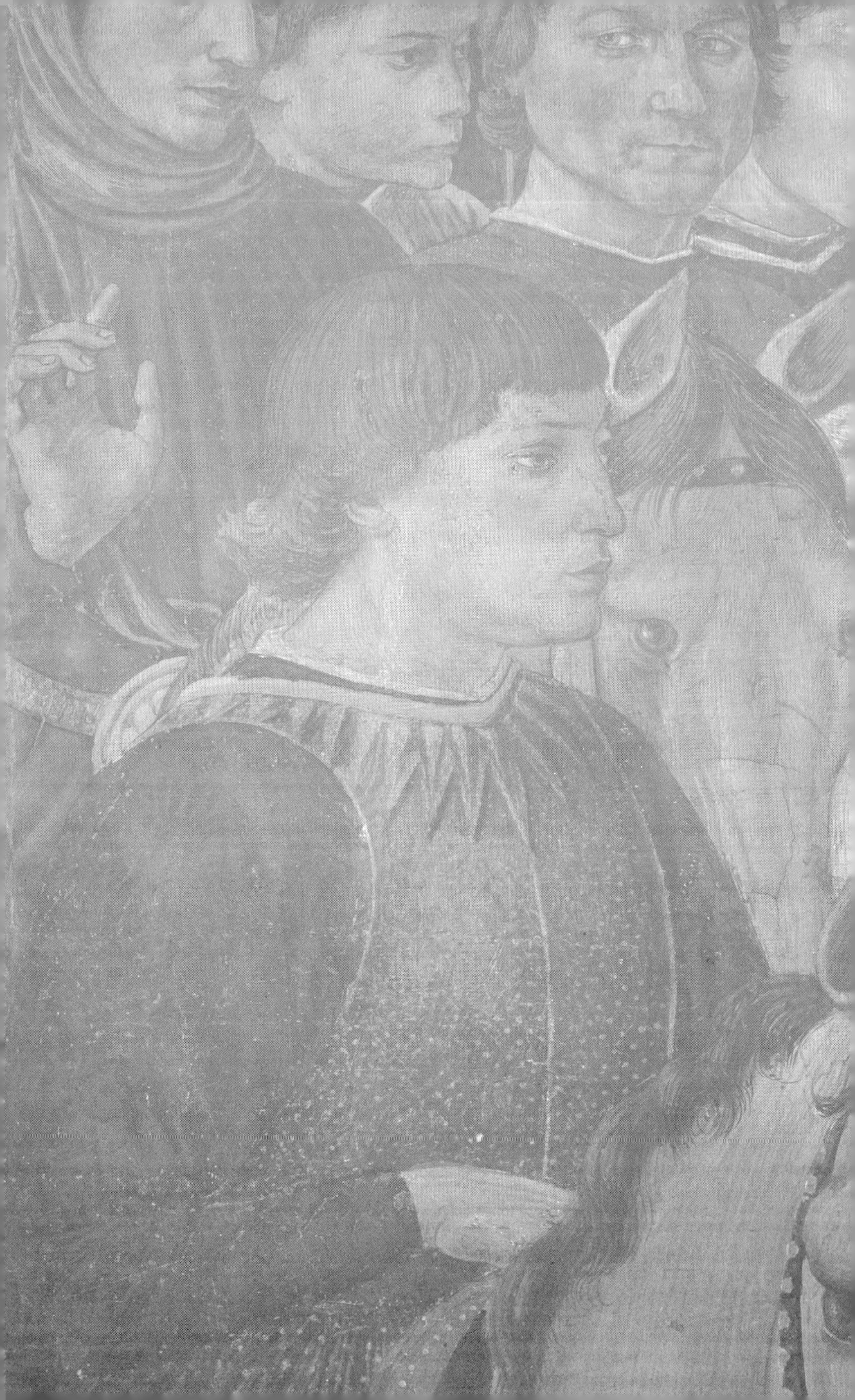

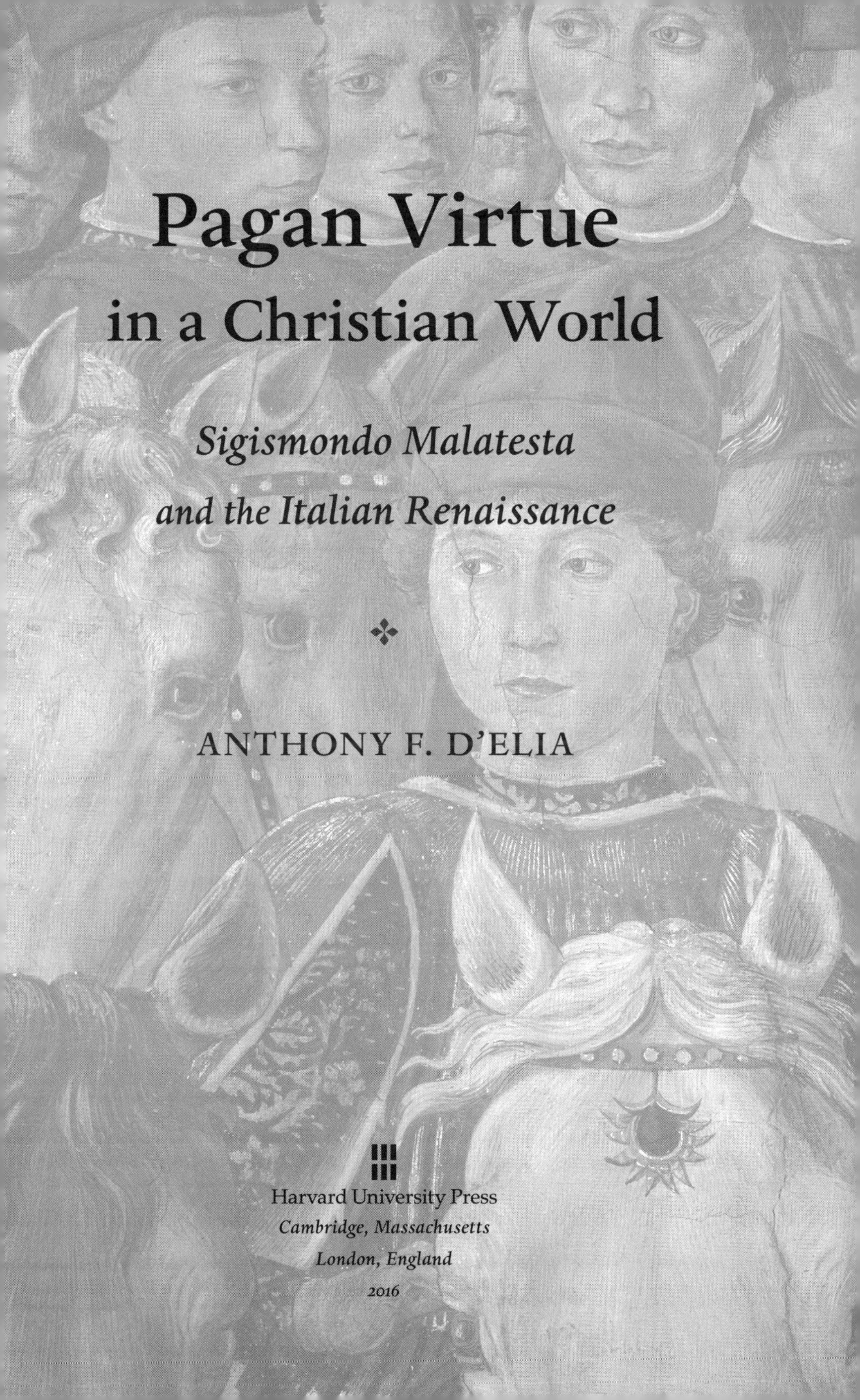

Pagan Virtue in a Christian World

Sigismondo Malatesta and the Italian Renaissance

ANTHONY F. D'ELIA

Harvard University Press
Cambridge, Massachusetts
London, England
2016

Printed in the United States of America

First printing

Title page background: Benozzo Gozzoli, Sigismondo Malatesta, detail of *Procession of the Magi,* fresco, 1459, Palazzo Medici, Florence. Photo: Erich Lessing/Art Resource, NY.

Library of Congress Cataloging-in-Publication Data

D'Elia, Anthony F., 1967–
Pagan virtue in a Christian world : Sigismondo Malatesta
and the Italian Renaissance / Anthony F. D'Elia.
pages cm
Includes bibliographical references and index.
ISBN 978-0-674-08851-1 (hardcover)
1. Paganism—Italy—Rimini. 2. Malatesta, Sigismondo Pandolfo, signore di
Rimini, 1417–1468. 3. Paganism in literature. 4. Italy—History—1268–1492.
5. Christianity and other religions. 6. Civilization, Medieval. I. Title.
BL432.D45 2016
945'.05092—dc23
2015015041

To my gorgeous girls, Lucy and Zoe,
who make life such a joy

Contents

Illustrations

PAGAN VIRTUE IN A CHRISTIAN WORLD

✣ 1 ✣

The Pope's Wrath and the Black Legend

On April 27, 1462, Sigismondo Malatesta (1417–1468), the lord of Rimini, was damned to hell. For on that day, Pope Pius II (1405–1464) performed a most unusual canonization: not to create a blessed man or woman a saint but to enlist Sigismondo Malatesta among the ranks of the damned and condemn him to hell while he still lived. That evening three life-size effigies of Sigismondo were burned in three squares of Rome. Each carried a placard stating: "This is Sigismondo Malatesta, king of traitors, enemy of God and man, condemned to the fire by the decision of the sacred college." Some Italian rulers were shocked and had tried to prevent it; others must have delighted in seeing a feared rival so utterly destroyed.[1] One ambassador called the whole affair a "carnivalesque masquerade."[2] Earlier popes had used excommunication as a potent weapon against recalcitrant rulers; subjects were no longer required to obey an excommunicated ruler, so the consequences could be dire. Pius had already excommunicated Sigismondo, but to little effect. The lord had not only kept his hold over Rimini but also reportedly dismissed the censure and "scornfully asked whether wine and food had flavor for the excommunicated."[3] Something stronger had to be used. No previous pope had ever performed a reverse canonization, nor has any pope done so since.

This anti-myth had a long afterlife. Before he was demonized, however, Sigismondo Malatesta constructed his own triumphal myth in the painting, sculpture, architecture, and literature that he commissioned. This book reconstructs the classical image of himself that Sigismondo Malatesta projected in fifteenth-century Italy (fig. 1.1). Pagan themes dominate Sigismondo's culture and imagined life from the revival of the ancient

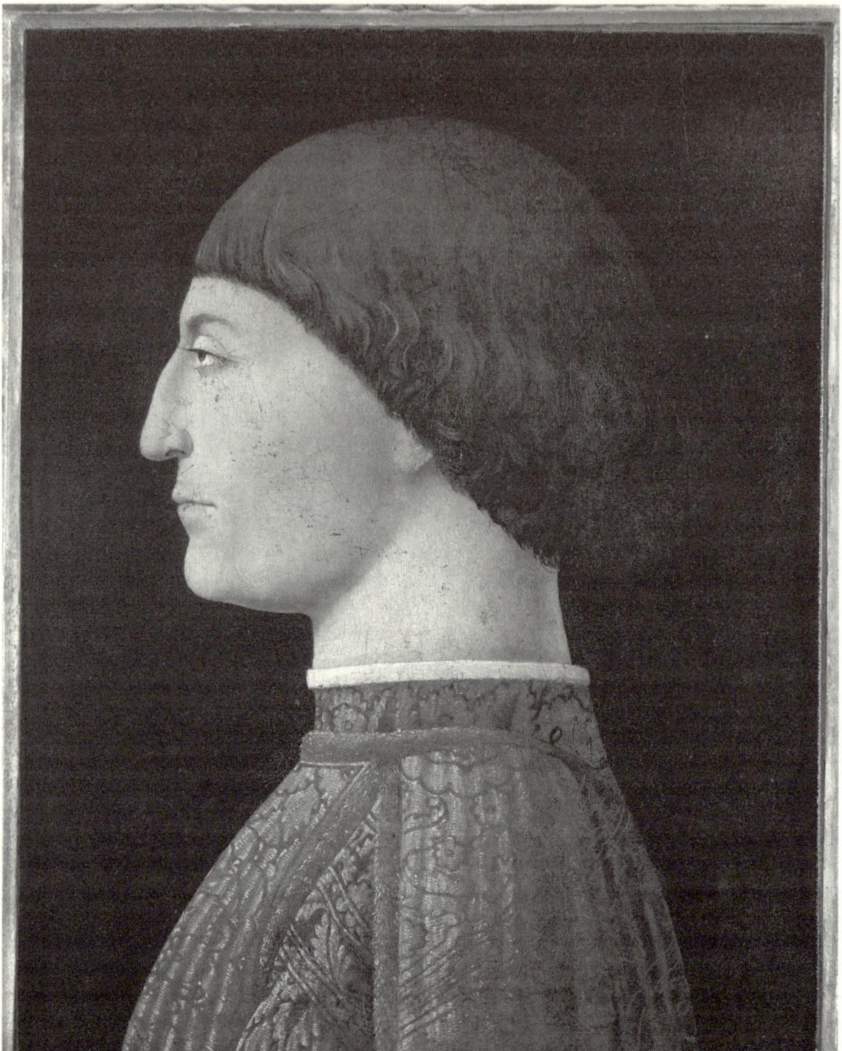

Fig. 1.1. Piero della Francesca, portrait of Sigismondo Malatesta, tempera and oil on panel, ca. 1452, Musée du Louvre, Paris. Photo: Erich Lessing/Art Resource, NY.

paideia, the Greek athletic ideal, and Sigismondo's Spartan upbringing to his sexual exploits and the astrological heights of his search for immortality, expressed in the sculptures of the Tempio Malatestiano and the epic verse of his court poets. Sigismondo nurtured a Greek revival in Rimini. Humanist writers used Homer and Plutarch to craft a portrait of Sigismondo as a classical hero who cultivated pagan virtue in hunting and the combat arts and who excelled in Homeric *arete* on the battlefields of fifteenth-century Italy. Classical literature, with all of its questionable pagan religious and moral images, was thus given new life in Rimini. Sigismondo's extremely pagan court culture is a prime example of the challenge to Christian values inherent in the very idea of Renaissance.

Damnation

A thirty-nine-page invective, known as the *Discipula veritatis* accompanied the bull condemning Sigismondo Malatesta. Pius II probably wrote it, but the fiscal canon lawyer Andrea Benzi delivered it in a public consistory. The formal bull, titled *Licet natura,* was much shorter.[4] The ostracizing and demonization in the *Discipula* are extreme. Pius warns the faithful that they cannot love Christ and Sigismondo. They must flee him "like a plague-carrier," since it is impossible to be with him "without the danger of infection." The pope dehumanizes Sigismondo:

> Drive away this poisonous beast. He is not a man, like it seems, but a brute beast born from a savage monster, a wild animal that has taken on human form, or perhaps a demon enclosed in an imaginary body. He is certainly the son of the devil . . . , whose mind he has and whose work he does. . . . Keep this monstrosity far from you, as if he were a precursor of the Antichrist.[5]

Now that Pius has taken the slightest shred of humanity away from Sigismondo, the violence of the spiritual murder of the reverse canonization seems justified and less cruel. "We know that he cannot be easily apprehended, since like a storybook monster he craftily changes himself into different forms."[6] After declaring him a heretic, rapist, murderer, traitor, gladiator, and other such epithets, the pope asserts:

> We excommunicate him again, call him anathema, and judge that he is to be cut from the body of the militant church like a putrid limb; and we forbid him to have any contact or commerce with the entire church of Christ, as if he were a sick and infected sheep. Unless he comes to his senses before leaving that muddy prison of the body, we allow his soul to be tortured by cruel demons and burned in the eternal flame. But while his body still has his soul within, we surrender it to the torments of evil spirits.

These tortures, however, are not given out of spite or a sadistic cruelty, for Pius says in the next line that this is a way to bring Sigismondo to his senses and salvation. But this is Sigismondo's last chance. "If," Pius says, "he retains his wickedness until the end, we order that his spirit be damned and his cadaver abandoned without any funeral, images, praise, or pomp; and that after being half burned on putrid wood his body should be torn apart and scorned by dogs and wild animals at night."[7] In Christian thought damnation is for the soul; the soul suffers physically only when it cannot sever its attachment to the body. Pius has let his classical imagination go and offers a Homeric damnation—that of the body left unburied, torn apart and humiliated by dogs. The ultimate humiliation for Christians comes in the form of the repulsive idea of cremation—but only halfway, in order to leave something for the dogs.

What had Sigismondo done to deserve such a fate?

In his *Commentaries,* Pius calls Sigismondo a "slave to avarice" and "so unbridled in his lust that he violated both his daughters and his sons-in-law." The pontiff focuses on sexual perversion: "As a boy he often played the bride; later, he who had so often taken the woman's part used other men like whores. No marriage was sacred to him. He raped Christian nuns and Jewish ladies alike; boys and girls who resisted him he would either murder or torture in terrible ways . . . he surpassed every barbarian in cruelty."[8] Pius's accusations against Sigismondo are legion. The pope demonized Sigismondo as savage, greedy, treacherous, and seized by an uncontrollable animal lust. Sigismondo's vanity and pagan belief in his own divinity gave Sigismondo no moral restraint. Pius accused Sigismondo of murdering priests and raping a German duchess. When a noble lady had rejected his advances, he bludgeoned her to death, then had his way with her corpse. He sodomized a young boy and made a brother pimp his sister. He had his first wife killed and murdered his second to make way for his mistress, whom he had seduced when she was twelve.[9] Few of these accusations had any but the vaguest basis in reality.

One of the most infamous crimes of which Pius accuses Sigismondo is murdering his half-brother. Galeotto Roberto Malatesta (1411–1432) was such a devout man that if he had not been forced to marry and rule Rimini, he would have gladly become a Franciscan friar and spent his life pursuing sanctity. As it was, Galeotto became a third-order Franciscan and neglected his duties to wife and subjects. Pope Eugenius IV (1383–1447) reprimanded Galeotto repeatedly; a ruler, he said, should spend his time listening to his subjects and caring for the state, not in prayer and isolation. Galeotto's single act of governance seems to have been his effort to take away privileges from the Jews and have them expelled from Rimini.[10] He was revolted by sex and could not perform his marriage duty, despite the urgings of his confessor. From an early age, Galeotto practiced extreme Christian asceticism. He wore a horsehair girdle, flagellated himself daily, and slept on a wooden plank. Galeotto spent his life helping the poor, and, although he miraculously healed the sick, he reveled in the pain of his own infected foot that never healed. He died at age twenty-one and was soon after beatified. Had Sigismondo not had such conflicts with the church, Galeotto might even have been canonized. After Galeotto's death, a local cult grew around his remains, and miracles were reported.[11]

When Galeotto became ruler of Rimini, Sigismondo, according to the entirely biased account of Pius, "tried by plots to depose him from his throne, persuading the people of Rimini that a man was of no use as head of a state who spent all his days and nights in church and, lost in contemplation of the divine, had no time for the society of men." Pius asserted that Sigismondo had poisoned his brother, called him a "foolish man," and complained about people "worshiping my brother."[12] This was, however, far from the truth. Sigismondo's devotion to his brother's memory was exemplary. In his renovation of San Francesco, Sigismondo probably initially planned to place his half-brother's tomb in the façade of the church to make it a pilgrimage site and help the canonization process.[13]

One of the only accusations with some foundation relates to this church—Sigismondo commissioned the rebuilding of San Francesco, which later became known as the Tempio Malatestiano. I refer to the church as the Tempio, because Sigismondo's humanists called it a *templum*. Pius accused Sigismondo of being a pagan of being so enamored of antiquity that he worshipped pagan deities and transformed a Christian church into a pagan temple that was dedicated to him and his mistress. Zodiac signs with their gods, ancient heroes, and the glorification of Apollo, the sun god, had replaced the Christian saints and God. This church, Pius says, "was so full of pagan works of art that it seemed less a Christian sanctuary than a temple where heathens might worship demons."[14] Though a Christian church, the Tempio Malatestiano is full of an unprecedented amount of pagan imagery.

Pius II himself was hardly a severe moralist or anti-pagan zealot. Before becoming pope in 1458, Pius was Aeneas Piccolomini. He was passionate about classical literature and happily answered the sexual needs of his body. He wrote to the imperial chancellor: "The caresses of a wife can be so enticing that it is easy to forget about work responsibilities. Nevertheless, you can keep your wife in a place close to the curia, so that she can often embrace you."[15] Sexual pleasure within marriage was both natural and good. But Aeneas did not condemn sex outside marriage. On the contrary, he enjoyed it himself on at least one occasion. In a letter addressed to his father in 1443, Aeneas waxed at length about an evening he spent with a Tuscan maid.[16] Like Moses, Aristotle, and all the other great men, he said, he fell under the spell of a beautiful girl in an inn, snuck into her room, and enjoyed sensual bliss. Instead of expressing shame, Aeneas praised his actions as a natural part of youth and boasted about the son that he fathered that evening.[17] The future pope's Latin compositions also contained romantic and vaguely pornographic stories of lovers in the tradition of Plautus and Ovid. In his bestselling *The Story of Two Lovers* (1444), Aeneas told a tale of love, seduction, and abandonment in the chivalric romance tradition. In the *Chrysis,* he described the lust of two clerics and their inability to maintain their vows of celibacy. The dialogue was lighthearted and comical, but Aeneas was actually making a serious argument for a more balanced view of human nature.[18] Given all this, it is surprising that a pope who had had such a positive view of sensuality should be so shocked by Sigismondo's alleged sexual exploits. Of course, most of Sigismondo's alleged sexual crimes involved use of violence and force that would have been unacceptable even in the sexist society of fifteenth-century Italy. The rape of a German noblewoman, for example, was seen as a terrible violation. Pius also accuses Sigismondo of sodomy, necrophilia, and other taboo acts.

As a cardinal, Aeneas had been somewhat of a rebel against the Church hierarchy. He had been an advocate of a more democratic church and wrote tracts in favor of conciliarism, the idea that a church council had greater authority than a pope. But even before becoming pope, Aeneas became disillusioned with these ideas, and as pope he sought to destroy the conciliarist movement and asserted a monarchic view of the papacy.[19] The invective against Sigismondo took place at the same time as Pius's attack on conciliarism. The pope saw Sigismondo's open defiance as a threat to papal power, as Sigismondo ruled over the papal state of Rimini but refused to pay dues and acknowledge the pope as the city's true master. Pius's eloquent Latin style in his autobiographical commentaries and frequent references to classical antiquity earned him the distinction of being called a humanist pope. In any other circumstances, Pius and Sigismondo Malatesta might have been friends, as they shared the same interests in classical antiquity, patronized classical architecture in Rimini and Pienza, and enjoyed learned company. Instead, their enmity became legendary.

Sigismondo's city, Rimini, was part of the Papal States, and the Malatesta had been papal appointed protectors of the city since the thirteenth century.[20] Sigismondo, who had ruled the city since 1434, had served two earlier popes as a mercenary captain and enjoyed great favor from the papacy. Starting at the age of thirteen, Sigismondo won a string of brilliant military victories. He fought for all the major city-states in Italy: the Church, Florence, Venice, Milan, Siena, and Naples.[21] Despite or perhaps because of his successes, however, Sigismondo spread himself thin, had too many different employers, and consequently lost trust. Then in 1447, after taking money from Alfonso of Aragon, the king of Naples, to fight on his behalf in Tuscany, Sigismondo reneged without returning his advance payment and joined the defense of Florence. If Sigismondo's switch saved Florence from collapse, his betrayal of Alfonso ultimately led to his own destruction. After this, Alfonso used every means possible to attack Sigismondo. He sent a mercenary army into Malatesta lands, negotiated the exclusion of Sigismondo from the 1454 Peace of Lodi, and incited the popes against the lord of Rimini.

Malatesta power nevertheless expanded and grew steadily until 1455, when Calixtus III (1378–1458) became pope. Calixtus was a Spaniard and allied with Sigismondo's enemy in Naples. The new pope demanded the payment of long-overdue tributes and the return of numerous papal territories that Sigismondo had seized. Sigismondo refused and managed to avoid serious punishment, but the frequent skirmishes and tensions with the papacy depleted his finances, and because of this, in 1458 all work on one of the greatest artistic monuments of the Renaissance, the Tempio Malatestiano, had to be permanently suspended. Matters for Sigismondo got much worse after the elevation of Pope Pius II in 1458. Pius II continued the battle with Sigismondo over land and tribute. Early in his papacy, Pius had tried to reconcile Sigismondo with the Aragonese, but the lord of Rimini was so recalcitrant that the pope lost his temper and purportedly shouted that no appropriate punishment could be found for his crimes.[22]

Pius II also had strong personal reasons for disliking Sigismondo. Pius was from Siena and showed great favor to his hometown. During his papacy, in fact, the Vatican was full of Sienese, and the only traditional canonization Pius performed was of Saint Catherine of Siena (1347–1380).[23] In 1455 Siena had employed Sigismondo to defend against a usurper. When for whatever reason Sigismondo did not immediately engage the enemy, the Sienese accused him of treachery and executed his second in command. Sigismondo barely escaped under darkness. Years later Pius still complained bitterly about Sigismondo's treatment of his native city.

Sometime in 1461 the pope called for a formal trial, charging Sigismondo with treachery, heresy, and immorality. No records of the judicial process survive, and most likely a trial never actually occurred. A formal process, however, is discussed in the papal invective. Pius writes that he wished to have a full judicial investigation of the accused, to see "whether [Sigismondo] could be shown guilty or innocent." He ordered Cardinal Nicholas of Cusa (Cusanus) (1401–1464) to conduct an exhaustive investigation, "to examine witnesses, inspect writings, and do everything necessary in such cases toward a sentence."[24] Pius was no theologian, but the man he put in charge of the Malatesta case, Nicholas of Cusa, was one of the foremost philosophers and theologians of the quattrocento.

Cusanus had himself been accused of pantheism and defended the late medieval mystic Meister Eckhart (1260–1328) on the same charge. He was a renowned Platonist, who used the mathematical certainty of numbers and geometry to understand God. He sought contradictions and saw God as the ultimate coincidence of opposites, in whom the finite meets infinity. Cusanus used the idea of a circle to argue his point. A circle is the opposite of a straight line: it is finite, as the straight line is infinite. But the bigger the circle, the straighter is the line of its circumference. When stretched to infinity, the circle's edge becomes a straight line; thus opposites coincide. God is like a circle in that he contains both the finite and infinity. Cusanus was a great exponent of syncretism and the perennial wisdom, which included doctrines from pagan antiquity. He did not reject the pagan deities as false or demonic but saw them as pre-Christian manifestations of God. They were another way in which finite man could understand infinite God. The pagan gods were just different faces of the same God. Cusanus's syncretic beliefs also included Islam. In *Sifting the Qur'an* (*Cribratio Alkoran*, 1461) he demonstrated how the Koran and the Bible were in harmony and revealed different shades of the same truth.[25] Few other Renaissance intellectuals would have had more in common and more sympathy than Cusanus for Sigismondo's blending of pagan and Christian religious ideas. Pius may have seen the irony of putting Cusanus in charge of the case against Sigismondo.[26]

In his *Commentaries*, Pius himself says that whereas Catherine's canonization "requires proof, Sigismondo's crimes are manifest" and therefore require no proof.[27] But the *Discipula* relates that after interviewing "trustworthy witnesses," Cardinal Cusanus "by public edict advised [Sigismondo] to present himself within thirty days in person to offer reasons why he should not be condemned for [his] crimes."[28] The summons was posted in numerous places, and there was "no doubt of him not receiving it. But Sigismondo disobeyed and scorned the orders of the vicar of Christ. . . . He neither came nor sent another in his place."[29] The cardinal nevertheless continued his investigation and confirmed by "reliable witnesses" the "popular rumor and hearsay" about Sigismondo's crimes. He then reported his findings in a secret consistory.[30] The papal invective drew on the cardinal's investigation and served as the public justification for what had been determined behind closed doors. No trial records survive. The *Discipula veritatis* therefore is the most complete record of the process.

Pius begins the invective with a description of Sigismondo's treachery, lying, and continual attacks on papal lands. He then relates his own experience of Sigismondo's mendacious character. This extensive story highlights the intensely personal nature of the pope's vitriolic hatred of Sigismondo.

The pope describes how on an earlier occasion Sigismondo had begged on his knees for mercy; "with tears and wailing, a dejected face and torn clothes, and a fake eloquent speech" of contrition, Sigismondo "deceived us."[31] For his robberies, adulteries, murders, sacrileges, and his perversion of divine and human law, Sigismondo "deserved a thousand deaths." But "his teary-eyed prayers convinced us into thinking that he had learned his lesson—we did not believe that he said one thing but had something else in his heart."[32] Pius thought of the ancient Malatesta house and "turned his eyes away from" Sigismondo's many crimes and forgave him. Sigismondo had sworn to all of Pius's conditions, which consisted in giving back a number of territories to the Church and his great rival Federico da Montefeltro, returning owed money, and not fighting for two years. If he had been content with "his part of the settlement," Sigismondo "would have been rich."[33] Sigismondo thanked the pope and promised to be good. But "although he confirmed that he had been polluted by every kind of sin, Sigismondo never confessed to telling lies." Pius thought the reason for this was "either because he had been trained in bad habits and thought there was no difference between true and false; or because these were mere words to him, so that what we called true he called false." So, Sigismondo's inability to make correct moral choices came either out of ignorance or purely out of moral relativism. "As soon as peace prevailed and he returned home, Sigismondo resumed his old way of life, his sordid pleasures, savagery, and infidelity. . . . He thus returned to his true character."[34]

The pope seemed most angered by the fact that Sigismondo had lied to him, manipulated him, and was ungrateful. Sigismondo wronged Pius personally. "We erred in thinking that the heart of Pharaoh had changed and Judas converted. . . . We thought that he should be forgiven and that the liar does not always lie. . . . We trusted him and believed that the worst kind of wild beast could show itself trustworthy and human."[35] Papal reprimands, excommunication, and ostracism had not been enough. In Pius's view, greed, violence, deceit, and lust so dominated Sigismondo's behavior that there had to be something diabolical. Sigismondo had allied himself with the devil and may even have been possessed by a demon. "Whatever comes from you is suspect," Pius writes. "Your letters are read as if they come from the house of Lucifer. Your words and writings hold as much trust as the utterances from demons' mouths."[36] Twenty pages later Pius returns to the subject of ingratitude: "Would that Sigismondo had recognized the gifts of God, and that he had lived his life, if not as a grateful man, at least not as an ungrateful demon."[37] Sigismondo was deemed inhuman; he was a "wild beast," who was incapable of trust.

Medieval theology and literature had certainly allowed for the possibility that some men were so evil that their souls had already been imprisoned in hell, while demons inhabited their living bodies. Dante placed the souls of Fra Alberigo and Branca d'Oria in the lowest circle of hell for fraudulent counsel, while demons wreaked havoc in the damned sinners' bodies among the living. Later, in a delightful novella, Machiavelli had fun with a devil inhabiting bodies to experience marriage.[38] Such literary depictions may be playful, but the Church took demon worship and diabolical possession seriously. The great witch-hunt centuries had their theoretical foundation in the fifteenth century, with the publication of the *Hammer of Witches* (*Malleus Maleficarum,* 1487). This manual vividly described how demons took possession of bodies in order to seduce poor women. Pius's references to the devil would have recalled more than a rhetorical trope of invective. Pius asserts that the devil was controlling Sigismondo and, in fact, among other nefarious acts had "driven him to murder his wife."[39] Pius's reverse canonization merely formalized Sigismondo's pact with the devil.

Pius was well aware of the novelty of his spiritual attack. He calls it an "ironic canonization by a new and unusual mode of speech." He immediately confesses: "I do not know whether these procedures are valid, but a different canonization was heard today than that of Saint Bernardino of Siena (1380–1444). Our predecessor Pope Nicholas enlisted him among the heavenly saints on account of his many good works, whereas Sigismondo Malatesta on account of his infinite wicked deeds was enlisted by Andrea Benzi among the worst demons."[40] Pius therefore sees the act as a reversal of a normal canonization. In his memoirs, he similarly compares it to his own canonization of Catherine of Siena. Bernardino and Catherine not only supplied the procedural precedent in their canonization processes, but their influential writings and sermons probably also helped shape Pius's view of Sigismondo and the unique punishment he devised for him.

Bernardino of Siena's Vision of Hell

When he imagined hell, Pius may very well have recalled Bernardino's vivid descriptions of the place in numerous sermons.[41] The Franciscan preacher had been the main form of public entertainment in Siena, when Aeneas (the future Pope Pius) was studying law there from 1425 through 1427. Like other Sienese, Aeneas was spellbound by Bernardino's call for spiritual and moral reform. Pius later said that Bernardino's sermons almost convinced him to become a Franciscan.[42] In his treatise on Europe, Pius praises Bernardino for his eloquence and outstanding learning, and calls him "another Paul."[43] Crowds of people gathered to hear Bernardino's sermons, Aeneas says, "as if he were a prophet."[44] In his bull for Catherine of Siena's canonization, Pius praised Bernardino extensively as eloquent and beloved of God.[45]

Bernardino had spearheaded the witch-hunt craze that began in the early fifteenth century. In the Middle Ages, Church authorities had focused on learned magicians who could conjure up demons and make them do their bidding. But starting in the fifteenth century the devil changed his tactics. Instead of enticing the learned, he now started preying on the weak—spinster females in particular, who because of their poverty and lack of family could be easily convinced to sell their souls and make a pact with the devil.[46] Bernardino was one of the first to recognize this diabolical shift. In 1426 he unmasked witches in Rome and watched with pride as the flames burned two women; one was not strangled, which was the normal procedure, but left to writhe in pain as her flesh cooked.[47] Nothing, he declared, pleased the heavens more than the incense of a witch's charred body. One witch, Bernardino claimed, had confessed without torture that she had sucked the blood of thirty babies, and after murdering her own son, made a magical powder out of him.[48] Such grotesque accusations drew upon the same kind of sick imaginings of sin that later fueled Pius's invective against Sigismondo.

Pius himself later recalled a technique that the preacher used to attract his congregation in Perugia in 1425: Bernardino promised to show the faithful the devil on an appointed day. Then, when a larger audience than usual attended and demanded to see the devil, Bernardino told them to look at each other. Bernardino described a world in which devils were not only constantly waging war for the souls of the faithful but often inhabiting their actual bodies and making them do evil. Sometimes multiple devils inhabited bodies, as when Bernardino upbraided a poor woman for spitting in church, saying that "she was one whose body contained thousands of devils." The forces of evil had such a strong presence in his sermons that a contemporary accused him of obsessing about the devil: "One hears coming from your mouth in your sermons the name of the devil no less than that of Jesus."[49] Bernardino saw the devil and his accomplices everywhere.

Bernardino was just as vivid when he talked about hell and damnation. In a sermon on the need for perseverance, Bernardino pointed a finger at a woman in the audience and yelled:

> O woman, when you burn your finger [at the stove], as you feel the pain, remember the hot house and think: "Oh how painful it must be to stay always in the fire [of hell]!" And when you prick your finger with a needle, remember the stings of the scorpions in hell, which torment the damned souls. When smoke gets in your eyes, remember the smoke of hell. When you smell anything disgusting, remember hell and be afraid.[50]

Bernardino insisted that the damned would be punished by a corporeal fire. Against the argument that the spiritual soul could not be harmed by a material flame, Bernardino asserted that anything was possible for an omnipotent God and that such a punishment was fitting for souls that clung to sensual pleasure and material existence.

Theologians had been troubled by the concept of eternal punishment, which a merciful God would surely not allow. And was it not unjust that a single injury done by man in time should be continually and eternally punished? Bernardino followed the scholastic argument that since the injury was against an infinite good, the punishment must be infinite. "By every mortal sin," Bernardino declares, "an infinite injury is done to God, and to an infinite injury an infinite punishment is due."[51] Such arguments about damnation and images of hell surely reverberated in Pius's mind, when he thought of the infinite sins that Sigismondo had perpetrated against God, the pope, and his church. Sigismondo's infinite sins had to merit an infinite and eternal punishment. Pius's radical demonization of Sigismondo—his belief that Sigismondo was in fact a devil—may very well have come from the vivid images and paranoid world of evil that Bernardino's sermons dramatically described in lavish detail.

These ideas may have also reverberated in Rimini, where Bernardino preached in June 1431. He praised Galeotto for his "amazing poverty of spirit," which, Bernardino wrote, "he himself had experienced." The meeting with Bernardino may in fact have had something to do with Galeotto's decision to become a third-order Franciscan on October 4, 1431.[52] (The official story is that Galeotto had a vision that he was to become Saint Francis's son, and for one day he received the stigmata wounds of Christ.) A fourteen-year-old Sigismondo, who was also in Rimini at the time, may very well have also been moved by the fiery preacher, who had such an influence on Pius II.

The Anti-Sigismondo: Saint Catherine of Siena

Less than a year before Pius performed his unique reverse canonization on Sigismondo, the pope canonized Saint Catherine of Siena on 29 June, 1461. In his memoirs, Pius explicitly compares Catherine's sanctity to the evil of Sigismondo.[53] Andrea Benzi, who delivered the damning invective against Sigismondo, also headed Catherine's case for sanctity.[54] The recognition of Catherine's sanctity inspired the pope to make a similar formal pronouncement about Sigismondo's wickedness. In addition to having performed the requisite miracles for canonization, Catherine was also a doctor of the Church. Her wisdom was "inspired rather than acquired," and she was so learned that Pius says that "she was a master before being a pupil."[55] She had the gift of prophecy and "foretold many things before they happened, and revealed the most hidden secrets."[56] She wrote numerous letters and a dialogue on Church reform and theology. Catherine's writings would have been key evidence in her canonization trial, so Pius would have been familiar with the oft-repeated themes in her work. She stresses the importance of obedience as the only redemption for humanity; the obedience of the sinner toward God, and toward His vicar on earth, the pope. In praising the obedience of Catherine, Pius could hardly have not thought of the disobedience of Sigismondo.

Catherine was her mother's twenty-third child and her favorite, as she was the only one the mother breast-fed herself.[57] She had an angelic upbringing. Every time she would go up the stairs of her father's house, Catherine would kneel on each step to praise the Virgin Mary.[58] She consecrated her virginity to Christ at seven and became a Dominican tertiary at sixteen. Already as a child, Catherine saw visions in which she would converse with Jesus. These divine conversations were frequent and intimate, and eventually during carnival in 1366 Catherine was mystically married to Christ. She practiced extreme asceticism, which included self-starvation and flagellation. She wore abrasive goats' hair under her clothes and slept no more than two hours a night. She beat her flesh with thick cords and was tormented by unremitting pain in her head.[59] Catherine "prevailed over diabolical temptations and the constant attacks of malignant spirits with the shield of patience and the helmet of faith."[60] She cast demons out of the possessed.[61] In the last year of her life, Catherine lived off of water and the Eucharist. She would also chew on bitter herbs and small bits of food, which often made her vomit. Shortly before her agonizing death in April 1380, she gave up water completely as an offering for Church reform.[62] When she tended to the sick, she would eat their filth and feast on the pus of festering wounds. On one occasion after sucking the pus from the putrid breast of a dying woman, she told her confessor: "Never in my life have I tasted any food and drink sweeter and more exquisite [than this pus]."[63] Such ascetic practices served to kill her own will and destroy her own ego so that she could be united with God's will and divine perfection. Fasting was central to Catherine's mysticism. She saw in her hunger a connection to Christ's suffering on the cross. Whereas Renaissance humanism tended to celebrate human nature, Catherine called her body a "dung heap."[64] She focused on overcoming human nature, destroying her human condition to make it divine. Catherine's grotesquely radical asceticism is the inverse of Pius's image of Sigismondo as a perverted hedonist. Both holy and unholy extremes run counter to societal norms—horrifying inversions to social values. There is a fine line between saints' lives and the demonic.

Whenever Catherine fell into a trance, scribes were always at hand to write whatever she dictated.[65] Four hundred of her letters survive, as well as a treatise, the *Dialogue,* which records conversations with Jesus. Catherine's *Dialogue* is unambiguous about the nature of sin and divine punishment. Just as the sinner is redeemed and reunited in the community of Christ by obedience, so is he damned by disobedience. She writes that Christ says that there are two ways to travel in life: one is the way of perfection and truth, which is on the bridge; the other is that of falsehood, under the bridge in the river, where sinners drown and "come to excruciating torments." The damned "drown by their own choice," by their own sins.[66] Through sin, she writes, the damned lose the life of grace; "pride nourished by sensual selfishness" brings them down and makes them "slaves of sin . . . pigs rolling in the mud" of lust.[67] Their arrogance makes sinners into "such animals that they have no respect for their own daughters and other relatives, but stoop to the meanest things with them."[68] "Like thieves, they steal what is [God's] and put it to the service of their sensuality." "All because of selfishness" and "disordered passions."[69] The damned soul, Christ says in Catherine's dialogue, "has made a god of itself and strikes at me with all sorts of sins."[70] Sigismondo was accused of all these sins: lust and rape, pride, envy, deceit, injustice, theft, lack of self-control, and believing himself a god. Pius could very well have seen Sigismondo's "disordered passions" in Catherine's image of the damned and their fruits.

It is not surprising that the only person Pius canonized during his pontificate was from Siena, his beloved homeland. Catherine's insistence on obedience also fit perfectly with the ideological needs of a papacy under siege. If Sigismondo Malatesta was encroaching on Church lands, conciliarist theologians and the French pragmatic sanction were also threatening papal authority. Pius dealt swiftly with both threats. His bull *Execrabilis* (1460) silenced promoters of conciliarism by affirming the pope's superiority over a Church council. Pius also demanded the repeal of the Pragmatic Sanction (1438), which would return the appointing of bishops and enjoyment of tithes in France to the papacy. Catherine was the ideal spokeswoman for papal monarchy. She had been devoted to the papacy and highly vocal in her conviction that the pope should move back to Rome from Avignon. She wrote letters and met with Pope Gregory XI (1329–1378) and his successor Urban VI (1318–1389). When the return of the papacy to Rome brought schism, Catherine argued for Church unity and loyalty to the pope.[71] In the *Dialogue* she says that the pope ought to punish corrupt clerics and those who rebel against papal authority. The popes, Jesus states, are only bound to the divine law. Temporal rulers and civil law have no authority over the anointed vicars of Christ. All rulers and Christians are bound to obey the pope, "Christ on earth . . . even to the point of death. Whoever refuses to obey him is . . . living in damnation."[72] In not heeding Pius and not relinquishing the papal lands that he had taken, therefore, Sigismondo embodied this notion of hellish disobedience.

Andrea Benzi stressed themes in the introduction of the bull for Catherine's canonization to which he would soon after return in his condemnation of Sigismondo. All creatures and natural objects, according to Catherine's bull, celebrate God and rejoice in their gratitude to God, except for man: "man alone among creation is found to be ungrateful, disobedient, and rebellious; he has imitated the ruin of the perverted angel. [Lucifer] was proud in heaven and desired to be like the creator; he was cast headlong into the abyss and paid the penalty for his wicked plan."[73] There follows a description of the fall of man in Eden, the banishment from paradise, the introduction of death, and then the flood, the tower of Babel, and the division of humanity. Abraham, then Jesus, saved the few good people. But many people sin against the Catholic faith and do not honor the Lord. Where are charity, justice, and religious piety?

> Some spread impious teachings and blaspheme against God; others are servants of pleasure and think of nothing except how to relieve their lusts. Some crave another's wealth; others thirst for human blood. Innocence is rare and hardly safe. . . . Everything serves passions and deceits to such an extent that the devil is rightfully called the prince of this world, since most of the globe is under his control.[74]

The Christians that remain, the author of this bull continues, have succumbed to heresy: "If we follow the commandments of God, we are without doubt children of God, but if we follow the devil, we belong to him."[75] Catherine came from God; she was holy, steadfast, chaste, and devout. Sigismondo was the polar opposite; he was the offspring of the devil: impious, disobedient, and a slave to lust and every sin.[76] The seminal moments in Pius's papacy canonized the split between the saints, Bernardino and Catherine, who had obeyed God's commandments, and the damned, Sigismondo, who had chosen to follow the devil.

The History of a Legend

The monster that the pope fashioned out of Sigismondo has influenced every description of the lord of Rimini since the Renaissance. Most historians in early modern Europe accepted Pius's charges and the black legend of Sigismondo that he created. They repeated the list of crimes and sometimes expanded on them. In his biography of Francesco Sforza (1475), Giovanni Simonetta repeated the charge that Sigismondo had had his second wife, Polissena Sforza, murdered. In his bestselling chronicle of world history, Fra Jacopo Filippo Foresti da Bergamo (1434–1520) based his portrait of Sigismondo on Pius's invective. His chronicle was published in 1485 and went through sixteen Latin and Italian editions. Franciscan martyrologies restated the accusation that Sigismondo tortured and murdered Franciscans for not revealing the contents of Polissena's confessions.[77] A later fifteenth-century humanist, Giovanni Gioviano Pontano, used the example of Sigismondo to define "immanitas," monstrous cruelty. Pontano expanded the list of Sigismondo's crimes to include the allegations that he had a child by his own daughter and his attempt to rape his own son Roberto—a triple mortal sin of rape, sodomy, and incest.[78] The dark legend had a life of its own. Local historians of Rimini, however, tried to clear the name of their city's great Renaissance patron. In the seventeenth century Cesare Clementini presented a heroic and learned Sigismondo, a worthy head of the Malatesta. Francesco Gaetano Battaglini (1753–1810) published the first real biography of Sigismondo, enriched with abundant archival sources. Battaglini rejected the charge that Sigismondo had murdered Polissena and dismissed most of the other accusations as calumny. In the nineteenth century this local pride joined the tide of nationalism, as historians looked to the past to support Italian unification against the Papal States.[79] Luigi Passerini tried to whitewash Sigismondo completely. He saw Sigismondo as a heroic precursor of the liberal secularists who were fighting against Pope Pius IX (1846–1878) and the Papal States.[80] Like Giuseppe Garibaldi (1807–1882), Sigismondo did not give in to the unjust pope and championed the cause of Italian nationalism. While these associations are obviously anachronistic, there is nevertheless a strong sense of Italian identity in the Renaissance literature of the Malatesta court.

More critical Italian historians also began to sift through the sources and reassess the issues. In a series of articles, Giovanni Soranzo systematically countered every accusation.[81] He presented strong arguments for dismissing most of Pius's accusations as unsubstantiated political propaganda. But whereas Italian nationalist historians sought to overturn the image of Sigismondo as villain, the father of modern Renaissance studies, the Swiss Jacob Burckhardt, praised Sigismondo, warts and all. Burckhardt's 1860 *Civilization of the Renaissance in Italy* formed the popular notion of the Renaissance as a secular age in which individuals could succeed on merit alone. For him Sigismondo was the Renaissance individual par excellence, an impious monster but a man of action and culture, who seized life and made his own fate.[82] He was the embodiment of Nietzsche's *Übermensch* who rose above the herd, followed no traditional morality, and battled the bourgeois forces of religion in the papacy. Like Burckhardt, who was his colleague at the University of Basel, Friedrich Nietzsche praised the "positive forces of the Renaissance," a time when "the spirit of antiquity was joined with the modern spirit;" the Renaissance brought a "liberation of thought, disrespect for authorities, victory of culture over the darkness of ancestry . . . and the unfettering of the individual." This "free spirit" Nietzsche believed had been stifled by the Reformation but was reemerging in his own time, late nineteenth-century Europe. For Nietzsche, the Renaissance was "the golden age of this millennium."[83] The English aesthete, J. A. Symonds, like Burckhardt, highlighted the contrast between high culture and extreme barbarism: Sigismondo "killed three wives in succession, violated his own daughter, and attempted the chastity of his own son. So much of him belongs to the mere savage." The Tempio Malatestiano, he wrote, was "more worthy of a Pagan Pantheon than of a Christian temple. . . . So much of him belongs to the Neopagan of the fifteenth century." He was a "most accomplished villain," duplicitous and cruel.[84] Symonds saw Sigismondo as the opposite of Renaissance civility. He epitomized the Renaissance individual completely detached from the bounds of religion and morality.

Whether seen as an Italian patriot and nationalist or a radically amoral individual, in both myths Sigismondo became a romantic hero, who fought against papal tyranny, unabashedly cultivated the pagan Renaissance, and glorified an extreme passion and devotion to his lover Isotta. The French journalist and travel writer Charles Yriarte popularized the romantic view of Sigismondo in his 1882 biography.[85] Yriarte did extensive research and uncovered many new documents for his sympathetic portrait of the condottiere. He expanded on Burckhardt's image of Sigismondo as the immoral but heroic individual—savage yet a great patron of Renaissance art. Yriarte's treatment of the Tempio and the romance of Sigismondo with Isotta degli Atti (1432–1474) was particularly influential on later writers. In 1445, Sigismondo was married to his second wife, Polissena Sforza (1428–1449), when he first noticed Isotta, who was only twelve years old. He fell madly in love, and she eventually returned his favors, with her father's consent. The mistress gradually takes center stage, as Sigismondo's wife Polissena, ignored and humiliated, retreats and eventually dies in 1449. At the time there was strong speculation that Sigismondo had her murdered, but Polissena probably died of plague, which was the officially reported cause. Sigismondo eventually married Isotta in 1453 or 1454.

Malatesta poets extensively and creatively celebrated the romance between Sigismondo and Isotta. Basinio of Parma (1425–1457), Porcellio (Pandone de' Pandoni) (1405–1484), and Roberto Orsi (1420–1496) composed numerous poems about their love, which are still available only in manuscripts or early printed editions. Only Basinio's poems have been edited and published in modern editions. Although this poetry is an obviously rich source for understanding Sigismondo and Isotta's romance, as discussed in Chapter 6, it was not widely read by later historians. Romantic writers instead looked to the church of San Francesco, which became known as the Tempio Malatestiano, for evidence of their great love, focusing on the central position of Isotta's sumptuous tomb and the "SI" insignia found everywhere inscribed in the church (fig. 6.1). Yriarte saw the Tempio as a monument of Sigismondo's love for Isotta. He popularized the claim that the "SI" stood for Sigismondo and Isotta and emphasized how the "S" was lovingly entwined around the "I." In 1909 Giovanni Soranzo proved that the "SI" was simply short for Sigismondo and pointed out that it was a common practice for rulers to abbreviate their names on monuments to the first two letters.[86] But the romantic view persisted. In 1924 the art historian Corrado Ricci tried to have it both ways. In Straussian fashion, he argued that the sign had two meanings for contemporaries: one official and referring only to Sigismondo, and the other "equivocal" that referred to both Sigismondo and Isotta.[87] The Tempio continued to be read as a monument to Sigismondo's love for his mistress Isotta and as a pagan glorification of Sigismondo.

The Italian poet and novelist Gabriele d'Annunzio (1863–1938) saw Sigismondo's passionate life completed in the art of the Tempio. He placed his poem about Sigismondo at the end of his play *Francesca da Rimini* in 1902. Francesca was famous for having an adulterous affair with her brother-in-law, Paolo Malatesta, in 1285. Francesca's husband, Gianciotto Malatesta, a distant relative of Sigismondo, caught them in the act and murdered them both. Dante immortalized the pair in the fifth circle of his *Inferno,* where the couple are continually and eternally whipped by torrential winds as punishment for their lust (*Inferno,* V.31–33). Nineteenth-century English Pre-Raphaelites loved the tale and retold it in art, poetry, plays, and opera. An oral tradition claims that the murders took place in the castle of Gradara in the Marches, where a feature film was made of the episode in 1949. The castle and its numerous faux-medieval decorations is still a major tourist attraction in the area. Like his ancestor, Sigismondo became similarly famous for his passion.

In his poem, D'Annunzio marks Sigismondo with the same illicit passion and plays on the storm image in the punishment of Paolo and Francesca. The "long haired Sigismondo" was a "stormy imperial soul," a "flower of eternity," and a "fated son of Desire and Death." This Romantic Sigismondo lives on in the art of the Tempio. D'Annunzio in particular meditates on Agostino di Duccio's sculpted triumphal profile portrait of Sigismondo (fig. 1.2):

> The roar of his learned mouth is silent. Intent on beauty, his lynx eye burns . . . so that through art the great tyrant conquers time, much more alive [now] than when he ran through cities and provinces. I wish to draw his voice of love and command from the marble, and his gestures. O sanguine poem, . . . I entrust you to Sigismondo Malatesta in the name of the two spirits, whom "la bufera infernal, che mai non resta" torments.[88]

D'Annunzio quotes Dante on the torrential winds of Hell that punish Paolo and Francesca (*Inferno,* V.31). As if living with the stain of an even more evil original sin, Sigismondo inherited their deadly passion. Like theirs, Sigismondo's passion destroyed him but also made him immortal.

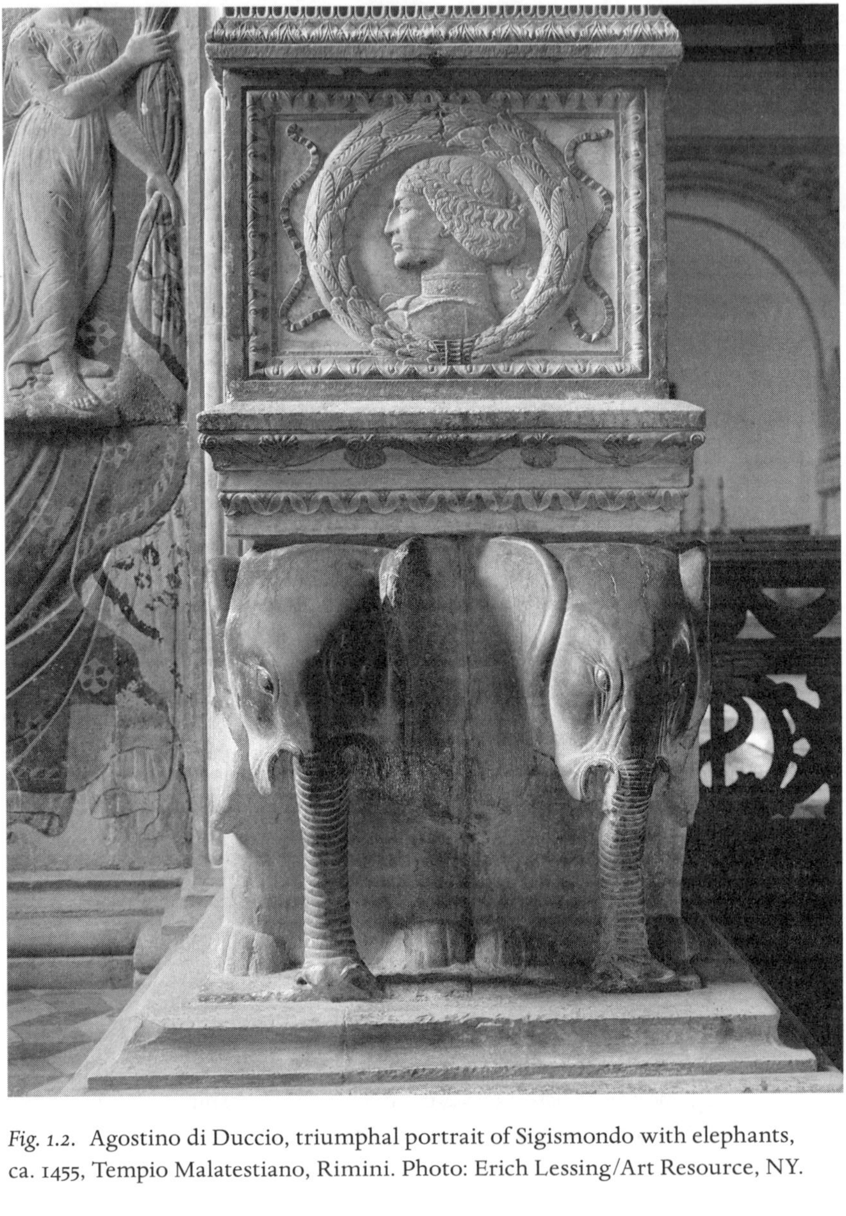

Fig. 1.2. Agostino di Duccio, triumphal portrait of Sigismondo with elephants, ca. 1455, Tempio Malatestiano, Rimini. Photo: Erich Lessing/Art Resource, NY.

This image of Sigismondo as a self-made superman, patriotic Italian, pagan, and lover dominated in early twentieth-century literature. In 1906, the English travel writer and art journalist Edward Hutton published a historical novel on Sigismondo, which was so popular that it was republished twenty years later. In a memorable scene, Hutton describes Sigismondo as a boy torturing a little dove in the woods: "[Sigismondo] caught it and in mere wantonness plucked it naked, a mere bleeding, grotesque little body, while it struggled now and then, and uttered tiny shrieks . . . , twittering in vain to itself or its companions, dying at last as the remaining feathers were torn away in the hands of Sigismondo covered with its blood."[89] Sigismondo's cruelty and sadistic tendencies inspired fear but also revealed something like a Greek demi-god's disregard for human weakness. Such images of unmediated action, violence, and force could hardly have fit better into the emerging ideology of fascism in Italy.

In 1912 Antonio Beltramelli wrote a popular little book on Sigismondo called *The Temple of Love*.[90] The book is written in triumphal stream of conscious poetic prose. Dreamy heroic descriptions conjure up the force that was Sigismondo:

> He was handsome, tall, and walked proud. His eyes were superanimated, and his leonine head covered in the thickest hair. His presence alone was imposing. By this and his rich eloquence he entranced the crowds. Strong in arms, untiring, and the first among his soldiers, in anger he was terrifying and in hatred unyielding. He knew no cowardice and was first to offer his life in battle as he launched himself alone into the enemy camp like a whirlwind . . . he had the bravery of legendary heroes and accomplished extraordinary deeds . . . Only force could subdue him. He had no faith.

Sigismondo embodies the Nietzschean power of the will in a dynamic struggle for dominance set against the emotive force of the Renaissance. Beltramelli's little book culminates with a description of the Tempio as a temple sacred to Sigismondo's love for Isotta and glory: "Sweet meditation and nothing more holds us. Our soul rejoices, is strengthened, and with fresh anxiety leaps toward life, as if towards a boundless good to be reconquered, drawn out of the profound voice of the Tempio, sacred to the beautiful humanity of love."[91] A decade later, in 1922, Beltramelli made the connection with fascism explicit in his biography of Benito Mussolini, the first biography of the Duce. Both Sigismondo and the Duce were from the Romagna. Mussolini came from Forli, which is a city near Rimini. In the Middle Ages and the Renaissance, the Romagna was notorious for its numerous petty warlords and constant battles. Beltramelli's biography of the Duce contains a brief historical sketch of the great men of the Romagna; Sigismondo is highly praised as a forerunner.[92]

The American poet Ezra Pound (1885–1972) used Beltramelli, Hutton, and Yriarte to craft his *Malatesta Cantos*. Pound was inspired by the Tempio, its poetry in stone, unfinished state, and mythic status as a monument of Sigismondo's love for Isotta, himself, and his revived paganism. Pound also incorporated published archival materials, which allowed him to blur the lines between prose and verse, fact and fiction. The romantic image of Sigismondo dominates, and Pound's own fascist leanings and devotion to the native spirit of Italy pervade his writing. In fact, Lawrence Rainey has convincingly demonstrated a connection between the composition of the *Malatesta Cantos* and Mussolini's march on Rome in October 1922, which began the fascists' rise to power. The eleven months that Pound spent writing the cantos were framed by his first visit to the Tempio in Rimini in May 1922 and Italy's turn to fascism culminating in the march in October of the same year.[93] His three cantos on Malatesta have been called a mini epic. Pound's image of Sigismondo comes through clearly in his use of Pius's attack in his *Commentaries:*

> and in the language of Pius
> built a church
> noble but impious
> with so many gentile
> works that it seemed
> no temple of Christians
> but of infidels, adorers of demons,
> and therein raised to his concubine
> a magnificent pagan
> sepulcher and inscription,

To the goddess Isotta,
sacro,
alla Diva Isotta.[94]

Pound quoted not directly from Pius's Latin *Commentaries* but from Beltramelli's bowdlerized translation of it into Italian. Beltramelli did not include Pius's phrase "built a noble church in Rimini to the honor of Saint Francis." Pound repeated Beltramelli's mistakes, then added a few of his own, including his mistranslation of the Italian "empì" ("filled") with "empio" ("impious").[95] Pound, of course, was a brilliant poet and classicist, and may have been consciously misappropriating his sources for his literary purpose. The image of the defiant overly masculine force of the immoral Sigismondo Malatesta appealed to the fascist convictions of Pound and Beltramelli. Sigismondo represented the strong individual in rebellion against the life-negating pope and his weak Christian collectivity.

A final picture of an angst-ridden Sigismondo emerged in the French playwright Henry de Montherlant's *Malatesta* in 1943. The play takes place in 1468, when in desperation Sigismondo decides to murder Pope Paul II. But the assassination is thwarted and Sigismondo descends into a deep abyss of powerlessness. Montherlant took great liberties with the history: Basinio, for example, who died in 1457, and Porcellio, who left Rimini for good in 1458, both have leading roles in the play. Montherlant has Porcellio poison Sigismondo. As he dies, Sigismondo has a vision of all the illustrious ancient Romans he admires—Pompey, Caesar, the Gracchi, and Scipio Africanus. But instead of welcoming him into a glorious afterlife, they fade, and Sigismondo surrenders unto great oblivion.[96] A right-wing existentialist, Montherlant emphasized the contradictions in life and the need for decisive action and violence against meaningless existence. The play *Malatesta* is grim: all the characters are selfish individuals who are deeply troubled by uncalculated acts of charity, and brutal self-interest and self-preservation are all that matter.

Sigismondo Malatesta had come to represent the pagan masculine heroic ideal, asserting itself against the crushing power of the ordinary. The contradictions made his life disturbingly appealing to fascists. He was a brutal sadistic warrior yet extremely cultured patron of the arts; a defiler of religion, enemy and would-be murderer of the pope yet admirer of ancient philosophy and pagan belief; an insatiable lover and serial rapist yet devoted servant of a single girl. These modern myths of Sigismondo have their origins in the Renaissance and the historical Sigismondo. Before Pius ruined Sigismondo's reputation for posterity, humanists and artists in Rimini had worked hard to fashion a myth of Sigismondo as an invincible warrior, a passionate lover, and a reborn classical hero destined to become a god, like Hercules, and earn a place in the heavens as a star, like the Caesars of the Roman Empire.

A Classical Life for a Renaissance Lord

The black legend and romantic and fascist views of Sigismondo Malatesta have cast a dark shadow over his legacy. Professional historians have nevertheless used archival sources to piece together the political wranglings and governing principles of Sigismondo's rule. In the 1920s Giovanni Soranzo used modern historical methods and unstudied documents to dispel much of the myth. In 1973 P. J. Jones published a meticulously researched monograph on the Malatesta family. It is a model political history, and the chapter dedicated to Sigismondo is enlightening about his role in Italian politics. Art historians have illuminated Sigismondo's artistic patronage, particularly of the Tempio Malatestiano.[97] In 1940 Jean Seznec pointed out the unusual preponderance of pagan imagery in Sigismondo's Church of San Francesco and concluded that in a Christian church the decorations were "impious," since in the Tempio "Christian thinking is subordinated to the classical imagination and to pagan sentiments."[98] More recent scholarship has complicated this interpretation, pointing to Christian aspects of the Tempio.[99]

The present study explores the pagan themes in Sigismondo's court culture but focuses in particular on the literature that he patronized. The two richest sources are an epic poem and a treatise on the art of war, both composed around 1455 and distributed by Sigismondo. In the *Hesperis,* the Latin poet Basinio of Parma defined Sigismondo as a classical hero, who uses divinely inspired prowess and pagan virtue to save Italy from foreign invaders and himself become a god (fig. 4.1). In his treatise on the art of war, Roberto Valturio (1405–1475) presented Sigismondo as the ideal commander, worthy of comparison to Alexander and Caesar. His treatise is available only in early printed editions from the late fifteenth and early sixteenth centuries.[100] The only translation is a sixteenth-century Italian one, which succeeds in making Valturio's convoluted sentences even more confusing. Some of Basinio's shorter works were edited and published in the early twentieth century, but his self-proclaimed masterpiece and the richest source for Sigismondo's public image, the *Hesperis,* has been published only once, in 1794. Basinio was an expert on Homer, and his Latin verse contains transliterations of Homeric Greek words and constructions.[101] The power of his poetry often depends on complex word order, obscure words, and classical references. Literary scholars have traced some of Basinio's classical sources, but no historians have used Basinio's poetry as a source for Sigismondo's biography and public image.[102] Classical values permeate the Latin language of Basinio's epic, which is a prime example of how the imitation of classical models shaped the way humanists read and presented contemporary events. Both Basinio and Valturio used classical Greek literature extensively as models and sources for their works. They benefited from the new availability of Greek authors and Latin translations in the early fifteenth century. Sigismondo commissioned these and other works of classically inspired literature and distributed them throughout the Italian peninsula, as gifts to such powerful rulers as Cosimo de' Medici, Francesco Sforza, and Sultan Mehmet II.[103] This is the portrait of himself that Sigismondo projected to his subjects, allies, and enemies.

The Renaissance that Sigismondo created in Rimini was spectacular. Piero della Francesca (1416–1492) painted Sigismondo in profile like a Roman emperor, with his elegant dogs sitting at attention, bathed in cool, crisp light (fig. 2.1). The architect Leon Battista Alberti (1404–1472) renovated the church of San Francesco and designed the quintessential example of Renaissance classicizing architecture (fig. 2.11). He used the form of an ancient Roman triumphal arch with richly-colored marble for the façade of the church, which was later rechristened the Tempio Malatestiano. Inside, Matteo de' Pasti (1420–1467) and Agostino di Duccio (1418–1481) filled the church with images of Sigismondo as a hero; they carved pagan gods and goddesses and astrological signs that transformed the sacred Christian space into a monument of Renaissance syncretism, if not revived paganism. Basinio immortalized Sigismondo in epic verse as a new Odysseus, and Valturio recovered the ancient art of war and made Sigismondo the ideal commander. The glorious heights of classical culture had returned and lived anew in Sigismondo's Rimini.

The humanist literature and the classically inspired reconstruction of the church of the Tempio Malatestiano in Rimini were all created in less than a decade (ca. 1448–1458). Sigismondo had led the defense of Tuscany against the Aragonese in the first Tuscan War and achieved his greatest victory in 1448. The fame of Sigismondo's victory as the savior of Tuscany marked the high point of the mercenary's career, and the triumphal theme runs through his cultural productions. He used his newfound wealth and status to gather the best humanists and artists of the day in Rimini. But the Renaissance in Rimini abruptly ended in 1458, with the death of Basinio, the departure of another poet, Porcellio, and the beginning of Sigismondo's fatal problems with the papacy. Thereafter Sigismondo's depleted finances prevented further patronage, and Pope Pius II's invectives soon brought into question Sigismondo's legacy. Work on the Tempio Malatestiano was permanently suspended. The church's façade was left incomplete, and Alberti's dome, which was meant to recall both the Pantheon of ancient Rome and Brunelleschi's dome in Florence, was never even begun. The Renaissance in Rimini was suddenly over. Sigismondo was ultimately defeated and humiliated at the hands of Federico da Montefeltro (1422–1482), and he died a sad, powerless prisoner in Rome in 1468.

Pagan themes are ubiquitous in the brief cultural flowering of mid-fifteenth-century Rimini. In his patronage, interests, habits, and crafted self-image, Sigismondo was a part of the Renaissance that dramatically transformed the art and literature of Florence, Rome, Venice, and the courts of northern Italy. But in Sigismondo Malatesta, the Renaissance engagement with classical antiquity takes its most extreme form. The art and literature that he patronized imitated the forms and appropriated texts and iconography from pagan antiquity. Pius was correct in that the imagery in the Tempio was unprecedented in its explicit references to pagan religion. Carved images of Apollo, Venus, Minerva, Diana, Saturn, Jupiter, Mercury, and the muses are in uneasy juxtaposition with the Christian saints, Jesus, and Mary. Pagan sibyls are depicted in other Christian churches, but in the Tempio, they outnumber the Hebrew prophets ten-to-two.[104] Such powerful pagan images could not be completely separated from their origins and original purposes. Despite their contemporary Christian context, the art in the Tempio and the humanist literature of the Malatesta court carried pagan ideas. On the exterior of the Tempio, Sigismondo placed the body of the infamous neo-pagan philosopher, Plethon (1355–1452/4), which he had recovered in Byzantine Sparta. Plethon's tomb sits alongside the tombs of Sigismondo's court humanists, making this Franciscan church a pantheon of classical thought.

The image of Sigismondo in his court literature, as a Homeric hero, a devout pagan, a passionate lover of Isotta degli Atti, an accomplished dancer, and a student of music, philosophy, and classical poetry contrasts starkly with but also in some ways mirrors the pope's vilification of him as a monster, reprobate, and devil incarnate, condemned to eternal hellfire. All of these features of the public and private Sigismondo make him the perfect conduit for understanding the Renaissance in fifteenth-century Italy. In Sigismondo we vividly see the clash of cultural and religious values brought on by the reintroduction of classical pagan literature into a Christian world. The accusations that Pius leveled at Sigismondo highlight the moral and religious dangers of pagan literature. Even though the pope demonized a mere caricature of the man, the heretical and moral topics in the papal invective follow the same lines as the image of Sigismondo that Malatesta humanists created and promoted. The pagan values in the hyper-classicizing literature and art that Sigismondo patronized conflict and contaminate his professed Christianity. In Malatesta literature glory and ambition negate Christian humility; nudity, sexual desire, and pleasure reject chastity and modesty; the muscular athletic body replaces asceticism; the body is a vehicle to the divine, not a tomb for the soul; and fortune and astrological fate rule over Christian providence and free will. Sigismondo projected an image of himself as an ancient hero, to his peril and ultimate destruction.

2

Court Culture and the Renaissance in Rimini

Sigismondo Malatesta presided over a court that was splendid with the medieval chivalric pageantry of tournaments and classical triumphal poetry, orations, philosophical debate, architecture, painting, sculpture, and medals. Rimini is a small city, separated from much of the rest of Italy by mountains, but cosmopolitan, as Sigismondo had ties to other courts—Venice, Florence, and Rome. Marriage between courtly families, festive occasions, diplomatic and cultural exchange, and even war brought Sigismondo into contact with ancient, medieval, and Renaissance art and literature. Ferrara, Florence, Venice, and Rome each had its own Renaissance and concept of antiquity. At a young age Sigismondo befriended two of the most important patrons of the fifteenth-century Renaissance. His brother-in-law, Leonello d'Este (1407–1450), and family friend and correspondent, Cosimo de' Medici (1389–1464), became powerful role models in Sigismondo's quest to define himself as a Renaissance lord and hero.

Sigismondo was the bastard son of a middling mercenary, Pandolfo III Malatesta (1370–1427). Pandolfo had fathered three illegitimate boys, Galeotto Roberto (b. 1411), Sigismondo (b. 1417), and Domenico (1418–1465, later known as Malatesta Novello). Pandolfo had moments of glory, as regent to the young Giovanni Maria Visconti in Milan and sometime lord of Bergamo and Brescia, before he met his maker in 1427, when Sigismondo was only ten years old. A renowned libertine, Pandolfo had nevertheless died on his way to the Marian shrine of Loreto to fulfill a vow that may have been connected to problems of impotence with his beautiful young wife.[1]

The three Malatesta boys were given to their uncle, the enlightened lord of Rimini, Carlo Malatesta (1368–1429), and his wife, Elisabetta Gonzaga (d. 1432), who were childless. Carlo later persuaded Pope Martin V to make them his legitimate heirs and ensured that the boys had a proper education, appropriate to future lords and captains of fortune. When Carlo died in 1429, the boys were suddenly thrust into their inheritance. Sigismondo's older half-brother, Galeotto, became the new lord of Rimini. The saintly Galeotto, however, was more interested in wearing a Franciscan habit and mortifying his flesh than ruling. The rival Malatesta family in Pesaro at once tested the young man's resolve by fomenting a rebellion and sending troops to take over the city.[2] They would have succeeded if thirteen-year old Sigismondo had not shown precocious courage and risen to defend his brother's rule and defeat both conspirators and invaders. After his brother Galeotto abdicated and then died in 1432, Sigismondo took over as ruler of Rimini and papal vicar of the city at the age of fifteen.

Pope Eugenius IV, who had been a close friend of Carlo, persuaded the holy Roman emperor, Sigismund, to stop in Rimini in 1433. For the imperial visit in Rimini, the streets were hung with tapestries, and three triumphal arches greeted the emperor. A humanist, Antonio degli Andarelli, delivered an encomium before the feast and dances.[3] As part of the festivities, the emperor knighted Sigismondo and his brother, perhaps in recognition of the virtue that Sigismondo had shown in liberating Rimini, but mostly to legitimize Sigismondo's fighting status and to ensure his loyalty to Pope Eugenius.[4] This imperial honor made such an impression on the young ruler of Rimini that he formally changed his original Italian name, "Ghismondo," to the more imperial "Sigismondo." Twenty years later Piero della Francesca evoked memories of the meeting and conferral of the knighthood in a fresco in San Francesco (fig. 2.1).

The fresco served several purposes. It first of all shows Sigismondo's devotion to Saint Sigismund, as it was next to the chapel dedicated to the saint. The painted Sigismondo could kneel and continually pray before his namesake. Piero's St. Sigismund is also a likeness of the Holy Roman Emperor, complete with imperial orb and scepter. The painting thus recalls the moment when Sigismondo, the bastard son of a petty mercenary, became a legitimate lord as a knight. The political rhetoric of this image confirms the divine and mortal rule of Sigismondo Malatesta.[5] The fresco depicts a

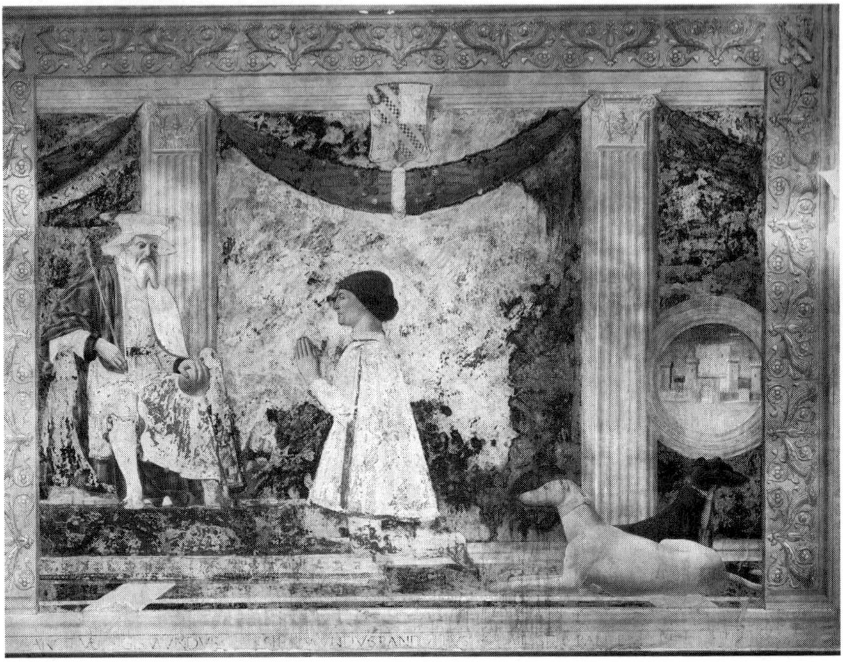

Fig. 2.1. Piero della Francesca, Sigismondo kneeling before Saint Sigismund, fresco, 1451, Tempio Malatestiano, Rimini. Photo: Erich Lessing/Art Resource, NY.

courtly scene. The setting is secular, and Sigismund's clothing is regal. The noble dogs, hounds of the hunt, the portrait of Sigismondo's innovative castle, and the classical profile of Sigismondo himself emphasize courtly grandeur and complicate, if not undercut, a purely pious interpretation of the image.

As a knight, Sigismondo could now fully participate in the medieval French chivalric culture that was popular in the courts of northern Italy. In Rimini, Carlo had hosted a number of tournaments with jousts and swordplay for weddings and other special occasions. For his brother's wedding in November 1395, Carlo had staged a mock Trojan War battle.[6] Sigismondo continued this tradition. Triumphs, tournaments, and sieges of an enormous wooden castle were staged for three days to celebrate the arrival of Sigismondo's first bride, Ginevra d'Este, to Rimini in 1434.[7] In 1437 a three-day celebration feted the birth of Sigismondo's son with dancing, jousting, and parading knights. In April 1442 another joust, banquets, and triumphal

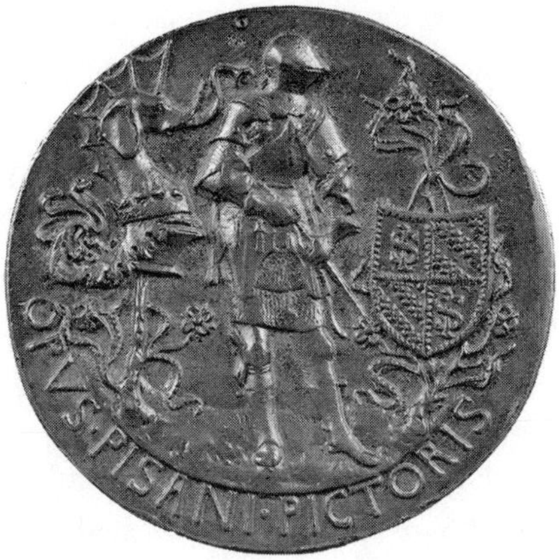

Fig. 2.2. Pisanello, Sigismondo as a knight, medal, bronze, 1443. Museo Nazionale del Bargello, Florence. Photo: Mondadori Portfolio/Electa/Art Resource, NY.

processions celebrated Sigismondo's marriage to Polissena Sforza.[8] The artist Pisanello (1395–1455) cast two medals of Sigismondo as a knight in armor, one on horseback and the other standing (fig. 2.2). These large, commemorative medals imitate the coins that Roman emperors commissioned in order to celebrate their reigns. Sigismondo is thus shown as a medieval armored knight on a classical medal. These images of Sigismondo both recall the Round Table of chivalric lore and the heroes of antiquity. In the same church Agostino di Duccio presented Sigismondo as a knight and as an ancient Roman emperor, complete with victory garlands (fig. 1.2). The presence of both medieval and classical styles does not reflect so much a transition from medieval to Renaissance as a purposeful association of two related warrior virtues, a melding of chivalric court culture and classical ideals. The noble excellence of Homer's heroes, the self-sacrificing virtues of the Roman soldier, and the prowess of ancient commanders found their complement in the honor-bound and battle-trained knights of medieval literature.

The Castle

By definition a knight was a nobleman who had his own horse and accordingly had land. In the Middle Ages, the highest mark of prestige on a noble estate was the castle. Sigismondo's first building project was the Castel Sismondo (1437–1444) (fig. 2.3). An astrologer declared March 20 the most propitious day for the first stone to be laid. Its innovative polygonal design made the fortress appear impregnable and enabled it to withstand artillery, which was being used increasingly in siege warfare. Its moat was twenty-five meters wide and eight meters deep.[9] Sigismondo's castle was one of the wonders of quattrocento Italy. Valturio waxes long about it. He calls the castle "so outstanding in such military ingenuity and knowledge of war that its beauty, place, and layout not undeservedly entice the eyes of all who behold it."[10] Valturio's description emphasizes the brilliance of its engineering by including measurements and stressing the thickness of the walls and their sloping design. Castles had traditionally been called by saints' names or geographic location. In labeling his castle the "Castellum Sismundum," Sigismondo broke tradition and revealed already his desire to promote a strong cult of personality.[11] The castle was a vivid sign of Sigismondo's uncontested lordship over Rimini. In the *Hesperis,* Basinio says that Sigismondo decided to build it in the aftermath of the 1431 rebellion, which almost succeeded in destroying Malatesta power. Successive papal interventions changed the castle's architecture in the sixteenth and seventeenth centuries, and in the nineteenth century it was converted into a prison and then left in neglect.[12] Today, the castle, with its angular walls, has been partially reconstructed.

The celebrated magnificence of the castle matched the literature performed within its walls and promoted the strength and superiority of its patron. Before the castle was finished, Sigismondo hosted a poetry contest in honor of the new edifice. Several major humanist poets competed, and in the end Maffeo Vegio prevailed. His Latin epigram, in which the castle itself boasts of its massive size and artifice, was inscribed on the façade.[13] The castle was a center of classical culture. In its main hall, humanists delivered Latin speeches, read out poems, and debated philosophical issues on the immortality of the soul and the literary merits of the Greek language.

Little remains of the castle's interior decorations, but they surely included the classical and chivalric themes that were popular in the castles and palaces of Sigismondo's peers. Palaces in northern Italy often had a painted series of famous men, a vogue ignited by the popularity of Petrarch and Boccaccio's catalogues of famous men.[14] In 1450–1455, Sigismondo's enemy, Federico da Montefeltro, had such a series depicted in his palace in nearby Urbino. Frescoes depicting equestrian knights and battles were a popular feature in other contemporary courts. In Mantua, Pisanello painted a cycle from the King Arthur legends for Lodovico Gonzaga in 1447–1448. Classical themes adorned the walls of the Este palace in Ferrara. In the late 1440s Sigismondo's

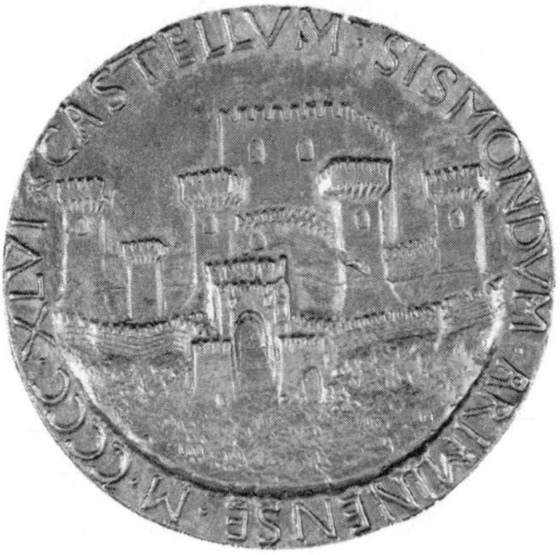

Fig. 2.3. Matteo de' Pasti, Castel Sismondo, reverse of a medal, bronze, 1446, National Gallery of Art, Washington DC. Photo: Samuel H. Kress Collection, National Gallery of Art, Washington, D.C.

friend and onetime brother-in-law Marquis Leonello d'Este had a room frescoed with scenes of Rome in the second Punic War, featuring Scipio Africanus and Hannibal. Piero della Francesca, according to Vasari, was the artist.[15] Sigismondo was often in Ferrara and would have seen the frescoes. In his younger years Sigismondo would have been exposed to the classical images favored in his relatives' palaces. In 1365 the Malatesta in the nearby castle of Montefiore Conca had a room painted with battle scenes from ancient Rome. A little later, in 1400–1401 in Pesaro, Malatesta "dei Sonetti" (1382–1429) had an image of Scipio Africanus in his atrium, Aeneas and other heroes in the Trojan War depicted in another room, and the story of Hector in a third room.[16] Similar classical themes probably adorned the interior of the Castel Sismondo. In particular, an image of Scipio Africanus would be expected, as the Roman hero had a prominent place inside the Tempio, and Sigismondo boasted of their shared ancestry.[17] Like his relatives, Sigismondo favored classically inspired subjects, but he nevertheless maintained the cultural pretensions of the Middle Ages. One of the rooms in his castle was called the room of Guinevere.[18] Likewise, despite its innovative design, the idea of a castle was also inherently medieval. The setting for Sigismondo's flowering of culture was both medieval and Renaissance.

Connections and Cultural Models: Ferrara

Allies were essential to Sigismondo's political and cultural power. The northern Italian courts of Mantua, Ferrara, and Rimini were intimately connected through marriage and culture. The Malatesta brothers' adopted father Carlo Malatesta was married to Elisabetta Gonzaga, who would have imparted some of the vibrant court culture of her native Mantua and the ruling Gonzaga family. The influence of this strong-willed and pious woman is seen in Galeotto's extreme devotion as a third-order Franciscan and later beatification.[19] Carlo and Elisabetta maintained ties with Mantua. When Gianfrancesco Gonzaga (1395–1444) inherited the rule of Mantua in 1407, Carlo acted as regent for the twelve-year-old ruler until he came of age. Under Gianfrancesco, Mantua became a center of the new Renaissance learning. In 1423 he invited the renowned humanist educator, Vittorino da Feltre (1378–1446), to open a school in Mantua. Vittorino ran his school for over twenty years. He taught the classical languages and inculcated a whole generation of children with Renaissance ideals. Basinio studied under Vittorino in Mantua and learned the skills he would later use to reinvent Sigismondo as a classical hero.

Ferrara and its Este rulers were the preeminent model for Sigismondo and his patronage.[20] In 1427 Galeotto was married to Margherita d'Este, and the alliance was further strengthened with the marriage of Sigismondo to her sister, Ginevra d'Este in 1433. Ginevra was the daughter of the ill-fated Parisina Malatesta, whom the Marquis Niccolò d'Este III (1393–1441) had decapitated for allegedly having an affair with his illegitimate son Ugo in 1425. Lord Byron wrote a poem about Parisina's uncontrollable passion (1816), which Gabrielle D'Annunzio later dramatized in a 1913 play.[21] Niccolò was a notorious brute, who may have used an allegation of adultery as an excuse to rid himself of an unwanted spouse and a potential threat in his son. The tragedy, however, evidently caused no bad blood between the Este and the Malatesta families, as Sigismondo was wholeheartedly welcomed into the Este clan. Throughout the 1430s the teenage Sigismondo was frequently in Ferrara at Niccolò's court, where he befriended the marquis's son and heir, Leonello d'Este, and his tutor, the great charismatic classicist Guarino Guarini (1374–1460).[22] When he became marquis in 1441, Leonello made Ferrara a center of the Renaissance.

Guarino assisted Leonello in establishing a sophisticated library of classical books. The library served as much as a location for performing humanist orations and poetry and debating literary and philosophical topics as for reading and correcting the numerous tomes it contained. Leonello tried to re-create the great libraries of antiquity in Alexandria, Pergamum, and Rome, where scholars copied Homer among others and argued over variant readings. Unlike the other famous libraries of the Renaissance in Rome and Florence, the Este library in Ferrara limited its holdings to only the true great classics. The ancient philosopher Seneca had written that one should have only as many books as one can read, since too many books distract the mind. Humanists in Ferrara therefore debated which books were the best and should be included in Leonello's library. Only classical authors were deemed worthy. Medieval and Renaissance authors were dismissed as unfit for the ideal library. Dante's *Divine Comedy* did not even make the cut, as it was judged appropriate only for women and children.[23] The formative experience that contact with this hotbed of classicism had on Sigismondo is evident in his patronage. At least three of the humanists in Sigismondo's court were students of Guarino (Tobia del Borgo, Giusto de' Conti, and Basinio), and several artists left Ferrara to work in Rimini, including Pisanello and Matteo de' Pasti.

Sigismondo probably recalled Leonello's ideal library in the construction of his own humanistic library attached to the Tempio. Valturio praises Sigismondo for "building a library for the use of his subjects and letting the humanists in his court acquire books for it." He says that Sigismondo "donated very many volumes of sacred and pagan subjects and on all the best arts" to the library. Before it was dispersed in the seventeenth century, the library contained about four hundred volumes. A catalogue from 1560 shows a variety of authors and subjects, including the early church fathers Augustine and Jerome and scholastic philosophers. Pagan philosophy was prominent in the works of Cicero, Seneca, Lucretius, Macrobius, Apuleius, and Diogenes Laertius. Ancient history was also well represented, with Herodotus, Plutarch, Livy, Sallust, and Valerius Maximus listed. The library also contained more recent humanist authors, such as Petrarch, Boccaccio, Dante, Valla, Basinio, and Valturio.[24] Many of these texts were probably in the library in Sigismondo's time, as Valturio lists and uses these and many other authors as sources in his tome on military science.[25] Although it was not the largest library in fifteenth-century Italy, its classical holdings would have delighted any humanist at the time.

In using bronze medals to extend his influence, Sigismondo followed the lead of his brother-in-law, Leonello d'Este.[26] As mentioned earlier,

Sigismondo had himself depicted as a knight on a medal. In 1446 the artist Matteo de' Pasti cast an image of Sigismondo's crenellated castle on the reverse of a medal (fig. 2.3). Such a portrait of the Castel Sismondo conveyed strength to resist enemies and power to dominate the Malatesta domain. The image of this marvel was so popular that nine different versions of it were cast. Unlike coins, medals had no monetary value but were works of art to be collected, displayed, and given as gifts. Ancient coins survived in the Renaissance and served as models for profile portraits, such as Agostino di Duccio's reliefs of Sigismondo in the Tempio. But none of them contained images of castles, and few had women, such as the ones that Matteo cast of Isotta degli Atti before she had even become Sigismondo's wife (fig. 6.2). The medals therefore demonstrate Sigismondo's transformation of ancient models to suit his needs. Sigismondo followed the ancient practice of burying coins in the foundations of his new edifices. Twenty-four medals with the castle image were found in the Castel Sismondo, forty-one in the Tempio Malatestiano, and no fewer than a hundred seventy-five in other Malatesta buildings. These buried medals carried Sigismondo's image of power into the distant future, as many were unearthed only when the church was bombed during World War II. He also gave the medals to other rulers.[27] They were the perfect gift: precious objects that reminded allies and potential enemies of Sigismondo's ingenuity and strength with an image of his impregnable castle. Just as he had used bronze medals to promote his image, Sigismondo later circulated copies of Basinio's Latin epic and Valturio's military treatise.[28] Both works provided flattering literary portraits of their patron as an ancient hero worthy of Homer and an ingenious commander, comparable with Alexander and Caesar. Accomplishments, as Sigismondo surely knew well, were only as impressive as the memory and the manner of their telling.

The Chapel of the Muses and the Liberal Arts in the Tempio is a direct example of borrowing from Ferrara. Agostino di Duccio, a Florentine sculptor, carved muses that follow the descriptions of the muses in a letter that Guarino wrote to Leonello on the cycle of the muses for his palace at Belfiore in 1447. Basinio lived in Ferrara from 1446 to 1449 and was also consulted on the iconography of the muses. Guarino emphasizes that Leonello himself had chosen the subject of the muses. Similarly, Valturio claims that Sigismondo was directly responsible for the iconography in the Tempio.[29]

Like Leonello, Sigismondo modeled his artistic patronage on his humanistic interests. There are, however, significant differences. The muses in Ferrara were meant for a private palace and stand alone, while the muses in Rimini are accompanied by the seven liberal arts and appear in a public space. It is extremely rare to have these pagan goddesses depicted so prominently inside a consecrated Catholic church, as Agostino's muses are. Each muse stands on a sphere, which when it turns creates music, and all the spheres together produce the sounds of cosmic harmony that Cicero had described in his *Dream of Scipio.*[30] The late Antique Latin poet Martianus Capella described how the muses accompanying Apollo each controlled a different planet: Polymnia guided the music of Saturn, Euterpe Jupiter, Erato Mars, Terpsichore Venus, and Clio the Moon. The astrological connection is particularly striking since the chapel is directly across from the Chapel of the Planets, in which Agostino sculpted the nominal gods of these planets. In contrast to the heavenly muses, Agostino showed the personified liberal arts standing on rectangular platforms to emphasize that they are earthly. Placing the muses along with the liberal arts is unusual and may have been meant as a defense of poetry and the secular arts.

Agostino, however, added subjects to the chapel that Guarino did not mention, such as the relief of Apollo (fig. 2.4). As Stanko Kokole has shown, Agostino followed Martianus Capella for specific attributes: the raven and a swan at Apollo's feet, a fillet binding his hair, and the laurel branch in his right hand. But what is not found in any images of Apollo since antiquity is the depiction of the three naked Graces on top of the lyre that Apollo holds. They dance to the music of Apollo, music that also turns the spheres of the muses. The only reference to the Graces on Apollo's lyre in ancient literature that Basinio may have seen is in Macrobius's *Saturnalia,* a work in which the late Antique author discusses among other subjects pagan festivals and mythology.[31] Renaissance images of the three Graces come later, including Botticelli's and Raphael's paintings of them, which were made for private residences. It is remarkable that the Rimini Graces were made for a Christian church.

In the *Hesperis,* Basinio frequently refers to Apollo. Before entering the underworld, Basinio prays for the gods' permission and assures them that Apollo inspires him.[32] In the underworld, the character Sigismondo visits the Elysian Fields. Fountains eternally pour forth waters that nourish the lush meadows, where "the muses lead with singing and plucking the lyre."

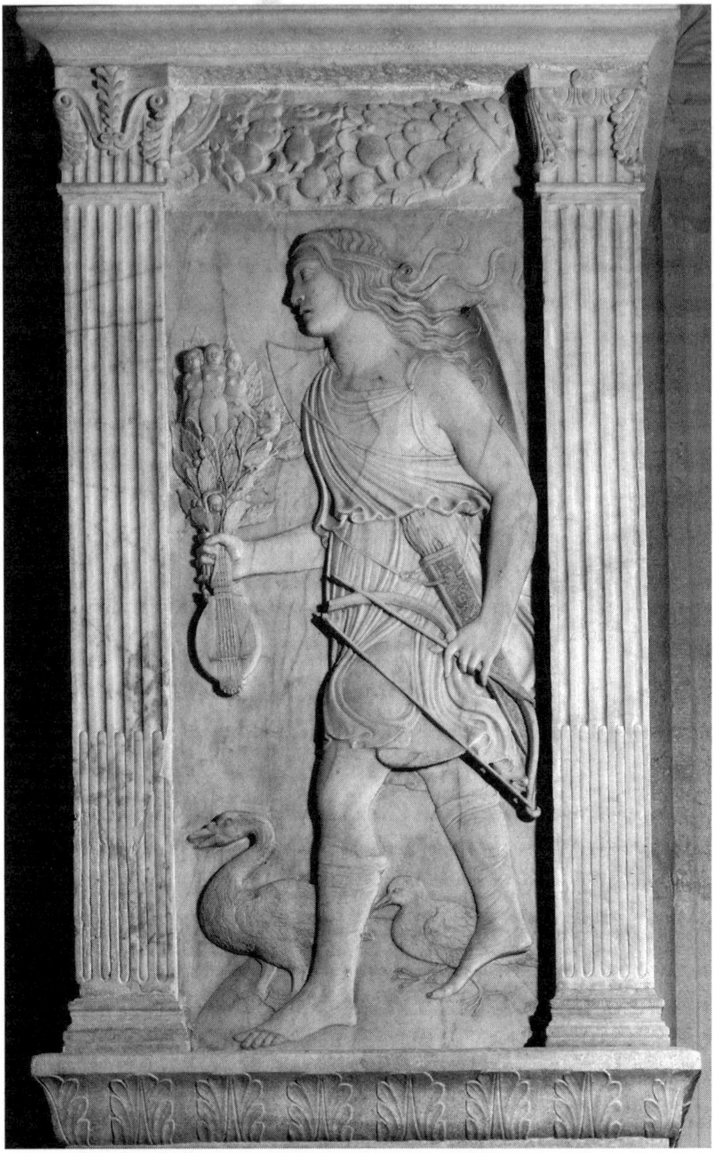

Fig. 2.4. Agostino di Duccio, Apollo, marble, ca. 1455, Chapel of the Liberal Arts, Tempio Malatestiano, Rimini. Photo: Scala/Ministero per i Beni e le Attività culturali/Art Resource, NY.

"Here," he writes, "are Apollo and his chorus, the most beautiful bodies, and divine poets: before all Orpheus, born of the muse Calliope, Homer, and Linus, whose father was Apollo."[33] The god Apollo was also associated with the sun.[34] In fifteenth-century Italy, Byzantine Greeks had brought over copies of the fourth-century *Hymn to the Sun* by Julian the Apostate. Drawing on this pagan hymn, Marsilio Ficino composed his own lengthy panegyric to the sun. Ficino avoids any charges of paganism by writing explicitly in the conclusion that he is using the sun as a metaphor, not a replacement, for God the Father.[35] In Rimini, Basinio compares Sigismondo standing in front of his army to Apollo:

> A new light filled the air. It shined with such great brightness that the land around them immediately smiled and the places nearby gave the Italians joyful hope. Just like when Apollo rises from the ocean at dawn and harnesses his horses, he spreads light over all the earth and the smaller stars become hidden by the new splendor, so illustrious was Sigismondo in his armor.[36]

Here Sigismondo is a "new light," giving hope to the Italians, like the sun at dawn and Apollo on his chariot. When Sigismondo returns after a prolonged absence, Basinio says that the people greeted him just as the Thebans welcomed Apollo "and crowned his head with ivy; such great love did all have when they beheld Sigismondo, their victor's shining face; hearing him speak once was not enough, and everyone had one mind to watch the one commander." His victories have made Sigismondo into a new Apollo, a sun king long before Louis XIV.[37] Basinio's praise of Sigismondo as Apollo and Agostino's relief of Apollo with the three Graces link Sigismondo's Rimini to the sophisticated culture of ancient Hellas, pagan mysticism, and Platonic philosophy.

Ferrara was an early center of the Renaissance of Greek studies in Italy. Under Leonello's tutelage, Guarino and other scholars translated into Latin such Greek authors as Plutarch, who had been little known in medieval Western Europe. The 1438 Church Council to unite the Western and Eastern churches initially took place in Ferrara. The greatest minds of the Byzantine world, including the Platonist Bessarion and Plethon, who was later condemned as a pagan, came to Ferrara to argue the finer points of orthodox theology. It is unclear whether Sigismondo ever met Plethon, but Sigismondo was so impressed by the Greek philosopher's reputation that he invited him to stay at his court. Plethon seems not to have accepted. Later, during his crusade in Sparta in 1465, Sigismondo found the body of Plethon, brought it back to Rimini, and entombed it in the Tempio. Placing the body of such an avowed pagan in a consecrated Christian church shocked Sigismondo's contemporaries in Italy.[38] If Plethon was brought to Rimini only after his death, one of his companions, Cyriac of Ancona, a founder of Greek archaeology and perpetual traveler in Greece, was several times in Rimini and the guest of Sigismondo.

Sigismondo's fascination with astrology probably grew out of his frequent visits to Ferrara and the court of Leonello d'Este, who wore different colored clothes every day to attract the favor of ascendant planets.[39] Fifteenth-century lords and princes sought the advice of professional astrologers for important political decisions. Court astrologers determined the most propitious day to engage in battle, to get married, or to build a church or palace. Belief in the power of the heavens to influence human activities was common, and even skeptical rulers used astrological readings to bolster their power and cull popular favor.[40] In Rimini, Carlo Malatesta had included the famous astrologer Iacopo degli Allegretti in his court, and Sigismondo himself tried to lure a celebrated astrologer from the court of Francesco Sforza.[41]

In Ferrara in 1442, Leonello expanded the studio into a full university, which included a chair of astrology.[42] At the council of Ferrara in 1438, Plethon dazzled Western scholars with his knowledge of Plato and may have also revealed his belief in sun worship and hope for a return to the pagan deities of Olympus. Leonello's successor, Duke Borso d'Este, commissioned frescoes of the months and their astrological deities in the Palazzo Schifanoia (ca. 1470) in Ferrara.[43] Unlike Borso's frescoes, the astrological gods in Rimini are in a church and carved out of prestigious marble. Sigismondo's gods are also decades earlier. Borso's astrologer, Pellegrino Prisciani, studied astronomy at the University of Ferrara and participated in the astrology discussions at Leonello's court in the 1440s. An inventory of Leonello's library in 1445 shows several books on astrology and magic. In 1449 a friar from Ferrara, Giovanni Cocchi, came to Rimini and participated in an all-day debate over the nature of the soul that Sigismondo hosted. Cocchi recorded the discussion in a tome on the immortality of the soul that is replete with astrological references.[44] Sigismondo was also linked to the astrological culture of Leonello's Ferrara through the humanist Basinio. After his student years in Ferrara, Basinio produced the *Astronomicon,* a Latin astronomical poem about the planets and constellations. In the poem, Basinio praises the positive influences of the moon and the sun and invokes the god Apollo to safeguard Sigismondo and his brother Novello as "custodians of Italy" against the Turks.[45] Basinio probably devised the conceptual scheme of the Chapel of the Planets in the Tempio Malatestiano and provided Agostino with descriptions of the gods to be carved.[46] These sculptures display the astrological legitimacy of Sigismondo's rule through his horoscope.

Sigismondo let it be known that he was born on June 19, 1417. His birthday's proximity to the summer solstice is celebrated with the keystone image of the sun and next to it a lion for Leo in the main arch of the Chapel of the Planets. Sigismondo's birth coincided with the sun being in the house of Leo, which meant strength. According to Macrobius, the late Antique authority on Neoplatonic astrology and a popular author in the fifteenth century, the summer solstice under the sign of Cancer was a portal through which souls passed from heaven down into mortal bodies. Sigismondo's birth placed him at the most propitious time for a soul to enter a body. According to ancient astrology, the soul descends from heaven through the Milky Way. On its way down, the soul drinks from the river Lethe, causing it to forget about its true home in the heavens. Then, each planet that the soul passes in its descent to earth imparts certain attributes that are more or less pronounced, depending on the soul's proximity to the planet. From Saturn, the soul gains reason and understanding; from Jupiter, prudence and the power to act; Mars, courage and a bold spirit; from the sun, sense perception and imagination; Venus, passion; Mercury, the ability to speak and interpret; and the Moon, the ability to grow and increase.[47] Agostino's reliefs in the chapel reflect this astrological idea and laud the attributes of Sigismondo's soul.

The front-facing pilasters framing the chapel contain six reliefs of the zodiac signs (Libra, Virgo, Cancer, Aries, Sagittarius, and Aquarius). Cancer, Sigismondo's birth sign, is depicted over the city of Rimini to show Sigismondo's protective rule (fig. 2.5). On the side of the pier, next to Cancer, is the Moon, shown as the goddess Diana, and next to her is the relief of the power of the moon with storming seas and the lone rowboat (figs. 5.1 and

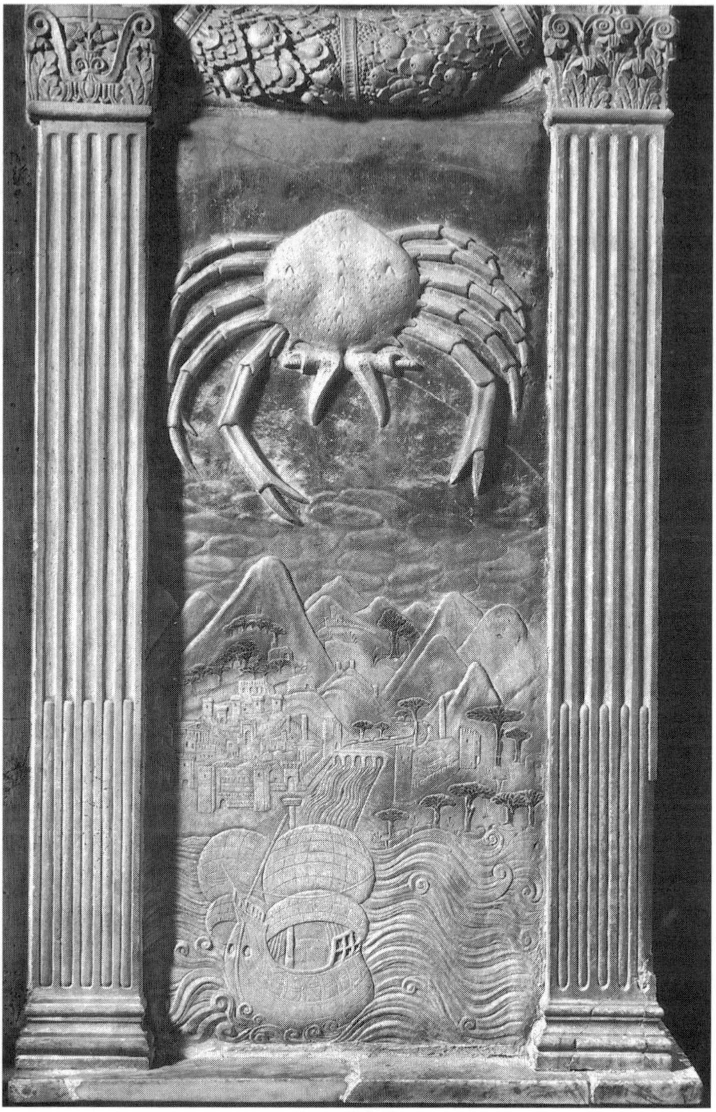

Fig. 2.5. Agostino di Duccio, Cancer, marble, ca. 1455, Chapel of the Planets, Tempio Malatestiano, Rimini. Photo: Alinari/Art Resource, NY.

2.15). In Roman antiquity, Diana was associated with royal power, and her favor was sought to bestow legitimacy on kingly successions.[48] Side-by-side, these three images emphasize Sigismondo's divine power. Like the moon and the tides, he steers the city of Rimini with the favor of Diana.

The six reliefs facing each other on the two pilasters stress the divine attributes of Sigismondo's soul. On the left pilaster are reliefs of Venus (fig. 2.6), Mercury, and Diana (fig. 5.1): passion, eloquence, and imperial power. Directly opposite these, on the right pilaster, are reliefs of Mars, Jupiter, and Saturn. The god of war, Mars, brandishes a sword and a shield on top of a parade chariot, a fluttering cloak underscoring his active engagement (fig. 2.7). Jupiter, ruler of the gods, raises his right arm menacingly, as the imperial eagle stands atop his head. Saturn was associated with Kronos, god of time, and is depicted here as an old man cutting the wings off Cupid with a scythe. The image is a reminder that the soul's abode in the body is temporary and limited. The three reliefs reveal the best qualities of a leader: courage and strength in battle, rulership, and the wisdom of time. The planetary gods and the zodiac signs in this chapel are unprecedented in a Christian church. Valturio insists that Sigismondo personally designed the chapel and that he drew from the "arcane knowledge of occult philosophy and humanists."[49] Regardless of whether he or his humanists designed the program, Sigismondo promulgated in this chapel and, indeed, the whole interior of the church a sophisticated knowledge of pagan mythology and the astrological beliefs of pagan religion.

From medal-casting to classical literature to art patronage and astrology, Leonello d'Este and Ferrara were foundational for Sigismondo's cultural interests and patronage. Sigismondo sought to outdo Leonello by having more medals cast on more varied and novel subjects, including depictions of his castle, the Tempio, and Isotta. Sigismondo's muses and astrological gods were made out of precious marble and placed inside a church. Sigismondo's patronage also focused more explicitly on himself: an entire chapel is dedicated to displaying his horoscope.

Florence

Sigismondo came into direct contact with the Florentine Renaissance when he was thirteen. In August, 1430, Cosimo de' Medici and his brother Lorenzo

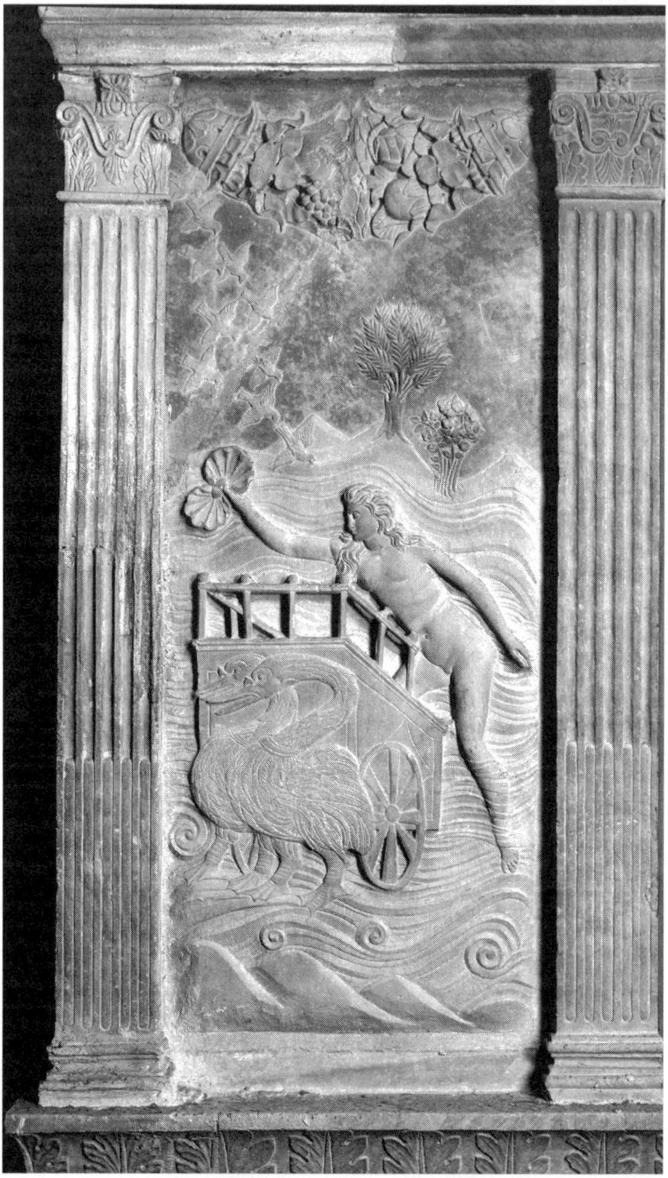

Fig. 2.6. Agostino di Duccio, Venus, marble, ca. 1455, Chapel of the Planets, Tempio Malatestiano, Rimini. Photo: Alinari/Art Resource, NY.

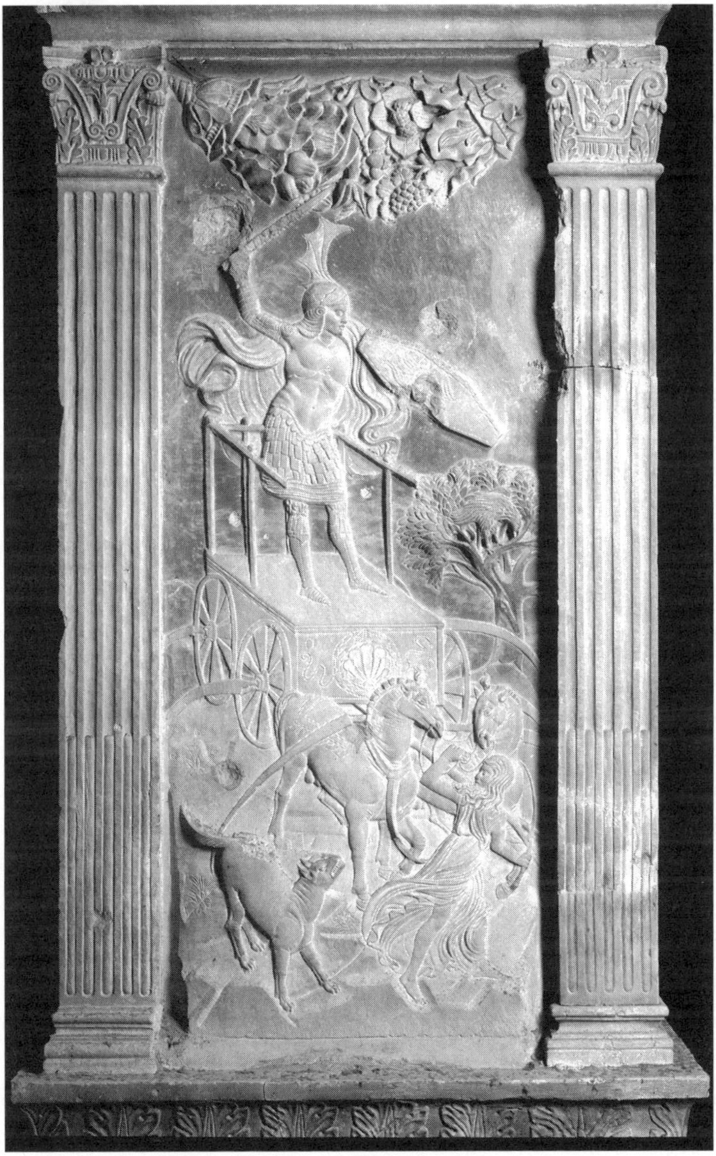

Fig. 2.7. Agostino di Duccio, Mars, marble, ca. 1455, Chapel of the Planets, Tempio Malatestiano, Rimini. Photo: Alinari/Art Resource, NY.

along with the humanist Carlo Marsuppini (1398–1453) stayed in Rimini in order to escape the plague in Florence. While there, Marsuppini translated Isocrates's *Ad Nicoclem* and dedicated it to Galeotto, the new lord of Rimini.[50] The works of the Greek sophist Isocrates (436–338 BCE) were little known in Italy at the time. The *Ad Nicoclem* is a lengthy letter about how to rule. Marsuppini also produced one of the first (partial) translations of Homer into Latin. In the preface to his Isocrates' translation, he refers to Agamemnon's leadership skills in the Trojan War and several classics of Greek literature, including a quote from Plato's *Laws*.[51] Barely a teenager at the time, Sigismondo benefited from exposure to such a first-rate humanist scholar and his patron. Marsuppini later returned to Rimini, when Sigismondo was lord, and wrote Latin poems on the dedication of the Castel Sismondo. Another Florentine humanist, Giannozzo Manetti (1396–1459), acted as Florentine ambassador in the Tuscan wars. In 1447 Manetti stayed in Rimini and convinced Sigismondo to leave the side of Alfonso of Aragon and lead the defense of Tuscany. In addition to Latin and Greek, Manetti was fluent in Hebrew and wrote a lengthy treatise, *Against the Errors of the Jews*. In Rimini, Sigismondo had him debate with local Jewish scholars about the merits of their religion. Later, in the second Tuscan campaign (1452–1453), Manetti again acted as ambassador and presented Sigismondo with the baton of command on the battlefield.[52] In his speech for the occasion (examined in Chapter 7), Manetti praises the long history of Florentine relations with the Malatesta family. The great sculptor of the Tempio, Agostino di Duccio, was a Florentine, as was the Tempio's architect Leon Battista Alberti; and Piero della Francesca was Tuscan.

Sigismondo stayed in Florence several times in the mid- to late 1430s, when he was in his teens. He was there to confirm relations not only with Cosimo de' Medici and the Florentine government but also with Pope Eugenius IV, who had based the papacy in Florence after he had had to flee a Roman uprising in 1434.[53] In March 1435, in the presence of Cosimo de' Medici, Sigismondo signed a contract to fight with his two hundred lances on behalf of the Church for six months.[54] Sigismondo was back in Florence a year later to renew the contract, and was present at the consecration ceremony for the great dome of Florence's cathedral in 1436.[55] The dome was justly celebrated for its dramatic size and Filippo Brunelleschi's brilliant solution to the engineering difficulties involved. In his treatise *On Painting* (1436), Alberti praises

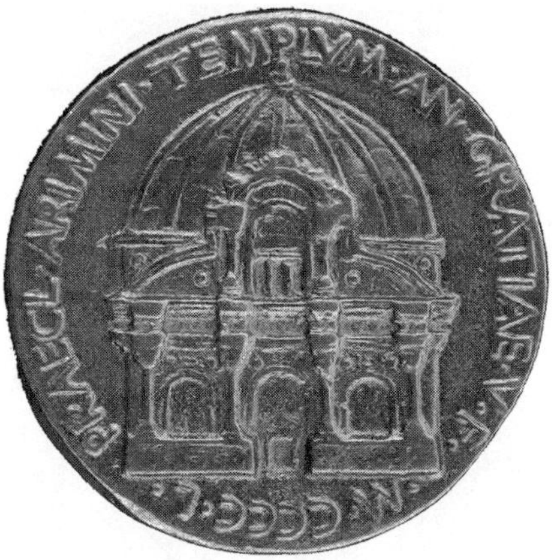

Fig. 2.8. Matteo de' Pasti, Tempio Malatestiano, reverse of medal, bronze, 1453, National Gallery of Art, Washington, D.C. Photo: Samuel H. Kress Collection, National Gallery of Art, Washington, D.C.

the dome, saying that it was "wide enough to cast its shadow all over the Tuscan people, made as it is without any beam or abundance of wooden supports, surely hard to believe as an artifice that it was done at this time when nothing of the kind was ever to have been seen in antiquity?"[56] Brunelleschi's triumphant creation must have been a major factor in Alberti's (as well as in Sigismondo's) later decision to include a dome in the reconstruction of San Francesco. The Tempio was never finished, but a medal struck in 1453 shows an enormous dome over the entire church (fig. 2.8).[57] Such a dome would have also connected the church to Rome's Pantheon, the ancient monument that most inspired Renaissance architects.

There is strong evidence that Brunelleschi was involved in the construction of the Castel Sismondo and that the Florentine architect spent at least fifty-five days in Rimini in 1438.[58] The 1440s and 1450s saw even closer ties to Florence, as Sigismondo commanded the city's defense in two wars (1448 and 1453). In 1459, Sigismondo stayed in Florence along with Pope Pius II on their way to the Council of Mantua. Sigismondo's presence in Florence was immortalized in Benozzo Gozzoli's portrait of him in the *Procession of the Magi* in the Medici palace (fig. 2.9).

Florence, the acknowledged center of Renaissance culture, played a pivotal role in Sigismondo's patronage and the cultivation of his self-image for political purposes. Although at the time Florence was in name a republic, Cosimo de' Medici controlled the government behind the scenes and expertly manipulated public opinion to present himself as father of the republic and first citizen. Medici artists and humanists presented Cosimo as a classical statesman who

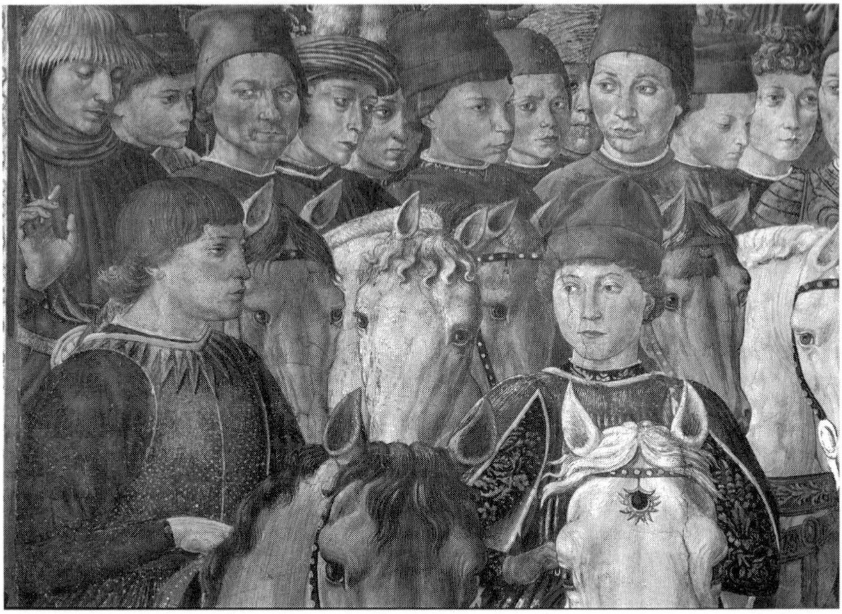

Fig. 2.9. Benozzo Gozzoli, Sigismondo Malatesta (lower left) in detail of *Procession of the Magi,* fresco, 1459, Palazzo Medici, Florence. Photo: Erich Lessing/Art Resource, NY.

restored Florentine liberty, a reborn Maecenas (the patron of Virgil and Horace), and the philosopher king of Florence.[59] Sigismondo maintained a friendship with Cosimo de' Medici throughout his life, and twenty-five letters between Sigismondo and Cosimo survive.[60] Sigismondo corresponded with Cosimo de' Medici about artists for his Tempio. As sole ruler of the Signory of Rimini, Sigismondo aptly drew on the imperial rhetoric of emperors and monarchs but nevertheless also made use of the republican heritage of ancient Rome and Renaissance Florence.[61] The resplendent humanist image of Cosimo must have been a central model for Sigismondo's cultural patronage.

Rome

Rome was a paramount model for Sigismondo, as a physical city full of relics of antiquity, a modern court, and a timeless idea. In ancient times, Rimini was the northern gateway of the Roman Empire. It was the endpoint of the famous Via Flaminia and the beginning of the Via Aemilia. The Emperor Augustus (63 BCE – 14 CE) marked the end of the Flaminia with a triumphal arch, the Arch of Augustus. Still today reliefs of the gods Jupiter and Apollo meet travelers entering Rimini, and Neptune and Roma greet those leaving (fig. 2.10). On the other side of the city, Emperor Tiberius (42 BCE – 37 CE) built a bridge over the river Marecchia at the beginning of the Via Aemilia. The Renaissance historian and antiquarian Biondo Flavio (1392–1463) praises it as the only surviving bridge on the Via Flaminia. Both the arch and the bridge were focal points in the fifteenth century city.[62] The stones of Rimini were a tangible link to ancient imperial glory.

Pope Eugenius IV was an early admirer, and, after witnessing Sigismondo's role in defending Rimini, the pope hired him, despite his youth, to lead the papal army in 1434, when Sigismondo was seventeen. This contract was renewed in person several times. After Eugenius finally returned from exile to the Eternal City in 1443, Sigismondo was often in Rome. We are told that a particularly nostalgic visit to Rome inspired Sigismondo to commission humanist poets to immortalize him in verse, as discussed in Chapter 7.[63] In the *Hesperis,* Sigismondo and his army are presented as being descended from the blood of the ancient Romans. Before the siege of Vada in the second Tuscan war, Sigismondo addresses his troops: "O pristine race of ancient men, I happily accept you [as my army], and do I not see my Romans in their antique names? Soldiers combined with my Rimini men in descent! A single race produced the fathers of Romulus, who, we know, divided themselves from the single blood at the origins of our ancient forefathers. Come now, noblemen, let us renew this ancient bond of love!"[64] Basinio emphasizes the importance of Rome and Sigismondo's ancient virtue in the Roman blood flowing in his veins.

In Rome, Sigismondo had contact with leading humanists on several occasions. The Roman humanist Biondo Flavio describes attending a dinner party hosted by Prospero Colonna for Sigismondo in 1446. The party was appropriately held in the gardens of the legendary ancient patron Maecenas. Sigismondo, Biondo writes, questioned Biondo extensively about Roman history and praised Leonello d'Este's casting of medals in imitation of the Roman emperors.[65] Cardinal Prospero Colonna (1410–1463) was a great patron of humanists in Rome. Biondo called him another Maecenas. Lorenzo

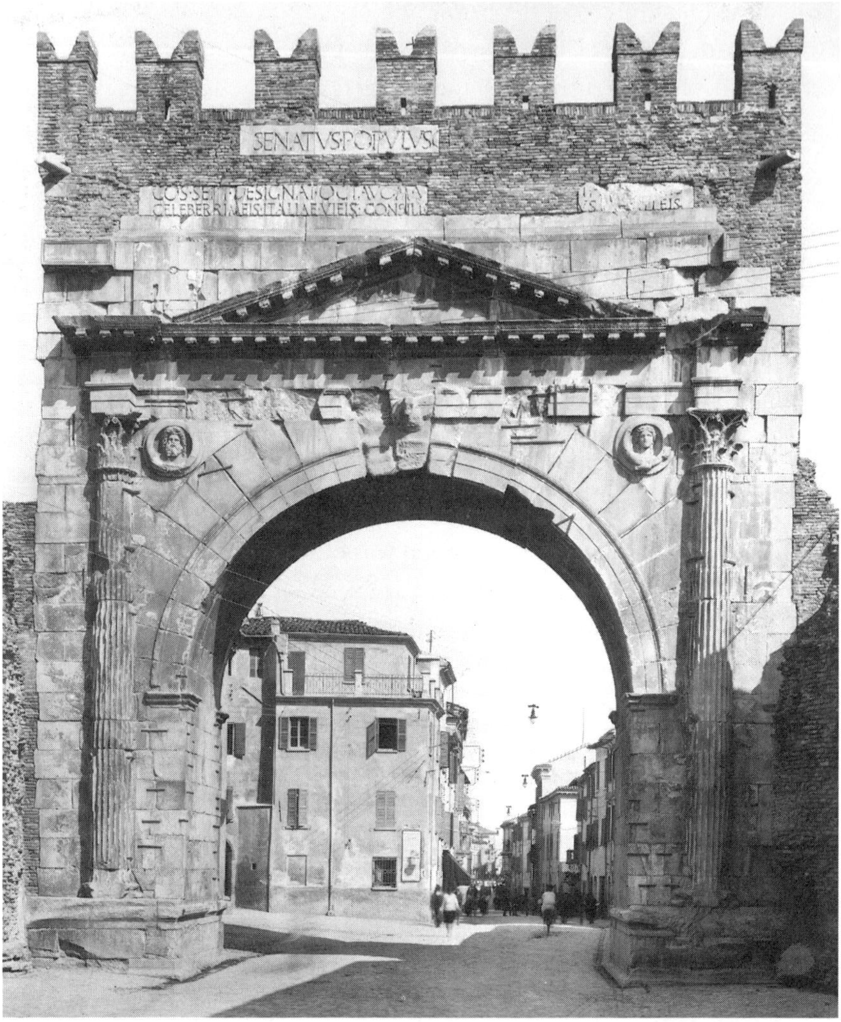

Fig. 2.10. Arch of Augustus, 27 BCE, Rimini. Photo: Alinari/Art Resource, NY.

Valla (1407–1457), Poggio Bracciolini (1380–1459), and Leon Battista Alberti, among others, enjoyed his patronage. The cardinal commissioned Alberti to raise a Roman ship found on the bottom of Lake Nemi.[66] Rome with its classical ruins and vibrant humanist culture presented Sigismondo with physical and literary remains of the ancient culture that he loved, and contemporary models of patronage in the person of Cardinal Colonna.

Leon Battista Alberti was a Renaissance man in that he was a master of many disciplines.[67] The illegitimate offspring of a Florentine exile in Genoa, Alberti was nevertheless given the best humanist education at the school of Gasparino Barzizza in Padua (1414–1418). Alberti composed several works in his twenties on classical themes that were related to his life, including a treatise on the hardships of the scholar's life, the value of work, and the glory to be attained from letters. In keeping with the classical values of his education, Alberti was also accomplished in gymnastics and horsemanship. He was said to have been able to jump over a man's head in a single bound without spreading his legs. Alberti composed works in the vernacular and in humanistic Latin. Most of his enormous output grew out of his fondness for classical authors, especially Greek. For his treatise *On the Family* (1432), for example, he looked to Xenophon's *Economics;* for his satire the *Momus* (1450), he adopted Lucian's style of irreverence; for his treatise *On Architecture* (1452), he started with Vitruvius; and for his work *On Painting* (1436), he took much from Pliny. Although Alberti refers often to the ancients in his writings, he includes contemporary examples and many of his own observations and often provides interpretations lacking in ancient sources. In his treatises on painting, sculpture, and architecture, he emphasizes the guiding roles of nature and mathematics. Alberti's building projects were formative in the development of Renaissance architecture. Although inspired by classical principles and extant buildings, Alberti's designs were innovative in their use of imperial magnificence for Christian churches and often adorned with unexpected fantasy.

Sigismondo had probably first met Alberti in the early 1430s. Alberti had been working for Pope Eugenius IV from at least 1432. He followed the pope to Florence in 1434 and, like Sigismondo, was present at the consecration of Brunelleschi's dome in 1436.[68] Sigismondo probably offered Alberti the commission to redesign San Francesco in Rome in 1446, as work started on the church soon after. It was likely Cardinal Colonna who recommended him to Sigismondo.[69] Alberti was not present in Rimini during the reconstruction of San Francesco in the early 1450s but corresponded with Matteo de' Pasti, who implemented Alberti's designs on the site. There is no direct evidence that Alberti ever stepped foot in Rimini. His use of Romagnole materials and imitation of local monuments for the façade of the Tempio, however, suggest that he visited Sigismondo's city in the planning stage.[70]

The exterior of the Tempio Malatestiano was Alberti's first major project (fig. 2.11). In his *Lives of the Artists* (1550), Giorgio Vasari called it "unquestionably one of the most famous temples of Italy."[71] During its construction, Alberti was composing *De architectura,* a Latin treatise, which both recovered ancient architectural theory and set the stage for Renaissance revival and innovation. The Rimini site posed a serious problem, since Alberti had to work within the constraint of a medieval gothic brick church. As the cathedral of Rimini, San Francesco was the central monument and could not be completely demolished. Three apses in fact contained frescoes by the great Giotto, which were purposely preserved and only later, in 1502–1503, white-washed.[72] Alberti's solution was to wrap the medieval walls of the church in a classical white marble shell. He took Rimini's Arch of Augustus with the round clipeae in the corners as the model for the façade of the church. The three arches with one higher central arch follow the form of many triumphal arches in Rome and elsewhere. The use of a Roman triumphal arch for the façade of a church was Alberti's invention. It reinforced the celebratory nature of the monument that, as two Greek inscriptions assert, was built to fulfill a vow that Sigismondo had made on campaign:

> Sigismondo Pandolfo Malatesta, son of Pandolfo, Bringer of Victory, having survived many and most grave dangers during the Italic War, in recognition of his deeds accomplished so felicitously and with such courage, for he obtained what he had prayed for in such a critical juncture, has erected at his magnanimous expense this temple to the immortal God and to the city, and left a memorial worthy of fame and full of piety.[73]

The language of inscription (Greek) and the form are unusual, especially on a Christian church. A dedication to Saint Francis would have been typical. The double dedication to God and the city had not been used since antiquity, when pagan temples were sometimes dedicated to a god and the country or city. The last clause of the dedication on the Tempio, "a memorial worthy of fame and full of piety," suggests Sigismondo's dual purpose. Alberti's design for the exterior of the church captures this triumphal votive theme and celebrates the magnificence of Sigismondo and the Malatesta family.[74] Alberti embellished the façade with triumphal garlands and medallions bearing Sigismondo's

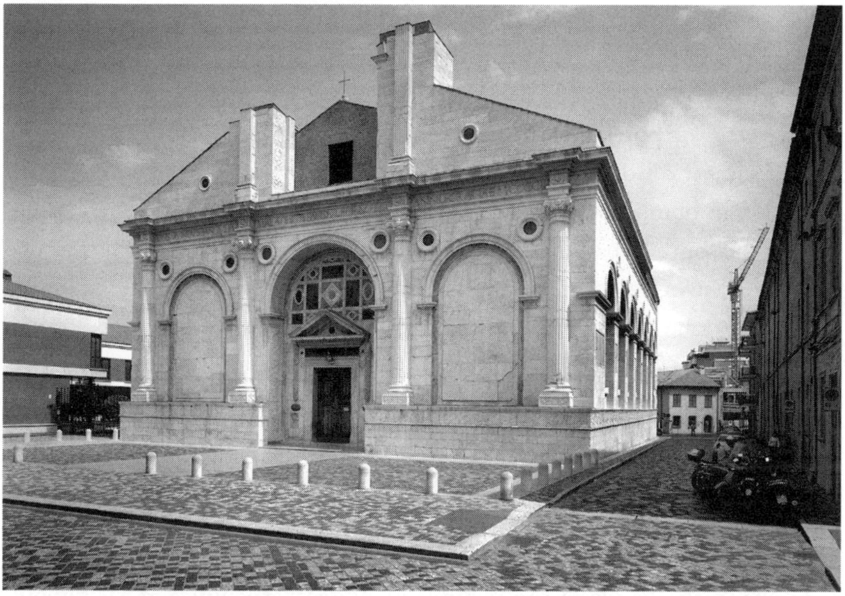

Fig. 2.11. Leon Battista Alberti, façade of the Tempio Malatestiano, designed ca. 1450, Rimini. Photo: Scala/Art Resource, NY.

coat of arms and images of elephants, palms, and roses. Elephants and roses were Malatesta emblems, and palms recall triumphs.[75] The porphyry above the main entrance pointed to the grandeur of emperors, since porphyry was the imperial stone; Charlemagne and his successors were crowned kneeling upon a slab of porphyry in old St. Peter's in Rome. Engaged columns show Alberti's fantasy and willingness to go beyond the classical canons of architecture, as winged putti faces adorn the tops of capitals. The Christian church is literally wrapped in imperial imagery of military and personal triumph.

The façade went through various stages of planning. Corrado Ricci argued that it was originally meant to have two sarcophagi on either side of the main door, one the Tomb of the Ancestors and the other of Sigismondo. Supporting the Romantic view of the church as a temple of love, Rudolf Wittkower proposed that the two tombs were to be for Isotta and Sigismondo. Both of these theories would support the self-aggrandizing theme of Sigismondo's renovations. Primary sources, however, refer to only a single tomb. Using this evidence, Helen Ettlinger proposes that the single tomb was meant to be placed over the main door and contain the body of

Sigismondo's brother, the Blessed Galeotto, thus making the church into a Christian pilgrimage site. Whatever the original plans, none were carried out, and what was finished left no room for any tombs. Furthermore, whereas the top portion of the façade was left incomplete, the area above the main door is the most finished part of the façade. It is encrusted with an elaborate design of multicolored marbles, including porphyry.[76]

On the south face of the Tempio are seven arches, each with a tomb. The fact that none of the tombs contain family members or have any kind of religious, let alone Christian, relevance, emphasizes the classicizing Roman imperial theme. Instead, Sigismondo's humanists fill the tombs: Giusto de' Conti, Basinio, and Valturio are joined by Plethon, whose body Sigismondo brought to Rimini, as noted previously. He may have been inspired by the recent tombs for humanists in Florence in the church of Santa Croce: Bernardo Rossellino's tomb for Leonardo Bruni (1444–1447) and Desiderio da Settignano's tomb for Carlo Marsuppini (1453–1464).[77] Although the inclusion of books in the hands of the recumbent effigies of Bruni and Marsuppini certainly signal their literary interests, the monuments commemorate their service as chancellors to the Florentine republic, whereas the tombs on the Tempio serve no such official purpose. Sigismondo was following classical precedent in placing the bodies of his court humanists in the same church as the tombs of the Malatesta. Scipio Africanus, Valerius Maximus (first century CE) reports, placed a statue of Ennius among his family tombs, as this poet had made his deeds famous.[78] Just as the ancient commanders had done, Sigismondo desired to promote his glory through letters. The way in which he enshrined his court poets shows how much Sigismondo valued humanism and saw literature as central to his lasting fame.

Rome and the triumphal theme are continued inside the Tempio, in the Chapel of the Ancestors.[79] The two reliefs of triumphs on the Tomb of the Ancestors recall the grandeur of ancient Rome. In antiquity, returning glorious commanders were paraded through Rome on the Via Sacra, under great triumphal arches constructed to serve no other purpose than to monumentalize their victories. Here too, after passing through the triumphal arch of the façade, we see ancient triumphs for a modern hero. The reliefs themselves, sculpted in a classical style, show the triumphs occurring under triumphal arches, one of which has carved winged putti faces on the capitals, mirroring Alberti's façade.

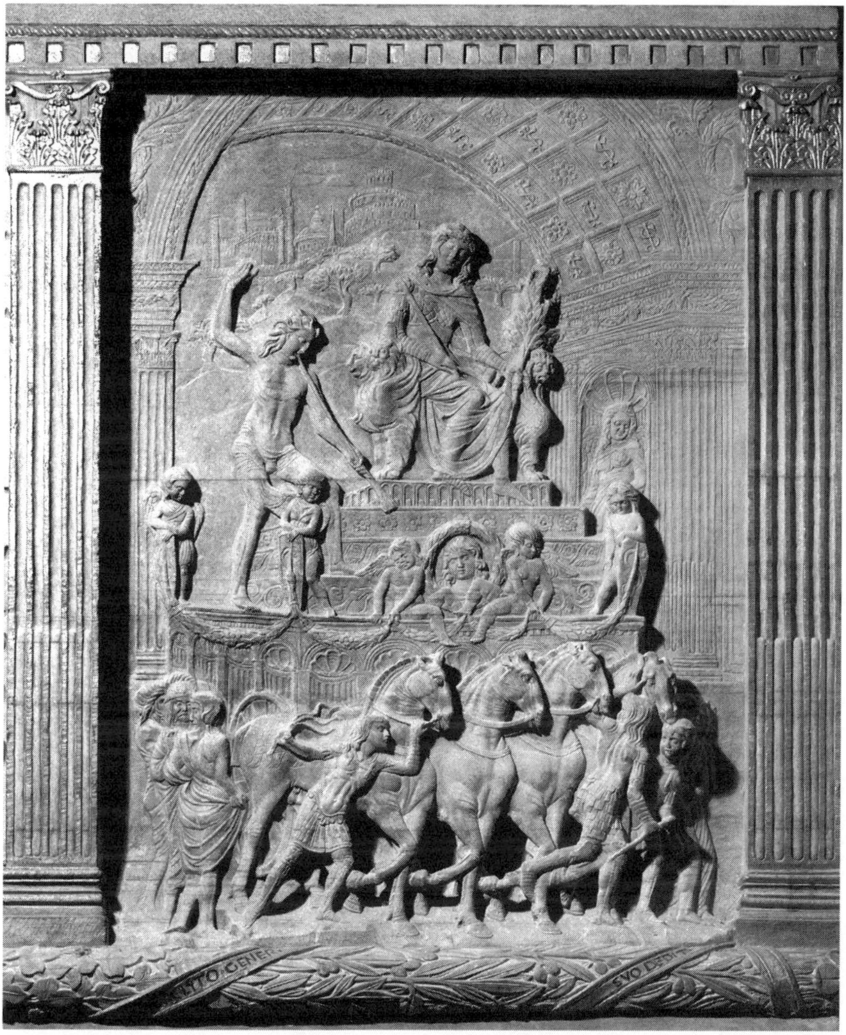

Fig. 2.12. Agostino di Duccio, the triumph of Sigismondo as Scipio Africanus, marble, ca. 1455, Tomb of the Ancestors, Tempio Malatestiano, Rimini. Photo: Scala Ministero per i Beni e le Attività culturali/Art Resource, NY.

One triumph is of Scipio Africanus, here given the features of Sigismondo Malatesta (fig. 2.12). In the *Africa,* Petrarch described the triumph held for Scipio in Rome after he defeated Hannibal in 202 BCE.[80] Scipio was one of the greatest generals of all time, celebrated for saving Rome. The other relief on the Malatesta tomb depicts the triumph of Minerva, the Roman goddess of wisdom and war (fig. 2.13). In order to make the connection to personal glory more apparent, Sigismondo's "SI" and rose emblems are carved dozens of times in the triumphal arches of both reliefs. Sigismondo's name and dedication are also inscribed both in a large panel between the reliefs and below on banderoles that wind around sculpted golden laurel, evoking the laurel wreaths worn by ancient triumphant commanders. The imagery of pagan triumph is particularly striking given that this is a tomb in a Christian church, usually a place for pious images about the Christian hope for redemption.

The chapel holding the tomb of Sigismondo's ancestors is framed by twelve sculptures: ten sibyls and two Hebrew prophets. Sibyls, female seers, were a central part of pagan religion. In ancient Greece, the sibyl at Delphi was frequently consulted on matters of state and war. She would fall into a trance and utter profound statements in a deep voice. Virgil has Aeneas use the Cumaean Sibyl as his guide to the underworld in the *Aeneid* (bk. VI). Instead of eradicating them, the early Christians capitalized on the prophetic authority of the pagan sibyls and insisted that, like the Hebrew prophets, the pagan sibyls had predicted the birth of Christ. In the fourth *Eclogue,* Virgil has the Cumaean Sibyl predict the coming of a savior, which Christians interpreted to be Christ. The early church father Lactantius (240–320 CE) describes ten of the sibyls and, as evidence of Christian superiority, he repeats the Erythraean Sibyl's pronouncement that there is only one God.[81] In ca. 1430 Cardinal Giordano Orsini had twelve sibyls painted in his palace in Rome. Sigismondo may have seen the room himself, as it was well known and listed among the monuments to be seen in Rome during the Jubilee of 1450. There was also a direct connection between the Orsini and the Tempio sibyls in the correspondence of Roberto Valturio, who asked the humanist Poggio Bracciolini for information about the cardinal's sibyls in 1454. Only Poggio's reply survives. He asserts the importance of having Latin phrases attached to each sibyl, a prescription that was followed in the Tempio.[82] Major differences in Rimini, however, are that the sibyls are marble reliefs, accompanied by the Hebrew prophets Isaiah and Micah, who both predicted the birth of the Messiah, and that they are in a consecrated Christian church. There are precedents for depicting sibyls in a church, notably on Giovanni Pisano's pulpit in Sant'Andrea in Pistoia (1301). In the Tempio, however, the sibyls are given new prominence, depicted in a large scale as equal to and indeed

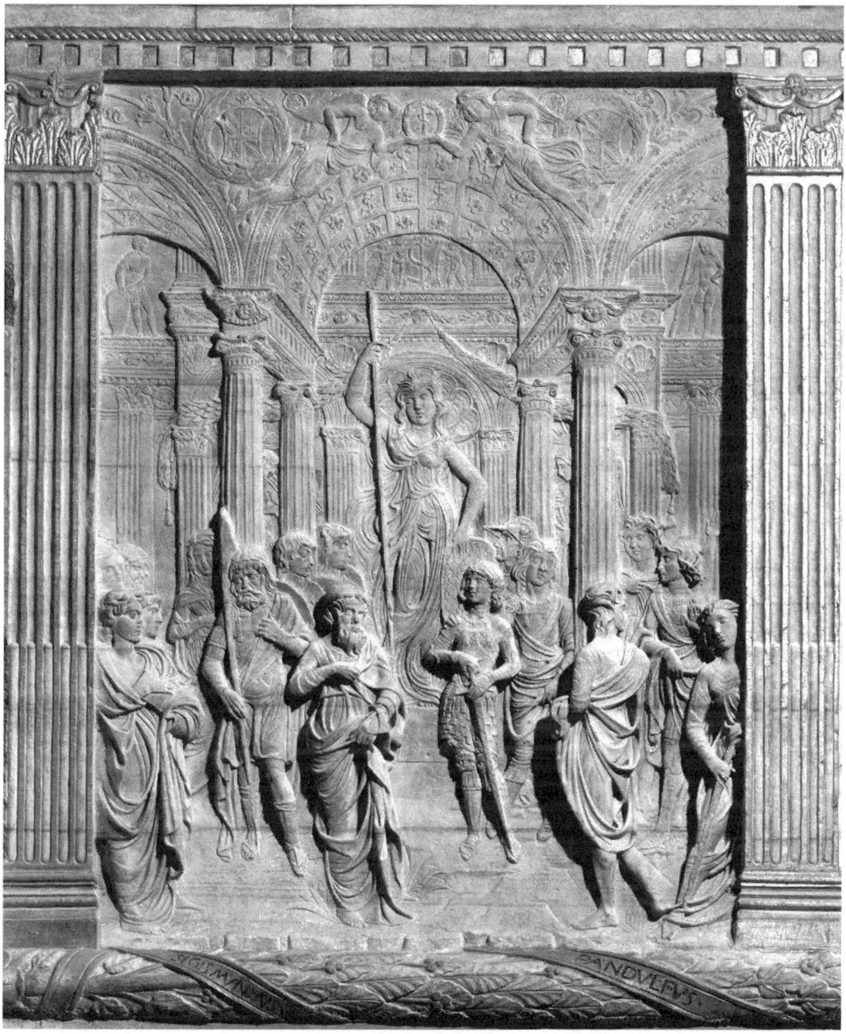

Fig. 2.13. Agostino di Duccio, the triumph of Minerva, marble, ca. 1455, Tomb of the Ancestors, Tempio Malatestiano, Rimini. Photo: Scala/Ministero per i Beni e le Attività culturali/Art Resource, NY.

predominating over the Hebrew prophets in terms of sheer numbers. Only later did sibyls play such a pivotal role in the interior of a church on the floor of Siena cathedral (1482–1483), in Filipino Lippi's frescoes in the Carafa Chapel of Santa Maria Sopra Minerva in Rome (1489–1491), and most famously in Michelangelo's frescoes on the ceiling of the Sistine Chapel (1508–1512).

The startling classicism of the Tempio does not derive from any single image but from the combination of so many pagan forms and themes: constellations, gods and goddesses, muses, triumphs and triumphal arches, and sibyls. The Tempio is classical in form as well as imagery, with figures in togas and other classical dress, and those that are nude or partially nude. The very medium, marble relief sculpture, which was not generally used to clad the interior of a church, recalls the ruins of ancient Rome, as well as the rich use of stone ornament in another lavish city, Venice.

Venice

Venice represented a different kind of grandeur to Sigismondo, one that evoked colored marbles, water, and extravagance. In 1437–1438 the city known as La Serenissima hired Sigismondo to fight its war against Filippo Visconti of Milan (1392–1447). Although Sigismondo actually appears to have lost the one important battle of the campaign (Calcinara sull'Oglio, July 22, 1437),[83] Basinio presents it as a victory and describes Sigismondo's triumphal entry into Venice. It is not clear if the triumph actually occurred, but Basinio paints a vivid picture of Sigismondo admiring the glories of Venice, which he certainly did—if not in 1438 then soon after. In the poem, the doge came out to escort Sigismondo in the Bucintoro, the famous large ceremonial ship of Venice:

> Innumerable skiffs covered the sea, and the waves became white and foamy from cutting prows. Seen from afar, such a great line of cheering ships raised Sigismondo's spirits. Covered in gold and yellow sails the ships looked like stars, and they shined all the more on the reflecting water of the sea, for the calm depths seemed to burn and flames to melt into the water. . . . The doge's galley, called the Bucintoro, received the jubilant Sigismondo and proclaimed a triumph with much praise of the victor. . . . Sigismondo set out to admire the noble palaces (of Venice), wondered at the eastern treasures of the empire, and gazed up at golden ceilings resting on golden columns.[84]

The jewel of the Adriatic and the gateway to the exotic East, Venice meant extravagance. The noble palaces along the Grand Canal and the Doge's

Palace seemed to float, and their multicolored marble façades reflected off the waters of the canals that make up the streets in the lagoon city. Nowhere else in Italy were buildings covered with as much colored stone, golden mosaic, and carved marble as the palaces and churches in Venice.

Sigismondo returned to Venice and led her army for two years, from 1449–1451. The extravagant use of marble in Venetian architecture must have left a lasting impression on Sigismondo, which is visible in the abundance of marble reliefs in the interior of the Tempio. Sigismondo's chief sculptor, Agostino di Duccio, had worked in Venice from at least 1446 until 1449. Agostino started life as a mercenary soldier before finding his path as an artist in Donatello's workshop. In 1441 he was accused of stealing silver from the church of Santissima Annunziata and exiled from Florence. Agostino then worked in Modena and Venice, and he arrived in Rimini in 1448 or 1449 to work on the first two chapels.[85] In Venice, Agostino trained in the workshop of Bartolommeo Bon, who was responsible for the richly ornate Porta della Carta (1438) and façade of Ca' D'Oro. The Porta della Carta was the main triumphal entrance to the Ducal Palace, and, if he did go to the palace in 1438, as Basinio claims, Sigismondo would have passed through the recently completed doorway.

At this time Venetian architecture and sculpture were Gothic, with ornate carvings covering whole surfaces of buildings. Agostino combined this Venetian taste for a lavish use of relief sculpture with the new Renaissance style. This was extravagant and unusual at the time, especially in Florence, where, for example, the sculptor Donatello was known for his restraint. Relief sculpture had been used in Florence and other centers on tombs, doors, and other spaces—but never to this extent. In the Tempio high and low marble relief cover large parts of chapels and the nave, an exceptionally expensive undertaking that displays Sigismondo's magnificence.

The reliefs in the Tempio may also recall the waterways of Venice. Agostino depicted flowing and spouting water in the Chapel of the Children's Games, where winged putti dance around a squirting fountain, ride sea monsters, row a boat, and play in waist-deep waves, squeezing water out of their hair (fig. 2.14). Agostino also carved water into several reliefs in the Chapel of the Planets. Aquarius unsurprisingly is surrounded by flowing water, and Venus's legs are caressed in foaming waves (fig. 2.6). Like Venice, Rimini was a port city on the Adriatic, where fishing and shipping

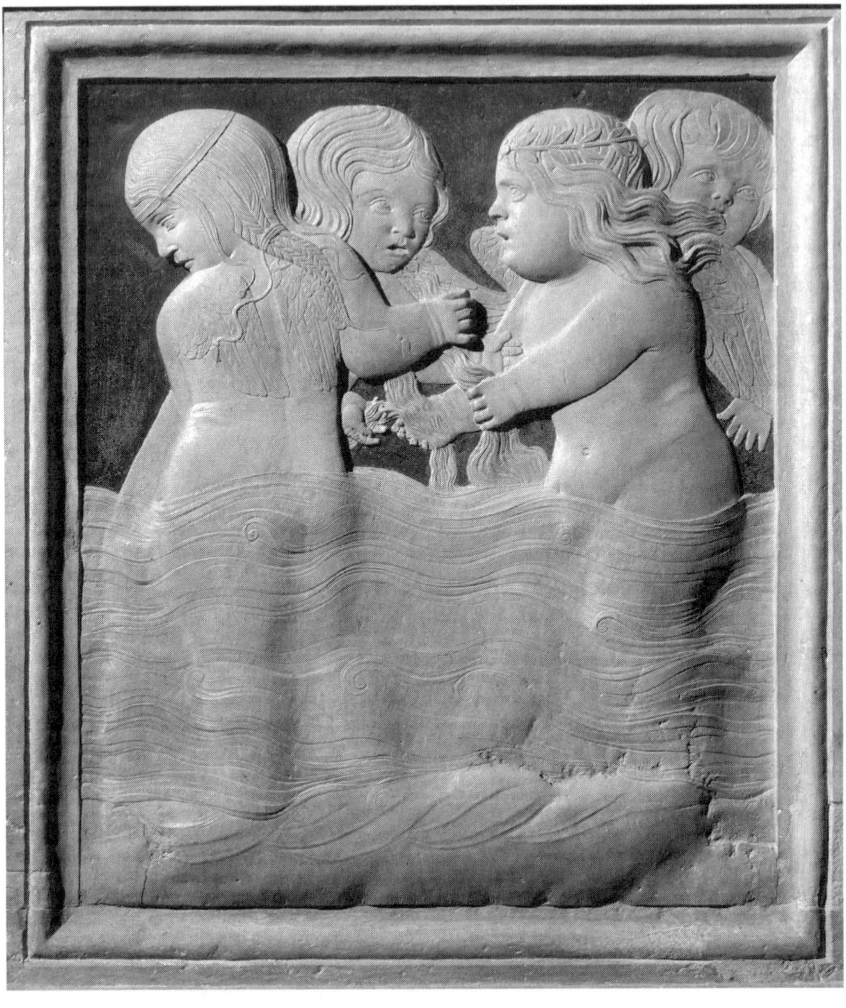

Fig. 2.14. Agostino di Duccio, children playing in the water, marble, ca. 1455, Tempio Malatestiano, Rimini. Photo: Scala/Art Resource, NY.

commerce were vital. In his relief of Sigismondo's sign, Cancer, Agostino carved the big crab over the cityscape of Rimini (fig. 2.5). The carved outlines of the Castel Sismondo, the Tempio, and the ancient Roman bridge all surrounded by extensive fortifications, celebrate Rimini. In front of the city Agostino depicted a galley with a billowing sail tossed about on a turbulent sea. Another relief shows the power of the moon in a stormy sea. Waves and menacing sea monsters threaten a lone naked man in a rowboat, as the

Malatesta emblem, an elephant, looks on from a small island, perhaps a representation of Sigismondo steering the ship of state through all difficulties (fig. 2.15).[86] The rich variety of ways in which Basinio described the water around Venice and Sigismondo's approach on the cerulean lagoon in the *Hesperis* find their complement in the dynamic variety of flowing water that Agostino captures in marble. Even if Basinio invented the scene of the Venetian triumph, Sigismondo knew well the splendor of the city on the water and aspired to a similar maritime glory.

The many places he visited and the intellectual company he kept shaped Sigismondo's cultural patronage. Sigismondo was clearly impressed by the culture of Ferrara, Florence, Rome, and Venice, and he obtained artists, humanists, and ideas for specific classical works from near and far. In imitating splendid centers of Renaissance culture, Sigismondo created a court that was more radically classical than that of any of his contemporaries. The tensions and contradictions of Sigismondo's extraordinarily pagan Renaissance are exemplified in the Tempio Malatestiano, a Franciscan church, clad in triumphal marble and porphyry, enshrining humanists and a pagan philosopher, and replete with classicizing reliefs of gods and goddesses.

Malatesta Novello (Lord of Cesena 1429–1465)

Sigismondo's younger brother, Domenico, had the same upbringing in letters and war, and apart from brief moments of separation, the two were close throughout their lives.[87] After Carlo died in 1429, Domenico inherited the city of Cesena, which he ruled until his death. In 1433 the Holy Roman Emperor Sigismund knighted Domenico at the same time as his brother. Domenico also changed his name and was thereafter known as Malatesta Novello, perhaps to emphasize his rebirth as an anointed knight. In a funeral oration for Malatesta Novello, the Cesena humanist Francesco Uberti recalled Novello's rigorous training regimen:

> He trained himself with great diligence to handle the sword and lance, and to mount fiery untamed horses. He knew how to wear armor like clothes, so as not to suffer from its weight or imposition. He trained his soldiers to follow him on horse or to jump over obstacles [and] ditches, one after another, wherever

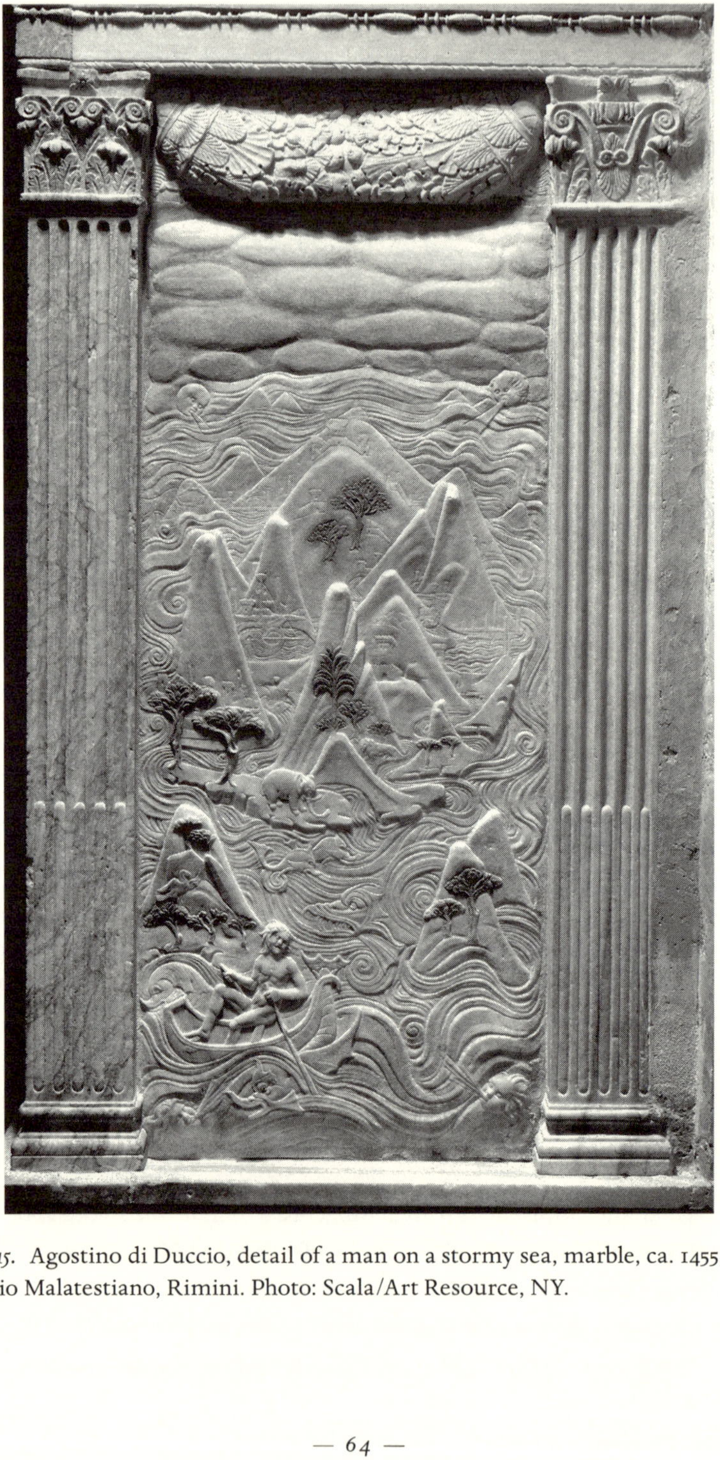

Fig. 2.15. Agostino di Duccio, detail of a man on a stormy sea, marble, ca. 1455, Tempio Malatestiano, Rimini. Photo: Scala/Art Resource, NY.

> they might be, to swim across rivers, to jump without stopping, and race on rough paths. He was passionate about reading history and the lives of the great commanders.[88]

As we shall see, Sigismondo shared in these exertions and early interests. Novello's career followed much the same trajectory as his older brother's; from 1434 he too led the papal army and worked for Venice and alongside the famed mercenary captain Francesco Sforza (1401–1466). Novello, however, experienced some devastating losses in battle; in 1438 he was overwhelmed by the Braccesche (the mercenary company of Braccio da Montone (1368–1424)), and in 1439 his horse went berserk and sent him into the enemy, who took him prisoner for two and a half months.[89] In 1446 Novello's life took a sudden turn from his brother's when a long-term illness forced him to quit the military life. Novello had a varicose vein, a tumor near his knee, and a deformed ankle. He was in much pain and could not move without the help of others.[90] He was still active in politics and used his faithful lieutenants Gian Francesco da Piagnano and Scario to lead his troops in several campaigns.

Crippled and virtually bedridden because of his leg, Novello sought to overcome the weakness and pain of his body with literature, history, and philosophy, both pagan and Christian. A near contemporary, Matteo Bosso, praised Novello:

> Far from pitying himself because he had lost his body's vigor and nimble movement, the illustrious lord knew how to raise his spirit in constant study of philosophy and sacred letters. He called the most learned men to his court and had a magnificent wonderful library, rich in art and cultural works, in fact the best books to be found in Italy, built in Cesena.[91]

Study and contemplation were apparently more than distractions for a disabled man, unable any longer to ride into battle. Novello was praised for becoming intensely aware of a higher philosophical and spiritual truth:

> Content and very wise [Novello] said of himself that once he had been cured of horrendous blindness he began to see and that if

> before he had always been strong in his body, now he moved his spirit; the one principally belonged to beast, the other the special, highest, and saving good of man. Oh magnificent progression, that that spirit raised itself from a wretched mortal body to such great light![92]

Novello is described as being Platonic in his intellectual striving to separate the eternal soul from the prison of the mortal body. Bosso's words recall Diotima's progression on the ladder from physical beauty to ideal beauty and the source of all light in Plato's *Symposium*.

Biondo Flavio states that Novello's "knowledge of history surpasses all the learned men of his age . . . and his library is equal in magnificence to other buildings in Italy, and it is not inferior in number of books."[93] Novello also showed a strong sense of Christian piety. One of the most cherished manuscripts in his famous library, the Malatestiana, was in fact a richly illuminated copy of Augustine's *City of God*. Carlo Malatesta had had it made long before the Malatesta brothers were born. Augustine had been a follower of Plato and a trained rhetorician before his conversion to Christianity in the fourth century CE. Although the *City of God* is a sustained attacked on the errors of the pagan philosophers, Augustine had paved the way for early Christianity's adoption of pagan philosophy. This Christian approach to the classical world was a model for Novello.

Novello completed his library in 1452. He had corresponded with Cosimo de' Medici about his recent renovation of the library of San Marco in 1441–1444. Novello's admiration for Cosimo is especially evident in the fact that he addresses the Florentine patriarch as "father" in numerous letters.[94] Cosimo's library was the first library open to the public. Niccolò Niccoli and Ambrogio Traversari, among other humanists, helped gather manuscripts and organize the collection for Cosimo. Tommaso Parentucelli was also involved in the project and, after he became Pope Nicholas V (1397–1455) in 1447, took it as a model for his founding of the Vatican Library. Novello was inspired by Cosimo in the construction of the building and in the acquisition of ancient authors. The Biblioteca Malatestiana in Cesena was particularly rich in medical and scientific texts and ancient historians. Novello especially prized translations of Greek authors, including Thucydides, Herodotus, Polybius, Plutarch, Appian, and Strabo.[95] He corresponded with the major humanists of his day. Francesco Filelfo dedicated his Latin translation of Plutarch's lives of Galba and Otho to him. In his dedication, Filelfo praises Novello for being prudent far beyond his youth and offers the two Roman emperors as positive and negative guides to ruling: the wise elderly Galba and the cruel Otho.[96] Among other manuscripts, the library held a complete Greek edition of Homer's *Odyssey* and a Latin translation of Plutarch's *Lives of Alexander and Caesar,* which together formed essential textbooks on leadership for Renaissance rulers.[97] It also contained an extensive collection of medical and scientific writings from antiquity and the Middle Ages, which belonged to Novello's personal doctor, the famed physician Giovanni Marcanova (d. 1467).[98] The design of the library, which survives today with its original furniture and books, reflects its purpose as a place for study and philosophical and theological contemplation. The wooden desks are slanted for often heavy manuscript tomes, which are chained down to prevent theft.

The Malatesta brothers shared the same education and upbringing. Yet although Sigismondo and Novello were born only a year apart, their personalities and lives were quite different.[99] In 1454 Francesco Filelfo (1398–1481) composed a Latin ode for Novello in the form of a dialogue among the gods. Disgruntled over Italy's prosperity, Pluto tries to persuade Neptune to raise stormy waves to destroy the peace and bring back war. Neptune hesitates, referring to the existence of one good man, Malatesta Novello, who has earned the protection of the gods because of "the force of his mind and the sweetness of his character." But strife nevertheless ensues, and all are at war, except for Novello, who "alone cares for the gods . . . fosters eloquence," and "cherishes the things of the mind." At the sight of Novello, Jupiter stops the war. The humanist's completely self-serving praise focuses on Novello's generous patronage of the arts—of eloquence and poetry in particular. Filelfo wrote a very similar ode to Sigismondo. He is praised for the same virtues: strength of mind, eloquence, love of the muses, and patronage of humanists. But, unlike in the ode to Novello, Filelfo recalls specific deeds: Sigismondo's saving of Rimini at thirteen, his battles under Francesco Sforza, his victories over Niccolò Piccinino (1386–1444) and Alfonso of Aragon (1396–1458), and his campaigns for Venice and Florence. Sigismondo's great virtue has subdued fortune.[100] Already an invalid in his late twenties, Novello could not match Sigismondo's famed valor on the battlefield, even in the most laudatory account.

In 1442 Novello married twelve-year-old Violante Montefeltro (1430–1493), the sister of the ruler of Urbino, Federico da Montefeltro, soon to be Sigismondo's greatest enemy and ultimate destroyer. Because of this family connection, Novello dealt very differently with his brother's nemesis, and on May 30, 1457, he made a pact with Federico da Montefeltro. Sigismondo was furious but could do nothing. The timing could not have been worse, as several setbacks leading up to 1457 marked the beginning of Sigismondo's long and painful downfall. Although they disagreed over how to handle Federico da Montefeltro, Novello and Sigismondo remained close, and cultural exchanges between the courts of Cesena and Rimini were fairly continuous.[101] Novello was married to one woman his entire life. When he died in 1465, the thirty-five-year-old Violante became a devout nun and eventually the abbess of a monastery. Such a religious and long-living spouse no doubt gave Novello a stability that his brother Sigismondo could never have experienced in his tragic first two marriages and the passionate romance of his third.

The Malatesta brothers were raised in the chivalric culture of the courts of northern Italy. The eldest, Galeotto, early on followed the lead of his adopted mother and dedicated himself to Christian devotion. If family pressures had not forced him to become a ruler, he would have preferred to live out his vocation as a Franciscan friar. In the end, neglect and extreme ascetic practices forced him to abdicate and succumb to an early death. His younger brothers, however, proved themselves more than capable to succeed where Galeotto had failed. The unfortunate Novello was a generous patron of classical learning, but Sigismondo alone would win fame in words, images, and deeds, as a pagan hero. Fueled by emulation of the classical splendors of Ferrara, Florence, Rome, and Venice, Sigismondo created a Renaissance in Rimini that was both of its time and distinct, a limit case in the revival of ancient pagan culture.

✣ 3 ✣

The Greek Renaissance and the Return of the *Paideia*

Sigismondo Malatesta was a generous patron to humanists and made the study of Latin and Greek literature central to the culture of the court of Rimini. Humanism was a catalyst for the Renaissance. Classical literature supplied the foundations for every discipline. Renaissance architects studied the writings of Vitruvius along with ruined buildings; painters and sculptors competed with both surviving ancient statues and the masterpieces described in Pliny. Renaissance poets imitated the meters, styles, and words in classical verse; philosophers started their enquiries into truth through recently recovered dialogues of Plato and other ancient philosophers; and Renaissance historians wrote the histories of their own times using as models ancient writers, especially Livy, Suetonius, and Polybius. Petrarch had revived the ideal of eloquence in the fourteenth century. He sought out the Latin texts of antiquity that had been lost in the Middle Ages, imitated their style, and applied their wisdom to his own life. The next generation of humanists took Petrarch's project a step further. Where he had failed to learn Greek and recover the classics of ancient Greece, Pier Paolo Vergerio (1370–1444), Leonardo Bruni (1370–1444), Guarino Guarini, and Basinio succeeded. Rimini was a center for this Renaissance of classical Greece.

The humanist movement was based on the belief in the transformative ennobling effects of classical texts of literature and moral philosophy. Much of this literature was unknown or known only by name to medieval intellectuals. Starting in the fourteenth century, humanist scholars recovered these lost texts from monastic libraries. They did this not merely to study a culture, as a modern-day anthropologist might, but to draw lessons from them and to absorb through imitation their eloquent language, whose very grammar and words they believed carried magnificence, empire, and success. The Florentine humanist Leonardo Bruni saw a link between political liberty and cultural efflorescence. It was no coincidence that the golden age of Latin literature, he said, was under Cicero and the Roman Republic and that decline began after the emperors curtailed freedom. Of course, Virgil's Latin, especially epic verse, could be and was used to serve an imperial ideology. Lorenzo Valla proudly declared that the Roman Empire was a direct result of the Latin language; one language united numerous different peoples and brought order and beauty throughout the world. Although the empire had fallen, he argued, its glory could be made to live again by reviving its language.[1] Both humanists stressed the importance of eloquent language for governments and individuals. Valla and other humanists not only imitated ancient eloquence but also tried to understand its grammatical underpinnings; imitation could then become appropriation, and a complex ancient language could be used to uncover and express the most sophisticated mental processes that wholly eluded the imprecise chaos of the Italian vernaculars. Inspired by the depth of Latin, Dante had tried to find a similar order in the vernacular, and in Sigismondo's time Leon Battista Alberti wrote the first grammar book for Italian.

Although writers had turned to the classics for inspiration and imitation before, Petrarch (1304–1374) was the acknowledged father of humanism. Throughout the fifteenth century, his writings were read and imitated. Frustrated by the arrogance of university professors and their scholastic method, Petrarch focused his attention on ancient Roman writers. For Petrarch, Virgil's *Aeneid* showed the fruits of virtue in glory. In imitation of Virgil, Petrarch composed a Latin epic about the ancient Roman hero Scipio Africanus and his battle with Hannibal in the second Carthaginian War (218–202 BCE).[2] Scipio Africanus was a cult hero in the courts of northern Italy. Sigismondo Malatesta later adopted Scipio as an ancestor and a personal model. Petrarch had also read Cicero, Livy, and other classical authors in new ways, as models for his own eloquent compositions, as sources for what he realized was a radically different historical time, and as living testaments of the authors' perspectives on life and the particular worlds in which they lived. Petrarch knew from his reading that there had been many other ancient writers, whose works were unavailable but might be recovered. He searched monastic libraries for manuscripts. When he discovered several copies of his favorite author for Roman history, Livy, Petrarch compared them, noted discrepancies, and corrected errors. His biggest find was the familiar letters of Cicero. Throughout the Middle Ages, Cicero was known through his philosophical works, which he had composed in exile. The medieval Cicero was a wise man, aloof from society and politics. But the personal letters were written before his exile, when Cicero was a major player in Roman politics. They are full of the kind of political wrangling so detested by contemplative philosophers and monks. Petrarch was shocked by this new Cicero: how could the greatest Roman philosopher have wasted so much time on politics and worldly power? Petrarch responded by writing a letter of disbelief and complaint to Cicero.[3] Writing to a man from an earlier age was logical, since reading for humanists was an active conversation with an author. Through formal and verbal imitation, and historical understanding of an ancient author, humanists summoned the ghosts of antiquity to help them navigate the moral and political decisions of their own time.

Cicero had defended the values of pagan Rome and made historical examples serve the state with the ideal of eloquence. Rhetoric was a philosophy focused on action. The Greeks had developed it, but Cicero excelled at it.[4] In antiquity, the art of rhetoric was seen as a form of magic. Mellifluous prose persuades, like a witch's charm. Balanced periods and rhythmic tricolons roll off the orator's lips and capture the listener's will and change his behavior. Rhetoric is the science of using words to move people. According to Cicero, true eloquence required both wisdom and style. Unlike philosophy, which concentrated on convincing the mind through reasoned argument, rhetoric aimed to move the heart of the listener toward virtuous action. By focusing on action, rhetoric aimed at instilling prudence. Humanists attacked scholastic philosophers not only for their lack of style and formal elegance but also for their neglect of practical wisdom, what really mattered for living in the world and developing one's fullest potential.[5] This concentration on language and behavior made the humanist program particularly appealing to upper-class and ruling families, whose children were brought up to be leaders and to rule over their cities in fifteenth-century Italy.[6] Pier Paolo Vergerio made the Ciceronian ideal of eloquence the guiding principle in his influential educational treatise *The*

Character and Studies Befitting a Free-Born Youth (1402–1403).[7] At his school in Mantua, Vittorino da Feltre educated the Gonzaga children and Federico da Montefeltro, and in Ferrara, Guarino Guarini taught the Este children the same ideal. After their classically inspired education, future rulers were apprenticed, as teenagers, to the great commanders of their age and learned the arts of war firsthand from experienced veterans. Leonello and Borso d'Este, for example, lived in Alfonso of Aragon's camps, and Sigismondo worked for years under Francesco Sforza. Humanist education espoused an ideal balance between the active life and the contemplative life.

The Renaissance of Greek

In his philosophical and rhetorical works, Cicero had to a large extent translated Greek ideas into Latin and simplified them for a practically minded Roman audience. He translated the Greek concept of *paideia* as *humanitas,* which, as Aulus Gellius clarified, meant training in the liberal arts. Italian humanists ascribed to Cicero's ideal of *humanitas,* which focused on the *studia humanitatis:* rhetoric, history, grammar, literature, and moral philosophy.[8] There was, however, also a revival of the original meaning of the Greek *paideia,* which became known in Italy with the recovery of Greek antiquity. The Greek system of education, the *paideia,* stressed the development of a child's character, of self-development, and an interior freedom that promoted the nurturing of a personality free from outside influences. It also stressed physical education and health of the body.

The revival of classical educational ideals and the *paideia* was directly linked to the reintroduction of the ancient Greek language and literature in Italy at the end of the fourteenth century.[9] Although some communities and a few monasteries in southern Italy still spoke Greek, for the most part Greek had been lost to intellectuals in medieval Western Europe. None of the great scholastic minds, including Thomas Aquinas, Peter Abelard, William of Ockham, and Albertus Magnus, had any knowledge of Greek.[10] Their understanding of Aristotle, whose ideas were so central to medieval thought, came through incomplete and imperfect Latin translations made in the twelfth and thirteenth centuries, mostly from Greek texts but also from some Arabic translations. Muslim commentaries from Spain were especially important for the reintroduction of Aristotle's ideas in the twelfth century. Ibn Rushd (Averroes) (1126–1198) in particular was known as the essential commentator. Many of his extrapolations on Aristotle, however, were seen as heretical to Christian doctrine. Whereas, for example, Christians believed that God created the world and that the individual soul continued to live after the body's death, Aristotle and Averroes saw the world as eternal and denied personal immortality.[11] Some of the reasons for the founding of the great universities (ca. 1190–1230) were to establish order, to protect orthodoxy in belief, and to combat heresy. Given their efforts to proselytize and protect the Church, Dominicans were a natural choice for teaching philosophy and theology, and by the late thirteenth century, they were the majority of the masters at the universities.

Dominican theologian and saint Thomas Aquinas (1225–1274) has rightly been seen as the star representative of the scholastic method and the pivotal figure in the development of medieval Catholic philosophy and theology. The scholastic method sought to reconcile competing authorities through logic and reasoned argument. Far from having separate truths, as Averroes would have it, philosophy was the handmaid of theology. It used logic and nature, which were after all God's creations, to prove what was accepted on faith. The growing popularity of the pagan philosopher Aristotle and the Muslim commentator Averroes prompted the University of Paris to proscribe the teaching of Aristotle in 1210 and again 1215.[12] Despite the edicts, Aristotle and Averroes were more popular than ever in the later thirteenth century. A Franciscan, Siger of Brabant, was even teaching Averroes's ideas right under Thomas's nose in Paris. Thomas was regent master of the University of Paris at the time (1268–1272) and wrote extensively against philosophical and theological errors. By reinterpreting Aristotle in a Christian framework, Thomas corrected the heretical conclusions of Averroes and others. Thomas, for example, subjected Aristotle's belief in the eternity of the world to Aristotle's own logic and concluded that there was no way to prove or disprove it. Ironically, Thomas's own works were condemned in 1277 for containing twenty propositions that limited God's omnipotence.

Neither Thomas Aquinas nor any of the other scholastics involved in the Aristotle controversy could read Greek. They relied on compendia and translations. Although Boethius (480–525) had translated a few of Aristotle's logical works into Latin, and later James of Venice, Michael Scot, Robert

Grosseteste, and others translated individual works, their translations were not as diffused, influential, or ambitious as William of Moerbeke's (1215–1286) almost complete works of Aristotle. His translation of the *Politics* (1260) among other works became the basis of scholastic political thought. William's translations, however, were clumsy, and his word-for-word method made them rife with errors. Latin grammar and syntax differed too much, and Greek philosophical terms often had no equivalents in Latin. These textual problems were magnified in the translations that came out of Spain. Gerard of Cremona and Michael Scot produced numerous Latin translations from Arabic translations, which themselves were based on Syriac versions of Aristotle's Greek. Ugly and unfaithful to the style and content of Aristotle's original Greek, medieval translations nevertheless created a technical Latin jargon that became the basis of scholastic speech and writing.[13]

Greek literacy was no better in the fourteenth century, when Petrarch and Boccaccio (1313–1375) tried in vain to expand their classical knowledge to include Greek. When Petrarch finally abandoned his effort, he bewailed that without a Latin translation "Homer is mute to me and I am deaf to him . . . O how I long to hear him!"[14] The situation, however, dramatically changed in the late fourteenth century, when Byzantine scholars started coming to Italy to garner support for their tottering empire. Byzantium had preserved the ancient Greek tradition almost intact. Unlike Western Europe, whose vernaculars had little in common with the Latin of Cicero's day, Byzantine Greek was quite close to the ancient language of golden age Athens. Manuel Chrysoloras (1355–1415) brought this tradition to Italy, when he taught Florentines Greek language and literature from 1397 to 1400. He was a gifted teacher and charismatic to the point that his students and later Italian humanists often marked the beginning of the Renaissance with the Byzantine's arrival in Florence.[15] Chrysoloras introduced Italian humanists to numerous Greek authors whose names had been barely known before, including Demosthenes, Plutarch, Xenophon, Polybius, and Isocrates. Leonardo Bruni, one of Chrysoloras's students, made translations of these texts into humanist Latin that became bestsellers in fifteenth-century Italy. In addition to translating most of Plato's dialogues, which had been previously unknown in medieval Western Europe, Bruni retranslated Aristotle's *Politics, Ethics,* and the pseudo-Aristotelian *Economics.* These works were immensely popular and mostly displaced medieval translations of Aristotle. Bruni and other humanists sought to correct the inaccurate and barbarous language of the medieval translations; they sought instead to translate Aristotle's Greek into eloquent Latin. Eschewing the medieval word-for-word literal method (*ad verbum*), humanists focused on translating the meaning (*ad sensum*) and style of the Greek original. Cicero was their guide in this method. In his writings, he had demonstrated how Greek ideas could be elegantly and forcefully expressed in Latin.[16] Only eloquent Latin could faithfully and persuasively convey the fullest meaning of an eloquently written Greek text.

Greek in Rimini

Rimini may have been one of the smaller courts of the Renaissance, but it was an important center for the study of the Greek language and literature. Located on the Adriatic, Rimini was closer to Greece than other Italian cities. Before Sigismondo's reign, the Malatesta family had forged strong links in the Morea, a semi-independent part of the Byzantine Empire, located where the Spartans had flourished in antiquity. Sigismondo's cousin, Cleofe Malatesta, who had also grown up in Carlo Malatesta's care, had been the empress of the Morea. As an early attempt to unite the Eastern and Western Churches, Cleofe had been married to Theodore II, the emperor of Mistra (next to ancient Sparta), in 1420. She had quite a presence in the Mistran court and was much mourned when she died in childbirth in 1433.[17] Cleofe's daughter became the queen of Cyprus. Basinio mentions both in the *Hesperis*. Another relative, Pandolfo Malatesta, was Archbishop of Patras from 1424 to 1441. Although under Venetian control, Patras was in the Morea, north of Mistra. Sigismondo probably never met Cleofe or Pandolfo, since he was much younger, but he would have heard about these family connections. Perhaps because of these ties to contemporary Greek culture, much of the humanist literature that Sigismondo patronized was distinctly Hellenic in inspiration.

In the fall of 1455 an argument broke out among three humanists at Sigismondo's court. As often was the case when humanists competed for the favors of a prince, the cause of the antagonism was style and grammar.[18] Basinio described the argument in a detailed letter to Roberto Orsi, and three invectives survive. According to his account, Basinio had originally recommended that Sigismondo offer patronage to the wandering Neapolitan humanist Porcellio. But as soon as Porcellio arrived in Rimini, he produced "puerile poetry that was most in need of serious censorship." In the words of the much younger Basinio:

> After I had corrected his poems two or three times, Porcellio exploded not with the divine madness that is usual with poets but with the purest kind of rage and the most extreme insults. He criticized my knowledge of Greek and said that my Latin was forced in many places; he spoke ill about me with the many butchers, cooks, poultrymen, and pimps that he keeps in his house. I could no longer tolerate his shameless impudence and therefore demonstrated in public and in the Castel Sismondo that his terrible, disordered, and ill-turned verse should be brought back to the anvil. Porcellio was so upset by this that he conspired against me with [another court humanist] [Tomaso da] Seneca and told Sigismondo that a Latin man had no need for Greek letters. They blabbed that I had wasted my time with Greek. When I heard this, I confronted them. I said that I would prove that the Latin language could not be known perfectly without Greek; they promised to argue the opposite. So, I composed a few verses to demonstrate with great ease that Latin could not be perfectly known without Greek.[19]

Basinio addressed his Latin invective in meter to Sigismondo Malatesta. Like his teacher Guarino, Basinio claims that Virgil took everything from Homer. He quotes or cites Horace, Quintilian, Statius, and other Romans who respected Greek; he also includes Jerome, Lactantius, and Augustine. Basinio lists the great Hellenists of his time: Vittorino, Guarino, Bruni, Theodor Gaza, Filelfo, Perotti, Valla, and Poggio Bracciolini. Basinio claims that under Sigismondo "in Rimini the Greek and the Latin languages are flourishing with great praise."[20] He then launches into his attack:

> But if you yourself, Porcellio, have been lazy, insipid, and dull, o Polyphemus content with one eye, why do you prevent others from learning the words known to the ancient poets? Go swiftly

> (young men); don't believe him; learn Greek! But if Porcellio stands in your way, be bold and plug up your ears.

Basinio says that it is impossible to know the names and immortal descent of heroes, gods, and men without Greek. He ascribes his own success to his knowledge of Greek literature and "the source and streams of the great Homer."[21]

Tommaso Seneca and Porcellio responded in kind. Their invectives center on arguments of Italian pride and the inherent machismo of the virile Latin language as opposed to the effeminate Greek. Seneca wrote:

> You madman think that no poet is illustrious without Greek books; according to you this is perhaps a law, you who have no ability except from Greek titles, and are ignorant of the Roman art. Do Dante, who was excellent only in his mother tongue, and Petrarch . . . seem completely worthless to you? What about the prophets, David and Job? They did not gain their power from Greek fonts.

Seneca's plea mixes patriotism and piety. He continues, "You are imitators and servile sheep, who do all things by example and lack a fertile mind. . . . We are strong in spirit and chest. We seek no help from outside." Seneca then refers to Leonardo Bruni's preface to his translation of Plutarch's *Life of Antony,* in which, following Cicero, Bruni argues for the superiority of Latin over Greek.[22] Seneca concludes by calling upon Sigismondo to "resolve the argument once and for all." As the arbiter and judge of such an erudite debate, Sigismondo is portrayed as having a strong foundation in humanism, a command of Latin, and perhaps some knowledge of Greek.

Porcellio's invective is fairly long and is mostly about how Latin authors are great and superior to Greek. Like Seneca, Porcellio turns it into a question of Italian pride and suggests how Sigismondo and Isotta should treat the pretentious Greek scholar, Basinio: "Italian voices and the sybils will drive you away from Roman shores and Rimini. Good-natured Caesar (Sigismondo), the son of Mars, will ridicule you; gentle Isotta will scorn your conceited head. Everyone will point their finger at you as uncultured and unskilled; to the Latin people you will be a ridiculous Greek." In the end, however, Porcellio invites Basinio to join him in "defending holy Rome" and finishes the poem with a flattering plea to Sigismondo and Isotta.[23]

Basinio was predictably offended by the suggestion that he would denigrate Latin letters:

> Instead of addressing the question, they argued with fallacy and deceit (since they had no learning or virtue) and tried to place Latin before Greek—as if I had praised Greek more than Latin and they had not seen my [Latin] verse. Hardly do I begrudge the most beautiful words of our language, the dignified sounds, rhythm, and polished prose; nor do I desire to place Greek before our language; but I have always taught and will always teach that without the help of Greek the Roman tongue has little strength.

Basinio got in the last word, as with his letter describing the polemic he supplied three pages of line-by-line criticism of Porcellio's and Seneca's invectives. He corrects their Latin grammar, nomenclature, and style. In the end Basinio turned to the perennial question of money:

> Porcellio and Seneca say that I have gained nothing from my knowledge of Greek letters. But they are certainly wrong about this, for Greek has won me the benevolence of a great prince, a most beautiful plot of land, and a very pleasant villa. All of which these starving parasites lack, dressed as they are in soldiers' rags, mad old men, who make everyone laugh.[24]

He concludes the letter: "Such is what these superficial blockheads wrote against me." Basinio won the debate: Sigismondo ruled in favor of Greek.

Homer on the Adriatic

Greek literature was an essential part of the humanist culture in Rimini. In the fall of 1455, when the supposed debate over the Greek language took place, with Sigismondo himself acting as judge, Greek had already been well established.[25] The debate in fact may well relate to the two prominent Greek inscriptions chiseled on the Tempio in 1455–1456. Basinio, who was probably the author of the inscriptions, had studied Greek under Vittorino da Feltre, Theodore Gaza, and Guarino.[26] He was one of the first translators of Homer and imitated the Greek bard in his lengthy Latin epic about Sigismondo, the *Hesperis.*

Homer was one of the authors that Chrysoloras taught in Florence, and Vergerio is believed to have translated the great poet already in 1400, but his work does not survive.[27] Humanist references show that Homer was being read in the early fifteenth century. In a 1430 dedication to Galeotto Roberto, Sigismondo's older brother, the Florentine humanist Carlo Marsuppini introduced his translation of Isocrates's *Ad Nicoclem,* with the example of Homer's Agamemnon, who was "despairing of ever taking Troy and so prayed to the gods not for gold, supplies, or more men or horses, but for only ten men who were equal to Nestor in council and wisdom."[28] Isocrates's short treatise on rulership could have no better introduction. Gaspare Broglio (1407–1483), Sigismondo's councilor and companion, produced a massive chronicle of his times, which he began before 1443 and finished at his death in 1477.[29] In the chronicle, he transcribed Guido de Columnis's 1287 retelling of the fall of Troy, the *Historia destructionis Troiae.* Guido, who probably could not read Greek, amalgamated stories from Homer as well as Virgil and has sections on such Greek heroes as Jason and Hercules. Broglio's inclusion of Guido's work emphasizes the importance of Greek culture in the Malatesta court. Broglio's chronicle is in the vernacular with transcribed parts in Latin; he probably did not know any Greek. Other Malatesta humanists, however, could read Homer's verse in its original. Homer and Greek culture are ubiquitous in Malatesta literature.

Roberto Valturio, who claimed to know Greek and used Greek sources in his military treatise, calls Homer "the font and source of all divine subjects." He urges Sigismondo to "meditate on and read intensively Homer's verse." Valturio actually disapproves of poetry as "weakening the nerves of virtue" but makes an exception for epic, especially Homer. Plato, he writes, cast out of the ideal republic all poets "except Homer, whom he recommended for honor, set up a temple and provided sacrifices."[30] Leonardo Bruni had called Homer the font of all wisdom in his *On the Study of Literature to Battista Malatesta,* and he had cited Homer already in his *Laudatio* (1404).[31] Valturio repeats the same two examples of practical advice from the *Iliad* that Bruni used. In one, Hector scolds Aeneas, saying that prudence is more important than boldness in battle. Tellingly, however, Valturio does not include Bruni's criticism of modern commanders who "ignoring this counsel and using rashness instead of caution, have brought great ruin and wretched slaughter upon themselves and their men."[32] Such a criticism would have been much too applicable to Sigismondo, whose professional life was characterized by impulsive decisions. Valturio also follows Bruni in using Homer's Iris as an example of the importance of vigilance. But Valturio includes other examples not used by Bruni and so must have been reading Homer directly. He argues that the Greeks' choice of Diomedes and Odysseus for a night raid shows the need for both force and wisdom in military actions. Valturio refers to Plutarch's stories about Alexander the Great and Homer, which are oddly missing in Bruni; how under Aristotle's guidance Alexander carried the *Iliad* with him into battle as a manual of war and always kept it under his pillow along with a dagger at night in a gold-encased and gem-studded box that he had gotten from the spoils of Darius. In his conclusion, Valturio reiterates the practical wisdom of Homer and his poetry as a primer for war.[33] As a mercenary and student of the art of war, Sigismondo would have an obvious interest in the preeminent poet of war.

Pope Nicholas V had asked Basinio to translate the *Iliad* into Latin, but Basinio declined, protesting that only his teacher, Theodor Gaza, could do the poem justice.[34] Nevertheless, translations, imitations, and appropriations of Homer abound in Basinio's poetry.[35] In his lengthy description of Sigismondo's shield in *Hesperis* XI.379–421, Basinio translates whole sections of Homer's ecphrasis of Achilles's shield in *Iliad* XVIII.478–608, including descriptions of Orion and the stars, the two cities, a wedding, dancing youths, the senate in session, and the battle scene with the two armies led by Mars and Minerva. Like Homer, Basinio concludes his description with a scene of bucolic peace, fields ploughed and cows tended. Unlike Homer, however, Basinio frames the shield with "one hundred snakes of the Gorgon [Medusa]" and in the middle places the Furies: "Discord and her sister Erinnys, followed by her dreadful sister Megaera. Impious Tisiphone summons her sisters to dark battles, bringing before her bloody slaughter (pitiful to see). Here is mad honor and the glory of a beautiful death."[36] By wreathing Homer's shield in snakes and filling it with bloody discord, Basinio competes with Homer and conveys more of the fury and chaos of war. He contrasts this violent image with a tranquil scene of Apollo calming Diana and the gods with song and lyre. In *Aeneid* VIII.626–731, Virgil had also modeled his description of Aeneas's shield on Homer, but he used the ecphrasis to recount Roman history. It is telling of Basinio's Hellenism that he appropriated and copied from Homer rather than Virgil in his description of Sigismondo's shield, even though this meant eschewing an occasion for a laudatory history of Rimini. Basinio also consciously competes with Homer and the *Iliad* in the *Hesperis,* when he has Athena declare that the Italians had already suffered as many casualties in their war, the second Tuscan War 1452–1453, as the Greeks had suffered in Troy "in their twenty year war in Asia."[37] Basinio wanted to be the new Homer and made the comparison explicit.

The *Odyssey* was Basinio's preeminent model. He calls Sigismondo a new Odysseus repeatedly. In the metered letters that Basinio composed in the names of Isotta and Sigismondo, the "divine Isotta" is several times compared to Penelope in her longing for Sigismondo-Odysseus.[38] In the *Hesperis,* a triumph put on for Sigismondo in Padua occasions a discourse on Odysseus's skill at Troy, which Basinio concludes: "But why am I recalling the deeds of ancient times? After Odysseus, no one is as renowned for his astute use of deceit as Sigismondo."[39] Known for his innovative siege tactics, Sigismondo could hardly have found a better classical comparison than with the inventor of the wooden horse that caused the fall of impregnable Troy. In the *Art of War,* Valturio uses Odysseus as an example of prudence and reviews the hero's adventures with the Cyclops, Scylla and Charybdis, the Lotus-eaters, the Sirens, and Circe. In the *Hesperis,* Basinio uses the same epithets to describe Sigismondo as Homer did for Odysseus: clever, eloquent, and skilled in deception.[40] An oracle reveals the trials that Sigismondo will encounter, including Scylla and Charybdis, and says: ". . . the muse hides this not from you, just as Circe instructed Odysseus and said such things as he traveled back to Ithaca." Like Odysseus, Sigismondo has help from the goddess Pallas Athena and is saved by the sea nymph Ino, after he is shipwrecked by a storm sent by Neptune. On shore another nymph, Psycheia-Isotta, helps Sigismondo just as Nausicaa did Odysseus. Psycheia takes Sigismondo to her father's palace and washes and dresses him. When they visit the Temple of Fame, Sigismondo contemplates marble busts of Odysseus and Aeneas.[41] Basinio translates whole parts of the *Odyssey* and the

Iliad in the *Hesperis* and then modifies them to accommodate his new hero. He uses Homeric epithets to describe Sigismondo in battle and copies lengthy similes, such as comparing the clash of arms to a forest fire or soldiers fleeing flames to locusts.[42] Basinio certainly had the ability to translate Homer, but he was not interested. Instead he appropriated Greek texts for his own creations, which probably would be more likely to win him patronage than a straight translation. Basinio's early works, the *Meleagris* and the *Diosymposeos,* also followed Greek models and were made to showcase Basinio's originality. In fact, in the same letter, in which he declined to translate Homer, Basinio asks the pope to look at his poem, the *Meleagris.*

Basinio's approach to Greek raises key issues for Renaissance humanism. He did not actually teach Greek to anyone, nor did he make the wisdom of Hellas available except through his own neo-Latin poetry. For him it was a mark of superiority, which he guarded closely. Virgil was his role model. In the *Diosymposeos,* Basinio calls Virgil "the greatest poet, the glory of the Roman language." In his letter to Nicholas V, he calls Virgil "no faithful translator" and praises him for "re-ordering the parts of Homer and changing themes; since he took many parts and left others on purpose and formed them, as if they were all his own verses, into a new well-connected single poem."[43] Basinio longed to be a new Virgil—an ingenious creator who, as Virgil did for Augustus, reworked Homeric epic to fit the hero of his own time.

Even though he has already recommended the translating ability of his old teacher Theodor Gaza, Basinio criticizes the whole notion of translation: "If you were to translate Homer," Basinio says, "his language would seem rustic and unworthy. For who would introduce Jove-born Mars with a whimper so that he sounds like a crying child? But there in that language he sounds appropriate."[44] Homer in any language but Greek is not Homer. Form was always central to the humanist project of imitation, but it is especially at issue in poetry as rich in synonyms and repetition as Homer's. Basinio understood and appreciated Homer's Greek verse so much that he believed it untranslatable.[45] As Virgil had done, he imitated Homer and created an epic in his own Latin. The neologisms, similes, and subplots in the *Hesperis* all reveal that Basinio had fully absorbed Homer's words in the original.

In the *Hesperis,* Basinio shows Sigismondo delivering a battlefield speech to his men, in which he refers to Homer's *Iliad* and compares the Aragonese to the Trojans, who broke a truce when the gods inspired a Trojan archer to let loose an arrow at the Greek Menelaus.[46] The comparison between the truce-breaking Trojans and the untrustworthy Aragonese places Sigismondo and the Italians in the role of the invading Greeks fighting the Trojans. It also creates an image of Sigismondo as the learned commander, who uses Homer to rouse his men in an eloquent battlefield speech. According to the Riminese humanist Pietro Parleo (1400–1463), Sigismondo himself was "an avid student of Homer, who delighted in debating about Homer with the learned minds of his court."[47] Parleo had studied under Filelfo and in Constantinople before returning to Rimini in 1453 as official Malatesta historiographer. He praises Sigismondo's interest in Homer in the preface of a life of Homer that is mostly a much-abridged translation of the second-century pseudo-Plutarchan *Life of Homer.* Like the ancient life, Parleo's piece mainly deals with the question of Homer's origins and birth, but about four pages offer a Neoplatonic interpretation of the epics. "These two poems [the *Iliad* and *Odyssey*] provide perfect instruction to man, since one treats the movements and virtues of the body and the other those of the soul. The *Iliad* concerns the body, while the *Odyssey* the soul. Virgil imitated this in one poem and in briefer order. The first six books of the *Aeneid* deal with the virtue of the soul, while the last six that relate the wars in Italy touch on the body."[48] Parleo's version of the *Life of Homer,* which is only about seven double-sided pages long in most manuscripts, is significantly shorter than the original Greek text, which besides disquisitions on Homeric grammar includes lengthy proofs for the Homeric origins of all philosophical ideas, such as the immortality of the soul and metempsychosis.[49]

When he prematurely died in 1457, Basinio left to Sigismondo his incomplete *Hesperis* and his "Homer in Greek."[50] Even though it is unlikely that Sigismondo could read them in the original Greek, Homer's epics were central to his court culture and public image. Homer appealed to Basinio for his mastery of epic form, rich language, vivid descriptions of war, and examples of heroic action. But most of all, Homer offered an ideal warrior code. Malatesta humanists used Homeric notions of virtue to present their lord, Sigismondo, as the ideal Renaissance warrior.

Homer and Pagan Virtue

In ancient Greece, the *Iliad* and the *Odyssey* were the essential primers of the warrior code and path to divinity.[51] Homer defined Greek *arete* as excellence, the key quality of a warrior and of nobility. For Homer *arete* is first and foremost heroic valor, athleticism, and prowess in combat. The indomitable Achilles is the prime example of *arete*. In the nobleman *arete* carried an obligation to be courageous and brave, to nurture manliness. In stressing the *vir* (meaning "man") part of *virtus* and defining virtue as manliness, Cicero recalled the original Homeric meaning of *arete*. Already in Homer, however, *arete* could also be intellectual excellence. Phoenix reminded his pupil Achilles that he had been brought up to be "both a speaker of words and a doer of deeds," or as later Greeks interpreted it, that human perfection came from the union of noble action and noble mind. Eloquent, clever Odysseus and strong Ajax, the man of action, represent the two sides.[52] *Arete* was associated with personal honor and also with social duty toward one's peers and subjects, and later toward one's city-state and fellow citizens. For Homer, honor is public; it is the recognition earned from brave action. This is the heroic goal. The *Iliad* centers on Achilles's anger at not being given his due honor. Unlike Homeric heroes who judged their virtue and self-worth on the opinion of others, Aristotle and later Greek philosophers focused on an inner strength and virtue that did not need external recognition.[53] In Homer, *arete* and fame were interlinked. Poets are thus necessary to publicize the fame of a hero's deeds and make him immortal. This sense of honor and ambition for fame lived on in later antiquity and the Renaissance, as, for example, the often-repeated commonplace of Alexander bewailing that he had no Homer to sing his deeds and make him immortal.[54] The stoic philosophers later insisted that virtue was its own reward, but the Homeric emphasis on fame and reputation as the public reward for virtue gained new prominence in the court of Rimini, where art and literature immortalized Sigismondo's heroic deeds.

"Let any commander," Valturio declares, "who wants to be like Achilles or Agamemnon, entrust himself to this poet [Homer] and never let his book out of his hands, just as Alexander always had the *Iliad* on campaign with him."[55] According to Valturio, Homer is the preeminent source for examples of "fortitude," bravery and strength.[56] Valturio also refers to Homer's

Odysseus to define prudence, another aspect of *arete*. The goddess Minerva personified prudence and always accompanied Odysseus. With her help, he escaped the Cyclops's cave, Scylla and Charybdis, the Lotus-eaters, the Sirens' song, and Circes's island.[57] Valturio says that of all the virtues, "fortitude is the most proper virtue of man; it alone is male among the other virtues, full of spirit, vigor and courage."[58] Starting with Aristotle's definition of courage, Valturio writes that fortitude denotes both strength of character and physical strength of the body.[59]

In ancient Athens, boys were brought up constantly hearing recitations of Homer. Their early education in math, music, and letters all contributed to their comprehension of Homer, since in particular the musical meter of Homeric verse made it easier for students to remember the famous exploits of heroes. Hearing these stories encouraged boys to imitate and strive for *arete,* "so that they too may be sung and admired by men of later times."[60] In reading aloud and probably translating parts of Homer's epics to Sigismondo, Basinio and other humanists re-created this tool to virtue in Rimini, as Sigismondo heard firsthand about the warriors who embodied the truest form of *arete.*[61]

Just as Homer had given Basinio the epic model for his neo-Latin epic, so did Plutarch supply Valturio with models of virtue in the biographies of great men. For his images of Sigismondo Valturio made ample use of Plutarch. Ancient biography and history were treasure troves of examples of heroic virtue in the great men of antiquity. The Greek revival in early fifteenth-century Italy brought new translations of Plutarch's *Lives.*[62] What was a better mirror of princes than the lives of the great Greek and Roman generals? Courtly libraries, including Sigismondo's, all had Latin translations of Plutarch's numerous lives. Plutarch was more than a source for ancient history and biography; he was a guide for rulers on how to act. Both Plutarch and Homer offered Renaissance Italians vivid examples of the Greek educational system, the *paideia,* which Vergerio and other humanist educators reintroduced into Italy in the early fifteenth century.

What was Sigismondo's role in this efflorescence of Greek culture? He was the judge in the debate between Basinio and Seneca on the value of Greek. He collected Greek books and invited the Greek Plato scholar, Plethon, to his court. His humanists portrayed Sigismondo as an avid student of Homer's verse and cited him as an authority on Homer, and Basinio left him his Greek Homer in his will. Although Sigismondo probably knew little of the Greek language himself, he certainly valued his reputation as a cultivated patron, surely knew enough about Greek culture to appreciate the many references to it in his court literature, and promoted an image of himself as a Greek hero.

Reviving the Greek *Paideia*

In appropriating Greek sources, Basinio, Valturio, and others ascribed the values of the ancient Greek *paideia* to their lord and patron. The athletic and clever warrior prince Sigismondo was seen as the culmination of a Greek educational ideal that was revived in the Renaissance. The learning of Greek and the recovery of the Greek classical canon constituted a second Renaissance that completed what Petrarch had begun. It was vital to humanist education not only in terms of learning the Greek language and its literature but also in augmenting the Latin Ciceronian ideal of eloquence that Petrarch advocated with the more holistic values of the Greek *paideia* that gave equal weight to physical education. In the early fifteenth century Italian humanists rediscovered two ancient Greek educational treatises that became foundational for the humanist movement. In 1411, one of Chrysoloras's students, Guarino, translated Plutarch's *On Education* into Latin.[63] This short treatise, which Plutarch had composed in 110 CE, advised a Greek-reading Roman audience on a proper Greek education. Plutarch's ideal education focuses on building character and good habits, self-control, and honesty. It also includes a general education in the liberal arts, as well as speech and memory exercises. Good morals, he writes, should be taught by example. Physical education is also very important for Plutarch, to develop a graceful and strong body, "for sturdiness of body in childhood is the foundation of a hale old age." Boys should be trained in the arts of war, including "throwing the javelin, shooting with the bow, and in hunting."[64] In his *Lives,* Plutarch offers concrete examples about how such an early education could lead to greatness.[65] Plutarch was one of Valturio's prime sources for his image of Sigismondo.

Another Greek educational treatise, St. Basil of Caesarea's *Letter to the Young,* was one of the most popular texts in the early Renaissance. Leonardo Bruni's 1400–1401 translation of it appears in four hundred and fifty manuscripts and ninety-one printed editions from the fifteenth century.[66] Writing in the fourth century, Basil urged young Christians to study pagan literature and philosophy. Without detracting from Christian superiority, Basil saw Homer and Greek literature as repositories of noble actions to be imitated and base ones to be avoided. "When," Basil writes, Homer and the pagan poets "recount the words and deeds of great men, you should both love and imitate them . . . but when they portray base conduct you must flee from them and stop up your ears, as Odysseus is said to have fled past the song of the sirens." Basil also recognized that Plato and pagan philosophy could teach moral behavior. "If we gain heaven through virtue," he continues, "then we should focus on the many passages in which the pagan poets, historians, and philosophers praise virtue."[67] Such pagan wisdom therefore provided an exemplary study for the Christian soul and its search for virtue and heaven.

The popularity of Bruni's translation of Basil's letter shows the extent of the Greek revival and perhaps a need to defend pagan wisdom from Christian opposition in fifteenth-century Italy. Bruni in fact made the translation for another humanist, Coluccio Salutati, who was involved in a polemic with a cleric over whether young men should be taught the classics. Other humanists also used Basil to defend classical authors from Christian censors.[68] Basil, however, is quick to condemn Homer's polytheism and scenes of lusty sensuality. Plato and Pythagoras are his sources for seeing the body as a prison for the soul. Basil nevertheless allows for the feeding and strengthening of the body, as beneficial for the soul. And his use of athletic analogies and examples promotes, if indirectly, the athletic ideal of the Greek *paideia*. Basil refers to athletes (and musicians) to stress the importance of determination and suffering:

> I have called to mind . . . the fighters. These men endure hardships beyond number, they use every means to increase their strength, they sweat ceaselessly at their training, they accept many blows from the master, they adopt the mode of life that he prescribes, though it is most unpleasant, and, in a word, they so rule all their conduct that their whole life before the contest is preparatory to it. Then they strip themselves for the arena, and endure all and risk all, to receive a crown of olive leaves or some other branch, and to be announced by the herald as victor.[69]

Basil transfers the athletic ideal to Christianity. The rigorous training, practice, and determination of the athlete is the same for the Christian, only the goal is different. In antiquity, stoic and cynic philosophers referred to athletic training as an example to follow for self-control and temperance. Paul (1 Corinthian 9:25–7) referred to the strict training of the athlete to emphasize what was needed to gain heaven. Paul's letters are in Greek, and he was addressing a Greek audience. Other Greek Fathers of the Church besides Basil also used the imagery of an athlete of Christ.[70] Basil's analogy, however, is much more detailed and shows an intimate knowledge of martial training. The Christian appropriation of the Greek paideia and athletic mentality found its way to Renaissance Italy through Basil's letter. Valturio, for example, refers to a passage in Basil's letter on the wrestler Milo of Croton and the pancratist Polydamas. Pankration was a combination of boxing and wrestling similar to modern mixed martial arts. Whereas Basil uses the famous athletes to stress the importance of preparation and training, Valturio refers to Milo and Polydamas as examples of great physical strength and fortitude.[71] Fifteenth-century humanist educational treatises contain numerous references to and quotations from Plutarch's and Basil's treatises.

The most popular humanist treatise on education was Pier Paolo Vergerio's *The Character and Studies Befitting a Free-Born Youth* (1402–1403). The treatise is found in three hundred manuscript and forty printed editions from the fifteenth century. Pier Paolo Vergerio (1370–1434) had become interested in classical studies at the University of Bologna, and, after reading Petrarch, he moved to Florence in 1398 to continue his studies with Coluccio Salutati and Manuel Chrysoloras. Vergerio's studies under Chrysoloras introduced him to the ancient Greek *paideia,* and his treatise did much to popularize it in Renaissance Italy.[72] Although Vittorino of Feltre, Guarino Guarini, and other later humanist educators had their own particular approaches, they all promoted the same Greco-Roman ideals that Vergerio summarized in his treatise.

For Vergerio, character and good morals were essential to the proper development of children; athletics and regular exercise of the body were a part of the curriculum, as a sharp mind required a healthy body. Each child has a different character and requires special attention to develop his particular gifts. As leisure leads to vice, children should always be doing some mental or physical activity. Premature sex should be avoided as it weakens the body and mind, as should dancing and contact with women. Solitude should also be avoided, as it makes children prone to vice and laziness. Moderation in food, drink, and sleep, and respect for the elderly and religion should be enforced. The ability to accept criticism and honestly correct one's flaws and vices is the only way to grow and eventually become wise rulers. Liberal studies teach virtue and wisdom. The best studies for "cultivating virtue and obtaining glory," Vergerio states, are letters and arms. Letters are important as a way to relax a tired body and mind, and as sources for examples of great men of action. In reading, we converse with the past, in writing, with the future. Vergerio repeats Cicero's assertion that honor and glory are the principal rewards of virtue: "Just as profit and pleasure are laid down as ends for illiberal intellects, so virtue and glory are goals for the noble."[73] These are the values celebrated in Malatesta court literature and art.

The Greek Athletic Ideal

Vergerio offered a balanced education of body and mind. The students' daily routine gave equal time to the study of letters and vigorous exercise. In stressing this connection between a healthy body and a healthy mind, Vergerio was transmitting the Greek athletic ideal, which not only contributed to the popular notion of the well-rounded Renaissance man but became elevated to the divine and joined to the Roman notion of glory. Vergerio praises the self-control that the Spartans instilled in their youth through rigorous exercise.[74] Another humanist educator, Vittorino da Feltre, also made physical exercise a requirement in his school in Mantua. According to a contemporary biographer, he scheduled the students' day so that "they would go from their studies to physical exercise." Such training, Vittorino believed, "made them good citizens whether at peace or war. A good citizen should know how to jump, run, ride a horse, throw a javelin, wield a sword, and aim a bow." As many of his students were princes and future rulers, physical power and the ability to fight in battle were an essential part of education at a time when wars were predominantly fought with swords and arrows at close quarters. But Vittorino also took physical dexterity as a sign of intellectual ability. "If while walking, hunting, or fishing, Vittorino saw a student in a single bound jump over a stream or a ditch, however wide, he considered him worthy of his teaching, because he said that a shrewd mind comes from an agile body."[75] His students included Sigismondo's arch-nemesis Federico da Montefeltro and the premier Malatesta poet Basinio.

The future Pope Pius II, Aeneas Piccolomini, also recommended physical exercise for boys destined to rule. He believed a strong sturdy body to be the best bulwark against the ills of old age and saw combat exercises as essential for preparing for battle against the Turks.[76] Leon Battista Alberti, who designed the Tempio, made education gender specific in his dialogue *On the Family* (1443). Boys, he writes, should practice the virile exercises of the ancients: "Let girls sit and grow lazy. Young men should naturally seek exercise, should move their persons and all their limbs—let them shoot, ride, and pursue other manly and noble sports." All these exercises, he continues, are "useful and necessary for civic life."[77] In antiquity, Aristotle had also stressed the importance of "physical education" for fostering "manliness."[78] Alberti's sexist ideas about female education were not shared by all humanist educators. Female students in Vittorino's school, like male students, were required to ride horses and do outdoor exercises.[79] Some of Alberti's bias comes from his reading of ancient sources, such as Xenophon's *Economics* (ca. 362 BCE), which reflected Athenian social norms, where girls' education was extremely limited, and women were kept indoors, separated from men. The upbringing of girls in ancient Sparta was much different. Spartan girls exercised and even wrestled virtually naked with boys.[80] The Dominican preacher Giovanni Dominici had also cautioned about the need for boys to have a particularly masculine education. In his 1402 treatise, he firmly states that "boys who play with toy swords will grow up to be soldiers, but boys who dance with girls will be nourished on fetid flesh."[81] While there was some debate on whether physical activity was good for girls, Alberti and other humanists agreed that boys learn to be manly by doing manly activities.

Renaissance writers continued the ancient debate over the health benefits of physical exercise. Medicine was largely based on the works of the ancient doctor Galen (129–216 CE). Galen called gymnastics a false art, unlike medicine. He said that it is dangerous and useless and that "it drags man down to the level of an animal, depriving him of the use of reason." Although he conceded that it could enhance strength, Galen believed that the risks of dislocation and bone fractures outweighed any health benefits. Galen's target was athletic trainers. He continually referred to their stupidity and denounced their "claim to represent Hellenic culture." Galen had his critics in antiquity, including Philostratus, who argued that athletics were an essential part of medicine.[82] Although they did not know the full details of the ancient debate, Renaissance writers were keen to stress the medical benefits of exercise. In his treatise on the family (1402), Giovanni Dominici encouraged his readers to do physical exercise in order to release dangerous humors. Bodies, he wrote, "need strain, sweat, and exhaustion, to prevent humors from becoming putrid."[83] Balancing the body's four humors was the standard theory of Galenic and medieval medicine.[84] Other writers noticed the endorphin effect of exercise. The sixteenth-century art theorist Paolo Pino advised artists to wrestle and exercise to dissipate melancholy.[85] Not everyone, however, was convinced of the health benefits of Greek athleticism. Girolamo Cardano (1501–1576) thought that the kind of exercise advocated by the Greeks was excessive and would weaken the body, dissipating its strength. More moderate physical exercise was needed, he said, for a long life.[86] The debate focused not on whether exercise was good for health but on how much and which exercises were best for the body.

In addition to health, the aesthetic benefits of physical exercise were recognized in the Renaissance. Ancient texts contained descriptions of athletes' bodies and movements, and the sculpted torsos and muscular limbs of gods and heroes survive in marble sculptures. Renaissance artists used this knowledge and their own observations to portray strikingly muscular male bodies. The vogue for Hercules in the fifteenth century is connected to a proliferation of images that stressed the ideal of muscular male beauty. In particular, depictions of Hercules wrestling Antaeus offered exemplary strength and athletic prowess. Strong male bodies were commonly depicted in violent acts on wedding chests and in parade art.[87] The omnipresence of muscular male bodies in art shows a taste for the ideal of Hellenic virility and the benefits of physical exercise.

The interior decorations of the Tempio are replete with male muscular bodies, only partially covered by clothing and displaying an aggressive male strength unparalleled in a Christian church in this period, where normally the only sculpted male nude is Christ on the cross. Drapery does not conceal the sinewy strength of Jupiter and Saturn. Even the lovelier Apollo and Aquarius display strong arms and legs and broad chests (fig. 2.4). The centaur Sagittarius pulls his bow, revealing the taut muscles of his conditioned

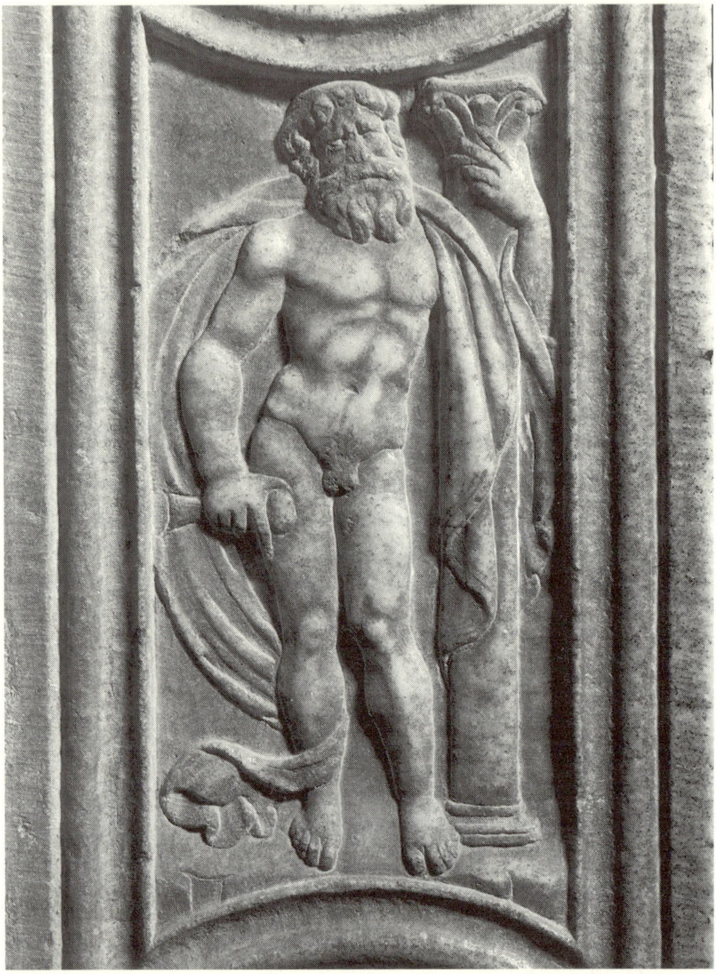

Fig. 3.1. Agostino di Duccio, Samson, marble, ca. 1455, Tempio Malatestiano, Rimini. Photo: Alinari/Art Resource, NY.

back and shoulders. Images of the Hebrew prophets in the Tempio conform particularly strikingly to this Greek athletic ideal. The prophets frame the door of a chapel that was in modern times rededicated to the war dead; the heroic male bodies around the entrance must have seemed particularly appropriate. Gideon, Samson, and Judas (?) are nudes depicted with strong, tensed muscles in movement (figs. 3.1 and 3.2). The identification of Judas is not definite since the nude bearded man with a big club over his shoulder

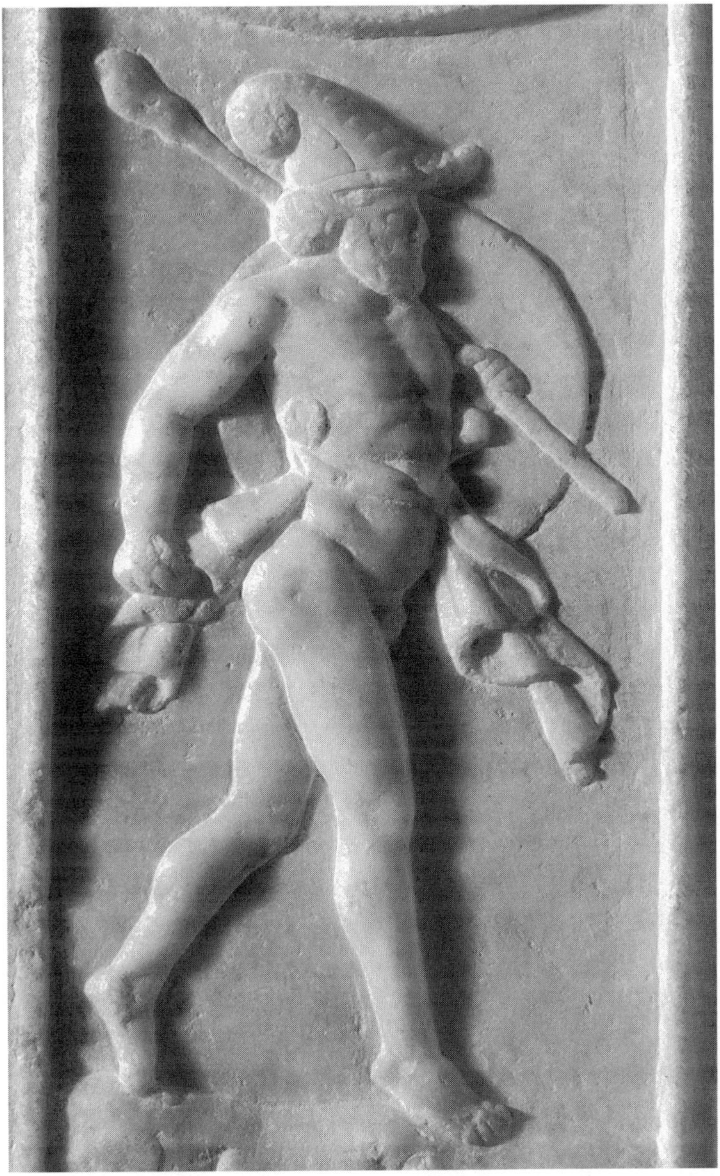

Fig. 3.2. Agostino di Duccio, Judas Maccabee or Hercules, marble, ca. 1455, Tempio Malatestiano, Rimini. Photo: Scala/Ministero per i Beni e le Attività culturali/Art Resource, NY.

has the same iconography as Hercules. These three prophets do not wear the traditional enveloping robes or have the long beards of sages but could instead easily be mistaken for Greek wrestlers, as their well-toned exposed physiques seem to be the products of extreme physical labor and exercise. The image of David also shows physical power in his stance, his aggressively pointed elbow, and his muscular large arms and legs (fig. 3.3). David is supposed to be young and small, as his triumph over the giant is in spite of his size and physical weakness. Here, decades before Michelangelo literally made David gigantic, he is depicted on a small scale but nevertheless made out to be a muscular giant, who turns his head in defiance and stands on Goliath's severed head. In republican Florence images of David were very popular. He was seen as a civic protector and linked to the struggle for liberty against tyrants.[88] The fact that a single ruler, Sigismondo, commissioned an image of David with Goliath's head is an example of how heroic imagery could be adopted for different political purposes.

A Hero's Education and the Art of Hunting

Like many other noblemen, Sigismondo was brought up hunting. In antiquity and the Middle Ages hunting was a popular literary topic. Homer famously described the scar that the young Odysseus received from a wild boar's tusk on a hunting expedition.[89] Boccaccio's first work of fiction, *Diana's Hunt* (1330s), was a hunting poem, and Basinio's first poem, the *Meleagris,* was a hunting poem dedicated to Leonello d'Este. It was fitting therefore for Basinio to use hunting as the first arena in which Sigismondo learned to fight and forged his character. Basinio emphasizes the dangers and the bravery the young Sigismondo showed in hunting: "He headed to the steep mountains with a light sprint and quickly returned a victor against shaggy wild boar and often wolves. Sigismondo complained that Lazio had no lions." Just as he will be later brave in battle, Sigismondo is shown fearless in the face of fierce animals. Basinio continues his account with a delightful image of the young lord's domestic bliss after the trials of the hunt:

> When the hunter returned to Rimini he brought from afar antlered stags to the halls and would enjoy at once the banquet gained by his sweat. He would then stand, content with little,

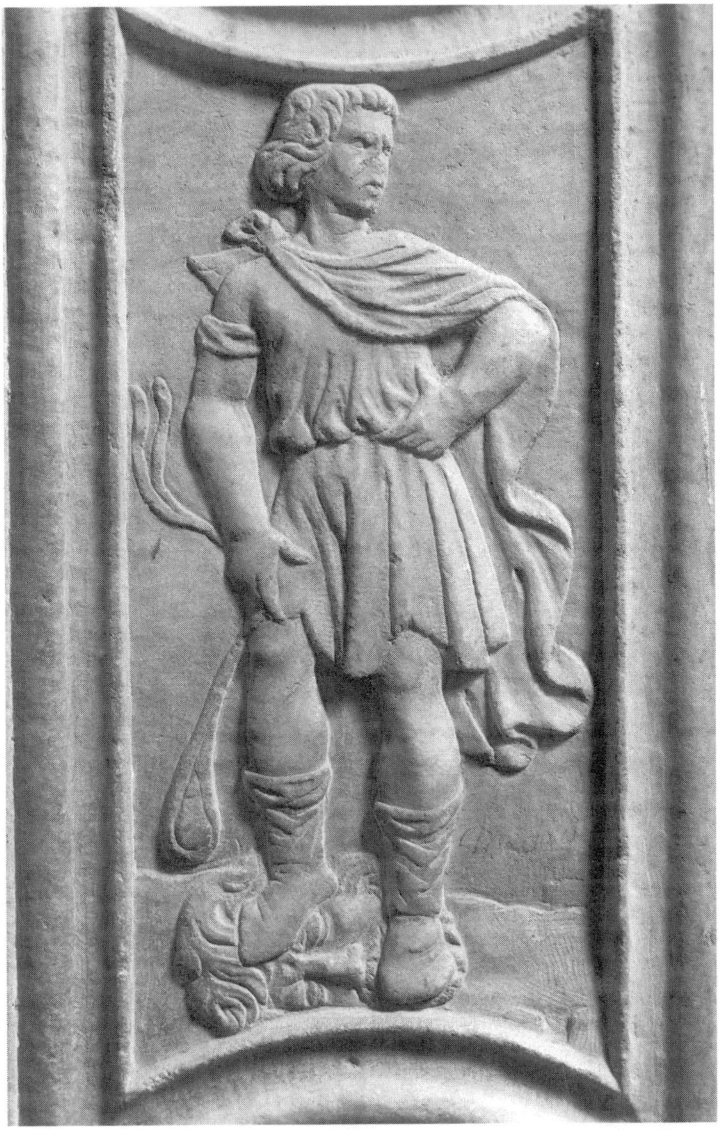

Fig. 3.3. Agostino di Duccio, David with head of Goliath, marble, ca. 1455, Tempio Malatestiano, Rimini. Photo: Alinari/Art Resource, NY.

> and read history, the monuments of ancient men. After wretched mortals began their sweet rest and others embraced black shadows, his dreams always brought horses and pleasant games. In the morning, when roofs resounded with birds' songs, the boy would get up and fill heavenly Olympus with prayers, and with much ceremony go at the same time to all the temples of the gods.[90]

The images recall the grandeur of both medieval and classical banquet scenes, complete with literary entertainments. The reading of ancient history and the deeds of illustrious men provide a preview of Sigismondo as humanist and patron. Elsewhere in the poem Basinio likens Sigismondo's pursuit of Alfonso to that of an African lion hunter.[91] The boy hunter of antlered stags has become the man hunter confronting the ferocious lion that is his enemy in war.

Hunting was a common activity of courtly youth in medieval and Renaissance Europe. In the Middle Ages, Charlemagne favored it both for relaxation and for training boys for war.[92] In his treatise *On the Family* (1443), Alberti told a story about how he ingratiated himself with Ladislas, the king of Naples. The king was desperate, cornered by a big bear on a hunting expedition. Alberti saved him by releasing two prize hunting dogs, who took the bear down by the throat. "The hunter's battle," Alberti remarks, "is like the soldier's struggle against enemies." That evening he and the king discussed hunting over dinner and noted that, as the dogs' collaboration had shown, hunting requires several men to locate and block prey off from flight. It was thus a worthy pursuit of princes and noblemen alike.[93]

Valturio repeats this common notion that hunting is a great preparation for war. He lists direct analogies between hunting and war, even asserting its value for hand-to-hand combat. Addressing Sigismondo, he says:

> You approve of hunting, which to you differs little from a just war, since one has to chase wild beasts in flight, move in rough, steep, and pathless terrain, suffer the greatest trials in pursuit, abstain from many things, endure heat and cold, suffer thirst and hunger, and be courageous, since one has to fight hand-to-hand and stay at close range with wild beasts.

Valturio refers to examples from classical literature to reinforce his point: Alcides transfixed a stag, Meleager a wild boar, and "Cyrus made his soldiers hunt for public utility and military discipline."[94] Xenophon's account of the education of the Persian ruler Cyrus was a favorite subject in humanist literature. Chrysoloras had reintroduced Xenophon to the Latin West in the 1390s. Leonardo Bruni translated several of his works and transcribed much of Xenophon's histories for his own Greek history. Lorenzo Valla translated the first four books of the *Cyropaedeia* in Naples and dedicated his work to Alfonso of Aragon in 1438. But the most popular translation was Poggio Bracciolini's in 1446 in Rome, which survives in thirty manuscripts. Hunting and its training of the skills for war was a centerpiece of Persian education.[95] Although Valturio's description of the benefits of hunting matches Xenophon's quite closely, he nevertheless credits his patron, Sigismondo, as the source. The humanists in Sigismondo's court thus elevated a common courtly activity by referring to classical models and presenting hunting as both the first testing grounds of Sigismondo's virtue and an education for war. Whereas Basinio presents Sigismondo as the heroic hunter in ancient epic, Valturio provides the classical rationalization of the utility of hunting.

Sigismondo and the Spartan Ideal

As previously noted, Sigismondo had family connections with Byzantine Sparta (Mistra). His cousin, Cleofe Malatesta, had been married to Theodore II, the emperor of the Morea, and knew the philosopher Plethon. In addition to his efforts to revive the cult of the Olympian gods, Plethon wanted to resurrect the glory of ancient Sparta. Using Lycurgus and the ancient civic model, he drew up guidelines to reform the social, political, and agrarian structure of Byzantine Sparta. Although he lived into his nineties, Plethon's project of reviving ancient Sparta had little success. His works were condemned for their paganism and mostly destroyed.[96] A frequent visitor at Sigismondo's court, the antiquarian Cyriac of Ancona (1391–1452) stayed in Mistra in 1447, had scholarly discussions with Plethon, and composed an ode in which he laments the fall of ancient Sparta and the loss of its virtue. Cyriac universalizes this decline, calling it "the pitiable ruin of the human race," and mourns the loss of that "pristine human virtue and renowned integrity of spirit."[97] As an antiquarian, Cyriac bemoans the physical ruin of pagan temples and art. But he also emphasizes the loss of pagan virtue, the spiritual values and character development of ancient Sparta. Back in Italy, Cyriac stayed in Rimini in 1449 and probably gave Sigismondo the idea to invite Plethon to his court.[98] The empress Cleofe, her teacher Plethon, and Cyriac's stories about his travels all assured Sigismondo that, although in ruins, the grandeur of Spartan civilization still endured in his own time and could be revived. The myth of ancient Sparta was very much alive in Rimini, and Malatesta humanists drew on Spartan lore to fashion their own myth of Sigismondo's Spartan upbringing and habits.

In antiquity, the Spartans were famous for training young warriors by exposing them to the hunting of wild beasts at an early age. In his educational treatise, Pier Paolo Vergerio praises the Spartans for training "their youth in exercises designed not only for physical endurance but also for mental self-control." In particular, he highlights their use of hunting as a training method for war.[99] Valturio compares Sigismondo's upbringing and education to Spartan practices and those of other ancient robust peoples in its extreme physical conditioning. He approves of the games that Lycurgus instituted for Spartan youth. From the age of seven boys slept, ate, fought, and trained for war together. Elders encouraged the boys to box and wrestle "so that they might learn by common struggle and competition each one's character, those who dared and those who declined to fight in the contests."[100] Such controlled violence revealed their strengths, bravery, and leadership abilities.

Valturio follows closely Plutarch's *Life of Lycurgus*.[101] Like the ancient Spartans, the Malatesta family took physical education seriously. Exercise and strengthening of the body trained it and accustomed it to hard work. Valturio addresses Sigismondo: "You cast aside the follies of youth and . . . learned not to grow stolid in laziness . . . and pleasure, but to strengthen your limbs, to endure military labors, vigils, hunger, thirst, cold, heat, and to tackle difficult hardships with the best soldiers and knights."[102] This is very different from the mortifications that his Franciscan ascetic brother practiced. Galeotto did what mortification literally means: he deadened the body, in order to eliminate it as a hindrance to the divine and ruin it to the point of spiritual transcendence. Sigismondo inured his body to hardship by strengthening it, building it up, and improving as far as possible the vehicle of the soul.

This early endurance training saved Sigismondo's life when Astorre Manfredi da Faenza ambushed him in the winter of 1446–1447. Knowing that he had to pass through hostile territory with only four soldiers in his escort, Sigismondo sent his men ahead of him, just out of sight. When Astorre attacked them, Sigismondo heard the din of the fighting and quickly escaped into a swamp. The chronicler Broglio reports: "When Sigismondo reached the wooded swamp, he jumped to his feet, drove his horse away, stripped off his armor down to his undergarments, and walked into the swamp. Seeing that Sigismondo was not with his men, Astorre ordered everyone to search him out with dogs. . . . as they reached the place where Sigismondo had hidden, he immediately put his whole body and even his head under the swamp water, suffering pain and grief. As night was coming, the search was called off." Realizing they had left, Sigismondo got out of the swamp and started walking "just as someone who understands from the stars which way to go for salvation." He walked all the way to Ravenna and found the house of a "poor man," whom he begged to take him that night to the house of the territory's marquis. Sigismondo hid his real identity from the man and in fact told him that he was an "escaped prisoner from Sigismondo" Malatesta![103] The man took Sigismondo to the friendly marquis, who rewarded him accordingly. The story reveals Sigismondo's craftiness and strong urge to survive, even to the point of dunking his virtually naked body in freezing swamp water in the middle of winter and quietly staying underwater for who knows how long. Then, of course, he had to walk probably miles in the cold through a dark forest. This anecdote in the much more sober chronicle of Broglio suggests that Valturio's praise of Sigismondo's Spartan endurance had some basis in fact.

To contextualize Sigismondo's training, Valturio recalls numerous examples of extreme exercise and endurance among the ancient commanders. A favorite example that Vergerio also cited is "Marius's mules": "On expeditions," Valturio writes, "Marius exercised his forces with continual work, distance running, and marches, and often ordered them to carry weights, and have baggage and rations placed in bundles on poles." His soldiers thus became known as Marius's mules. The Stoic sage Cato the Censor taught his son by example and himself practiced "bodily exercise, spear-throwing, arms-handling, horse-rubbing and riding, fist-fighting, bearing heat and cold, and swimming across rapids and rough rivers." The other famous Cato, of Utica, who sided with Pompey and committed suicide rather than accept the end of the republic under Caesar, also "exercised in the gymnasium and was so tolerant of hardship that he wore no hat either in sun or hail." Even at age sixty-two, Pompey exercised alongside his men in jumping, running, arms, and horseback riding: "Pompey would have been no match for Sertorius (in Spain) had he not prepared himself and his soldiers for battle with frequent exercises." A somewhat odd example of physical excellence is the Numidian king Masinissa, who "at ninety never covered his head in hail or cold, and stood in the same place without moving for hours."[104] The message in all these examples is the importance of discipline, of training the body to endure the hardships of war by conditioning it in analogous ways. Skill is taught and necessary, but self-control in a very stoic sense is the mark of a true warrior.

The Spartans also served as a model for their advocacy of dancing as preparation for war. Sigismondo was an enthusiastic dancer. Referring to Seneca's praise of Scipio Africanus's manly way of dancing, Valturio compares Sigismondo to his ancestor:

> Nor do you, Sigismondo, consider the study of dancing disgraceful; you usually exercise and perform in public, and you sometimes put on a show both unmasked or in costume; and you often use this reasoning that in dancing no part of the body should be at rest but that the neck, ankles, and hands should be exercised all together by him who wishes to have a body most agile and ready for every military movement and speed.[105]

The image of Sigismondo wearing a mask and dancing in public has great comic value, but Valturio's point is well founded, since dancing not only brings grace and charm but also body control and flexibility, which are essential in close combat.

Valturio cites the Spartans' approval of dancing as "a useful exercise for war." He quotes Socrates's assessment that it was "not shameful but necessary, since dancing was done with arms." Cicero's contemporaries Gabinius, Caelius, and Licinius Crassus "not only studied dancing but boasted of their great skill at it." And of course Scipio "would move his triumphant and warrior body not to soft and weak rhythms, as the habit is nowadays, with flowing movement that is beyond feminine softness. But as the ancient men used to dance ceremonially in such a virile way that they would cause no shame, even if seen by the enemy."[106] Sigismondo's dance is similarly masculine, a part of his heroic image.

In the *Laws,* Plato defined gymnastics as consisting of wrestling and dancing. "Of dancing," he wrote, "there is one branch in which the style of the muse is imitated, preserving both freedom and nobility, and another which aims at physical soundness, agility and beauty by securing for the various parts and members of the body the proper degree of flexibility and extension and bestowing also the rhythmical motion which belongs to each."[107] Although he condemns non-functional wrestling and the use of boxing gloves as they are useless for war, Plato allows the softer kind of dancing in times of peace in order to express joy. For this "pacific" kind of dancing, Plato elaborates on the differences between the "proper, noble kind of dancing that befits law-abiding men" and "questionable" dancing, such as Bacchic and lust-inducing revels. In general and especially in times of war, however, Plato stresses the importance of war dances and "mimic" fighting in armor and bearing weapons in civic processions at festivals, referring in particular to the sword dance of the Spartans. In antiquity, the Spartans were famous for their skill at the Pyrrhic war dance.[108] This kind of dancing trains the body for the motions of war and strengthens its limbs for combat.

In all his examples, Valturio is keen to stress manly dancing as a preparation for war. He credits Sigismondo for seeing it as a form of exercise, but other images of Sigismondo's dancing betray another reason. In the *Isottaeus,* Basinio has Sigismondo declare to Isotta a different reason for his dancing:

> If my looks emit soft Syrian scents and the hand of an artisan combs my hair; if I wear clothes heavy with inlaid gold, if a hand-painted Phrygian cloak falls from my shoulder; and if we perform artistic festive dances, or I put on my face new masks, I do all of this out of extreme love, so that I may be pleasing to you, my dear girl.[109]

Yet another image complicates the picture of our manly mercenary. Doused in oriental perfumes, done-up hair, golden-disco sparkles with a graphic-art cloak, and dancing with different masks, Pius's savage monster is unrecognizable. Yet Spartan warriors come to mind, combing each other's long-flowing hair and themselves accomplished dancers.[110]

In the Renaissance there was much debate about the morality and utility of dancing, especially for men. Although he acknowledged its value as exercise, Vergerio condemned dancing in mixed company because it excited sexual urges.[111] But fifteenth-century Italy also saw the revival of dance as a serious art form. Dance masters, who were predominantly Jewish, traveled from court to court to teach their craft. The humanist Giovanni Mario Filelfo (1426–1480) celebrates in a poem the most famous master, Guglielmo "the Jew":

> So much grace and angelic harmony is in the sweet music of Guglielmo Ebreo. So much elegance is in the beautiful dancing that it would make Maccabeus put his weapon away, Solomon lose his wisdom, and King David be embarrassed. Were it Judith, she would dance, and Socrates, Aristotle, Plato, and someone born more rational. Dancing would captivate Cato, make Diana bow to her followers, and make Scipio quit his noble enterprise.[112]

Giovanni Mario alludes to a quasi-magical quality of dance that captivates and entices. The god Apollo was the originator of sacred dance. The Greek poets celebrate the muses of Mount Helicon, dancing in delicate feet at the altars of the mighty son of Cronos to Apollo's lyre.[113] Plato, Cicero, and Macrobius had all seen the most graceful dance as reflecting the movement of the heavens and therefore magical.[114] Dancing putti and the Graces in the Tempio could allude to this tradition of dance. When Sigismondo's son Roberto Novello was born in 1437, "the shops were closed for three days and there was dancing in the streets."[115] Valturio also stresses the public nature of his patron's dancing. In saying that dance made "Scipio quit his noble enterprise," Giovanni Mario inserts a dangerous opposition between heroic virtue and the corrupting influence of dance, an opposition that neither Valturio nor his source Seneca admit in Scipio's manly dancing.

Music is also a point of comparison between Sigismondo and the ancient Spartans. In the *Laws,* Plato defined music as a form of gymnastics for the soul. Just as physical exercise trains the body, so does music the soul. Aristotle had also made music prominent in education as "it frees the spirit and ennobles the soul."[116] Vergerio refers to Socrates, who encouraged youths to learn music "to moderate the movements of the soul under the rule of reason." Vergerio emphasized the benefits of music for "relaxing the mind and calming the passions." Love songs, however, he said, should be avoided in favor of songs about heroic men.[117] Valturio tells us that Sigismondo took pleasure in listening to music after battle in order "to relax and rest his spirit." But he also used music to spur his men on to courage in battle:

> The trumpets, horns, tubas, bugles, and drums in our legions serve nothing but to sing for those going out to battle and returning, by exciting those too tired or reigning in those too excited. The Spartans marched to rhythm and pipes; their infantry was not employed except to the anapest measure. Their appearance was beautiful and formidable, as they marched to pipe tones; they would not break the order of the phalanx nor lose heart, but calmly and happily from the music they would head into battle. Because of this music, they did not have too much fear or rage, but a firm and constant spirit mixed with hope and daring.[118]

An example of Sigismondo's use of this Spartan technique in an actual battle came in 1461, during a surprise attack on the papal forces' encampment at Nidastore in the Marches. It was early evening, and Sigismondo and his men had been fighting "most ferociously" since dawn. They were outnumbered, four men to one, and exhausted. "Sigismondo called to his brave soldiers at the enemy's gate: 'when you see me enter the enemy camp, bravely follow me in and we will force them to abandon their posts.' He then ordered the trumpeters to double up their playing and the pipes to do their work, thus encouraging [*inanimando*] his infantry." Sigismondo then launched himself "with such great ferocity that it would be impossible to describe and encouraged his brave men to follow his lead."[119] The vital role of music to enliven and encourage tired warriors was an essential part of this long and bloody battle, Sigismondo's last great victory, as discussed in Chapter 8.

The association of music with fighting is unsurprisingly the theme of Valturio's music chapter in his treatise on the art of war. "Everyone," he writes, "admires how you have wisely joined this kind of music to courage in war. In doing this you especially imitate Mercury, who taught wrestling and first discovered the lyre."[120] Valturio, however, repeatedly cautions Sigismondo about the dangers of music, that it can excite lust, weaken the muscles, and lead to effeminate men. "Bacchants and their lutes" and theater music should be avoided, since "their aim is pleasure." He calls this music "effeminate," with "shameless beats and excessively broken rhythms, neither wild nor varied." This kind of music is bad because it is "soft" and "makes the body useless for war or civic service." Valturio also condemned singing as leading to destructive obsession, as shown by the example of the mad emperor Nero. Instead, Valturio advocates "simple, gentle, prudent, masculine, and modest music that praises the deeds of the brave." Different modes affect minds differently. For war, Valturio says that Sigismondo should use the virile Doric mode or the violent Phrygian "to excite, distract, seize, inflame, and encourage men to fight." When a musician played a Phrygian mode at a banquet, "Alexander grabbed his sword and jumped up but then returned to the banqueting when the beat changed." Valturio refers to Achilles, who played music to relax after battle, "not singing about love but about the deeds of brave men." In Sparta the poet-singer Terpander "settled civil strife" with music, and the medical musician, Thaletas, cured the Spartans of plague.[121]

Ancient Sparta offered Sigismondo an ideal masculinity and a model for his hunting, wrestling, and extreme physical conditioning. Sparta also provided a manly justification for dance and music, which were essential for preparation and success in war. But the reception of Sparta in Rimini was not wholly positive. Valturio is critical of the Spartans for neglecting the humanist liberal arts education. "The Spartans," he abruptly declares, "were mistaken, when they made their youth into savages with constant labor, as if this were useful for bravery." True bravery, he says, requires humanity. Valturio continues:

> The Spartans did not achieve what they intended, for we do not see bravery present in other animals nor among wild peoples, but rather among the gentle habits of the lion. There are many peoples who attack in order to slaughter men and devour them, like the [cannibals] around Pontus [Black Sea], and other peoples in the Mediterranean who secretly pillage with traps, but are no good at fighting. All these wild peoples, like wolves, can neither

> serve nor command, for they do not possess the power of the human character but of a wild and unmanageable nature.[122]

Valturio here expresses a humanist belief in the value of classical literature for the development of character and also a classical xenophobia about other "uncivilized" peoples. He was also probably thinking of Sigismondo, who was ferocious in battle and often compared to a wild bear, yet enjoyed music and the literature produced by the humanists he supported in his court. Sparta and its masculine ideals certainly had its Renaissance in Rimini, but it could never replace Athens or Rome in terms of character development and eloquence.

A Renaissance of Classical Wrestling

Sigismondo matched the strengthening and conditioning of his body with the intricate techniques of martial arts. "When you were growing up," Valturio writes, "very many masters of such matters [arts of war] were summoned throughout Italy, who were not dismissed by you until you had equaled or surpassed them . . . , and given them many riches and honors."[123] After emphasizing Sigismondo's bravery and skill in hunting, Basinio turns to gymnastics, wrestling, jumping, and endurance of hardship:

> Sigismondo often threw a heavy discus into the air with his right arm. No other boy anywhere could beat him at full-force wrestling. Nor could any youth beat him at jumping over large ditches, nor did the cold and snow depress his spirit.[124]

Diligence and constant activity in his youth marked Sigismondo for success. Even if Sigismondo did not actually do these things, his portrayal as a wrestler and an athlete is revealing. Two of the manuscripts of the *Hesperis*, which the artist Giovanni da Fano embellished with illustrations at Sigismondo's expense, include a miniature that shows Sigismondo wrestling (fig. 3.4).[125] This does not make Sigismondo base or gross and overly attached to the body (as opposed to the spirit) but elevates him as a classical Greek hero, like Hercules whose amazing physical feats made him divine.

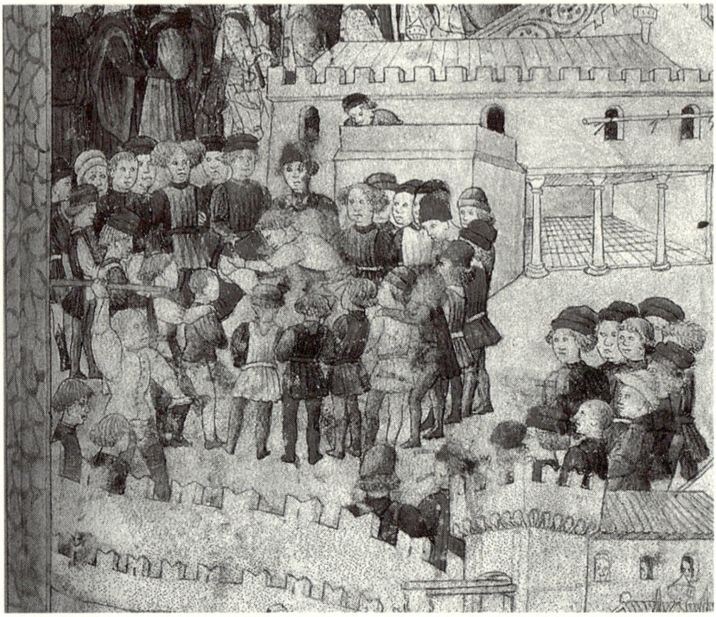

Fig. 3.4. Giovanni da Fano, Sigismondo wrestling (detail), manuscript illumination (Canon Class lat. 81, fol. 61r), Basinio, *Hesperis,* ca. 1460, The Bodleian Libraries, Oxford. Photo: The Bodleian Libraries, University of Oxford/The Art Archive at Art Resource/Art Resource, NY.

According to Valturio, Sigismondo was a strong advocate of the value of wrestling for warfare. Sigismondo, Valturio says, "imitated . . . Publius Rutilius, who was the first soldier to accept that not only strength and daring, which he excelled at, were necessary in fighting but also technique and diligent [study]." Valturio used several of the same ancient examples as Vergerio. Both follow Plutarch in describing how, in Valturio's words, Marius "as an old worn man . . . wrestled daily with the youth in the forum. He knew that when practiced from a tender age this kind of pretend fighting in peacetime was a valuable preparation for the great dangers of real battles of war." Valturio argues for the value of martial arts training and competitive wrestling for strengthening the body and dealing with the pressures and strain of actual combat in the field. But he does qualify this assertion with the following sentence: "Although this kind of training, which is sought in such exercises, is by far unequal to that learned amid the tumults of war in all its terrors, it nevertheless wonderfully and easily renders the body very light for riding horses and heavy armor."[126] In calling wrestling the "image of war," Plato had stressed both its practical and symbolic value.[127] In antiquity, martial arts could be more directly effective in warfare, but in the new age of gunpowder and artillery, they were still useful for their physical strength conditioning and agility training.

Vergerio had said that combat sports were good to train the body "so that it can endure with fortitude and obey with ease." His caveat about combat "games" is similarly worded to Valturio's: "To be sure," Vergerio writes, "this kind of training which takes the form of games is very different from what one learns in the tumult of battle, when everything is wanting and fear is real." But Vergerio sees its value in learning courage, leadership, and tactics. He also specifically connects training with the theoretical knowledge in books: "It is widely repeated," Vergerio writes, "that these things are better learned from practice than from oral teaching or books, yet there do exist books on military affairs written by great men, which you should certainly not neglect."[128] Vergerio adopts a pagan perspective when he asserts that "we should not fight for the sake of plunder or greed, but for power (imperium) and glory."[129] This is more imperialistic than Plato, who ascribed the same goal to rhetoric as to martial arts. In the *Gorgias,* Socrates asserts: "Rhetoric is like pankration, boxing, and wrestling; one learns it not to attack friends, but to protect friends from enemies."[130] Plato is describing rhetoric, but he nevertheless assumes that fighting is for self-defense. Valturio and Vergerio advocated wrestling as an endurance exercise with little connection to the horrors of combat, but other writers were more confident in the value of wrestling for fighting on the battlefield. In the *Book of the Courtier* (1528), Baldassare Castiglione had the character Lodovico da Canossa declare: "It is of the highest importance to know how to wrestle, since this often accompanies combat on foot."[131]

Interest in classical antiquity brought a new awareness of ancient athletics and martial arts in Renaissance Italy. In his panegyric of the city of Florence, Leonardo Bruni compared Florence to the strength and physical beauty of the great wrestler Milo of Croton and the pancratist Polydamas.[132] There were, however, critics. In the *Tusculan Disputations,* Cicero asserts that "this love of men [homosexuality] had its rise from the gymnastics of the Greeks, where these kinds of loves are admissible."[133] Plutarch summed up the negative Roman view of Greek athletics:

> The Romans considered nothing to be the cause of the Greek's enslavement and degeneracy as much as the gymnasia [and wrestling schools], which gave rise to much time wasting and laziness in the cities, and also profligacy, pederasty, and the ruin of the youths' bodies through sleep, strolls, eurhythmic exercises, and precise diets, because of which they stopped practicing with weaponry and were happy to be called nimble and wrestlers and handsome instead of hoplites (Greek infantry men) and good horsemen.[134]

Yet again, the question of manliness and effeminacy were subjects of active debate. The same practice, wrestling, was seen as quintessentially masculine in some sources and soft and degenerate in others. In the Renaissance, Petrarch had dismissed wrestling as enslaving one to the ephemeral body and advocated Augustine's call to train the mind to move beyond the corporeal to incorporeal truth.[135] But such puritanical thinking was not widespread. Even Plato, whose negative view of the body is often overstressed, may have wrestled competitively as a boy and definitely saw gymnastics as essential to the health of the soul and mind in his ideal republic. But Plato distinguishes between the good kind of combat sport that prepares men for war and the bad kind of wrestling and boxing that teaches techniques that are worthless on the battlefield.[136] Athleticism for him should never be practiced as an end in itself but always as a means to defend the state and to develop the soul through exercise. Similarly, the ancient champion of rhetorical education, Isocrates, saw rhetoric and philosophy as a form of mental gymnastics. Orators and philosophers, the ancients said, teach forms of speech and logical arguments, just as a wrestling coach teaches winning positions.[137] A feature of ancient education, especially in Greece, is the balance of physical conditioning and mental study. Socrates after all had some of his most intense philosophical debates amid the grunts of physical exertion and the odor of male sweat at the wrestling gym.

Renaissance writers learned from classical literature and art, which describe and show Greek wrestlers doing elaborate holds, take-downs, and joint locks.[138] Sport, especially wrestling, boxing, and pankration, was a staple of Greek education and became a patriotic symbol of Hellenistic culture both for Alexander the Great, who exported Greek culture to the lands he conquered, and during the Roman occupation, when sport distinguished the Greeks from the dominant Romans. In the *Odyssey,* Homer described a boxing match between a beggar and Odysseus disguised as a beggar. Forced to fight for the entertainment of the suitors in his house, Odysseus chooses to knock out his opponent by a well-placed blow on the side of the neck below the ear. In the *Iliad,* Odysseus wrestles Ajax at the funeral games for the fallen Patroclus. As in judo, the object was to throw the opponent to the ground. Ajax relies on his strength, while Odysseus uses specific techniques.[139] The passages in Homer show that wrestling and boxing were already considered arts, techniques that could be learned, not thoughtless mayhem. The richest sources on ancient combat arts come from later Greek writers living in the Roman Empire, who look nostalgically back to the independence and pride of Greek antiquity and decry the current state of Greek youth, who still wrestled in the *palestra* but had become soft and effeminate.[140]

Despite their occasional jibes at effeminacy, Romans admired Greek boxing and wrestling skills and so adopted and expanded the Greek myth of Heracles, the ultimate strongman wrestler. The Roman Hercules defeated the monster Cacus outside Rome and was venerated as a protector god by Mark Antony and the Emperor Commodus. The Roman poet Statius (45–96 CE) described the boxing and wrestling techniques that a Spartan boy used to beat a much stronger man.[141] But the clearest proof of Roman approval of the Greek art of wrestling is in the great repository of Roman religion and culture, the enormously influential *Aeneid.* In addition to singing and dancing, Virgil describes the blessed in the Elysian Fields, "exercising their bodies in a grassy gymnasium [and] competing in sports and wrestling on yellow sand."[142] Sweaty wrestlers and body-builders: pagan heaven never looked so different from Fra Angelico's ethereal angels dancing and singing in fifteenth-century Christian churches! Both Virgil and Statius were canonical authors in the medieval curriculum.[143] Their descriptions of technical fighting would have been on the lips of every schoolboy.

Like the ancients, Sigismondo is described as training his body and mind in martial arts and the skills necessary to lead armies and win the battles of Renaissance Italy. He excelled in everything, as Valturio reported:

> Before the others of your time you learned how equally to be ruled and to rule; to lead armies, set up camps, organize battle

> lines, knock down defenses, wound enemies, raise war machines, strengthen ramparts, launch missiles, throw javelins, knock shields, and to wield your sword into incredible places; you did not like to mount horses in the Persian manner, but to raise yourself without any step-ladder, to jump lightly and easily onto horses, your hands tied behind your back, and often moving rapidly in the fastest runs to lead your men; sometimes pulling the reins and outstripping others in the middle of a ride with a slight movement, other times climbing mountains, or jumping across ditches. You were so well versed in all the military arts that no one could easily escape you, whether soldier or knight, and you were considered the greater and better-trained officer and commander.[144]

Here, Valturio presents Sigismondo as both embodying and surpassing the classical warrior ideals. Cyrus and the Persians were renowned for their archery and horse skills, and Valturio recalls Plutarch's *Caesar* in his description of how Sigismondo rode horses with his hands behind his back, but adds an extra feat not in Plutarch, that Sigismondo would mount horses by a light jump without the usual help of a step.[145]

Valturio saw the classical ideal balance of mind and body in the person of Sigismondo, who was both a warrior and a humanist scholar. He claimed that Sigismondo took the ancients as models for this kind of training: "I believe that you have imitated Alexander Severus, who, they say, wrestled after studying letters."[146] Although he personalizes and adds new terms and references, Valturio's categories of excellence correspond to what Vergerio says that young men should learn.[147] In appropriating so much of Vergerio's educational treatise for his portrait of Sigismondo's education, Valturio is purposely presenting his patron as the ideal Renaissance prince, heroic warrior, and learned patron of the arts. Sigismondo was no doubt consciously competing with his rival, Federico da Montefeltro, who boasted throughout his life of the humanist education that he had received at the school of Vittorino da Feltre in Mantua, and in fact had a portrait of his old teacher in his bedroom to inspire him.[148] In the words of his humanists, Sigismondo embodied all the virtues and accomplishments of a Renaissance lord, educated according to the Greek *paideia* and trained in the library, the arena, and on the battlefield.

Despite classical and Christian condemnations of Greek and the Greek athletic ideal as effeminate, extreme, decadent, and leading to sexual perversion, Sigismondo embraced the Greek ideal. He had his humanists cast their patron as a wrestler poet and sculptors fill his church with muscular bodies. Greek and Homer in particular were well represented in fifteenth-century Rimini and were central to the humanist culture that Sigismondo patronized. Basinio and Valturio spun Sigismondo's upbringing into a tale of Chiron and Achilles, of Spartan trials, and Roman triumph. Here was a man who enjoyed conversing about classical literature and history with the intellects in his court and who had himself inserted into that history as a Greek hero fighting under the protection of the gods. His life as it appeared in his humanist sources was a living testament to the value and power of the Greek *paideia* and the classical conception of virtue in the active life.

✣ 4 ✣

An Ancient Hero on Renaissance Battlefields

Renaissance education was about engagement; it was about action. Young men were taught how to speak in public with persuasive force and how to apply the lessons of ancient history to their own lives. In Italian courts, Sigismondo and other boys who were destined to rule and have military careers learned from ancient history and classical literature how to win a place in the pantheon of antiquity's great heroes. They strove after that particularly masculine virtue so well exemplified in the works of Homer, Plutarch, Virgil, and Livy, and later to be famously redeployed by Niccolò Machiavelli (1469–1527), a true manliness that the pagan world had produced. The Malatesta humanists, Valturio and Basinio, described the key events that marked Sigismondo's transition from boyhood into manhood and made him the man of legend. In doing so, they defined classical virtues that are often in conflict with Christian values.

The record of his military victories, though much embellished by his humanists, was indisputable. Starting at age thirteen, Sigismondo proved his mettle in battle, and his continued successes ensured him lucrative contracts from Pope Eugenius IV, Francesco Sforza, Florence, and Venice. Most of the art and literature that Sigismondo patronized centered on his military triumphs and glory. In his treatise on the art of war (1455), Valturio often refers to Sigismondo as an example of a great commander. He praises war for revealing Sigismondo's "famed heroic and divine virtue" and calls him the greatest commander of his age because of his efforts to emulate the ancients. "Tuscan, French, and Northern tongues everywhere," Valturio assures us, "have celebrated and will celebrate for centuries to come" Sigismondo's exploits.[1] But Valturio provides few details about actual campaigns. In contrast, Basinio's massive Latin epic poem, the *Hesperis,* focuses on Sigismondo's battles and victories in the field. Although he embellishes, exaggerates, and adds the Olympian gods and a mythological context, Basinio bases his poem on the actual battles and events of Sigismondo's life. The *Hesperis* is contemporary history writ as classical epic.

Humanists in other courts also composed Latin epics about potential or current patrons and their times.[2] Francesco Filelfo's *Sforziad* (begun in 1451) about Francesco Sforza in Milan was one of the first and has received the most attention from scholars.[3] Soon after the conspiracy of Stefano Porcari against Pope Nicholas V in Rome in 1453, Orazio Romano produced the *Porcaria,* in which he presented Porcari as another Catiline and Pope Nicholas V as the savior of Rome, ushering in a new golden age.[4] Sigismondo's nemesis, Federico da Montefeltro, the lord and later duke of Urbino, was the subject of two Latin epics, Porcellio's *Feltria* (1464–1475) and Giovanni Mario Filelfo's *Martias* (1464). Giovanni Mario even wrote a Latin epic about Mehmet II, the *Amyris* (1476), in which among other events he glorified the Ottoman sultan's siege and sacking of Constantinople in 1453.[5] All of these humanists imitated classical epics, and in particular used the *Aeneid* as a model. Most of these epics, for example, include extensive interventions from the pagan gods, and the *Hesperis* and the *Porcaria* describe trips to a classical underworld. Just as Basinio does in the *Hesperis,* these humanists present their subjects and contemporary history with the language of classical epic.[6] Basinio and Filelfo were accomplished Hellenists (unlike Orazio Romano and Porcellio) and so could take as their models not only Virgil's but also Homer's epics. The classical form and content of the *Hesperis* thus participates in a Renaissance genre, but it is also integral to the particular culture that characterized Sigismondo's court.

Sigismondo cultivated a public image of himself as a classical hero, boasting that he was a descendent of the Roman commander Scipio Africanus, who had defeated Hannibal and saved Rome.[7] Just as humanists throughout Italy produced hyperbole in order to please and promote their patrons, so Malatesta poets and writers flattered their patron by presenting him as semidivine and invincible.[8] They were especially concerned with historical detail and anchored their portrayals in Sigismondo's actual accomplishments on the battlefield. In casting Sigismondo as an epic hero, Malatesta writers applied pagan values to the realities of contemporary life—an age of mercenaries, shifting allegiances among city-states, and gunpowder.

The Making of a Classical Hero: Sigismondo's Childhood and Virtue Revealed

Book IV of the *Hesperis* begins with a scene of utter despair. Sigismondo has just roundly defeated Alfonso of Aragon and forced him to raise his siege of Piombino and flee. A despairing Alfonso is shown alone in the middle of the night, floating on the dark sea, contemplating suicide. Apollo consoles Alfonso with a speech about the amazing virtues of his adversary, Sigismondo, who was, even as a boy, a natural ruler:

> To relieve your pain a little, I will recite in order all of Sigismondo's achievements, and, great king, you will not be ashamed to have fallen to so great a leader. . . . He was a mature boy from an early age and already ruled peoples in placid peace. He seemed to everyone to carry manly worries and mighty passions before his time. He terrified many dangerous peoples, who were different from his own, and savage tyrants.[9]

As a boy, Sigismondo purportedly had overpowering virility and a natural predisposition to rule and defend his interests. These qualities, however, made some uneasy and caused them to plot his demise: "Struck with fear, every part of Lazio trembled at the wars of the future leader and at the power developing in the young Sigismondo. Many conspired in deceit and pressed him constantly; others exposed him to wild beast chases."[10] Classical precedent abounds as the young Sigismondo emerges triumphant from the snares of his enemies, just like Romulus and Remus, Hercules, and even the god Dionysus, who all escaped early attempts at their lives to fulfill their destinies.

Valturio says that he dedicated his treatise on the art of war to Sigismondo because he alone cultivated the military art of the great commanders of Antiquity and "strove to emulate their lives and deeds."[11] Valturio says that Sigismondo, like the great commanders of Antiquity, was born with innate bravery, prowess, and genius in arms. "Scipio Africanus," Valturio writes, "at age eighteen saved his father's life as he lay wounded and dying at the battle of Ticinus against Hannibal, and in the same battle, as a boy Aemilius Lepidus, whose statue was placed on the Capitol, killed an enemy and saved a citizen's life."[12] Valturio follows these examples with a lengthy account of Sigismondo's first decisive act of bravery:

> But, lest we begrudge you your praises, o Sigismondo Pandolfo, you should not be . . . considered inferior to these two in any way, since you were barely thirteen years old when that horrible conspiracy erupted against your brother Roberto. . . . The entire Malatesta family and the state of all the citizens would have been finished, if you had not . . . in one day fought with iron, force, and arms against innumerable very strong men, bent on our city's destruction, with the greatest danger to your life. In that rabble of lost men it would have been amazing enough for a veteran to have escaped from that place, one most skilled in arms, horsemanship, and the entire art of war, [but] you did it at that age. Because of your vigilance, shrewd intelligence, and outstanding courage, you earned a triple crown for saving both your brothers and the fatherland, a most outstanding beginning for a most invincible future commander.[13]

The 1431 rebellion was the defining moment of Sigismondo's youth and career as a warrior and mercenary captain. This account comes in Valturio's section on gymnastics, in which he talks about the ancients and their practice of the martial arts; Valturio sees this incident as Sigismondo's training put into action.

In the epic version of the events, Basinio is pagan in his terms, even calling the blessed Galeotto "most holy and dear to the Thunderer." Seeing the enemy soldiers invading Rimini, Galeotto is too scared to escape and instead laments "in his trembling heart." The thirteen-year-old Sigismondo consoles his brother and urges Galeotto to "cast fear from your heart and put aside your worries" before "bravely riding his quick steed out into the enemy." "Defended by the spirit of the gods," Sigismondo rides "across the frozen Rubicon to Cesena." Citizens come out to meet him there, and the "crowd embraces the victorious boy." Sigismondo stirs the crowd and encourages them to defend Galeotto's rule: "Now there is need for arms and for all to help. The traitor, Labienus, has seized Rimini and is besieging my scared brothers. I alone dared to break through the enemy soldiers and to cross fields at a mighty gallop to come here. Oh you, men faithful to me, return our uncle's ancient kingdoms, which were taken away by deceit."[14] Both Valturio and Basinio present the 1431 rebellion as Sigismondo's transition from education to action. Basinio also gives Sigismondo a rousing speech to signal his abilities in classical rhetoric, even at the age of thirteen.

The citizens "wash the tears from their eyes and promise their loyalty" and rush to gather weapons to expel the rebels. When all is ready, Sigismondo "summons the gods of vengeance to battle," and "unexpectedly leads the army of rough farmers to Rimini." As they climb the walls of Rimini, the enemy "sees Sigismondo daring to do deeds worthy of a great man to be." Labienus (Giovanni di Ramberto Malatesti) realizes his defeat and escapes on the Adriatic in a rowboat. By calling the rebel Labienus and referring to Sigismondo's crossing the Rubicon, Basinio explicitly presents Sigismondo as Caesar. Labienus (100–45 BCE) was Caesar's lieutenant in Gaul. When Caesar crossed the Rubicon with his army, set on Rome, Labienus deserted and joined Pompey and the republicans. Sigismondo's bravery, Basinio concludes, brought him "fame and glory with outstanding praise; [but] he excited envy with his virtue, he whom the great spirits of the gods protect, whom Jupiter sent from high heaven, so that his example might reveal the power of human virtue."[15] Exaggeration is to be expected in a Latin epic about the poet's patron.[16] But the bravery of the young Sigismondo in rallying the people to protect his homeland was easy to couch in classical terms. These texts reveal more strain, when they praise the epic heroism of Sigismondo's later career as a mercenary soldier, who shifted allegiances and used deception and modern firepower as a part of his violent campaigns.

In the 1430s and 1440s Sigismondo fought and trained under Francesco Sforza, who worked for Pope Eugenius IV. Like Sigismondo, Sforza was the son of a mercenary. His stellar rise to power from nothing has made him emblematic of the belief in nobility based not on family lineage but on personal virtue and merit.[17] Sforza's skill and success rate were so great that the Duke of Milan, Filippo Maria Visconti (1392–1447), made sure that the mercenary would not ever fight against him by offering him his daughter's hand. Sforza's marriage to Bianca Visconti later justified his takeover of Milan in

1450. Sigismondo's close relationship to the mercenary soon-to-be ruler of Milan was cemented by a marriage to Sforza's daughter, Polissena, in 1441. Sigismondo might have easily remained a middling mercenary captain with skill and experience but hardly the stuff of legends, if it were not for the Tuscan Wars of 1448 and 1453. The two greatest triumphs of Sigismondo's adult life were in these wars, at Piombino and Vada. Basinio extensively celebrates his patron's exploits at these sieges, and the triumphal theme in the art of the Tempio recalls the victories in these wars, when Sigismondo defended the Florentines from Aragonese forces in 1448 and 1453. Sigismondo's liberation of the city of Piombino from a vicious siege in 1448 was a turning point in his career. He proved himself a generous patron, eager to have his victories immortalized in image and word.

Italy and the Barbarian Invasion

Nationalism may have been born in the nineteenth century and Sigismondo's legacy appropriated by fascists in the twentieth century, but there was nevertheless a strong sense of Italian identity, if not nationality, in the Renaissance. In the fourteenth century, Petrarch bewailed "Italia mia," and in the sixteenth century Machiavelli tried to unite Italians against the French and Spanish.[18] In the fifteenth century, Basinio's *Hesperis* is outlandishly nationalistic. Its very name, the *Hesperis,* is an ancient word for Italy. The star in Basinio's epic is Sigismondo Malatesta, who defends Italy against the foreign Spaniards, the Aragonese in Naples. The words "Italia" and "Itali" appear throughout the poem and are contrasted to the "Celti" "Iberi" and "barbari." As Pope Eugenius IV declares: "No one except you, Sigismondo, wishes to keep evil wars from our lands; in your ancient devotion you alone defend Italy."[19] Mercenaries from all over Italy unite under Sigismondo to expel the Spanish out of Tuscany and Italy. This clash of races and atavistic pride was a centerpiece of the epic before Basinio even began it. In 1450, when he was still in Ferrara, Basinio wrote to Sigismondo, requesting patronage in a metered letter, which contained sample scenes of the heroic Sigismondo in classical epic. Basinio shows Sigismondo encouraging his men before the battle of Piombino:

> All the gods favor you; you are all Italians. Dare now to boast of your ancient lineage and the first Romans. Defend this great

> name for yourselves, draw your swords, and flatten these barbarian armies. We do not see here Hannibal and the arms of savage Carthage, the tough Numidians, or the wild Jugurtha. This barbarian race and mob is the lowest dregs of humanity.[20]

Italian pride, built on ancient history and blood ties, would lend historical importance to Sigismondo's recent victory in the first Tuscan War. The idea pleased Sigismondo, who hired Basinio to write the poem, even before his victories in the second Tuscan War. This letter was the nucleus of the *Hesperis,* a book proposal that was faithfully executed.

In another poem, Basinio has Sigismondo explain to Isotta why he must leave her to save Italy. Italian pride is paramount:

> If Alfonso captures Italy, he will not tolerate the Italian commanders. For no barbarian people has ever been a friend of the Latin name or our people. But we will not be beaten nor will the Italian people learn to be conquered, for they do not fear barbarian arms. . . . Scipio, the glory of his fatherland, sent Hannibal back to his native shores, and great Camillus flattened the Gauls and took the standards back from the enemy. I, Sigismondo, will drive out the Spanish and come as a great glory to my homeland.[21]

Basinio writes that after his speech, Sigismondo thought of the three hundred Trojans who fought against Turnus to protect the first walls of what would become Rome. The *Hesperis* (1455) elaborated the same ethnic and nationalist themes. Before describing a battle in the second Tuscan War, Basinio compares the two armies. The Italians, he says, "obey Sigismondo on their own accord . . . they all had the same love of fighting . . . and bore themselves with great virtue." The Spanish, however, were shocked by Sigismondo and his well-ordered ranks: "They growled noisily in a sad mob scene and lost their courage in great fear, for they had neither the same customs nor the same language but came from all parts of the world."[22] The Italians are a single people fighting for their homeland, while the Aragonese are foreigners, an army of barbarians with nothing in common. In reality, both armies would have comprised a mixture of local troops and mercenaries from other lands.

In stressing the different natures of the Spanish and Italian armies, Basinio follows Virgil's *Aeneid* but also recalls the ancient historian Livy's description of the Romans led by Scipio Africanus and Hannibal's Carthaginian army in the second Punic War (218–202 BCE). Machiavelli later compared Scipio and Hannibal in order to explore mercy and cruelty in leadership. Scipio initially did not have success because his men loved him and took advantage of his leniency and mercy. On the other hand, through cruelty and fear, Hannibal united an army of different cultures and languages into a deadly fighting force. Valturio also used Livy and other classical sources to explore this theme, but he included Sigismondo's opinion on whether it is best to be feared or loved: "When people criticize you [Sigismondo] for being both too lenient and sometimes appearing too severe and cruel, you usually respond that cruelty is unbecoming in a prince but that in order to be victorious the commander of an army has to be feared more than the enemy."[23] As Machiavelli would do later, Valturio uses the example of Scipio and Hannibal to illustrate the importance of military discipline. In contrast, Basinio appropriates the same ancient source, Livy, but in order to stress the ethnic unity and thus superiority of Sigismondo's Italian army and its just cause against the barbarian Aragonese invaders.

Basinio also sees these nationalist or ethnic differences in political terms. He writes that during the second Tuscan War, Alfonso sends ambassadors to Sigismondo to bribe him into surrendering and accepting an Italian appeasement to the Spanish king. Alfonso says that kings have rightfully and divinely ruled Italy from Aeneas and the Alban kings to Caesar and the emperors. The gods, he says, have shown through auspices that he shall rule the Latin lands. Sigismondo responds with a proud assertion of Italian independence: "Jupiter has not consented at all for the Latin people to be slaves to the Spanish king, which Alfonso believes was foretold to foreign kings; let him expect nothing owed to him, but another fate, by which every barbarian will leave Italy and take up no further arms . . . let him not think that Tuscans will be enemies of kings, but that they oppose cruel and violent tyrants."[24] The words *foreigner* and *barbarian* show a classical ethnocentrism, a cultural and ethnic dividing line. The distinction between a just king and a cruel tyrant emphasizes the beneficial single man rule of Sigismondo and his relationship with republican Florence. Basinio makes his poem truly epic by setting two different peoples against each other in a grand battle for the soul of Italy.

The First Tuscan War and the Siege of Piombino

War had broken out on the Italian peninsula after Francesco Maria Visconti, the Duke of Milan, died in 1447 without a male heir. Because he was married to Visconti's daughter, the mercenary captain Francesco Sforza claimed the duchy. Visconti, however, had named Alfonso of Aragon, the king of Naples, as his successor. When Alfonso heard that Florence and Venice sided with Sforza, he started planning an invasion of Tuscany. In 1447 Sigismondo offered to lead the defense of Florence but was flatly rejected, possibly because Florence was afraid that Sigismondo would threaten its liberty and take control of the republic.[25] The scorned Sigismondo signed a contract with Alfonso, who promptly invaded Tuscany. With Sigismondo's help, Alfonso planned a two-pronged attack on Tuscany by sea and land. When, however, Alfonso began besieging the strategic Tuscan port city Piombino, ruled by Rinaldo Orsini, Florence abruptly changed its attitude, panicked, and sent envoys to Sigismondo.

Giannozzo Manetti, the famous Florentine humanist, made the case to Sigismondo in an eloquent speech and convinced him to abandon Alfonso's side. In his biography of Manetti, the contemporary Naldo Naldi says:

> Had we been attacked by two armies [Alfonso's and Sigismondo's] at the same time we would have been overwhelmed; the liberty of our homeland would have been finished. The fact that we are still alive, free, inhabiting this city, safeguarding our home, maintaining our laws, breathing, and living, is all because of Giannozzo, since his eloquence held sway in Rimini.[26]

Rarely does a man of letters get such high praise for the practical application of his art. Eloquence aside, Manetti's task was easier, since he had the support of Sigismondo's trusted councilor, Roberto Valturio. Sigismondo, Valturio insisted, owed neither money nor allegiance to Alfonso. The king of Naples, Valturio argued, had refused to pay the remaining money owed, and Sigismondo had already spent the advance on assembling troops and garrisoning castles.[27] Efforts nevertheless were later made to repay some of the money. The issue of the contract with Naples may have been resolved in his mind, but Sigismondo was not happy with joining the same side as his archenemy Federico da Montefeltro, lord of neighboring Urbino, who was also hired to defend Tuscany. The two rulers were in the middle of a territorial war. Sigismondo gave as a condition that he be the sole captain general of the Florentine force. According to his biographers, upon hearing Sigismondo's concern, Manetti immediately jumped onto his horse and rode to Urbino, where he obtained Federico's approval and temporarily reconciled the feuding lords.[28]

Sigismondo's stunning success at Piombino made his reputation as a shrewd military tactician and brave warrior. But his decision to betray Alfonso of Aragon and join in the defense of Tuscany eventually destroyed him. Vespasiano da Bisticci (1421–1498) calls this decision the "salvation of Florentine liberty and the ruin of the house of Malatesta." Similarly, despite his vitriol, Pius admits that "Sigismondo's treachery was the salvation of the Florentine cause."[29] Alfonso was determined to have vengeance on Sigismondo. Six years later, in 1454, Alfonso refused to sign the Peace of Lodi unless he was permitted to attack Sigismondo. It was granted, and Alfonso sent Jacopo Piccinino to attack him. Both for Florence and for Sigismondo, Piombino was a turning point.

In the first part of the *Hesperis,* Basinio describes Alfonso's siege of the Tuscan port city of Piombino in 1448. The city is about to fall to the barbarian Celts; all looks lost, but then Sigismondo arrives, fights bravely, inspires all, and forces the Aragonese to raise the siege and sail back to Naples. Basinio's version of the events is somewhat different from that in other sources. First of all, he elides completely the messy circumstances of Sigismondo's contract. In the poem, he was never employed by Alfonso nor did he accept money from the king. There is not a whiff of treachery or profit motive. Instead, Jupiter sends Mercury to tell Sigismondo to defend Tuscany against the foreign invaders: "Lead the Latins against the Celts, as all the gods favor this."[30] Sigismondo tells Mercury that he will fight for no other reason than Italian pride: "My Italian birth and the shores of our plundered land rouse and compel me to join the battle."[31] Here Mercury, not Manetti, persuades Sigismondo, who responds with a patriotic apologia utterly divorced from the mercenary's reality.

Obeying Jupiter's command and patriotic pride, Sigismondo makes his way to Tuscany and gathers troops:

> Like numberless birds, many thousands of people flocked to you . . . so many brave Italians from all cities poured into the field by the Arno. Sigismondo stood in his beautiful armor in the middle of the field and the nobles. . . . Screaming and pushing on all sides, they [thousands of armored men] admired Sigismondo and approached him like the roaring of the high sea, resounding waves crashing on cliffs, and the bubbling sea. . . . At the command of Sigismondo's right arm, so many brave Italians put themselves into quiet formations.[32]

Here is the fearless leader of Italy against the foreigners. Apart from the mention of the Arno, there is no indication that the war is limited to Florence and Naples, a mere skirmish compared to the later French invasion of Italy in 1494. The image of a volunteer army of patriots also contrasts sharply with the reality that the army consisted predominantly of mercenaries. When night comes, Venus sends Sleep to comfort the "handsome Sigismondo," and Jupiter commands Iris to send him "nectar and ambrosia, and whatever food a divine man eats: it is lawful for him to know the gifts of the gods and it is lawful for him to breathe divine air."[33] Already the chosen one before the biggest tests of his virtue in battle, Sigismondo enjoys the delights available only to the immortals. The picture here is not of the humble Christian who attributes his success to God but of a pagan hero lavished with favors from the gods, favors that Sigismondo happily accepts.

A pagan incarnation occurs when divinity infuses Sigismondo's body and makes his mortal frame immortal:

> The goddess poured the divine comforts into Sigismondo's heart and strong limbs. Pristine vigor suddenly filled his great joints; the sweet quivering breath of scented air inspired his vivacious heart and filled his entire body, and renewed ancient flames in his bones.[34]

This is an utterly physical image of the Renaissance that Basinio fashioned for Sigismondo. In Rimini, classical antiquity was a lived pagan prowess, virtue earned on the battlefield that begins with divine favor and ends in the hero himself becoming divine. At its core Homeric *arete* is divinity expressed in mortal terms.

To avoid greater bloodshed, Jupiter makes Alfonso challenge Sigismondo to a single combat duel to decide who will rule Tuscany. Sigismondo recognizes Jupiter's plan and tells his men to gird themselves for war "as if Mars calls them to arms" and to look out for "traps, lest the barbarian hoard is planning hidden deceits and the enemy has woven frauds in a dark hiding place."[35] "Now," Sigismondo continues his speech, "let us test the force of severe Mars so that I may see who throws sturdy spears, who better nourishes his horses with rich meal, who runs better on foot, is prepared for deception, rides a two-horse chariot lighter, puts on armor, and seizes a helmet and shining shield."[36] These are all the skills that Sigismondo has practiced for years—throwing spears, riding horses, wearing armor, and being deceptive. Basinio uses the phrase "furtoque paratus," which vividly recalls Spartan education. The Spartans forced teenage Spartiates to steal for their food, as preparation for stealth warfare. Without reference to the Spartans, Machiavelli would later characterize this kind of *virtù* as that of the fox, who wins battles by laying traps and using deception.[37] Sigismondo exhibits this virtue in his unorthodox and ingenious battle strategies. In Malatesta literature, Sigismondo is repeatedly compared to Odysseus for his craftiness—hardly a Christian virtue. "After Odysseus," Basinio declares, "no one is as renowned for his astute use of deceit as Sigismondo."[38] Like Odysseus, Sigismondo succeeded in uniting the power and charisma of the lion with the craftiness of the fox. Whereas Dante had placed Odysseus in the eighth circle of hell for the fraudulent counsel of the Trojan horse, Basinio praises Sigismondo for his ability to deceive.[39] Pius later attributed Sigismondo's military successes to base trickery. He belittled Sigismondo's valor in battle as nothing more than setting traps and tricking his adversaries:

> He boasts of himself as the one commander who can equal the famous ancient commanders, Scipio, Marius, Pompey, Julius Caesar, Alexander, Hannibal, and Pyrrhus. Nor would he measure up, if military matters depended on bravery and courage and not deceits and lies alone, for he is a marvelous master of frauds and traps.[40]

The trickery that Pius condemns is precisely the quality that Basinio praises in Sigismondo. Although he cautions his men to beware of the "traps," "hidden deceits," and "frauds" of the "barbarian hoards," Basinio's Sigismondo lists deception as a necessary art of war.

Alfonso's trusted colleague Antiphates tries to persuade Alfonso to refuse the duel, but the king refuses, refers to an augury, and proudly goes ahead with the duel. Both sides carry out pagan sacrifices right out of the *Aeneid*.[41] The Italians arrive led by Sigismondo, who "handsome and armored, was first before the others. Just like a bull . . . well[ing] its neck up and challeng[ing] the winds, such an ornament, o Sigismondo, did the ruler of Olympus grant you to be for the Latin peoples."[42] From high Olympus, Jupiter hears the prayers of both commanders, looks down on the "brave and better looking Latins," and tells his wife Juno that Sigismondo and his men have surpassed the ancient Romans.[43]

The actual duel is short. "Like a bull destroying woods and fields," Sigismondo rushes on Alfonso. When a spear breaks Sigismondo's shield, he throws it down and fires a spear back, breaking the king's shield and lightly cutting into his chest. Now they pull their swords out and strike each other three, then four times in turn. Sigismondo smashes Alfonso's helmet:

> Pressing forward Sigismondo wounds him a third time, but the fourth time he pounds his tired sword on Alfonso's heavy armor the sword breaks in half and falls heedlessly, fragments glittering on his shoulders. But young Sigismondo is not deterred by his fallen sword or lost weapons, and more savagely enters the fray. Roughened by anger he raises himself and with his right arm chases down the threatening king; he clinches his hands together and squeezes the king's throat, and Alfonso could draw neither breath nor light.[44]

Here we get an image of Sigismondo's barehanded fighting. Even more aggressive without his sword, Sigismondo clinches and chokes his armed opponent to submission. Lying in defeat, Alfonso yields to Sigismondo: "O greatest commander of the Italians, whom Jupiter himself commands me to beg, and swiftest fortune of battle, which has granted you to look upon me as a vanquished king, spare me further enmities; let me live, I beg you, good man. I yield to you as victor and willingly leave all the kingdoms which have been given me on different shores."[45] The duel, which has no historical foundation, is a poetic conceit based on the duel between Aeneas and Turnus in *Aeneid* (bk. XII). What could be more classical and flattering than to have King Alfonso on the ground, begging Sigismondo for his life and giving up all his land? Alfonso's assertion that Jupiter and Fortune have orchestrated his defeat both lessens the king's responsibility for the loss and emphasizes Sigismondo's divine favor. How much does this favor, however, detract from Sigismondo's virtue? Fortune, fate, and divine favor certainly tip the scales, but the best pagan virtue contains the charisma that attracts divine favor. The problem, which Machiavelli later debated, was whether this kind of virtue could be learned or whether it was a part of one's unchangeable nature.[46]

This is only the first book of Basinio's epic, and the war was far from over. As in Homer's and Virgil's epics, the goddess Juno spurs the Spaniards to break the treaty. Accepting Alfonso's surrender, Sigismondo agrees to let the king live and wants only what he has earned with his arms. Alfonso is about to sign a new treaty to liberate the Italian people when a hidden archer shoots Sigismondo with an arrow, and Alfonso escapes. Alfonso is deceitful with the gods' help, and to take advantage of Sigismondo's injury, the Spanish immediately attack, but the Tuscans fight bravely: "The arrows and arms of Apollo's bow resounded to some; bullets roared with melted lead to others. But the Tuscans kept the mad Celts at bay with missiles and huge rocks rolled from on high."[47] Ancient weaponry of the gods is mixed with modern firearms. Apollo comes to Sigismondo's rescue and leads him back to the safety of his camp. There is little distinction between Sigismondo's clever trickery, favored by the gods, and Alfonso's treachery, abetted by the gods. This is hardly a Christian universe with clear-cut virtue and vice.

While Sigismondo recuperates in Volterra, Alfonso lays siege to the Tuscan port city of Piombino. Slaughter and bloodshed abound, until the Spanish knock down a passage through the city walls: "Just as a wolf enters an open stable and silently drags out the sheep before the shepherd comes, no less was the savage Alfonso about to take the walls of the dejected Tuscans."[48] But night has fallen, and Alfonso decides to wait until morning to enter the city. In the meantime, Apollo convinces Jupiter to allow him to heal Sigismondo more quickly: "I certainly believe that this commander of the Italians and the Etruscan people by his fame approaches the gods and touches the stars. Therefore send Paeon (doctor) down from serene Olympus to heal his mortal wounds." With Jupiter's consent, Paeon comes to Sigismondo in his sleep and fills his wound with herbs. Immediately "the pain is forced out by the sweet ointment and goes away. Sigismondo pulls his lightning sword out of its hilt, ardently tests his skills, turning and slicing the tender air."[49] Far from the miraculous healings that Jesus or Saint Peter performed, the pagan gods use actual medicine to heal wounds. What separates the human and the divine is the knowledge of what and where to find these herbs. Like Prometheus bringing fire to humanity, it is through knowledge that man can become like the gods.

Sigismondo is now ready for action, "like an injured lion . . . terrifying in anger and fury."[50] Meanwhile, Alfonso has started the final siege of Piombino. He rides his steed into the defenders and furiously cuts them down, while his cannons blast the remaining defenses:

> The bronze machine was filled with hard stone, enclosed with sulphur, and sent burning smoke of dust into the air. Then everything shook at the din from the sudden movement, the mountains echoed the crash, and the sound thundered in the air, rolling broken voices through the shaken lands. The Greeks did not throw stones on the great walls of fated Troy with a catapult; neither did powerful Rome, brave Hannibal and the Carthaginians, nor the great king Pyrrhus of Epirus, nor Alexander the Great; but such a weapon was invented by others on different shores and has filled the entire world. When with a terrible sound and a sudden crash the stony mass was shot out of the flaming cannon and forced the tottering outer walls against the inner walls, people were struck with fear, pressed their spirits with freezing heart, and had no hope for salvation. They prepared themselves, their families and property for the final fate; no Tuscan could evade death.[51]

Basinio's description of cannon fire is an early account of the new technology of gunpowder used in warfare, couched in hexameter verse and faithful classical Latin.[52] How would you describe a cannon in ancient terms? Like Cicero and Caesar, Basinio uses *ballista* for a catapult, and, like Livy, Frontinus,

Tacitus, and Sallust, he employs *machina* for a warlike engine.[53] War machines, as the ancient military theorist Vegetius notes, were especially useful for fomenting panic and terror in the besieged.[54] Such a *tour de force* is emblematic of the entire Renaissance humanist project. Basinio expresses his own world through a classical lens, even the cannon that ruptured walls and the gunpowder that exploded the previous ways of waging war.

Cannons are so loud that "they resound in vast Olympus" and are devastating, but no matter how advanced the weapon, according to Basinio, success in war rests on the strength and ability of the soldiers: "the bronze machine that launched stones did not prevent the defenders from threatening on the high walls. They struck and killed Euphilus with a heavy boulder as he tried to climb the wall."[55] Machiavelli later dismissed artillery and asserted the superiority of the virtue of soldiers to technological advances.[56] Sigismondo embodied this prowess and particularly pagan virtue in the face of devastating modern firepower. Piombino is lost and about to fall, when Sigismondo's imminent arrival is announced. The defenders take courage, turn on the offensive, and push the enemy back. Sigismondo drives the Spaniards from the walls.

Watching from Olympus, Jupiter points out Sigismondo to Mars:

> Do you see how Sigismondo rushes against the enemy and how, mindful of the violated treaty, before all others he hurries to entrust himself to the rough battle? Indeed he comes from your blood, a certain descendent of Quirinus, from the early origins of the people. For the goddess Venus slept with a mortal man and gave birth on the Trojan shores of Phrygia . . . whence the greatest hero Aeneas was born, from whom descended the founder of Alba Longa, the Roman commanders, and the great Julius Caesar, author of the long empire, and Augustus, all the princes of Italy, from whom the race of nobles has flowed into the entire world, including the heroic son of Pandolfo, the Trojan commander, Sigismondo in his ancestral arms.[57]

Sigismondo's divine lineage is explained. This racist view of Roman history, which Virgil masterfully forged in antiquity for Augustus, is extended to include all the noble, presumably hereditary, princes of the world. Although not unique, since all nobles share it, Sigismondo has the divine blood of Venus in his veins. Just as Mars assisted Aeneas in the Trojan War, so does Jupiter want Mars "to give Sigismondo eternal glory, the certain prizes of fresh labor, to be his companion alone on the front line and to confuse the wavering Spaniards."[58] Mars dons his armor and flies down to assist Sigismondo.

Accompanied by Mars, Sigismondo arrives on the battlefield in glory and downs rows of Aragonese besieging Piombino. When Sigismondo sees a frenzied Alfonso in the heat of battle, he encourages his men:

> We Italians have always had the bravest hearts, and Fortuna has desired us to drive proud peoples from our lands of Hesperia. That awaited day is now here for us and the time when Jupiter ordered men to take up just arms. We must dare to do this. Victory first! Men, do not stop! For yourselves, our dear household gods, esteemed elders and the sweet children above all, and for my battles that are already famous throughout the world, I beg you, Italians, do not gather spoils, while the battles are still being fought, nor let any booty left behind delay the Tuscans. Prizes shall belong to all. Equal to a man let us seize arms, horses, and this Tyrrhenian land.[59]

Basinio's rendering of Sigismondo's battle speech encapsulates the flattering literary portrait of the entire poem. The battle is nationalistic, and there is heroic camaraderie: all are equal, and the spoils will be equally distributed, but they all fight for Sigismondo's fame. Above all, Basinio gives Sigismondo a Spartan eloquence. Rhetoric should be functional, and Sigismondo's words will move his men to fight bravely. Such rhetorical feats may be more than a literary conceit based on classical epics, as Pius later accused Sigismondo of showing off his eloquence in Latin and Greek.[60] Images of the eloquent Sigismondo in poetry underscore the importance of rhetoric for the ideal commander. Rhetoric, Valturio asserts, moves soldiers and inspires them to courageous deeds.[61]

Sigismondo's words had the desired effect:

> Great-hearted Melanippus drove his horse into the ranks of the great Alfonso. . . . After breaking a spear, Sigismondo turned

> his lightning sword and amid enemy arrows made a path with his iron through the wielded weapons: everything yields to him pressing forward; double horns covered his bare helmet, a terrifying sight![62]

A battle scene worthy of the *Iliad:* the commander inspires courage in his heroic men, then accomplishes himself the pinnacle of valor. One of Sigismondo's men falls to Alfonso's sword and curses the king with words that are at once classical and nationalistic:

> O Spaniard, have now that Italy, on which you have been raging wars, and wretchedly seize another's land. You will arrive at another world, where neither your Iberian fleet can save you nor any loud-stepping beast will tread on desired land. Unburied you shall wander still by the rivers of Styx.[63]

The wandering soul and unburied body of Alfonso recalls both Hector and Palinurus in classical epic. In the *Iliad,* King Priam begs Achilles for his son, Hector's body, so that he can give it a proper burial and stop his soul from wandering. In the *Aeneid,* the helmsman Palinurus falls off the ship and dies on the shores of Italy. In the underworld, Aeneas finds Palinurus's soul wandering and unable to cross the river Cocytus because his body was left unburied.[64] Although the idea is classical, Basinio uses the wandering unburied soul in a different context, that of a curse on the illegitimate foreign invader.

The battle rages on. Italians and Spaniards fall in epic gore. Shining like a god, the armored knight Sigismondo hunts down his prey. The Italians press on and, following Sigismondo's plan, they surround the Aragonese and attack them on both flanks:

> So many times the horrid barbarians were ensnared in the field, just like the close-quarter battles the cautious Picenes fight against an excited wild boar. They surround the beast and drive it out with barking dogs and confused noise. Then they catch it in a net or a group of youths and drag it out in its confusion. The injured beast flees in vain. So many times the Spanish troops fell

> hesitating over which enemy to attack. As soon as Sigismondo saw them failing in the cacophony and tripping themselves up in the confusion, he shouted: "We have won! Jupiter has placed a routed enemy before me. Now let there be close combat, and before you the love of praise and the sweet triumphs of a defended Italy." Having thus spoken, Sigismondo launched himself against a stunned enemy, like a lion intent on slaughtering cattle.[65]

Sigismondo outmaneuvers Alfonso, showing his tactical superiority on the battlefield in trapping Alfonso's men. The ingenious and charismatic commander Sigismondo also shows his Spartan eloquence by seizing the moment and rallying his men to victory. His words, however, find their greatest power in his personal example, as he fearlessly throws himself into the melee, like a lion.

The Spanish are all but lost, when Jupiter takes pity and sends Apollo down to convince Alfonso to abandon the siege and return to Naples. Apollo warns Alfonso that if the Spanish stay they will die, since the gods have decreed this; and he offers to lead the Spanish secretly to their ships. Alfonso is livid at this and bewails his fate.[66] The image of Alfonso's bravery in the face of ruin is surprising in a laudatory work about Sigismondo, but it nevertheless follows a standard trope and makes for a better read, as the worthier opponent makes the hero shine all the more.

When he notices the Spanish leaving the battlefield, Sigismondo orders his men to cut them off before they reach the cost: "Just as a fierce wolf inside a fence scatters sheep (every sheep suddenly and silently falling in the shepherd's absence), so did the barbarian formations leave their posts, let themselves be captured, and cease cruel wounds, for Sigismondo halted the bloodshed." Some were used to barter for prisoners, "others Sigismondo kept for the great triumph."[67] The Aragonese are both a worthy enemy and mere sheep. The wolf, almost always a negative figure, encapsulates Sigismondo's ferocity.[68] After performing funeral rites, the victors leave Piombino triumphant: "Sigismondo on a snow-white horse, followed by a thousand heroes on horses, head for their tents, and the captains sing your praises, o Sigismondo."[69] As a golden epic hero, Sigismondo still shines in personal strength and manly virtue amid the modern artillery and complex political maneuvers.

Valturio, surprisingly, barely mentions Sigismondo's victory at Piombino in his tome on the art of war. Sigismondo's victories are listed in a chapter on ancient triumphs in a discussion of the siege-victory crown. On the Piombino campaign, Valturio focuses on the triumph that Florence awarded him:

> Like lightning, you devastated the Aragonese encampment. For the splendor and pomp of the man who saved them and the returning army, a crowd of inhabitants and townspeople came out, and everybody admired your soldiers and you alone Sigismondo, among so many captains and outstanding commanders. All Florence turned her eyes to you, every mouth cheered you, and, when they considered your victory, they beheld you as if you were divine and sent from heaven. They praised you for saving their homeland and wondered how a single prince was so important that, when its ancient domain and liberty had been extinguished by a king, you alone were the author of its return.[70]

Valturio makes up for his brevity and lack of details with the image of the Florentines beholding the victorious godlike Sigismondo, the restorer of liberty to republican Florence.

Basinio describes the Florentine triumph in much greater detail. Sigismondo leads a long line of captive Aragonese to the city walls, including one of Alfonso's captains, who bewails his fate to the gods and having to march "like an old weak ox attached to the plow." When the parade reaches Florence "numberless lines of citizens come out to meet the conqueror." The Florentines then crown Sigismondo with laurels and celebrate his victory in song, processions, and a horse race, which includes Alfonso's beloved steed. Sigismondo stands in appreciation and praises the Florentine connection to ancient Rome and the pagan gods: "Let the temples of Florence be festooned and libations poured for Jupiter."[71] In the triumphal procession, Sigismondo is led through Florence by nobles decked out in shining outfits, and senators in white, on top of golden chariots pulled by brilliant snow-white horses. Sigismondo's chariot is gold and silver, with glittering bronze spokes, and pulled by four horses. Church bells ring continuously. Men marvel at Sigismondo and the paraded spoils of war, and "mothers and girls lean out of high windows" to see him.[72] There is, however, no evidence of any triumph for Sigismondo in Florence. None of the Florentine sources mention it, nor do any of the Malatesta chronicles. Only Basinio and Valturio describe a triumph held in Florence for Sigismondo. The Florentines in fact refused to pay him, and immediately after the battle Sigismondo left and took up a condotta for Venice against Francesco Sforza.[73] Sigismondo's success may have made him even more of a threat to Florentine liberty, and honoring him with a triumph in Florence would have only augmented the danger.

Other contemporary sources presented the siege of Piombino differently. The official biographer of Federico da Montefeltro unsurprisingly places Federico at center stage. With few lines, Pierantonio Paltroni says that Federico scouted out the territory, "guided some of Sigismondo's men," and forced Alfonso to retreat.[74] Sigismondo's adviser and historian Gaspare Broglio says that Sigismondo used "clever inventions and explosives" and "by his high virtue and knowledge" raised the siege. Broglio nevertheless places the "most illustrious lord Federico" by Sigismondo's side.[75] A citizen of Piombino, Antonio di Agostino, wrote down his experiences of the siege as an epic in Italian verse. The poem starts with lengthy invocations to the "false" pagan gods, which the eighteenth-century editor chose not to include in his edition, since this part of the poem was "useless."[76] The gods nevertheless appear throughout the piece. Sigismondo is not the hero of this poem; rather, Rinaldo Orsini, the Lord of Piombino, and an otherwise unknown condottiere named Cecco di Modigliana are celebrated for withstanding the ferocious Aragonese siege. Cecco's bravery is the subject of the majority of the poem: when Alfonso digs a tunnel under the city's ramparts, Cecco heroically destroys it; he sets fire to a wooden siege tower; and he encourages the defenders by calling the Aragonese cowardly dogs from the walls.[77] Described merely as *valente,* Sigismondo arrives only at the very end of the poem. He scouts the area, then rages against the enemy like a "ferocious bear." A Spaniard notices Sigismondo and other famed condottieri from afar and points them out to Alfonso. "His [Alfonso's] face immediately changed color."[78] At this sight, Alfonso consults his generals and decides to abandon the siege and leave. Other sources similarly ascribe Sigismondo's victory to a psychological defeat. During the final ferocious Aragonese assault on Piombino, Sigismondo reportedly rode on horseback to a high promontory in order to be seen and thereby encourage the city's defenders. At the sight of Sigismondo, the king was dismayed and raised the siege.[79] In his book of epistolary poems about Jupiter's love for Isotta, Porcellio has Mars praising Sigismondo's exploits in Tuscany. Mars calls Sigismondo, the offspring of ancient Rome, which succumbed to discord and corruption and then in the absence of Caesar and the Roman emperors was overrun by barbarians, until Sigismondo came. "Only Sigismondo's virtue and virile courage" saved Rome and Italy from the barbarians. As in Antonio's poem, Mars-Porcellio says, "at the sight of Sigismondo" (*quo viso*) Alfonso "turned his army to the woods and shore in fear and fled in disgraceful flight."[80] Basinio's *Hesperis* is different in this respect. Alfonso does not show fear. He cries that he would gladly fall courageously in battle rather than be seen leaving as a coward.

In stark contrast to the epic versions of the battle, Machiavelli presented the siege of Piombino as wholly lacking in violence and heroism.[81] He says that the Tuscans suffered from lack of supplies, especially wine and potable water. In desperation, he says, more than two hundred Florentine soldiers deserted and joined the Aragonese. If it were not for the stubborn Neri Capponi, Machiavelli contends, Florence would have agreed to surrender Piombino and pay Alfonso a ransom. (Machiavelli was probably using Capponi as a source.) In the end, Machiavelli insists, Alfonso retreated with his superior troops not because of Sigismondo's prowess but because his army was devastated by swamp diseases and lack of supplies. Machiavelli's estimation of fifteenth-century Italian warfare is often mistaken. His history of the battle accords with his criticism of Italian warfare and the mercenary system as bloodless battles and pageantry. In describing the famous battle of Zagonara, for example, Machiavelli says that only three men died after falling from their horses and suffocating in the mud. Similarly, in describing the battle of Anghiari, which, he claims, lasted only four hours, Machiavelli writes that only one man died after he fell from his horse and was trampled.[82] Other more reliable sources claim losses of 3,200 cavalry for the Florentines at Zagonara and 900 men on both sides at Anghiari.[83] Machiavelli was concerned with deflating the notions of epic confrontations and the classical images of heroism that Basinio and other humanists had crafted for their patrons. Modern historians, however, have largely corrected Machiavelli's dismissals and stressed the intensely violent nature of fifteenth-century Italian wars. Following nonliterary primary sources, they have corroborated much of the violence of Piombino.[84] They see Piombino as a stunning military success for Sigismondo. Sigismondo was captain of 8,000 to 9,000 Florentine men, whom he led against 15,000 Aragonese. The Florentine commissioners thought the situation impossible, and, apart from Capponi, wanted to accept Alfonso's terms. Federico da Montefeltro wanted to attack Alfonso immediately and head on. Sigismondo, however, insisted on waiting and won the day by attacking from both flanks. The battle was ferocious.[85] Sigismondo's performance in the first Tuscan War made his reputation as, depending on your point of view, either a brave and crafty commander or a treacherous and ferocious beast—a mercenary Odysseus with modern firepower.

Gradara, October 1446

Shortly before the first Tuscan War, Sigismondo proved his battle skills at the siege of Gradara in 1446. Although the battle took place before Piombino, Basinio places it after and dedicates book V of the *Hesperis* to Gradara. Basinio begins his epic with Piombino because Sigismondo's crushing victory changed his life, and after the siege of Piombino, he was proclaimed the savior of Tuscany. A couple of years earlier in 1445 Galeazzo Malatesta, the lord of Pesaro, sold his city to Francesco Sforza and his brother Alessandro. Francesco Sforza, who had married Bianca Maria Visconti in 1441, did not take control of Milan until 1450, three years after his father-in-law, the duke of Milan, died. Before this, in the mid-1440s Sforza sought to carve out a territory in the Romagna. He placed his brother, Alessandro, in charge of Pesaro, and, with the help of Sigismondo's nemesis, Federico da Montefeltro, invaded Malatesta lands.[86] Several towns had already fallen to Sforza's large army, and despite its high walls Gradara seemed lost. The siege was long and tough.

Sigismondo arrived with his army, but they were outnumbered. Basinio shows Sigismondo surveying the scene and then praying for the gods' help. Mars flies down to the battlefield with Apollo's bow and slaughters great numbers of Sforza's men. He sends sickness and famine into their camp. Sforza recognizes the divine origins of these misfortunes: "From that time on, Sforza knew that Sigismondo was the offspring of the gods, as the spirits of the gods had stood on his right side; and Sforza feared the unnatural omen's effect on trembling souls. . . . Suddenly disturbed by the sad image of Mars's arrival . . . Sforza sensed that the wicked fates of the gods were returning."[87] Shocked by this vision, Sforza resorts to traps. He sends men into the woods and up the hills surrounding the battlefield, then orders other men to fire cannons on Gradara and attack in the open field. The ploy works. Sigismondo hears the noise "from his cave," sees the small contingent besieging the fortress, and launches himself into battle in the open, "like a proud lion, who, bringing slaughter to silent cattle, sends disaster and death across the wide fields, and, summoning the tough bulls into battle, does not see the erect Molossian hounds coming behind him; so was brave Sigismondo rushing against such great enemies and measuring his huge honors."[88] As planned, Sforza's men come out of the woods and down the hills, and surround Sigismondo and his men:

> . . . with his bloody arm, Sigismondo cut his way through the slaughter, arrows, waves of blood, and between the dense corpses and bodies of great hearted men . . . then he wrecked seven others, who ran in from the vast formation and blocked the way out. But after he had overcome the crowded enemies and escaped, Sigismondo flew back again into the hostile swarm with his own swift formation. He felled all the men and with his sword tore up their staggering backs.[89]

Sigismondo is at the center of this vivid, gory battle scene. He is an unstoppable force, strong enough to render Sforza's trap useless. He is a headstrong lion rather than a crafty fox, in this image, an Achilles heedless of personal danger, not a cautious Odysseus. Sigismondo escapes Sforza's trap and returns to his men. Night falls, and sleep comes upon everyone except Sigismondo, who with the help of Pallas Athena sneaks into the besieged fortress of Gradara with reinforcements. Inside, Sigismondo comforts the defenders, who "cry at his arrival," and comes up with a plan to surprise the enemy in the morning with a frontal assault. Meanwhile, realizing it is pointless to go against the gods' will, Sforza decides to abandon the siege.

In the invective, Pius II focuses on Sigismondo's actions in the battle of Gradara. But rather than as an example of the hero's bravery and the gods' approval, the pope sees Gradara as damning proof of Sigismondo's cowardice and brutality:

> He secretly invaded the town with an army, pillaged the inhabitants' property, raped their women, and murdered very many of them. He burned down churches and private houses, and did not spare the church treasuries. While a peace treaty was being worked out, Sigismondo returned to the town, drove out all the inhabitants and, as they ran away, he set the wretches on fire from behind. He forced them headfirst into the Centauro river and the water engulfed men, women, children, and elderly alike. To the present day Gradara remains deserted. This is the noble trophy of Sigismondo.[90]

Rather than the glorified violence of noble combat, this is the basest of crimes. Another Malatesta source, Broglio, presents a version of the events between these two extremes. Rather than sneak into the castle, Sigismondo sends his brave soldiers to fight for him and deliver his encouragement. Sigismondo remains on horseback on a cliff above the fray, urging his men to fight bravely. Far from divine intervention or battlefield prowess, Sigismondo raises the siege by convincing Duke Filippo Maria Visconti to recall Francesco Sforza. For Broglio, Sigismondo is a crafty behind-the-scenes hero, whose men are passionately loyal.[91] (The eighteenth-century historian Lodovico Muratori simply writes that Alessandro Sforza raised the siege because he ran out of gunpowder and makes no mention of Malatesta heroics or cowardice.)[92] In contrast to Broglio and later Machiavelli, Basinio and Pius describe the brutal violence of Renaissance warfare, either decrying it in Christian terms as sin or elevating it in pagan rhetoric as heroism.

The Second Tuscan War

In June 1452 Alfonso's illegitimate son, Ferrante (1423–1494), and Federico da Montefeltro led 12,000 Aragonese soldiers into Tuscany.[93] They took Foiano and encamped in Chianti; from here they raided Florentine territory, causing much havoc and coming within six miles of Florence. "So formidable were these armies and so dangerous those wars," Machiavelli surprisingly writes, "that towns that today are abandoned as places impossible to defend were then defended as places impossible to take."[94] Machiavelli's comments should be taken especially seriously given his general disparaging opinion of

Italian warfare. Among other towns, the Aragonese had taken control of the strategic previously impregnable fortified city of Vada.[95] The shocked Florentines hired Astorre Manfredi and Sigismondo Malatesta to lead their army of 8,000 soldiers against the Aragonese and defend Tuscany.

By the 1450s the most sought-after condottiere was Federico da Montefeltro, whose reputation for caution and fidelity to his employers made him more attractive than Sigismondo, who was regarded as the better soldier.[96] Federico had led the Florentines before and would lead them again, but now he was employed by the Aragonese. The Malatesta had a longstanding friendship with Florence and the Medici family; Sigismondo had saved Tuscany at Piombino, and his military genius was needed for the recapture of Vada. On September 30, 1453, the Florentine ambassadors Giannozzo Manetti and Bernardo de' Medici met Sigismondo in the field below Vada to hand over formal control of the Florentine army.[97]

Basinio starts his narrative of the second Tuscan War long before Sigismondo's appearance on the battlefield. He shows Alfonso years later, still bitterly blaming the loss at Piombino on the "fortune of the gods and Jupiter's fates, which were contrary to my desires."[98] The king wants revenge and the Tuscan victory that unjustly eluded him before. When a rumor circulates that Sigismondo has drowned, Alfonso seizes the opportunity for a second invasion of Tuscany. Alfonso puts his son, Ferrante, in charge of the army, which departs immediately from Naples.[99] Disturbed by this new invasion, Jupiter sends Mercury down to tell Sigismondo to leave the island of Fortunata and return to defend Tuscany once again.

Ferrante and the Aragonese began the invasion with a brutal siege of Foiano (June 2, 1452). Without Sigismondo's help, this outnumbered and outgunned small Tuscan city near Siena was doomed. Artillery blasted the walls and cut down the city's defenders. Invaders began to scale the ruined walls with ladders. All seemed lost, until the god Mars filled the role of Sigismondo and rallied the defenders: "Oh Tuscan people . . . remember your love of liberty and the glory of Mars; do not yield to the Spanish." After pointing out Ferrante's youth and inexperience, Mars jumped down from the walls and rushed into battle: "smashing terribly the tough Spanish ranks and slashing many to their deaths with his sword, he seized Ferrante by the arm and took him far away from the high ditches." The goddess Athena, however, did not like what her brother was doing and decided to encourage the disheartened Spanish, saying: "This is not the Leader of the Italians, the hero Sigismondo! Do not delay the attacks! There is need now for strong arms, outstanding courage, and the force you used to take down these walls. Rush now and fight! Let fear be gone from the Spanish against few Italians!" This episode reveals how Basinio does not need Sigismondo heroically present in a battle in order to praise him. Only a god, Mars, could be as effective and courageous on the battlefield as Sigismondo. With this clever device, the poet can thus show off his verse in a lengthy and exciting description of a battle in which Sigismondo took no part while still maintaining the celebratory focus of the work on his patron.

At the goddess's words, the Spaniards fight with renewed vigor. Both sides now rage in battle. But the Italian defenders again gain the advantage:

> The defenders rain arrows and rocks down on the invaders, shout encouragement to one another, pound the approaching enemy, and force them into the open with their hard spears. One held a shield, while the other stabbed [at the enemy's] groin repeatedly. No Spaniard was without blood. Brave and coward fell; there was no difference between virtue and fear. One after another unworthy javelins overwhelmed entire formations of worthy men; no one died from a single javelin, as black blood poured out of many holes.[100]

The defenders are systematic. The ordered line of shields and spears recalls the battle formation of the ancient Spartans, who held shields to protect the soldier on each one's left. In an epic poem glorifying war and the great prowess of Sigismondo, the hero, on the field, Basinio's collapsing the distinction between virtue and fear, even bravery and cowardice, is surprising. It nevertheless captures the actual chaos of war. The unworthy javelins taking down worthy men is similarly negative. In its unfair chaos and sudden death, war is hardly the arena for virtue. Such laments about warfare had been around at least as early as the first uses of projectiles in antiquity, and became commonplace with the greater use of guns in early modern Europe, when one coward could kill ten noble warriors with a lucky gunshot.[101]

Ferrante tries to shame his men into fighting harder: "If only Alfonso came to this war and saw his men, so many lines of his choice noblemen, yielding and rushing back in fear! What laziness is slowing you down? The Italians have no hope of salvation. Fight and before long you will hold their lands as conquerors, and the rich countryside of vanquished Italy will belong to you!"[102] His words then became even more effective by his example:

> [Ferrante] ran swiftly to the wall and with an iron-hooked stake dragged an imposing defender down to the ground . . . placed his knee on the lying Tuscan, and raised his lightning sword, twisting it high in the air. The beast then called out a challenge and at the same time cut open the man's jugular. The Tuscan rolled to the ground and expelled dark gore from his mouth.[103]

This graphic violence is worthy of Homer. It shows the cruel Ferrante at his worst. This display of brutality both encourages the invaders and disheartens the defenders. Such a theatrical use of ferocity brings to mind Machiavelli's later praise for Cesare Borgia's smart use of cruelty in the staging of Remirro de' Orco's execution. Cesare had Remirro do all the dirty work in his pacification of the Romagna and then, when the minister was most hated and seemed unstoppable, Cesare had him sliced in half and placed in the central piazza of Cesena for all to see. "The ferocity of the spectacle," Machiavelli writes, "left the people at once both satisfied and stupefied."[104] Basinio's image of the young Ferrante's cruelty is prescient: after he inherited the throne of Naples in 1458, Ferrante had a reputation for sadistic violence. In 1465 the king feted the mercenary Jacopo Piccinino on his recent marriage for a whole month, only to throw the condottiere out of a castle window to his death, reportedly toasting his health as he fell. One legend relates that after murdering his enemies, King Ferrante had them stuffed and seated around a banquet table.[105] But Basinio could have had no knowledge of any of these later events and rumors.

In another passage in the *Hesperis,* Sigismondo defines true honor and bravery in war by contrasting himself with Ferrante: "Whoever loves war and encourages arms for the people, is wicked, monstrous, and impious; but whoever defends his endangered and oppressed homeland, is brave, just, and innocent."[106] Unlike Ferrante, Sigismondo for Basinio is no warmonger. Sigismondo, however, could be every bit as cruel as Ferrante in war. Valturio, for example, praises Sigismondo's successful siege of the "unassailable" fortified city of Crema. He "burned fields, destroyed houses, and took prisoners and livestock; he devastated every part of that land, then dried out its marshes. Its walls had never before fallen under any attack, even an imperial one. The inhabitants obeyed you as their conqueror and many other difficult places caved under your efforts."[107] Here, Sigismondo is lauded for razing a city in terms that are not far from Pius's accusations about his conduct at Gradara. Despite the realities of Renaissance war, in the *Hesperis,* the character Sigismondo stands for the true glory and virtue of protecting the fatherland. But even this encomiastic text betrays a tension between violence and virtue, the hero and the rapacious wolf, and fortune and justice.

To continue with the epic version of the battle, as if to startle the defenders out of their shocked horror, the Spanish immediately fire their cannons and topple the remaining walls. Raging and screaming, they rush forward, a dense mass into the city. The defenders

> fled everywhere through houses and temples, as the enemy took control of the city and the defeated Tuscans. They slaughtered many and sent others bound as captives to the ships. There was screaming everywhere, and heavy afflicted groans from the wretched. Vows and prayers were doubled, and laments tossed at empty ears. Others despaired, asked the gods unspeakable things, and blamed them indecently . . . so great was the fear everywhere, and its great infamy moved through the mouths of all men.[108]

Foiano had fallen, and its people were enslaved. To celebrate the victory, Ferrante and "several thousand men plundered the countryside, the fields, and destroyed nearby castles. There was no great honor or glory in this. He destroyed everywhere, burned down houses, and murdered farmers."[109] This more than anything else prompts Jupiter to anger. He calls the Spanish an impious people and sends favorable winds down to fill the sails of Sigismondo's ship and hasten his return to Italy.

Sigismondo lands in Genoa and is greeted with shocked celebration, as the rumor of his death is dispelled and the "savior of Italy" returns. From the Ligurian mountains, Parma, and Modena, he gathers an army. "When the report [of Sigismondo's return] reached the trembling ears of the Spaniards, they were stunned in great fear. Some angrily refused to believe it, others feared deception and a trap, and others were tormented by the unfair fortune of the Latins against foreigners." The Italians, however, rejoiced at the news. At each city he visited, Sigismondo raised hope and filled everyone with the zeal for war, "just as Mars coming across the ocean and returning a victor to the shores of Thrace." The Italian nobles address him as the sole hope of Italy and their savior: "From you, above all glory, it is right that they learn from you how great is virtue, so that they might be able to win a just war."[110] In response, Sigismondo assures the nobles that he will fight and win, since theirs is the just cause.[111]

Swords, arrows, and spears at the ready, the armor-clad Italian youth mount horses and prepare for battle. Sigismondo addresses the men in another example of classical rhetoric on the battlefield:

> Great-hearted noblemen, flower of experienced youth, young men outstanding in war, if I recall ancient battles, if I remember ancient force, the very many wars waged under a favorable god . . . now all of you mark my words in your firm minds, commanders, and do not fear the empty dangers and threats of the Spanish. What kind of force do they have? How great? All of them are before my eyes. I know that the Spanish pray for wicked destruction upon the Italians. May the great gods destroy them for composing such words! How much should we value them? Do not value them as more than words, companions. Deeds are needed. Here is labor; here is the glory and the great honors of great virtue. A few of us scattered Alfonso's ranks on the Tuscan fields. The best part of them and their strong companies are held in bronze chains. Many of their men have been cut down. The vanquished Spanish are threatening the unvanquished Italians. . . . Come on then, noblemen, use your usual force, and engage your minds in the ancient study of war! Now is the time to turn your cleft-footed horses on warm dust; now weigh your shoulders with decorated armor; now the sorting of gold and silver in fresh spoils entices! Let all the barbarian arms and wealth, which we capture on the Tuscan field, be shared![112]

Ironically, Sigismondo dismisses Spanish valor as all talk, mere rhetoric, in a well-balanced eloquent classical oration. Without any specific historical examples, Sigismondo excites his men with the image of antiquity and the "ancient study of war." He reminds them of the victories in the previous Tuscan war, and concludes with the promise of rich booty. The speech starts in an abstract call for classical glory and ends in the very real material spoils of war.

Soon after Sigismondo's speech the trumpet sounds and the Italian army rushes together: "just as the numberless waves on the stormy Adriatic rise and engulf the vast shore, so did the Italians flood into Tuscany."[113] Both armies encamp nearby and prepare for battle. Sigismondo is anxious to hunt down Ferrante: "Just like when a gnashing lion awakes himself in anger, studies the rough terrain, and dominates the high forest searching for the horned bull. No differently was Sigismondo's fervid anger swelling up over the great Ferrante." Switching animal comparisons, Basinio now makes Ferrante the "bull" and Sigismondo the "lion." After a seven-day march, Sigismondo rejoices at the sight of the enemy and addresses his men:

> What joys, passions, and courage, have you gods given us! Even if there are no divine spirits and no gods watching over the earth, which I do not think, the Italians, whom I have taught for so many years and in so many battles not to yield in a just war, will still not yield to the Spanish. Whoever turns his back to the enemy is not one of my men—strike him down, Italians, with many spears, like a Spaniard![114]

Sigismondo is thankful for the gods' support but hubristically announces that the Italians do not need help from the gods. As in antiquity, the gods were seen as important, but in the end, wars were won by personal virtue, courage, and preparation. Basinio is not merely invoking a Christian God through a classical gloss but instead reveals an entirely different attitude toward the divine.

From atop a hill on horseback, Sigismondo orders his men into formations. The Aragonese are at first terrified at the sight of radiant Sigismondo and the Italian army, but then the Spanish commanders and Ferrante rush into battle "like the stormy south wind." Sigismondo sees Ferrante killing brave Italians, and "kicking his horse with strong feet, launches himself against his savage enemy and challenges him: 'Do not flee Sigismondo, if you want victory. Seek either the kingdom of Italy by your arms or the sweet honor of death in the wounds I will give you." Now it is Sigismondo's turn to cut down the Spanish youth. The enraged Sigismondo fights: "just like a shark on the Tyrrhenian sea darts furiously into fish and swiftly torments them with its great open mouth; and, as the fish flee everywhere, the shark devours whatever fortune gives him." When he sees a companion fall, Sigismondo jumps into the melee, "just as when in the wild an eagle from high above . . . sees a hare hiding in a bush or a deer cub left on a mountain, and dives down low . . . snatching its prey, and returns to the clouds." Sigismondo tries to protect his companion's body, fighting with "his head bare and spurning repeated blows."[115] The fighting continues with noble and numerous deaths on both sides.

Although Sigismondo has declared that the Italians do not need divine help, the gods have not abandoned them. The Greek gods join the fray: Ares comes down to lead the Italians "in the form of an handsome youth, faithful to strong Sigismondo, and distinguished with a heart eager for virtue." Then Athena with the "Gorgon's snakes on her shield" comes down and encourages the Italians:

> Take Italy and her sweet kingdoms back from the foreigners, and put an end to these evils. In its twenty year war in Asia on the shore of Troy, Europe did not lose to the Trojans as many men as Mars sent down to Orcus at the cruel hands of the Spanish. Therefore fight together and do not turn back, but all of you burst forth in tight formation against them, where daring and virtue are calling you.[116]

Like the entire poem, the comparison with the Trojan War is overkill, as Basinio himself seems to emphasize by including the "twenty years" in his description.

Ferrante fears the enraged Sigismondo and tries to hide:

> Just as the crafty wolf slaughtering sheep recognizes the hound coming to kill him, drops the sheep and flees the pursuing

> Molossian mastiff, rushing and trembling in fear. Oh memorable youth, this would have been your last day, if great Apollo had not saved you. As you shook in fear, he surrounded you in a huge fog, which covered your eager horses and barbarian standards.[117]

In this image Ferrante, the devious wolf, is chased by Sigismondo as the Molossian hound. In antiquity, Molossian hounds were famous for being rabid and tough. Sigismondo, previously a wolf, now hunts the wolf Ferrante. The mixed bestial metaphors—Sigismondo as wolf, lion, shark, eagle, and Molossian hound—all point to Sigismondo's ferocity, a quality heroic but on the edge of bestial. By showing Sigismondo in constant action, a wild animal with unstoppable fury in battle, Basinio recalls the heroic vitality Homer gave to Achilles in the *Iliad*.[118] But, unlike the multiple compelling heroes in the *Iliad*, Sigismondo for the most part is the sole hero and guiding force of the *Hesperis*. Here, Basinio uses the gods to explain why Sigismondo did not fight Ferrante in the battle.

Angry at being robbed of his prey, Sigismondo "dove into the enemy, a terrible sight to behold; swollen with power, he held his strong spear in front and great ruin followed. He raged furiously against all the Spaniards, striking at their weak knees, then taking off their heads with his sword."[119] The violence is too much even for the gods, and Jupiter decides to end the war by forcing Ferrante to flee Tuscany just as his father, Alfonso, had done in the previous war. Juno tries to persuade Jupiter not to interfere but to let the fates decide the outcome. She sends down Iris to create a huge storm to end the fighting and save Ferrante. Meanwhile, Sigismondo continues to dominate the battlefield. The Spanish are hard-pressed until the hero, Haemonides, raises their hopes. Sigismondo pretends to flee, turning his horse this way and that, and the Spaniard pursues him unaware of the trap. Like a "vulture," Sigismondo encircles his prey, turns suddenly, and "violently plunges his entire sword into his opponent's chest and breaks his ribs with a second blow. Haemonides collapses and his armor rings out in devastated ruin." Again, Sigismondo's trickery fells a brave warrior.[120] The battle has turned in the Italians' favor but continues to be intense.

Basinio appropriates Herodotus's description of the battle of Thermopylae when the Persians threatened to shoot so many arrows at Leonidas's outnumbered Spartan warriors that they would blacken out the sun: "The shade of spears covered the day," Basinio writes, "and a repeated hissing from a melodious cloud came violently into the air. No face of evil was lacking in the flying spears."[121] "Chest to chest" the men are locked in hand-to-hand combat, when lightning and rain fall suddenly on them in a storm that the goddess Iris starts at Juno's command. Sigismondo rages on and cuts down Spanish hero after hero; "he would have killed Ferrante, if Iris had not darkened great Olympus with a tornado" and brought hailstones. Sigismondo calls out to the gods in anger: "What injury have we done the gods . . . ? Why, father of the gods, have you saved the Spanish from death twice?" Ferrante escapes in the fog to the mountains, leaving his men behind to drown in the floodwaters. While they favor Sigismondo, the gods still protect Ferrante either to prolong the war in order to create a greater arena for Sigismondo's virtue, or out of respect for the warrior Ferrante. Seeing the Spanish fall, Sigismondo recalls his men: "High Jupiter has given us this sweet victory and . . . in their efforts to save Ferrante the Aragonese are dying."[122] Here at the conclusion of this battle the ambiguities are resolved, as Basinio compares the two commanders: one brave, the other a coward.

The war is almost over. Sigismondo easily retakes Foiano for the Tuscans and heads to the port city of Vada (fig. 4.1). The city had a well-fortified castle, which was surrounded by swamp and marsh, so that Sigismondo could not effectively use artillery. The castle was also strategically placed on the Mediterranean coast, so the enemy had a constant flow of fresh troops and supplies. These problems seemed insurmountable, and many of the captains were disheartened until Sigismondo devised a way to mount his cannon and cut off the castle from the sea.[123]

> Minerva gave Sigismondo the following idea: he shook the hard walls with terrifying stones and from a high side cut the approach off from rafts. His bronze war machine thundered from the ground and flung rocks; it beat the air with crashing movement, and pounded the walls with a tumbling boulder, and his catapult hurled huge mill-stones . . . [124]

Here again, Basinio uses classical words to describe cannons. It is ironic that a modern invention is described as Minerva's idea. A cannon mounted on a raft and the catapult are clearly seen in a manuscript illumination to the *Hesperis* (fig. 4.1).

Cut off from reinforcements and supplies from the sea, the Aragonese were now stranded inside the fortress. Instead of starving out the occupants, as was normal practice in Renaissance warfare, Sigismondo built a wooden rampart and stormed the isolated fortress.[125] The Aragonese defended well but in the end could not fight Sigismondo's onslaught. When night comes, a Spaniard, Palerma, tries to convince his fellow defenders to flee the fortress before it is too late:

> Black night has fallen, and night is fit for escape and silent stealth. . . . Come therefore, while the fates allow, and quickly flee the dark unspeakable death that promises to smash us all against the sea and give us to the wild dogs of Tuscany. . . . O gods, turn such fates against Sigismondo. But if life remains more unfortunate than death itself, what pleasure will it be to have dragged out our life in darkness, pale horror in our bones, sad hunger in our words, filthy mouths to suffer endless thirst? All of us have death as our punishment, but wretched hunger above all is the worst kind of death.[126]

Convinced of their imminent loss, the Spanish secretly abandon Vada and head for their ships. But the Tuscans discover their escape, set fire to the harbor, and rush into battle. Mars and Athena take opposing sides and end up attacking each other on the battlefield. After much bloodshed, the Spanish escape. Sigismondo enters the city in triumph, takes down its walls, and orders proper burials for the fallen.[127]

Valturio praises Sigismondo's siege tactics in Foiano and Vada in his chapter on ancient triumphs. He succinctly states that Sigismondo drove the Aragonese out of Foiano, and, after a lengthy and tough siege, forced its inhabitants to submit again to Florence. Vada receives longer praise from Valturio. Ferrante had control of the key fortified city. Four miles of walls, ditches, towers, and an endless supply of resources made the city unassailable: but "your quick wit thought up a way more powerful than arms, so that the city was added to the Florentine empire, against the judgment and opinion of everyone, who had planned the death and flight of many, and the

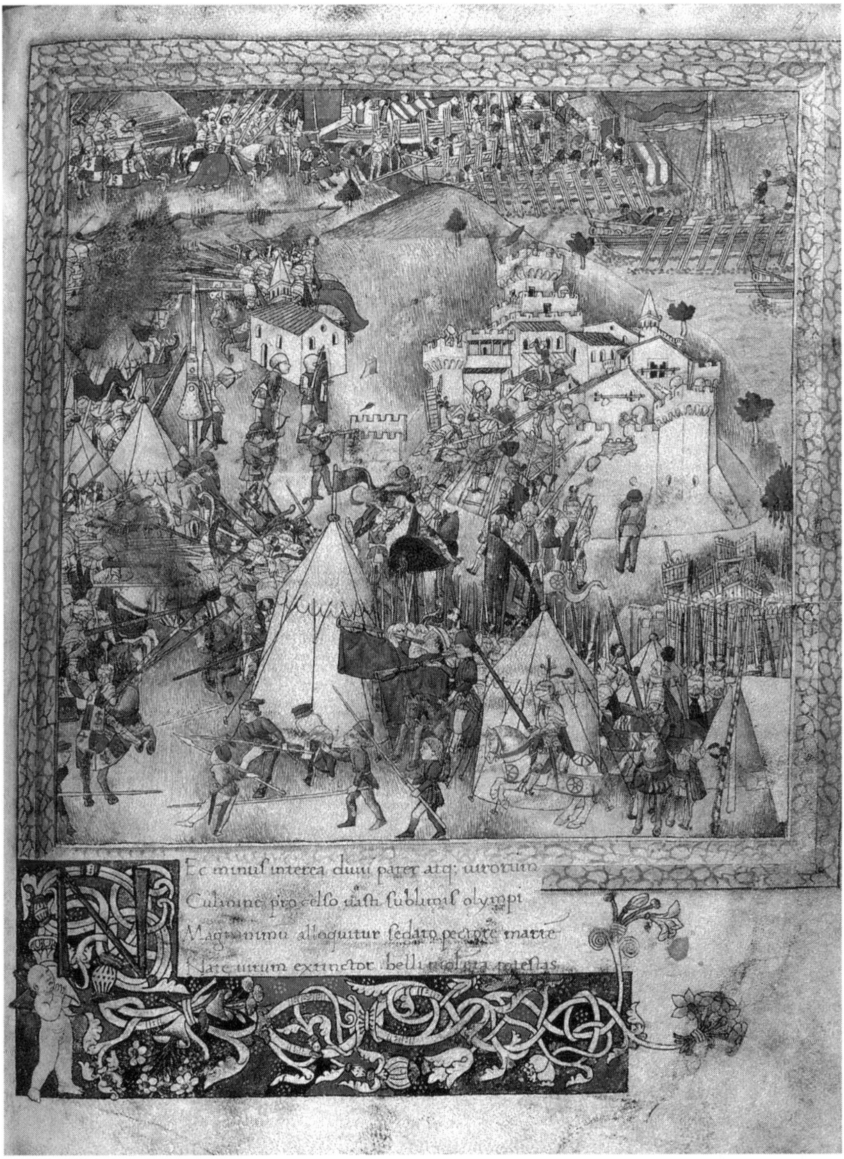

Fig. 4.1. Giovanni da Fano, siege of Vada, manuscript illumination (Canon Class lat. 81, fol. 112v), Basinio, *Hesperis,* ca. 1460, The Bodleian Libraries, Oxford. Photo: The Bodleian Libraries, University of Oxford/The Art Archive at Art Resource/Art Resource, NY.

demolition of the place."[128] Valturio highlights Sigismondo's ingenious tactics in taking the fortress. Basinio also stresses how Sigismondo built elaborate, unusual siege engines and managed to cut off the castle defenders from their supplies. Sigismondo was at the forefront of fifteenth-century innovation in military engineering, which included complex field fortifications.[129] Unlike with the Piombino battle, there are few details in nonliterary sources about the siege of Vada, apart from the laudatory accounts of Basinio and Riminese historians. Machiavelli only refers to brief skirmishes, and the modern historian P. J. Jones ascribes Sigismondo's success to "the laziness and improvidence of the enemy."[130] In Basinio's account, Sigismondo combines the ingenuity of Odysseus with the courage of Achilles to conquer a ferocious foreign enemy in an epic battle that left thousands dead.

In his epic, Basinio praises Sigismondo for all sorts of unchristian virtues, including trickery, violence, and ferocity. The Tuscan Wars were the high point in Sigismondo's career as a commander. The fame and myth of Sigismondo's military power depended to a large extent on self-promotion. In this Latin epic, Sigismondo wanted such an outlandishly classical and pagan image of himself; otherwise, he would not have hired Basinio to write the laudatory epic that the poet had promised. Basinio's untimely death and Sigismondo's financial ruin denied Achilles his Homer and toppled the myth before it could fully take root.

✣ 5 ✣

Astrology, Plato, and Pagan Worship

In the papal invective, Pius II accuses Sigismondo of every kind of intellectual immorality, including atheism, pagan idolatry, blasphemy, and heresy; Sigismondo's intellectual culture was indeed rich with pagan ideas and images. In Rimini, humanists reverently proclaimed astrology, pagan ideas about the soul and its fate after death, and Plato, the Elysian Fields, and the transmigration of souls. Pagan gods fill Malatesta poetry and art, including the Franciscan church that was described as a "temple." In his court literature, Sigismondo is shown as an avid student of the occult arts and fully immersed in pagan worship, praying and sacrificing to the gods, incensing altars and pouring libations, reading omens, and predicting the future using auguries. Even if he surely did not actually perform pagan sacrifices or literally worship pagan gods, the philosophy and attitudes toward the divine of pagan antiquity—in an uneasy relationship with Christianity—shaped how Sigismondo's humanists presented him to the world.

Accusations

Pius II accused Sigismondo of being an atheist and a heretic. Denying God's existence, the pope argues, is the worst kind of heresy, and this denial is the origin of Sigismondo's many blasphemies against the Christian Church:

> He denies serious matters in public and swings an axe at the root of the faith. He often dares to argue about the faith with the

> most learned men. What does he not allow himself? His arguing has reached such insanity that he asserts that the human soul is destroyed with the body, that hell does not exist, and that it is an empty fear given to mortals.[1]

These are all arguments of the ancient philosopher Epicurus. If the soul dies with the body and there is no hell, then mortals are free of the greatest anxiety and can enjoy life. Furthermore, Epicurus argued that even if there were gods, they would want nothing to do with weak mortals. The first century BCE Roman poet Lucretius had popularized Epicurean ideas in his poem *De rerum natura*. After Poggio Bracciolini had rediscovered this poem in 1416, Epicurean ideas popped up all over the place and may have been a decisive influence on the worldly Renaissance.[2] Against these Epicurean ideas that he attributes to Sigismondo, Pius adopts arguments from the natural order, pagan and Judeo-Christian authority, and human nature, and indulges in pure ridicule:

> Although the entire school of pagan philosophers confesses that there is a certain force, which guides this great and most beautiful machine of the world, and has given it the name of God; although the words of the Old and New Testaments and the Greek and Latin doctors [of the Church] strive to bring us nothing other than the worship of the true God, and to show us the way to understand it; although no people can be found so barbaric, so inhuman, so uncultured, and so wild that they do not worship some divinity; this little ass walking on two legs, wiser in his judgment than all mortals, nevertheless argues that there is no God. As the prophet writes: "The fool said in his heart that God does not exist." Or he follows Epicurus and claims that God does not care about mortals.[3]

In addition to being himself damned for his impiety, Sigismondo is a danger to the entire Christian community. For, Pius further asserts, "this little ass walking on two legs" has not kept his disbelief to himself but has led others astray by ridiculing the Church and leading an openly lewd life:

> What should I say about his blasphemy? About the abuses he has thrown on Christ and his most blessed mother, the Virgin? Sometimes he laughs at the most sacred Trinity; other times he scorns the procession of the Holy Spirit. He jeers at the ranks of the saints, detracts from the choirs of angels, and declares our entire religion ridiculous.

Pius even alleges that Sigismondo replaced the Holy Water in one church with ink so that when crossing themselves, the faithful would leave deep black ink marks all over their faces. Such an evil practical joke could only have been the act of the most wicked man who had ever lived and surely proved that Sigismondo should be eternally damned by Pius's reverse canonization. In the *Commentaries,* Pius relates how Sigismondo's blasphemy against a miraculous image of the Madonna gave rise to divine intervention. Sigismondo despised the image so much that he ordered the monk custodian to take it down. When he refused, Sigismondo sent "assassins" to drag the bound monk to Rimini to be punished. But after walking all night, the assassins found themselves again in front of the Madonna's chapel. Enraged, they hanged the monk "on a high cross," but as soon as they left, the rope broke; the monk survived.[4]

Pius paradoxically accuses Sigismondo of both atheism and heresy:

> Sigismondo is therefore a heretic. He has chosen no approaches to religion, imagined nothing, and follows no sect. But nothing is as heretical as to destroy the foundations of the faith and question divinity. Nor does he choose nothing at all, whoever believes nothing about God. For he chooses this about God, that he believes nothing, and Sigismondo has gained the first place in this sect of the fools. Do not think that Arius and Nestor were worse than Sigismondo. They believed that God existed; he denies it. They betrayed immortal souls; he says that they are mortal. At least they apparently lived cleanly and purely; openly and in the dark he shows himself impure and dirty. These heretics dragged men into error only with words. Using his lordship, Sigismondo has forced men with fear, threats, and bribes into the most dissolute life.[5]

Pius refers specifically to Sigismondo's lordship and his abuse of power. Few theologians would follow his argument about Sigismondo's heresy, since a heretic is by definition a Christian whose theology is in contradiction to the orthodox beliefs of the magisterium. If Sigismondo denies God's existence, then he is no longer remotely Christian and can therefore not be a heretic. The contradictions in the pope's arguments are rife: as evidence for Sigismondo's heresy, the pope says that even after he was excommunicated, the lord of Rimini continued to receive holy Eucharist "and not out of ignorance or necessity." This accusation implies that Sigismondo was a practicing Christian, even if imperfectly.

Sigismondo's purported heresy was ultimately political. "On many occasions," according to Pius, Sigismondo said that he agreed with the "the Hussite heresy, which was condemned at the council of Constance for among other errors asserting that priests should not be allowed to have civil dominion." This accusation suggests that Sigismondo might have used heretical ideas to question papal claims to temporal power and justify his refusal to relinquish his control of papal territory. Once, the pope continues, at the palace of Cosimo de' Medici in Florence, Sigismondo said to a poor widow that "the pope should be content with wealth alone" and not castles.[6] Pius had been systematically reclaiming Malatesta strongholds. Sigismondo's questionable Christian orthodoxy may have become an issue for the pope only when it turned political and threatened the rationale behind the Papal States and its ever-expanding territory.

Pius refers to Sigismondo's arrogance about his command of law, philosophy, and theology:

> In governing a city and passing laws he yields neither to Solon nor to Lycurgus. He judges Moses unworthy, to whom he compares himself, and whose laws he calls nonsense. In eloquence, if he has to speak in the vernacular, he yields neither to the Latins nor to the Greeks. If the conversation falls on philosophy and the humanities, he believes that he alone can understand the arcane senses of Plato and Aristotle; and that he knows how to unravel the knots of Chrysippus; nor is he silent on sacred letters, though he despises them. Nothing is so obscure among theologians that he thinks is not open to him.[7]

Chrysippus was a famous stoic, who delighted in logical problems. Although mocking him, Pius lists Sigismondo's accomplishments and intellectual interests: good government and justice; rhetoric and humanism; Plato, Aristotle, and pagan philosophy; the Bible and theology; and ethics.

Sigismondo's councilor and resident humanist, Roberto Valturio, offered a very similar assessment of his patron's intellect and intense involvement in humanist debate, but for the purpose of flattery rather than defamation:

> Your abundant reading and listening, discussing and patiently refuting, o great-hearted prince Sigismondo, brings the greatest and richest praise to your name. Although you know very many things, and the common opinion of all the learned is that all the seeds of the good arts have been divinely bestowed upon you, you nevertheless continue to learn every day in your free hours, to attend to the conversations of wise men in private and public meetings, to delight in the most serious and deepest questions and arguments of natural science, and to support the most illustrious minds of the orators and poets of your time.[8]

Valturio adds key elements lacking in Pius's invective, including praise for Sigismondo's intellectual curiosity, continual learning, patient listening, and patronage. But the image of a political leader immersed in intellectual conversation is still remarkably similar. Valturio's treatise was published six years before the invective. Pius may have been reacting to this and other panegyrics of Sigismondo's intellectual pursuits. If the pope bolsters the image of the erudite prince, this is not ultimately redeeming for Pius:

> Finally, Sigismondo declares himself the best in every kind of conduct, whether good or evil, nor does he lie about the evil. He is the master of all wickedness . . . vices please him more, and letters do not easily reform an ill-educated character, although they do show off a well-instructed one.[9]

The pope does not question Sigismondo's erudition, only his character. Declaring a humanist education useless for leading a moral life is quite an admission for the humanist pope. In the end, Pius sees Sigismondo's learning as pure arrogance:

> If anyone is arrogant, full of himself, a bigheaded windbag with a great opinion of himself, talks about himself while listening, and uses high-flown language and yard-long pedantic words, that person is Sigismondo. He not only thinks that he is the equal of the greatest men, but he also puts himself before God himself and thinks that he himself is God.[10]

Pius's insults and criticisms ironically present Sigismondo as the humanist that he wants to be. In the pope's words, Sigismondo was (or at least tried to appear) learned and eloquent, and enjoyed intellectual discourse. Cicero himself was accused of being arrogant. Pride is the common sin of intellectuals. As far as we know, Sigismondo wrote no philosophy or theology, but Pius's insults place him as an active member in learned exchanges. The violent mercenary and sex fiend was also an intellectual. In his arrogance, Pius asserts, Sigismondo thought that he was above all men and divine. Even for the humanist pope, a classical education is at the root of Sigismondo's overweening pride and heresy.

The Soul in Rimini: Astrology

Pius's jumbled accusations of atheism were simply wrong. Sigismondo did not believe that the soul would perish with death; the amount of money and care he put into renovating the church of San Francesco and the highly religious content, albeit fairly pagan, at his court alone suggest that he believed in some form of afterlife. What mainly prompted Pius II to accuse Sigismondo of turning a church into "a temple dedicated to demons and pagan worship" was the sculptures of pagan deities and zodiac signs inside the church carved by the exiled Florentine artist Agostino di Duccio. The walls of the church, Valturio said, were covered with:

> the most beautiful sculpted reliefs of the holy fathers, four virtues, the signs of the celestial zodiac, the wandering stars, sibyls, muses, and many other images of noble things. Because of the

> sculptor's skill and the recognition of their forms—you, the shrewdest and most famous prince of our age, invented images from the hidden recesses of philosophy—the reliefs especially appeal to beholders learned in literature and those almost completely separate from the vulgar.[11]

The humanist credits his patron with devising the intricate iconography. It seems likely that Basinio and Valturio supplied the details of the iconographic program for the reliefs of the zodiac planet-gods, the muses, and the sibyls.[12] They were based on descriptions of the gods in ancient texts, but their deeper meanings were meant to be hidden, accessible only to the learned elite.

Because of Sigismondo's interest in astrology and its popularity in Renaissance Italy, Valturio dedicates an entire chapter to the subject in his book on the art of war (1455). His treatise outlines all the different skills needed to become a successful general, including discussions on eloquence, poetry, history, medicine, law, music, and gymnastics. These are all deemed essential for a commander, but none has its own chapter, except for astrology. Valturio calls astrology a "most profound discipline, which many think is especially useful for predicting the outcome of battles."[13] But, already in the beginning, he highlights a problem with astrology. If, as they claim, astrologers can predict everything according to the stars, then our accomplishments are worthless since there is no individual free will. "The greatest minds," he says, "have debated whether the art of predicting the future is an art at all or rather a most groundless joke."[14] Valturio nevertheless tries to present a balanced account of the role of astrology in antiquity. Not just philosophers but also emperors and kings, he writes, would not do anything without consulting astrologers.

Valturio's use of sources is anything but critical, despite his disingenuous declaration: "I am on purpose passing over everything that either is fiction [fabula] or smacks of fiction."[15] This assertion comes after he refers to Cassandra and Troy. He nevertheless includes any and all ancient exempla. The Babylonians and the Egyptians "first noted and discovered the varied paths of the sun and moon, and the movements and effects of the stars." The Chaldeans and the Assyrians also introduced the use of entrails, birds, and lightning. Valturio mentions Thessaly, Britain, and the druids of Gaul and refers to the works of Aristotle, Lucan, and Cicero. We hear about the practice of human sacrifice among the Galatians; the Greeks' refusal to embark on any wars without consulting their gods; Etruscan, Phrygian, Cilecian, Arabic, and Spartan priests; the famous necromancers Tiresias and Amphiaraus from Homer; and the Sibylline verses and portents in Rome.

Valturio's critique of astrology is multifaceted. This plurality of arguments creates confusion, which is magnified by the nature of his sources. The ancient exempla and pagan authors that he uses also carry assumptions that undercut a Christian argument against astrology and the occult. Valturio makes the distinction between astrology, which is based on superstition and ignorance, and astronomy, which is based on science and can expose superstition and be useful. If the Athenian general Nikias loses an entire fleet because of an irrational fear of the moon, Pericles calms the Athenians by explaining the cause of an eclipse. If Julius Caesar argued for heliocentrism and worked out a scientific calendar by referring to the stars, the corrupt emperors Nero and Eliogabulus used the knowledge of the stars for dark purposes.[16] Elsewhere in the treatise Valturio counts as an essential skill reading the stars for purposes of weather prediction. He also comments on what the moon does to the waves of the sea.[17] Valturio's problems with astrology have to do with religion, human presumption, and efficacy.

Astrologers, Valturio declares, "with clever arguments and arts pervert the idea of the true triune God among all peoples. These disciplines concerning the knowledge of the stars are superstitious; association with demons should be feared and avoided." To be successful, astrologers and diviners need the help of demons, and those who deal with demons "immerse themselves deeper and deeper in the manifold snares of this most pernicious error." As Augustine did, Valturio emphasizes the evil of curiosity as a vice that leads the faithful to sin. Those who meddle in occult arts are called "curiosi." Valturio tells us about Moses's injunction against the arts of divination and Paul's warning to the Romans not to "enquire about things above you nor to examine matters more powerful than you." Isaiah and Ecclesiastes add their condemnation of fortunetellers. Valturio quotes the Church father Lactantius on the madness of stargazers, who cannot know about what they dispute, since only God knows the truth.[18] The occult arts trick people into worshiping idols, and as a result they "throw their lives into confusion, disturb their sleep, torture their limbs, destroy their health, provoke illness, and terrify their minds."[19] Valturio especially warns against the Chaldeaen arts since they claim "to explain past and future events by studying the effects of the twelve planets, five stars, and the sun and moon on human reason."[20]

Both the pagans and the Christians condemned astrology. The "teachings of our religion and the sayings of the poets," Valturio declares, "are similar." He quotes the Roman poet Lucius Accius: "I do not believe in augurs who fill the ears of others in order to enrich their own homes with gold," and refers to the poet Ennius's tirade against greedy charlatans, who offer false predictions for money. Horace and Lucan attest that men's minds are "blind of their future fate." Statius cautions against reading the future, and Juvenal declares: "the oracles at Delphi have ceased, and a foggy future condemns the human race." Valturio concludes with the wisdom of Socrates that man should "suspend searching" for the unknowable higher causes and "turn his attention to virtue and duty," ethics.[21] Only a god can know the future. It is presumptuous for mortals to try to know what will come.

The next argument takes for granted the accuracy of fortune telling. Valturio asks: What good it is to know the future, if, as must be assumed, one cannot change it? Only pain, Cicero says, can come of knowing the future. Valturio wonders how it would have helped Crassus to know that he would be killed by the Parthians, or Pompey that he would be slain alone in Egypt, or Caesar that he would be slain in the senate below the statue of Pompey. But Valturio saves the strongest argument for last, that of human weakness in interpretation. It is virtually impossible to determine the exact position and brightness of stars at someone's time of birth. There are also an infinite number of stars, and some are not visible in some places. As Cicero asserts, gods do not fail in the signs they leave; men have failed.[22]

Valturio's attempt to dissuade Sigismondo from pagan belief in the occult arts is ambiguous, to say the least. The dense chapter is based primarily on pagan sources. There are a number of possible reasons for this. Both Valturio and Sigismondo were obsessed with antiquity and valued the wisdom of the ancients. This is especially clear in the frustratingly few references to his own times that Valturio makes in the treatise. The Christian argument may also have been well known, and Valturio stole some of his pagan sources from Augustine's discussion of them in the *City of God*. As a humanist bent on showing off his erudition, Valturio probably also considered it an act of virtuosity to use pagan authorities to argue against pagan belief in the occult arts.

For all these reasons, Valturio concludes, Sigismondo should avoid astrology as it is either foolish, useless and disconnected from reality, or dangerous, involving commerce with demons. His final warning leaves no doubt that Sigismondo practiced astrology in his court. Fortunetellers and astrologers, he says:

> know nothing about what they promise; [they are] delirious as if drunk on their foolish and false predictions . . . Do not, Sigismondo, in any way rely on the superstitious judgments of such men! You yourself are well-versed in their disciplines, you indulge in such studies and favor and delight in their sharp intellects, especially since you have always and continue to have by your side the most renowned mathematicians and supreme horoscopists and astronomers in order to foretell the future for military purposes as the ancients did.[23]

Valturio condemns astrology and the occult arts, even though he admits that they are favored by Sigismondo. This suggests that his treatise is not simply knee-jerk classicism and straight praise. It also suggests that astrology was both the most practiced and, for Valturio, pernicious pagan art in Sigismondo's court. Other princes consulted astrologers and used astrological imagery to exult their rule, but Valturio, at any rate, considered Sigismondo's devotion to astrological studies to be particularly fervid.[24]

Omens and Oracles

Valturio begins his chapter on astrology with Figulus's speech in Lucan's *Pharsalia,* in which the augur affirms that the civil war was inevitable due to the malice of Saturn and the doom-bearing stars, clear signs.[25] This example of functional astrology is quickly followed by skepticism. Valturio singles out the foolish belief of the ancient Romans in auguries:

> You may wonder why I did not mention that the father of Rome was the greatest augur. But I regret to recall and am ashamed to

> think that Rome, the undoubted head of the world, was founded and flourished with augury, that Rome preferred to entrust the fate of a powerful people to birds and not God. For many centuries under the kings and the consuls nothing could be done without auguries, no assemblies, senate appeals, equestrian councils, infantry conscriptions, or anything having to do with the military. It is astonishing to think that such celebrated and magnificent men succumbed to the flights of birds and their fallacious chatter.[26]

The "father of Rome" is probably Numa Pompilius (753–673 BC), the second king of Rome. Numa founded the Roman religion; he introduced Vestal Virgins to Rome, built temples, and instituted sacred rites, which he claimed were revealed to him in frequent meetings with the nymph Egeria.[27] If Valturio grants some efficacy to astrology, he does not offer the same respect for the art of augury. Hannibal and Caesar, Valturio reminds us, famously refused to believe in auguries.[28] The tension present in Valturio's ridicule of Roman religion and at the same time great respect for antiquity is a constant dynamic in his astrology chapter.

Despite Valturio's warnings, Sigismondo was reported to have asserted his belief in omens on at least one occasion. In his sober chronicle of Malatesta history, Gaspare Broglio reports a speech that Sigismondo delivered on the battlefield before his troops in 1461:

> If victory is ours, consider how yesterday evening a gentle eagle landed on our encampment. The brave ancient Romans put great faith in these signs, called auguries. I take great comfort in this, since I descend from the progeny and blood of the most illustrious noble Roman, Publius Cornelius Scipio Africanus, and God Almighty made this sign to show that I was correct.[29]

This commentator, who was much less of a classicist than Valturio, not only does not condemn augury but also has Sigismondo praise it as a link to the antiquity of his ancestors. The references to Scipio Africanus and the ancient Roman augury underline Sigismondo's connection with the pagan classical world. The passage also demonstrates that Sigismondo could declare without scandal that the Christian God worked through the omens and auguries of paganism.

Malatesta poetry is also rife with images of auguries and omens in the Renaissance. In a poem addressed to Isotta, Basinio has Sigismondo assert his belief in the power of dreams to foretell future doom. The poem starts with a disquisition: "Who would deny that dreams portend true events? Who would deny that they are prescient of evil to come? Who would deny that ghosts bearing lament appear at night during sleep?"[30] Sigismondo then describes the nightmare he had in which a sickly Isotta appeared to him, begging for help and about to die. Waking up startled, Sigismondo immediately opens a window to find the sky in complete darkness, with neither moon nor sun. He calls the nightmare and the black sky omens, and they are soon verified as a messenger appears with dire news of Isotta's fever.

Omens, both true and false, have a central place in Basinio's *Hesperis*. Beneath the walls of Gradara in 1446, Francesco Sforza reads his soldiers' losses in war and the appearance of plague as signs that Sigismondo is divine and has the approval of the gods. In the end, he decided to abandon the siege.[31] Omens can be tricks of the capricious gods. This suggests the problems in interpreting omens and whether they could be considered true portents. Perceptively favorable omens initiate the first Aragonese invasion of Tuscany. Jupiter sends false visions through the goddess Iris to Alfonso's personal diviner, Phorbas, "who was the greatest at knowing the gods' designs at that time and scrutinizing dreams. He alone guided Alfonso to the shores of Italy, relying on an augury, which Phoebus Apollo had given the soothsayer. From his first years he had as a boy dedicated his stringed lyre to the god."[32] Phorbas's interpretation of an omen is what had convinced Alfonso to invade Tuscany in the first place. Before the battle of Piombino, Jupiter decides to spare mass bloodshed by having the commanders fight a single combat duel. Against his companions' advice, Alfonso agrees to the single combat, proudly referring to the omen that occurred while his high priest was at the altar:

> It is not long since Jupiter's priest bound in gold cloth lit holy flames on the altars under the branches of a shady oak . . . twin doves sat on the highest peaks of two trees; the one that sat on a green pine was scared by the flight of an eagle and hid itself in

> the dark branches. The eagle circled it seven times, and on the seventh turn the dove fled and took off into the air. The holy eagle seized it in the southeast wind. Then the eagle attacked more swiftly the other dove, eviscerated it with its claws, and sat victorious on a high branch. Have hope then proud people: from high heaven Saturn has shown us this end to the war. The seven circles show seven years, and in the seventh year the fighting will fall to the great hearted Spaniards; the second dove is Italy, which you will conquer with little effort for your grandchildren to hold as kingdoms.[33]

The problem, as will become clear, is not the omen but the interpretation of the omen. Sigismondo could have interpreted the same occurrences otherwise, as a sign of his own victory, and it would have come true. Sixty years later Machiavelli praised how the ancient Romans used favorable auguries to inspire their soldiers before every battle.[34] In the *Hesperis,* Alfonso's interpretation of the omen had the desired effect and served to rally the troops behind Alfonso's acceptance of the single combat challenge and, later, to encourage them to fight. Machiavelli would have approved of this effective use of pagan religion to unite a large army.

In the *Hesperis,* at the outbreak of the second Tuscan War, the Italian nobles praise Sigismondo as their savior and then describe recent omens:

> Behold portents of an impending doom are given now already: never has the air been so thick with fog, never have the setting sun and returning moon opposed each other with such great strain. Now Jupiter is planning something great in high heaven: you yourself [Sigismondo] see that the comets are promising much death.[35]

These omens foretell the devastating war that has just started and the need for Sigismondo's protection and leadership.

Basinio and Broglio were not alone in ascribing power to omens.[36] Even Valturio, after dismissing ancient augury as the "fallacious chatter" of birds, ponders the role of oracles in antiquity and appears to concede under the weight of historical authority. "Who," he asks, "except a madman, would not believe in oracles, when he sees not only the greatest philosophers and masters of life but also the largest countries and renowned peoples and kings running to Delphi, Dodona, and Ammon? Who would scorn the sibyls, whom the Roman Senate and people consulted in the gravest dangers?"[37] Valturio continues referring to the Spartans' belief in dreams and to the wise men of the Persian Empire. Hannibal dreamt of his imminent blindness. Anchises appeared to Aeneas in dreams and foretold the Trojans' arrival in Italy. But dreams and oracles can also mislead. Both Croesus and Pyrrhus followed oracles and lost everything. Following Cicero, Valturio, like Basinio, asserts that the problem is not the oracle but the interpretation of it. King Croesus was told that if he crossed the river into Persia, a great empire would perish. The prediction came true, but Croesus's empire was destroyed, not the Persian Empire. The oracle at Delphi told Pyrrhus a sentence in Latin that could mean either that Pyrrhus could beat the Romans or that the Romans could beat Pyrrhus.[38] Valturio says that Jupiter and Apollo purposely made oracular pronouncements ambiguous in order to deceive depraved listeners. The skeptic Cicero ridiculed this anecdote about Pyrrhus and said that Apollo never spoke Latin. Cicero believed it an invention of the poet Ennius, the original source of the story. In a rare criticism of the ancients, Valturio says that he is "not moved by Cicero's reasoning, since the ambiguity of the oracle could also be translated from the Greek."[39] Multiple ancient examples of the efficacy of oracles and the problems of interpretation follow from Philip of Macedon to Nero. So many illustrious examples might convince the reader to believe in oracles. But Valturio writes of banning the practice: "Why was belief in the Pythian oracle scorned and abolished only long after Caesar's empire and the birth of Christ, our savior? It was scorned because it was empty, false, and uncertain."[40] The ancients believed in oracles, he concludes, because they were often correct, but only because divine providence allowed this. Things changed, however, in the Christian world:

> Then divine vengeance pursued the human race and deservedly put a stop to heaven's tolerance of human superstition. The splendor of divine grace has illuminated us, and it is fitting that we embrace another kind of life and other rites. We should also consider [all the occult arts, including] augury, examining

> entrails, dreams, inspiring prophets, lightning bolts, casting lots, and the other ways by which we know the future, to be done with the compliance and help of demons. For these things are full of deceptions.[41]

Despite such condemnations, all of these occult arts remained popular in Renaissance Italy, as a century later the Council of Trent (1534–1564) felt the need to reassert the church's condemnation of such practices.[42]

Plato and the Pagan Soul's Afterlife

Sigismondo and his court had numerous links to sophisticated Greek pagan culture. He may not have ever met Plethon, but Sigismondo clearly admired this influential thinker on Plato and paganism, as he enshrined his body in the Tempio. As discussed previously, Sigismondo's cousin, Cleofe Malatesta, had been married to Theodore II, the emperor of the Morea, and a student of Plethon. When she died in childbirth in 1433, Bessarion, who was to be a key advocate of the reintroduction of Plato to the West, composed elegiac verses for her, and Plethon himself wrote a lengthy funeral oration, in which he used Plato to prove the immortality of the soul and to argue for Cleofe's continued existence in a higher realm. In the funeral oration, Plethon advocated a Platonic view of the body and an unchristian acknowledgment of the benefits of suicide.[43] Plethon's connection with Sigismondo's cousin was well known and surely was a factor when Sigismondo visited her palace in Mistra in 1465 and arranged to have Plethon's remains transported to Rimini and reinterred in a tomb in San Francesco. As a member of the Greek delegation at the council of Ferrara-Florence in 1438–1439, Plethon lectured on Plato to interested Italians, including Cosimo de' Medici. As a parting gift, he left a Greek manuscript of Plato's writings, which Marsilio Ficino later used to complete the first Latin translation of Plato's complete extant works.[44] The peripatetic antiquarian Cyriac of Ancona stayed in Mistra in 1447 and had frequent discussions about Greek geography and antiquity for several months with Plethon, whom he called "the most learned of the Greeks of our time." Plethon's treatise *On the Laws,* which was later condemned for advocating a return to paganism, was already in circulation in 1444, so Cyriac would have been exposed to the philosopher's arguments for the

Olympian deities and other pagan beliefs. On his return to Italy, Cyriac stayed in Rimini and would have talked about Plethon to Sigismondo. This is probably when Sigismondo wanted to invite the philosopher to teach in his court in Rimini.[45]

The fifteenth century saw the reintroduction of Plato's thought in Western Europe, as Italians were finally able to read his original Greek dialogues, understand Plato in his own words, and translate his thought into eloquent and mostly faithful humanist Latin.[46] The Christian concept of the soul borrowed much from Greek philosophy, especially Plato, but also Aristotelian metaphysics. There were nevertheless important differences, which Augustine and the early Church fathers took pains to emphasize. But when the original texts of pagan learning and literature became available in the early quattrocento, humanists appropriated pagan ideas in their discussions of religion. Christian critics certainly objected to pagan morality and to deterministic astrology, but the heresy battles of late antiquity had been long before fought and won, and at least in the early quattrocento, there was no urgency to distinguish Christian beliefs from pagan and define Christian orthodoxy. Malatesta humanist literature is a prime example of the messy appropriation of pagan religious ideas in the humanist imitation of pagan form for a Christian subject.

Sigismondo's early interest in the philosophical nature of the soul is shown in a little-studied treatise on the immortality of the soul by Giovanni da Ferrara (Giovanni de' Cocchi, 1409–1462).[47] In 1449 Sigismondo invited Cocchi to Rimini to participate in a debate on the nature of the soul. The debate took place in the Castel Sismondo and lasted all day, until the night. Cocchi recorded the discussion in a treatise. The original manuscript contains a dedication, in which the author describes the debate in Rimini and stresses Sigismondo's participation. A few years later, Cocchi rededicated the treatise to Borso d'Este (1450–1471) with the addition of a fourth section on paradise, which was then published in 1494.[48] The manuscript of the Rimini debate is a scholastic compendium on the soul. The first book offers various definitions of the soul, such as where it is located and its relation to the body; the second deals with various ideas about the soul; and the third discusses hell. Cocchi takes several arguments for the soul's immortality from Plato's *Phaedo, Meno,* and other dialogues. Although he also quotes Augustine liberally, Cocchi adopts a definite Platonic view of the body as a prison for the soul: "If we believe in agreement with almost everyone that the dead and their shades remain in bodies; what else is understood than the death of the soul, when it is plunged into the lower realms of the body; whereas living is when the soul escapes the body to the heavens."[49] The soul can be said to die only when it is overly attached to the mortal body.

Macrobius, the pagan philosopher of Plato and astrology in the fifth century CE, was one of Cocchi's main sources.[50] In his commentary on Cicero's *Dream of Scipio Africanus,* Macrobius describes in great detail the soul's place and how it comes into and leaves the body. According to Macrobius, the ancient sage Pythagoras revealed how the soul descends through the Milky Way, imbuing the characteristics of each planet it passes in greater or lesser amounts, according to proximity. Once inside a body, the soul has forgotten about its true heavenly abode. Only a true philosopher can regain this abode by breaking the cycle of reincarnation as the soul passes from one body to another body. Although he copies whole sections of Macrobius, Cocchi puts a Christian reading on the pagan soul: "For the followers of Pythagoras and Plato assert that there are two deaths of the soul, one when it leaves the body, another when the soul is given over to die, when it is scattered from the simple source of its nature into the body's limbs. The first death is known to all, the second happens to everyone except the wise."[51] There is no mention of Pythagorean transmigration of the soul. Instead, Cocchi seems to impose an Augustinian reading that traps sinners inside the prison of their bodies even after death.[52] Just as Cocchi contaminated his Christianity with pagan philosophy, so did the Franciscan friar misread pagan philosophy through his Christianity. Cocchi's treatise and the 1449 debate that it commemorates show Sigismondo's personal interest in the soul and the theories of Plato and Pythagoras, before Basinio and Porcellio arrived in Rimini, and before Valturio composed his military treatise in 1455. Basinio, however, displays greater knowledge of pagan philosophy than Cocchi.

Basinio recounted that he had studied Plato under his teacher, the Byzantine Theodore Gaza. He thanked Theodore for introducing him to the "books and secret knowledge of Plato."[53] Platonic ideas about the soul and the afterlife appear in several of Basinio's works. In the poetry he wrote for Sigismondo, Basinio often grapples with ideas about the soul. Life after death, the underworld, and Pythagorean and Platonic theories about the transmigration of souls are all topics in the *Isottaeus.* This is a book of epistolary poems that Basinio composed, which focus on love, death, and the afterlife.[54] In one poem, Isotta asks Basinio if she will live after death, so that she can continue to love Sigismondo:

> Do we live after we are released from the body? Are we tossed about in light or darkness, our body and its shade completely silent? And if we are sent to another world and live again, will our mind remain the same as it was? . . . but if the whole life perishes with the body, and no shade survives for the dead, then we will live out joyful years in love until our time is up.[55]

It is odd that Isotta ends her questions and the poem with an acknowledgment that there might not be life after death, which, she implies, would not be so bad.

In the next poem, Basinio answers. He asserts that the soul is immortal because it is not flesh, and it has its own motion: "When bodies are taken away from souls, in my opinion the souls live without end. Whether the same mind remains in souls released from their sad frames, I think, can be explained in a few words."[56] Basinio then refers to the example of Sychaeus, Dido's deceased husband, in Virgil's *Aeneid,* who even after death was still himself:

> We are something after death, and we always live in memory of an earlier life, whatever place it has. For who would think that souls drink the oblivion of Lethe, then go again into new bodies? Pythagoras would never convince me of this . . . God does not will that divine souls, coming from the heavenly abode, be common with wild beasts.[57]

Basinio's objection to Pythagoras seems limited to the idea that human souls could inhabit animal bodies. Pythagoras's doctrine of the transmigration of souls is not condemned outright.

Platonic ideas about the soul and the afterlife appear in several of Basinio's poems that were meant to console Sigismondo after the imagined death of Isotta, his lover. (Sigismondo in fact predeceased Isotta by six years.) Basinio uses reincarnation to answer the distraught Sigismondo's query about whether he will see his lover again: "I will tell you the divine precepts that sacred Plato taught me in Greek. He thinks that souls will return again into mortal bodies to fulfill their time and after this return to the Elysian fields and be drawn back by their eternal condition."[58] Basinio does not condemn Platonic reincarnation; in fact by using it to console Sigismondo, he seems to approve of it. Literature again serves as evidence for life after death: "If your dear girl (Isotta) desires to address you, she can appear before your face." To prove this, Basinio refers to the ghostly image of Aeneas's wife, Creusa, who "slipped through his trembling hands." "Do not doubt," Basinio concludes, "that she can return to you and comfort your worries with her sweet voice."[59] In both scholarly debate and love poetry, the immortality of the soul is debated but ultimately affirmed.

In the *Hesperis,* Basinio has Sigismondo himself proclaiming reincarnation. Sigismondo has organized funeral rites for the fallen after the battle of Piombino. In tears, he insists on "sending the bodies to the earth, so that the dead might reach the stygian waves of Acheron safely and worthily be decorated with honor." Sigismondo and his men zealously cut down cypresses and pine trees. "They set up elaborate pyres and put the fallen cadavers with their cold limbs on top of the pile." Loud laments accompany the flames. Sigismondo intones: "Be well innocent souls; be well divinely and eternally pious souls. Cross the swampy Styx, hope for the Elysian fields, hope to return again into human limbs with better fates."[60] The two "hopes" seem to contradict: hope both for pagan paradise and to live a mortal life again. Both rewards are odd in a funeral oration after an actual battle among Christians. Of course, the passage is in Basinio's epic poem, but the battle was nonetheless still a real and recent memory. This is dangerous territory even for poetic conceit or intellectual debate.

Basinio's underworld in the *Hesperis* is Platonic and Pythagorean. In book VIII, the blessed Galeotto appears to Sigismondo in a dream and describes souls in heaven:

> After death, souls cannot doubt but see everything with a pure mind, which they could hardly see while they continued in the shadows of their prison. Once freed from their bodies they fly above the stars and leave the squalid earth. . . . Therefore come now, conqueror of the great Spanish, do not hesitate to come

> when God summons you and the certain door of a better life lies open to you, where the high ether is free from earthly clouds and the heavy mass of limbs and the blind shadows of a body, needing to be left behind . . . The divine mind returns to reborn souls.[61]

The body is a prison, which prevents the soul from flying and thinking or seeing clearly. Platonism offers a blatant dichotomy: at the separation of death, the soul will be pure mind, and the "blind," "shadowy" body and all matter are squalid interference to enlightenment. This is far from incarnational Christianity and the corporeal reaffirmation in Jesus's birth and resurrection. According to Basinio's Galeotto, resurrected bodies contain different souls, which smacks of Pythagorean reincarnation, not Christian resurrection. Galeotto concludes the speech with a call not to fear death but to embrace it: "Go quickly and bravely, o nobles, to dark death. . . . If they want to see a joyful future, men should not fear death, which is worth but little time."[62] Death, after all, is the doorway to their ultimate happy future. After seeing his ancestors among the blessed in the fields of Mars, Sigismondo encourages them:

> Be well my elders and famed crowd of venerated ancestors, hope soon to return again into human bodies with better fates. But, nevertheless, long fame has kept you alive, so that you survive, my holy father, and the name of our ancestors remains to bestow eternal honor on the worthy.[63]

Even though they are dead and hoping to live again, Basinio stresses that fame has kept them alive in the world. He heralds the Malatesta name and provides the "eternal honor" for the worthy. But the dead hope for something more than memorial. The hope is not for reincarnation, which is a given, but for "better fates" in their new bodies. The reference here must be to reincarnation, since, although Christians will receive their pristine bodies again at the second coming, they will not live life and be subject to the fates again and again.

Other poems combine pagan and Christian images of heaven. Basinio consoles Sigismondo on the death of his son—this time not an imagined loss but an actual bereavement:

> Stop soaking his tomb with tears and disturbing the pious spirits (Manes). If the dead have any sensation, which I myself believe, your son will be pained by your grief. Liberated from its mortal prison, his life will soon be happily delivered to the supreme gods. There he more happily enjoys eternal peace, exciting envy for his good fortune. Joining the holy choirs and accompanied by your brother Roberto, he ever offers prayers to the gods. Although enclosed in a bitter tomb, your son has here a way to live.[64]

Basinio refers to the body as a mortal prison, from which the soul is liberated in order to return to the gods. Even though gods are in the plural, there is no talk here of reincarnation and the heavenly choirs singing praises and continuously praying is a very Christian image of heaven, reminiscent of Dante's *Paradiso* and the hand-holding dancing and singing blessed in Fra Angelico's paintings. Even in consoling Sigismondo over the painful real death of his son, Basinio still conflates Christian and pagan notions of heaven.

Basinio shows Sigismondo expressing a variety of philosophical and religious beliefs about the soul. At times Plato and Pythagoras dominate the discourse about the soul's immortality and eventual return to another body.[65] Other times a Christian heaven and pagan underworld appear. Skepticism fills some poems on the question of life after death, and Epicurean arguments are voiced about pleasure, love, and the soul dying with the body. Even if these texts ultimately affirm the immortality of the soul, Pius was right in that this fundamental belief was openly questioned in the literature of Sigismondo's court.

Sigismondo, Devout Pagan: Sacrifices

Pagan sacrifices are an essential part of Basinio's *Hesperis*. This is not just Christian worship in pagan dress but reveals a relationship to the divine that is antithetical to Christian beliefs. Pagan cult and practices, surely poetic fiction, are a startlingly prominent part of the public image that Sigismondo crafted in literature. We read that because of their connection to the blood of the ancient Romans, Sigismondo and the Italians have a special relationship with the gods. Sigismondo's pious devotions and respectful sacrifices help him to gain and maintain the favor of Jupiter. After the Aragonese victory at Foiano, Jupiter looks down in disgust as Ferrante plunders and devastates the city's surroundings. Only with Sigismondo's help, he says, will the Tuscans prevail:

> They [the Italians] first performed sacrifices for me, nor was the pious worship of the gods lacking from their forefathers. On the other hand, nothing is sacred to the Spanish, and they usually have no priest perform the divine office on account of their ill-fated hearts . . . a very wicked people and forgetful of the gods, they boast and revel in unjust frenzy in their desire to draw human blood. My judgment will certainly disappoint them now, since the gods are determined to save the pious, and prayers and vows do not fly empty in vain under the high heavens, for the father of the gods hears whatever men pray.[66]

Offering sacrifices is a way to gain the favor of the gods. Before battle, "Sigismondo piously performs sacrifices to Mars and the other gods."[67] Sigismondo uses sacrifices and divine honors as leverage both with the gods in his prayers and with his soldiers in battlefield speeches as a means to instill confidence. In the second Tuscan War, Sigismondo asks in one speech:

> How much further will you, o highest Father, exalted Jupiter, tolerate the raging Spaniards? Do we renew our sacrifices for you every year and eternally honor your altars, so that we may be forced to abandon the temples, as Alfonso thinks, as refugees, we who are born from Trojan blood? Do the gods want Italians to seek their home realms in foreign lands?[68]

Sigismondo's plea reminds the gods to keep up their side of the bargain, which is a central part in pagan prayer, the *quid pro quo* pact between the mortal supplying payment in sacrifices and the god granting favor in exchange. Such logic encourages acts of bravery. The gods, after all, owe their worshippers a victory. Looking down on a bloody battle from Olympus, Jupiter says as much to the other gods:

> I do not hate Ferrante; it is right for a son to obey his father. But the prayers of the men in Italy are just and do not move me in vain. . . . The Tuscan people have never deprived us of our feasts nor cheated the gods . . . for we gods alone receive such honors. Therefore, since a virtuous mind makes the pious equal to Olympus, I have decided to save the Italians from the jaws of Alfonso, and force the king to flee again.[69]

With the help of Jupiter and the gods, Sigismondo eventually wins the second Tuscan War. A true faith and worship will bring him to Olympus. The gods protect those who maintain pious worship of the gods in prayers, vows, and sacrifices.

In his book of epistolary poems about Jupiter's love for Isotta, Porcellio repeatedly shows Sigismondo sacrificing to the gods and performing the duties of a good pagan. In her response to Jupiter's love letter, Isotta warns Jupiter that if Sigismondo discovers the letter, "he will no longer give sacrifices and pious incense to Jupiter." Isotta's threat appropriately has a pagan perspective on worship: the gods rely on mortals to feed them with sacrifices and incense. To counter Jupiter's advances, Sigismondo pleads with Mars for help. Sigismondo says that he has always followed Jupiter's commands: "I built a marble temple to high Jupiter [the Tempio] and gave him solemn altars and incense. I fear the god's lightning bolt, whenever it comes out of the clouds, and as a supplicant I give pious prayers to Jupiter." This is a wonderful image of Sigismondo, cowering in fear of lightning and praying with incense to the gods. Sigismondo credits Mars for his kingdom and success in battle. If Mars helps him, Sigismondo promises to incense his altars and to place garlands on the god. He also promises to have two statues of Mars made: one armed and out of gold for his triumphal chariot, the other unarmed outside the temple to promote peace: "Fat gifts will be burned for Rome's birthday and bloody sacrifices will fall for Mars."[70]

In the next letter, Mars tries to help Sigismondo by enlisting Apollo's aid. After praising Sigismondo's exploits in the first Tuscan War, Mars argues that the gods owe the mercenary because of his worship and sacrifices. Sigismondo, Mars says in a letter to Apollo, "sacrifices a bull on the altar for me and rich incense burns on sacred hearths. Am I to fail him, who preserves me and my spirit? Who will continue to give prayers and vows to an ungrateful god?" In antiquity, devotees regularly sacrificed bulls to Mars. "Sigismondo has done all this," Mars says, referring to the victory in the first Tuscan War, "for the liberty of Italy, and for my name and yours [Apollo]. He has served me . . . and in his sublime triumph he sings paeans to you, for he cultivates poets and the gods of augury."[71] Apollo tries to convince Jupiter to abandon Isotta by again referring to pious Sigismondo: "weighed down with the spoils of war Sigismondo worships at the temple of god and fells bloody sacrifices before our altars."[72] It makes sense that Sigismondo's patrons should be Mars, the god of war, and Apollo, the god of poets and the arts.

All the gods try to avoid the war that Jupiter's infatuation is threatening to start. Jupiter's father, Saturn, asks Luna to help in the next poem. He praises Isotta's piety and devotion to the gods: "Isotta often walks to the sacred altars of the gods, and the goddess rejoices in true religion." Saturn tries to hatch a plan with Luna to take the goddess Isotta, as she sleeps, to his son. Luna, however, protests that she will not be involved in deflowering a pious virgin: "Are you commanding me to use deceit and give a friendly modest nymph to Jupiter? Then who will give incense, who will do and cultivate chaste honors, and who will light torches with a pure flame? Am I, the goddess Diana, devoted to modesty, to deceive the modest heart of a virgin?" (fig. 5.1). The same argument is used for Isotta that Mars used for Sigismondo. The gods depend on the sacrifices and devotions of mortals. Luna then protests that, if she did this, she would hurt Sigismondo, "than whom no one is better in piety and brave arms, and no one is before him in faith and religion."[73] Both Isotta and Sigismondo are shown as faithful pagan worshipers. In one of the final poems, Mercury calls an assembly of the gods to make peace. He sums up the situation and the consequences of Jupiter's insistence:

> I am seeing a crime done, a virgin kidnapped, and trust in Jupiter and the gods lost. If love conquers us, if the life of the gods is shameful, who would be so out of his mind to worship our spirits? For whom will they sacrifice an animal? Who would adorn the temples with green garlands? Who will give pious prayers before the gods? Who will slaughter a calf at solemn altars? And in what hearths will manly incense burn?[74]

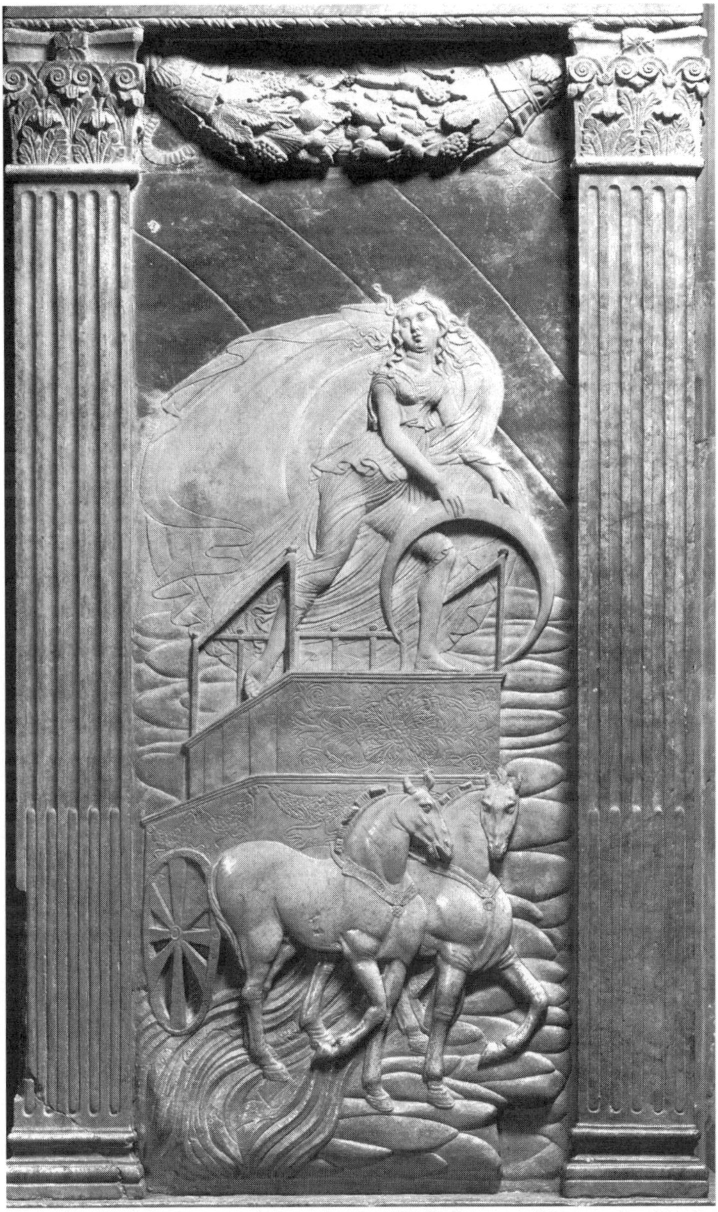

Fig. 5.1. Agostino di Duccio, Diana-Moon, marble, ca. 1455, Chapel of the Planets, Tempio Malatestiano, Rimini. Photo: Scala/Art Resource, NY.

Again, Mercury's chief concern is the gods' loss of adoration and sacrifices from mortals. Only later in the speech, does Mercury address the moral problem in Jupiter's actions: "If Isotta is given to Jupiter, an injustice will be done to her lover against the laws, justice, and honor of the heaven-dwelling gods. What just man will perform sacrifices at unjust altars? Who would want to be more just than the gods? Humans live by the gods' example: justice and piety."[75] The gods are better than humans and serve as role models. They, therefore, have to act accordingly. (The injustice here, in Renaissance fashion, is against Sigismondo, not against Isotta, who for the most part is a passive pawn.)

In some ways, all this is just a pagan gloss—a pagan way of saying that Sigismondo is pious and dutiful and goes to mass. But the *quid pro quo* aspect is very different from Christian belief, although Luther would later argue that it was all too characteristic of Catholic devotions. Unlike Basinio, Porcellio describes Sigismondo's sacrifices as "bloody," which was one of the chief complaints of early Christians against pagan sacrifices—the shedding of an innocent animal's blood.[76] The gods here are arbitrary, dependent on human offerings, and need to be reminded to uphold a moral standard. Even if pure fiction, the fact that both Basinio and Porcellio publically presented Sigismondo as an active enthusiastic worshiper of the pagan gods and repeatedly showed him making sacrifices at their altars suggests the fascination with and tolerance for pagan religious beliefs and practices in fifteenth-century Italian culture.

Oaths

Machiavelli praises the role of the pagan religion of ancient Rome in making oaths and treaties. Fear of the gods ensured that soldiers would keep their word and fight, and citizens would not steal or harm each other. Maintaining oaths sworn before the gods was a common theme in the *Iliad* and *Aeneid*. In the *Hesperis,* Sigismondo actively participates in this central feature of the pagan religion. When Sigismondo and Alfonso sign the agreement before their single combat, they each give multiple speeches to mark the solemn occasion. Alfonso calls for proper sacrifices to confirm the treaty: "Let the Spaniards and the Italians confirm this treaty with sacred rites. Noble men, bring a black sheep here; carry a white heifer to the earth for me and perform sacred rites for the Sun, and we will sacrifice another elegant sheep to Dis, lest anyone rashly desire to break the rites of Jupiter and hide in the thick of battle."[77] Basinio has Alfonso emphasize the inviolability of his word, precisely because he and his men will break his oath and the agreement. In his address, Sigismondo insists that if victorious, Italy will return to the Italians, and the Spaniards will go home.[78] The gods control everything. Pagan fate replaces agency. Instead, the goddess Fortuna either bestows gifts or turns her evil eye to cause disaster, and Jupiter decides which life to take.

The themes continue when both commanders perform the required sacrifices:

> Italian and Spanish youths prayed to the gods and goddesses, performed the sacrifices, and lit the sacred altars with fire. Then king Alfonso, who had daringly come to distant shores, stood and poured the cups of Bacchus. He first raised the sweet gifts of nourishing earth in foaming cups, and the sweet nectar (the gift of nurturing Silenus) fermented in pure gold. . . . But neither music, altars, or gods were favorable, when he himself first prayed the following: "If I break this agreement with hands or arms, then may another's hand take this head of mine from my severed neck, and carry it as victor to foreign shores."[79]

Wine is poured, sacrifices are made, and pagan altars are lit with fire. Again, Basinio stresses Alfonso's future betrayal of his oath to the gods, as his prayer is all about the consequences of breaking the treaty. Sigismondo's prayer is more extensive and focuses on his request for divine favor and his promise to honor the god by building the Tempio and filling it with statues. He also prays to avenge the treaty, if broken:

> "O Jupiter, most holy cultivator of the Tuscan woods, you who rule from high heaven, let the sun not leave Olympus and fall onto the watery waves of the ocean before the Spaniards have been beaten on the Tyrrhenian shore and flee. O greatest of the gods, allow me to defile Alfonso's head and tear it with my own

> hands from the bloody ground, and allow me, o Father, to drag in the dust and twist with hot metal his well-groomed and myrrh-perfumed hair. Let these pirates leave Italy, and let the Italians not fear the Spanish on land and sea. For you, I will then build temples of white marble and wonderful carved statues, brilliant in Daedalian design, and I will dedicate a temple in the middle of the city of Rimini, which will stupefy every barbarian and Italian. Let us only prevail and cast out this evil." Sigismondo spoke and poured sweet wine from a bowl to the ground, saying "thus may the seat of his broken brain slip and fall, whoever breaks the treaty, just as wine falls through wet grass never to return to the cup."[80]

The violence of what Sigismondo wants to do to Alfonso is shocking but in keeping with classical epic. Homer and Virgil describe the intimate details of blood and guts and the sadistic actions of battle. Pagan as opposed to Christian prayer is usually seen as a barter exchange, a legal agreement whereby the supplicant promises something in return.[81] In the Renaissance commanders and rulers continued to promise Christian churches in thanks for victory in battle. Ludovico Gonzaga in Mantua built the Madonna of Victory church to celebrate his victory in 1495. Sigismondo is promising to build the Tempio Malatestiano, which he in fact did dedicate as a token of thanks for his victory in the Tuscan Wars, as the twin inscriptions in Greek on the side of the church state. Even in Basinio's hyper-classical epic, the lack of any Christian reference in Sigismondo's vow to build the Tempio is surprising. The dedication to Jupiter could be taken as a reference to God, were it not for this pagan context. Couched between the utter violence of his petition and the poured libation to the earth, this is exceptionally pagan.

In this warfare full of trickery, far from any Christian moral values, oaths are a way to establish moral order and piety, to distinguish in the shifting allegiances the righteous warrior from the impious traitor. These issues of loyalty and piety were particularly pressing for the mercenary Sigismondo, especially after his earlier betrayal of Alfonso. In placing such emphasis on oaths and the terrible consequences of breaking them, Basinio risked calling attention to this dubious chapter in Sigismondo's life.

Malatesta Heaven: Immortality and the Path of Glory

The intellectuals at Sigismondo's court played with different ideas about the soul, but they broadly agreed that the soul is immortal. When these authors discuss the divine nature of the soul and what makes a man worthy of a good afterlife, they dwell not upon Christian virtues but upon military triumph and physical strength. The glory that Sigismondo wins in battle, they assert, makes him immortal and that this heroism is what gains him entry into heaven. In an imagined speech below the besieged walls of Gradara, Basinio has Sigismondo encouraging his men by recalling the example of pagan antiquity and declaring how ancient warriors had earned Olympus and become divine through heroic virtue: "Let love, piety, the glory of the Latin name, and the examples of ancient men move us . . . Virtue, for which it is fitting to fight, made them equal to the gods and educated them for high Olympus. This is the love of praise, by which I and you are equally inflamed."[82] Bravery in battle leads to immortality and heaven.

Military prowess and glory in battle were explicitly connected with the soul and the divine in Giovanni Cocchi's treatise on the immortality of the soul, which he dedicated to Sigismondo. Two chapters in his second book are particularly appropriate for a ruler, famed condottiere, and man of action. In book II.7, Cocchi argues that the attainment of glory and praise makes the soul immortal. At first he seems to limit his discussion to poetic immortality—that heroes live on in the fame of the poet's verse. He quotes Cicero, saying "the desire for praise spurs us all to obtain glory."[83] The role of art as commemoration and inspiration is emphasized: Scipio Africanus used to meditate on images of great men, and Julius Caesar looked at an image of Alexander. The seven pyramids of Egypt and triumphal carved columns served this purpose. "Among the ancients," Cocchi writes, "the desire for glory was so great that day and night it excited and stimulated mortal minds."[84] They feared no dangers.

The topos of immortality through letters and monuments leads Cocchi to find a deeper meaning in Homer's praise for heroes as divine. Homer, he writes, said that men who had lived a divine life were immortal. He believed that because of their great virtue, heroic warriors were transferred into heaven and are called gods.[85] Hercules, Castor, and Pollux, among others, are mentioned:

> After their souls return, they enjoy eternity and are rightly considered gods. Certainly, if in this brief life their souls had not foreseen anything for the future, and if all thoughts had ended in this life, they would not have broken themselves with labors nor been troubled by so many concerns and vigils, nor would they have fought so often over life itself.[86]

The soul will thus continue to live after death in a real sense, not just by reputation. Men reach heaven and themselves become divine through heroic acts of prowess.

Cocchi elaborates on this idea in the next chapter, which explores bravery as an argument for immortality. The kind of bravery that is divine comes not out of necessity but is freely chosen. The brave, Cocchi says, "long for death to save the state or out of zeal for the faith."[87] Although he refers to martyrs, there are no Christian examples in the bulk of the chapter; only at the end does he briefly mention the athletes of Christ, the martyrs of the early church who competed with each other and endured all manner of torture and eventual execution for their refusal to renounce their faith in Jesus Christ. Although there was certainly an element of fame involved in their self-sacrifices, Christian martyrs bore witness and suffered not so much to impress the living and ensure their fame as to gain the heavenly reward that God promised his faithful servants. Cocchi's examples are almost all classical, and he praises in particular the Roman civic ideal, as found in Cicero and Macrobius. "What is more illustrious," he asks, "than to prolong the life of the republic with one's own life?" He refers to Horatio at the bridge, Brutus's decision to execute his sons, and Leonidas of Sparta: "For what is more excellent and magnificent than to end life with a triumph . . . ?" The personal gain of winning such glory, however, is still linked to the idea of fame and the memory of posterity.[88] Hector, he says, held the line against the Greeks because he feared that the poets might ridicule his flight. The Romans, Cocchi writes, had eight military crowns that they used to encourage heroism. The civic crown was awarded to those who had saved the republic. Cicero was awarded the civic crown when he saved the republic from Catiline. Cocchi's brief description of ancient triumphal wreaths highlights the courtly context of his piece, where both antiquarianism and military prowess were especially prized. Six years later Valturio included a lengthy discussion of the crowns in his military treatise, and such descriptions may have been background to Basinio's description in verse of Sigismondo's triumphs and Agostino di Duccio's relief portraits of Sigismondo with a Roman crown of laurels.

Bravery, triumph, and glory provide Cocchi with a double argument for life after death, that heroes and martyrs would not willingly choose to die, if they did not believe that their souls would go on living and that there must be a reward for virtue: "Virtue cannot exist without a reward," he reasons, "and the soul will, therefore, always be living."[89] This argument is straight out of Cicero's *Tusculan Disputations*.[90] Basinio used a similar kind of argument in a poem in answer to a query from Isotta about what remains after death. He says that if there were no life after death, then the sacrifice of soldiers for their country would be in vain. Cocchi no doubt stressed this pagan vision of the soul and immortality for his audience. The Homeric hero who becomes a god through great prowess and deeds is precisely the image Sigismondo projected of himself.

Sigismondo's Journey to Heaven

In *On the Republic,* Cicero described the dream of the ancient Roman republican hero Scipio Africanus. Scipio is shown the heavens. He hears the divine music of the revolving planets and sees the blessed in paradise. Cicero offered a distinctly Roman pagan notion of heaven, in which the blessed were not desert hermits or martyrs who had given up everything for God but the benefactors of humanity, civil servants, politicians, and generals who had built up the commonwealth and sacrificed their lives to protect it. Glory on earth led to paradise.[91] Malatesta writers follow the ancient Romans in joining the Greek athletic-heroic ideal to civic patriotism: Basinio's blessed are not devout Christian saints but warriors who sacrificed their lives fighting to protect their homeland. Sigismondo earned his divinity by heroically defending Italy against the foreign invaders.

This heroic ideal, that outstanding virtue makes a warrior divine, and Sigismondo's demi-god status are the central themes of Basinio's *Hesperis*. In book VIII, after visiting the temple of fame and looking at the statues of ancient heroes, including Odysseus and Aeneas, and the poets who inspired them to achieve glory, Sigismondo studies reliefs of the four ages of man: the golden age without war, the silver, the bronze, and finally the iron age, "when the offspring of the gods, the heroes, lived and died at Thebes and under the great walls of Troy." Lost in thoughts, Sigismondo falls asleep, and his deceased brother Galeotto speaks to him in a dream. Sigismondo is about to visit the underworld, and Galeotto tells him about his place in the afterlife and the nature of heaven. Galeotto was beatified and thus is described as being in heaven. "The Milky Way surrounds me," he says, "and I look down on high ethereal Olympus. Here the face of God shines bright to me . . . Priests on earth have built an altar to me and dedicated a temple in my name, but I am not moved by their incense. My greater glory is to be among the holy choirs and to take in the Thunderer of the gods in his unmediated light."[92] Basinio's Galeotto rejoices in being among holy choirs contemplating God in all his splendor, a Christian idea of heaven that brings to mind Fra Angelico's dancing choirs and the explosion of light in Dante's *Paradiso*. But the references to the Milky Way (with all of its Macrobian connotations), Olympus, and the gods reveal the presence of a more pagan conception of heaven, onc that Basinio must have thought would please his patron, even when putting words into the mouth of his saintly brother. Indeed, the paradise that Galeotto inhabits overflows with pagan imagery, especially when he describes to Sigismondo what fate awaits him in the afterlife:

> O hope of your Italy, brother, you must take courage. . . . Do not refrain now from looking upon Tartarus, and from crossing the infernal rivers, the waters of burning Phlegethon, high Cocytus, and the swampy Styx. God has brought you to Styx for no other reason than for you to seek and find as a conqueror the longed-for Olympus. For the way that leads to the walls of great heaven is varied. Many have arrived at this goal, but all have not taken one path. . . . Different kinds of men with me contemplate the ruler of heaven: those who defended the besieged shores of the fatherland, those who cherished faith and the gods with a pious tongue, those who took pity on the poor, who spared the conquered, and [did not succumb to revenge]. All have an equal love.[93]

In Basinio's poem, the Franciscan Galeotto stresses the different paths to heaven and emphasizes in particular the heroic way.

After Galeotto recedes into the shadows, the nymph, Isotta, tells Sigismondo more about heaven and his divine fate:

> Your brother is pious and very similar to you . . . he inhabits the abode of the gods, enjoys the council of the gods, and beholds himself in the highest stars. But you defend Italy, and, if the fates call, do not hesitate to repulse the enemy and fall for your country. You, the best man, can know that this is the one good. Afterwards, when you will have climbed the starry orbs of heaven and the moon, looking down as conqueror on the stars of the Titans, the august shores of sea and land, and the smallest lonely place, then you will be permitted to know how greatly the human and the divine differ. You cannot know this before you climb great Olympus. Therefore turn your eyes here, look at this abode and eternal home. The solid adamantine force of men does not fell it nor does the long passage of time. Nothing is mortal here, age deteriorates nothing here, and its structure is changeless. Eternal youth remains here. All enjoy the single love of watching the great Thunderer.[94]

Basinio here directly compares the life of the saintly Galeotto and Sigismondo's pagan valor, which is "the one good" that will allow him to climb, using his own strength and will, to heaven. Dante's image of paradise is echoed in the perfection of changeless heaven and the blessed whose greatest joy and reward is to look upon the face of God in all its glory. Sigismondo's bloody and determined scaling of the walls of Olympus is very different, though, from Dante's rapturous ascent with Beatrice as his guide.

After describing Apollo and the divine poets in the Elysian Fields, Basinio lists other professions that have earned men the celestial abode:

> Here are Greeks and Italians, whoever was a chaste priest in life, whoever fell for his country, whoever tried to understand the causes of things, who shared wealth with others, and whoever thought that one Thunderer ruled, not others. All of their heads were crowned with Apollo's wreath.[95]

The list of the blessed is revealing: first the poets, then chaste priests, just warriors, philosophers, philanthropists, and monotheists. This is an instance of Basinio perhaps protecting himself from accusations of impiety by asserting his belief in Christianity in such an excessively pagan poem, even by humanist standards.

After observing the blessed in the Elysian fields, Sigismondo sees a battle being fought among the greatest warriors of all time, including Hector and the Trojans and Ajax and the Greeks, and when he sees Theseus killing the great hearted Creon, Sigismondo draws his sword and rages against the shades. The shade of Pandolphus stops him, and Sigismondo weeps at the sight of his father, the "glory of our family." Pandolphus then shows Sigismondo a panoply of ancient heroes in the "fields of Mars." The lengthy list goes from Fabius Maximus, Julius Caesar, the Assyrian King Ninus, Saturn, Evander, Aeneas, Romulus, Numa, and the kings of Italy to the Malatesta ancestors.[96] Far from the placid dancing lights of Dante's paradise, Basinio's heroes and warriors continue to do battle in heaven, continually demonstrating their prowess and reliving their glory. "The death that comes with praise," Sigismondo declares to the "most holy" nymph Psycheia, "is blessed."[97] Death is not evil, only the death that comes without praise. Glory is immortal. "No road," the nymph responds, "is difficult for the brave man; nothing is left unfinished to him who wants it, as long as he wants what is right."[98] Such a can-do mentality is at the heart of the optimism in pagan virtue. The warrior can fight his way to heaven.

By ending the tour of heaven with warriors and the Malatesta ancestors in the fields of Mars, Basinio stresses the heroic path to heaven. Those who fought to protect the homeland and demonstrated virtue on the battlefield are assured places in the afterlife. Poets and heroes take center stage in this land of the blessed. It is perhaps not surprising that in an epic dedicated to a warrior, we should have so much emphasis on the heroic. But Basinio goes further than decorum and presents a kind of warrior's religion, that the way to achieve immortality is through the heroic; divine favor is won, as opposed to divine grace being bestowed. The most grossly flattering of verses proclaiming Sigismondo a god—both promised beforehand and delivered by Basinio—show an extraordinary latitude in decorum. Tensions between earthly fame and heavenly immortality abound. Basinio tries to reconcile these tensions by putting Sigismondo's divinization into the words of the saintly Galeotto.

Porcellio takes the flattering image much further than Basinio and turns Sigismondo into a deified follower of Mars receiving the prayers of faithful soldiers. In his poem about Jupiter's love for Isotta, Porcellio has Mercury declare in an assembly of the gods that "after the end of his holy life Sigismondo should return his weapons to the god Mars, and himself become a god, shining forth as a follower of Mars," and "let the soldier offer his prayers to this god."[99] Although the "miles" in the last clause of the Latin sentence could also refer to Sigismondo "as a soldier" praying to the god Mars, the context of deification makes it more likely to be about soldiers praying to Sigismondo. Just as the Christian faithful pray to a saint who lived a divine life by following Christ, so should soldiers pray to Sigismondo, who followed Mars in life, indeed lived a "holy life," and earned divinity through his prowess in battle.

Pagan philosophy and religion are omnipresent subjects in Malatesta literature. Valturio shows Sigismondo as a student and an avid practitioner of astrology. The chronicler Broglio describes his patron reading omens on the battlefield. Basinio and Porcellio emphasize Sigismondo's piety in sacrificing bulls and worshiping the Olympian gods, in swearing oaths and building a temple to Jupiter. Friar Giovanni de' Cocchi describes Sigismondo participating in philosophical debates on the immortality of the soul and the nature of the afterlife. Basinio presents Sigismondo touring the pagan underworld and seeing the Olympian abode he will occupy after death as a divinized hero made into a star. And for Porcellio it is Sigismondo's "holy life" as a follower of Mars that makes him a god worthy of worship.

Sigismondo surely did not perform pagan blood sacrifices, but a *quid pro quo* relationship with God and the practice of astrology and augury were central to the literature and art of his court, and possibly to his political decision making. Both Valturio's condemnations and the potentially heretical musings about the soul after death in Basinio's poetry demonstrate the real danger that such practices could contaminate Christian belief. In a sense, Pius was right, in that some passages hint at atheism, and much of the literature at Sigismondo's court was so contaminated with paganism and implicated in his military exploits that it could be deemed heretical. Even the laudatory Valturio felt the need to reprove such pagan beliefs and practices as demonic and dangerous.

✣ 6 ✣

Pagan Sex and Heroic Virtue

Hercules may have chosen virtue over vice at the crossroads, according to the famous myth, but his amorous exploits and occasional effeminate manners brought his manhood into question.[1] Unlike the hero of myth, Sigismondo is presented as not having to choose between love and valor—as being as ardent and strong in love as on the battlefield. Basinio might show instances of Sigismondo brought to his knees by love, but the dominant trope in Malatesta poetry is that of the ancient love poet Propertius, who insisted that sex made the ancient heroes no less fierce and effective in battle: "What about when Achilles left Briseis's arms? Did the Trojans run from the Greek javelins less? When fierce Hector rose from Andromache's bed, did the Mycenaean fleet not fear the battle?"[2] Like Achilles and Hector, Sigismondo fought harder, triumphed, and earned greater glory in battle because of love.

In the papal invective, Pius presented Sigismondo as a sexual predator, without restraint and bent on gratifying his most banal physical urges on other men's wives, nuns, virgins, and even the cadaver of a noble lady, whom he strangled for refusing his advances. Such an image hardly fits the heroic noble warrior of Basinio's verse, who earns Olympus and becomes a god through bravery and outstanding virtue. Basinio, however, also shows a Sigismondo who is a passionate lover, devoted to Isotta yet focused on satisfying urges that are decidedly physical and this worldly. Like virtue, the soul, and the afterlife, love had a particularly pagan Renaissance in the culture of Sigismondo's court.

After carrying on a lengthy affair with Isotta degli Atti, Sigismondo refused desirable alliances and eventually married her for love. This romance is celebrated and described in pagan terms in court poetry. In Basinio and Porcellio's verse, Sigismondo's passionate physical longings for Isotta are matched by her desires for him. Isotta is presented as a sexually assertive woman, yet she was also a powerful ruler, who governed Rimini when Sigismondo was away and successfully kept the papacy out of Rimini after Sigismondo's death.[3] The erotically-charged Isotta in the literature of Sigismondo's court is antithetical to the typically virginal image of the female Renaissance ruler. Malatesta poetry presents Sigismondo as devoted to one woman, Isotta, but in reality he continued to have sexual relationships with other women and in fact made Isotta take care of the illegitimate children that came from those affairs.[4] Despite these dalliances, the widespread acceptance of male philandering, and the reality of arranged marriages for Italian elites, Isotta's central place in the myth Sigismondo promulgated remained undiminished. The descriptions of Sigismondo as Isotta's devoted, passionate lover are not a straightforward mirror of reality but a consciously crafted part of his public persona as a modern pagan hero.

Husband Gone Mad: From Lust Fiend to Uxoricide

According to an anonymous Spanish author of a poem against Sigismondo dedicated to Pius II, Sigismondo was born from the Fury Tisiphon and the infernal river Phlegethon. He was educated in all the vices by the infernal gods and imbued in particular with the poison of Pleasure-Voluptas. Pleasure taught him how to defile virgins and to dedicate his life to luxury. Almost one hundred lines of the poem are dedicated to Sigismondo's amorous exploits.[5] Sigismondo's unbridled sexuality also dominates the papal invectives against him. His vicious character, the pope stressed, thrived on mad lust. He had a demonic need and a passion that knew no bounds and thus committed heinous acts of sacrilege in raping nuns, pimping girls, and molesting his own son. In the pope's eyes, Sigismondo's theology was willfully corrupt: "He says that the vow of virginity and continence is foolish and the sacrament of penance is an invention of clerical greed."[6] Pius's Sigismondo denied the Church's teachings on sex and morals, not only by committing numerous sexual sins but also in explicit pronouncements against Christian ideals.

Long before Sigismondo, the Malatesta family had already earned a reputation for their lack of sexual restraint. Sigismondo's ancestors appeared in Dante's *Inferno* as negative examples of the power of lust. Francesca da Polenta (1255–1285) was married to Gianciotto Malatesta but fell in love with her husband's younger brother, Paolo. When Gianciotto discovered the couple exchanging amorous looks and a fatal kiss, he slayed them both. Francesca takes center stage in the circle of the lustful, and her story of how she and Paolo fell in love and committed adultery makes Dante cry and faint. Lust drove Paolo to betray his own wife and to cuckold his brother. Lust and his wife's adultery drove Gianciotto to murder.[7] Sigismondo's much older cousin, Laura Malatesta (1404–1425), also failed to control her lust and met a similar end. Known as Parisina, she was unhappily married to the Marquis of Ferrara, Niccolò d'Este III, who was twenty-one years her senior. But she found true love with the marquis's son, Ugo d'Este, and the two carried on a secret romance for at least a year. When the marquis discovered their affair, he had them both imprisoned and then beheaded.[8] Parisina's daughter, Ginevra d'Este (1419–1440), became Sigismondo's first wife in 1434. Lust and adultery were therefore somewhat of a Malatesta specialty.

Sigismondo's marriages were all politically motivated until Isotta became his bride after a nearly decade-long romance. Before his marriage to Ginevra, Sigismondo had been betrothed to the daughter of the mercenary captain Francesco Bussone (Carmagnola, 1385–1432), who had enjoyed great success as the captain successively of both the Visconti of Milan and the republic of Venice. After persuading Venice to declare war on Milan, Carmagnola played the powers off each other, dillydallied on the battlefield to prolong his commission, and failed to bring a decisive victory to Venice. Eventually, the republic lost patience, summoned the captain, and decapitated him in the Piazzetta for treason. Although he had already received a steed, a silver helmet, and a stunning suit of armor as a prenuptial gift, Sigismondo promptly broke off the engagement and did not return the armor.[9] Soon after this, in 1434, Sigismondo married fifteen-year-old Ginevra d'Este, when he himself was seventeen. Ginevra linked him to the powerful Este rulers of Ferrara, who were very important for the development of Sigismondo's cultural interests, as discussed in Chapter 2. Ginevra died in 1440, and in 1441 Sigismondo married the thirteen-year-old daughter of Francesco Sforza,

Polissena Sforza (1428–1449).[10] Sigismondo had fought under Sforza's command and learned much from this star mercenary, who would later brilliantly orchestrate the takeover of Visconti Milan and the establishment of his own ruling dynasty. Sigismondo's relations with Sforza, however, turned sour over the fate of the strategic port city of Pesaro. The ruler of Pesaro, Galeazzo Malatesta (1385–1461), was nicknamed "the inept." The humanist Filelfo called him "sluggish" and "effeminate," and another contemporary accused Galeazzo of cowardice, saying that "he preferred to live as a private citizen in shame to the life of a lord in fear." The Malatesta of Pesaro had helped foment the 1431 rebellion against Galeotto in Rimini, which the thirteen-year-old Sigismondo was celebrated for quelling. So there was bad blood between the two family lines. When the weak Galeazzo inherited Pesaro in 1441, Sigismondo asserted his own claim for the city. He tried to stir up conspiracy and at first convinced his powerful ally Francesco Sforza to let him lead a military attack on the city. But after a few years of skirmishes and negotiations involving major players in the area, including Federico da Montefeltro, Pope Eugenius IV, Alfonso of Aragon, and the condottiere Niccolò Piccinino, Sigismondo was undone when Galeazzo secretly sold Pesaro to Sforza in 1445.[11] The Malatesta family would never again rule Pesaro.

Already in 1445, Sigismondo was accused of violence motivated by lust. His longtime enemy Federico da Montefeltro wrote a letter in which he listed Sigismondo's crimes of passion. When a noblewoman refused his advances, Sigismondo reportedly had her stripped naked, whipped, and paraded through the streets of Rimini. He beat an unaccommodating girl to death with his gold-studded silk belt. He raped a Jewish girl, which, Pius II later emphasized, showed the depths of his immorality, as Sigismondo had no qualms about copulating with non-Christian women. Sigismondo, Federico's list continues, murdered a brother for not pimping his sister, refused to return the dowry for Carmagnola's daughter, and poisoned his first wife, Ginevra d'Este.[12] It is unknown whether Pius used this letter for the composition of the invective, but the pope refers to the same stories with the same details. The pope dwells in particular on Sigismondo's violation of Jewish women and Christian nuns. "In Rimini," the pope says, "and Sigismondo's lands there is nothing more pernicious to citizens than to have a pretty daughter or wife."[13] Pius expresses particular horror about the time when in the countryside around Verona, Sigismondo came upon a group of German pilgrims on their way to Rome for the Jubilee in 1450. When a beautiful noblewoman refused his advances, "excited by lust," he reportedly dragged her off her horse and beat her until she was "soaked with blood," and all the time she was "imploring the saints and not resisting the blows." This particular charge may have some basis in fact. Indeed, Sigismondo returned immediately to Rimini and sent emissaries to Venice to answer the scandal and charges. Another contemporary source, the Duke of Monteleone, places the attack in Rimini, inside Castel Sismondo. He says that Sigismondo killed two of the noblewoman's defending knights and struck the noblewoman repeatedly. He writes that when Sigismondo puts his arms around her, she "bites him and pulls off bits of flesh with her teeth, so that he loses his temper and stabs her in the chest and kills her." Even Soranzo, Sigismondo's twentieth-century defender, had trouble exonerating him from this charge.[14]

In addition to his sexual crimes, Sigismondo was accused of murdering his first and second wives. Pius calls Ginevra a "chaste and holy woman" and elaborates:

> But this pure girl was badly joined to an impure man, a chaste woman to an adulterer, an innocent to a noxious man; this lusty most squalid debaucher and thief could not tolerate the habits of a most modest wife. The two different natures could not bear to live any longer together. The stronger sex and the one more daring in every criminal act prevailed. The unfortunate wife perished in no time from a poison prepared by her husband.[15]

Federico's accusations and the papal invective, the only other source that speaks of Ginevra's murder, are of course biased. Because there were no immediate accusations of foul play and Sigismondo continued to have good relations with the Este family, the charge must have been false and politically motivated.[16] The most notorious charge against Sigismondo was that he strangled to death his second wife, Polissena Sforza, and that he had the Franciscan friars "tortured to death" for not revealing Polissena's and other matrons' secret confessions.[17] Polissena died in 1449, probably from plague.

Sigismondo had been on bad terms with Francesco Sforza since 1445, but two years after Polissena's death, they signed a pact, which cancelled all previous points of contention, specifically the sale of Pesaro and Sigismondo's attempts to keep Sforza out of Milan when he commanded Venetian forces in 1450. There were no rumors about Sigismondo murdering Polissena until 1461, when Milan and Rome were at war with Rimini. Sforza turned on Sigismondo for inviting the French back into Italy and supporting the Angevin claim to Naples. Pius II, as we have seen, wanted to chastise Sigismondo and regain the Malatesta lands for the church.[18] This accusation must be seen in the political context in which the charge was made, when the pope and his ally Sforza were using every weapon they could muster to defame and defeat Sigismondo.

Sigismondo's most celebrated and long-lasting love affair was with Isotta degli Atti (1432–1474). In a poem that Basinio composed in her name, Isotta says that Sigismondo first noticed her in 1443, but the earliest evidence of his attention is a 1445 love poem.[19] The date 1446, however, is celebrated on medals that Matteo de' Pasti cast of Isotta after 1452 and on the original epitaph of Isotta's tomb in the Tempio (figs. 6.1 and 6.2).[20] That a ruler had extramarital affairs is not remarkable for the time. It is, however, striking that Sigismondo's adultery was so publicized and celebrated, while he was still legally married to Polissena (who died in 1449).[21] Isotta would have been about fourteen years old in 1446, which was the legal age for marriage and, therefore, an acceptable age for romance. In May 1447 Isotta already gave birth to a son, who died prematurely and was buried with full pomp in the Malatesta family church, San Francesco. In September 1447, Isotta asked permission of Pope Nicholas V to renovate the Chapel of the Angels inside the Tempio. With no dowry nor family wealth, Isotta claimed to be able to use "certain possessions and properties." Sigismondo no doubt provided these funds and supported Isotta's planned renovation, which he eventually took over. In February 1448, furthermore, Sigismondo knighted Antonio degli Atti, Isotta's brother. The original marble inscription on Isotta's tomb, which contained the date 1446, was discovered under the bronze inscription in 1912.[22] It was probably carved when the tomb was completed in 1452–1453 and meant to mark the beginning of their love affair. The second inscription, in bronze with the date 1450, was probably placed sometime after the private marriage in 1453 or 1454, when Isotta had gained official status as the *donna*

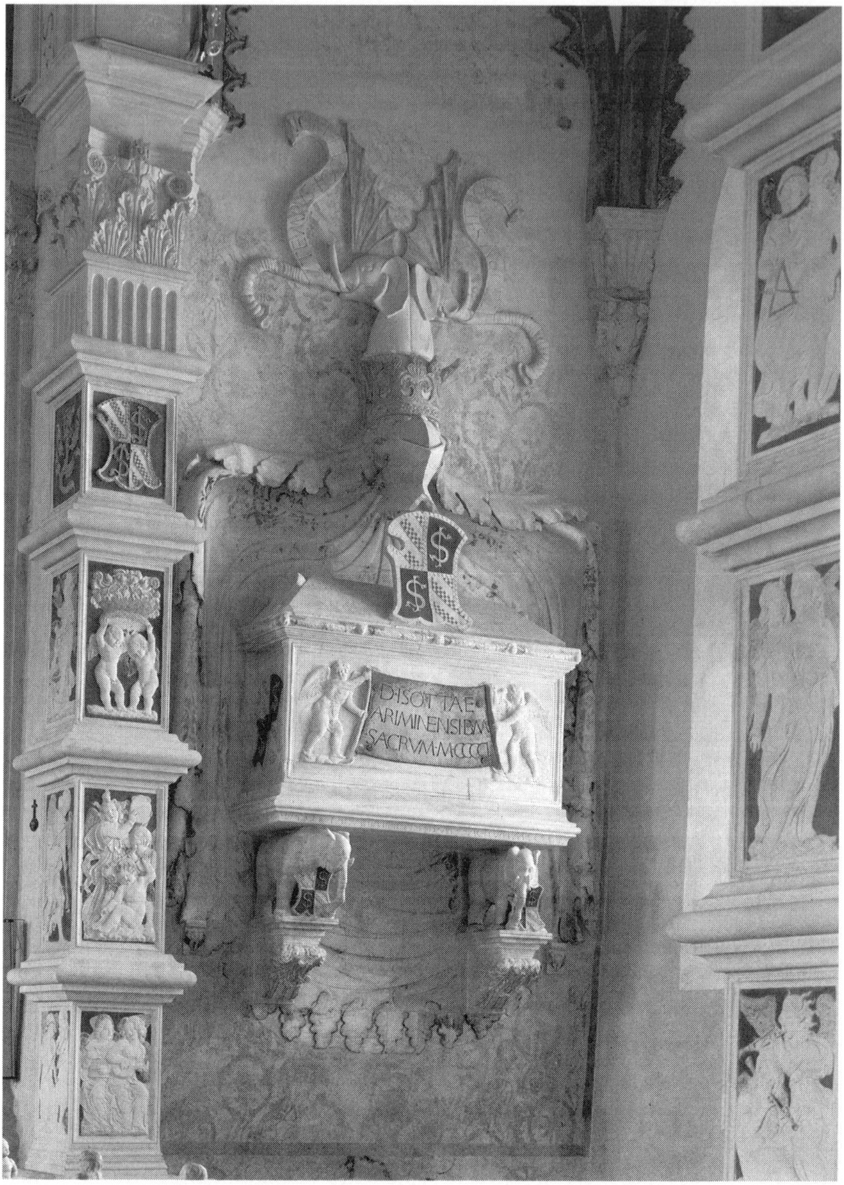

Fig. 6.1. Agostino di Duccio, tomb of Isotta degli Atti, ca. 1452–1453, Tempio Malatestiano, Rimini. Photo: Scala/Art Resource, NY.

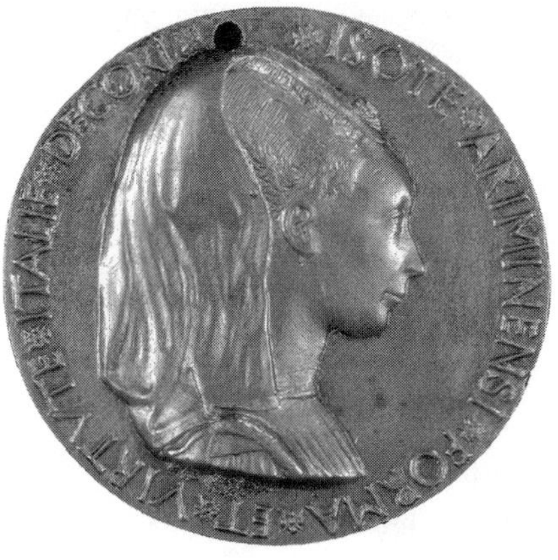

Fig. 6.2. Matteo de' Pasti, Isotta degli Atti, medal, bronze, dated 1446, National Gallery of Art, Washington, D.C. Photo: Samuel H. Kress Collection, National Gallery of Art, Washington, D.C.

de' Malatesta.[23] The date change to 1450 avoids the scandal of adultery, as Polissena was still alive in 1446, and reflects the official status of Isotta as Sigismondo's wife.

In his *Commentaries,* Pius objected to the prominence of Isotta's tomb in the side chapel and to the use of the epithet *Divae* in the second inscription, which reads *D(ivae) Isottae Ariminensi b(ene) m(erenti) sacrum. M.CCCCL.* "Sigismondo," Pius writes, "built for his lover a tomb, most beautiful in craftsmanship and stone, and in the pagan manner gave the title to it: 'a sanctuary for goddess Isotta.'"[24] In antiquity, mortal women were made immortal for copulating with gods. The epithet *diva* could mean "goddess," but in later centuries it referred to a particularly holy person, a saint.[25] Even so, Pius thought its use for Isotta was inappropriate, since Sigismondo's concubine was far from a saint. In Malatesta poetry, Basinio and Porcellio use the term *divus* to refer to pagan gods or the divine Sigismondo and Isotta, each made into gods through their virtue. It was one thing, however, to use such an epithet in poetry but another to have it prominently displayed on a tomb in a church.

After his second wife died, an ambitious lord would have married into another powerful family. Instead, Sigismondo continued and publically celebrated his love affair with Isotta degli Atti, whose family had little to offer the mercenary in terms of status, wealth, or power. In the *Isottaeus,* a book of epistolary poetry, Basinio has Sigismondo proudly list all of his potential brides and thank Cupid for providing him with the perfect consort:

> A thousand girls celebrated weddings because of Cupid; my brother married a royal wife. Sforza and Este girls, and Bianca, the only offspring from the powerful duke of Milan, were present; and the only surviving girl of Montefeltro, the singular hope and sole glory of so great a house. There were one hundred Helens and one hundred Briseis, who indeed could have summoned Jupiter from heaven. But my mind immediately returned to my dear girl, and all my care was for Isotta . . . although you will find many girls equal to her in birth, in my opinion you will not find any girl in Italy equal to her in beauty and virtue. Shall I compare her eyes to Apollo's, her hair to Diana's, and her lips to the red of Cybele? Her words do not sound mortal; neither does Pallas Athena have more arts nor nourishing Venus more play. Whatever she does pleases me; I like this girl alone. As a soldier following your encampments, Cupid, I rejoice in this lot.[26]

Sigismondo surely could have found a third wife, but Basinio's account does not quite tally. Malatesta Novello had married Violante Montefeltro in 1434. Although Bianca Maria Visconti was betrothed to Francesco Sforza in 1430, her father broke the engagement and tried to wed her to Carlo Gonzaga or Leonello d'Este in 1434, before relenting and allowing the marriage to Francesco to be made in 1441. Sigismondo's name may have appeared as a potential suitor before his marriage to Ginevra d'Este in 1434 or just after Ginevra's death in 1440. Sigismondo could not, however, have been thinking of Isotta at those points, as she was far too young, even by Renaissance standards. Basinio emphasizes Sigismondo's options by shoring up the mixture of contemporary brides with classical beauties. Briseis was Achilles's war booty and the cause of the great tension between Achilles and Agamemnon in Homer's *Iliad*. In the opening lines of the poem, the famous "wrath" is due to the hero's loss of his beloved prize. All of the love poetry from Sigismondo's court focuses on Isotta, who is constructed as a fictional character, just as Sigismondo is.

Isotta's Sacred Grove

In books VII–IX of the *Hesperis*, Sigismondo is taken on a tour of the underworld by his lover Isotta, in the form of a nymph. Sigismondo meets the shades of the ancients, including Cicero, Dido, and Homer, and he witnesses the punishments of various pagans. This use of pagan form and content reflects Dante's *Inferno* without the Christian framework. But Sigismondo's entrance into the divine realm is unlike anything in Basinio's ancient or Christian models. Homer had Odysseus raise the blind seer Tiresias with a blood offering. Virgil had the Cumaean Sybil accompany Aeneas, who had to use a golden bough to enter the underworld safely. The spiritual love of the chaste Beatrice saves Dante and guides him through the heavens. In Basinio's poem Sigismondo enters heaven through the erotic.

The nymph "Psycheia," who is actually Sigismondo's real-life lover, Isotta, cannot resist the beautiful body of the hero. Physical copulation provides Sigismondo with an entry to the divine: "After he took possession of the goddess' wedding bed and experienced such great love-making, Sigismondo gladly left [his] happy tree for the thick grove."[27] In the last line Basinio includes an erotic joke: Sigismondo goes from or through the sensual pleasure of his penis (*arbor*) to the "thick groves" of philosophical-religious truth (*densos lucos*), which is the path to the underworld and heaven. In fact, another way to translate the last lines could be: "Taking possession of the goddess' wedding bed and such great love, Sigismondo gladly entered [her] thick groves by means of [his] happy tree." In classical Latin, *lucus* means "sacred grove of a goddess." This impious joke stresses the poetic fiction of what is to follow but may also hint at a serious connection between human sexuality and the divine.

In the underworld, after seeing the orators and before encountering the poets in the Elysian Fields, Sigismondo witnesses the fate of unfortunate female lovers. Helen and Pasiphae show the power of lust; Dido and Lucretia are martyrs for love; and Calypso, Circe, and Medea are examples of unbridled passion that drove women mad. Just as in Dante's *Inferno,* their improper love has given them no rest in the afterlife: "they wander in uncertain abodes. There is no rest, no order, and the insane pain of mad lovers . . . cruel love destroys them in more than one death."[28] The fact that all the martyrs for love are women betrays the misogyny of classical literature, which predominantly presents the female as the weaker, more sensual sex. Unlike Dante, who faints, "falling like a dead body falls," after hearing Francesca's tale of woeful love, Sigismondo does not react to the vision of tormented lovers.[29] Instead of driving him mad and destroying him, the physical passion that Sigismondo feels for Isotta/Psycheia inspires him to pursue virtue and raises him to the Heavens.

An Imagined Romance: Sigismondo and Isotta

In the *liber Isottaeus,* Basinio penned ten Latin poems in Sigismondo's name and eleven in Isotta's.[30] Most are presented as letters exchanged between the lovers, and some are exchanges with the poet (Basinio) on the nature of love and the afterlife. In one poem, Sigismondo describes to Basinio how he first fell in love with Isotta:

> Isotta moved me to love her by her divine habits and first put me under her will. Honest goodness above her years saved this love, and beauty, along with a long unblemished trust, increased it. She had not yet matured in age nor had her soft cheeks pressed mine. Embracing her with all my heart I said: "you will be my mind's only rest and care." Although her tender years made her useless, she was superior to great goddesses in character . . . her eyes competed with heavenly flames, sweet yet chaste. I therefore dedicated myself with entire mind and decided to desire and live by her wishes. The hope was not vain, since as she grew in years she dutifully accepted my requests.[31]

Basinio uses the fiction of this letter to deal with the potential scandal of a romance between a grown man and a girl about twelve years old. In calling Isotta *inutilis* (useless) because of her "tender years," Sigismondo must be referring to her inability to bear children because of her youth. The statement is perhaps meant to show that Sigismondo did not try to have sex with her before she reached puberty, when she "dutifully accepted" him as her lover. Whether or not true, this could be a public assertion that Sigismondo was no child molester, at least as far as Isotta was concerned. More cynically, it could also just mean that she was too young to conceive, no matter what Sigismondo did.

Another court humanist, Pietro Parleo, described the first moment of erotic attraction between the lovers in a Latin wedding oration for Isotta's brother, Antonio degli Atti:

> When the queen of the Amazons, Thalestris, saw the regal majesty of Alexander the Great, she at once desired to sleep with him and bear his children. In the same way did Sigismondo react when he saw Isotta's lineage and beauty, heard her voice and laughter, and observed her walk. He thought that there must be the spirit of kings in her body and something more than human in her mortal person. He burned with an unbelievable fire of love and longed that Isotta might burn with an equal flame so that they might be joined in joyous and perpetual love.[32]

Although most aristocratic marriages in fifteenth-century Italy were contracted for political and economic reasons, wedding orators in Italian courts promoted an ideal of romantic passion and love, in addition to the more practical concerns of lineage, wealth, and family status. Ignoring the issue of Isotta's age, Parleo asserts that Sigismondo fell in love with her at first sight and longed to have sexual intercourse with her. In this epithalamium, Parleo emphasizes that both sexes should feel passion by comparing Sigismondo's desire with that of an Amazonian queen's. Although Amazons were often described as manly in arms and virtue, it is odd that Parleo compares the hyper-masculine Sigismondo to a woman.[33] Other humanists, Valturio and Manetti, compared Sigismondo to Alexander the Great, but never to a lusty Amazon queen wanting to have sex with Alexander, an image that suggests tensions between masculinity and all-subjugating desire.

Both the poem and the wedding oration stress reciprocal love. Sigismondo in Basinio's voice is self-deprecatingly surprised and thrilled that Isotta "chose" him as a lover: "Although there were many handsome rulers equal to me in lineage, this one girl, her beauty famed in Italy, this one girl, courted by many nobles, chose me alone from many lovers as the object of her devotion." Sigismondo's humility and the image of him caring about what a girl thinks about him is striking in contrast to Pius's portrait of Sigismondo as a savage and selfish rapist. Basinio's Sigismondo writes of how his culture and even his military success all came from Isotta:

> I owe more to her, for her love has dared to perfect in me what nature could not. She has turned my soul to the delicate arts and

> wetted my mouth with the waters of Parnassus. I have learned poetry from her, music from her, and from her the noble work of crested Mars. For whenever I dare to besiege a walled enemy, fight in battle, and attack enemy forces, I think about how I can please my Isotta. . . . If I have any virtue, it is indebted to her, and all my praise depends entirely on her merits. She has created genius, power, and courage in me.[34]

The ennobling power of love is a standard trope in ancient and Renaissance literature. In the *Decameron,* Boccaccio showed peasants turned overnight into nobles and cowards becoming heroes because of love.[35] It is hard to imagine the real Sigismondo ascribing all of his accomplishments to a girl. He was already a well-known successful mercenary, who had rebuilt a castle and held poetry contests, before he had ever laid eyes on Isotta, though his stunning successes in the Tuscan wars occurred when they were already engaged in their adulterous affair.

The humanists in his court claim that Sigismondo himself wrote poetry to Isotta. In addition to listening and questioning humanists, Valturio praises his patron for "writing something that future men will read, of which very many are vernacular poems on human and divine matters most eloquently produced by you, and already sung on many shores and various regions."[36] The stress on "vernacular" is an important distinction, one that would not have been made had the image of the love poet Sigismondo been an entirely laudatory fiction. Elsewhere in the *Isottaeus,* Basinio refers to Sigismondo's poetry by having Isotta tell how Sigismondo has celebrated her:

> I confess to owe more to such a great lover than he owes to me; for my eternal fame has come from his attention, and I alone have been celebrated in his poetry. Although there have been many spirited and beautiful girls, who could certainly move the great gods, I have always pleased him and I alone have appeared worthy of his cult and affections. He has cast my face in gold and silver, and built an empty tomb for my ashes, so that he might offer the gift of a true lover and, after death, I might be known to you, posterity.[37]

Isotta refers both to the poetry and the art in her honor. Whereas the poetry is clearly penned in Sigismondo's own hand, as the possessive *suo* is added to *carmine,* the medal-casting and sculpted tomb are memorials that he commissioned from artists. Matteo de' Pasti cast several bronze (not gold or silver) medals featuring Isotta's profile, and Agostino di Duccio carved a tomb for Isotta, surrounded by putti and angels playing instruments and dancing, in the Tempio (figs. 6.1 and 6.2).

In a poem addressed to Sigismondo, Basinio praises his patron for doing deeds worthy of great poetry and fighting "wars that have to be celebrated for ever and sung by a new Homer." But in the same poem, he calls Sigismondo himself a "divine poet," a *vates.* He says:

> Twin laurels compete in you, my king: Mars and Calliope favor my commander. But, if you were a famous king only in arms, my eloquence would not prefer you. Behold your monuments to winged love that will be read long into the future. Although she is dead, the shades of the dead (Manes) will not hold your Isotta. She has escaped the funeral pyres. Because of your poems, she remains and will remain for eternity.[38]

Although Isotta lived until 1474, the poetic fiction in several of these poems is that she becomes sick and dies, leaving a distraught Sigismondo. This conceit imitates Petrarch's *Canzoniere,* in which the poet pines over his deceased Laura. The distinction, however, is that Basinio's dead Isotta eventually becomes a goddess and returns in the flesh with glory. In this poem, Basinio presents Sigismondo as such a good poet that he will be able to keep Isotta alive. His verse makes her immortal. No poems to date have been unanimously attributed to Sigismondo. In 1882 Charles Yriarte claimed to have found four poems. But in 1911 Aldo Massèra proved that they were the work of other poets.[39] Other vernacular poems written in Sigismondo's name also survive, but these too may well have been composed by ghostwriters.[40] They are fairly typical Petrarchan verse in which Sigismondo is portrayed as overwhelmed with love and desire for his Isotta. Whatever its truth, the public image of Sigismondo as a love poet is at odds with Valturio's portrait of the ideal warrior, who is solely interested in virtue and glory, an epic hero rather than a lyric poet.

In several poems Basinio explores how love affects virtue and the idea that it weakens the warrior. In a verse letter addressed to Basinio, the fictional Sigismondo asserts the power of love and its superiority over war:

> Venus taught her tough brother [Mars] to become soft, and love upset his heart with good feelings. The crafty goddess opens closed gates and thresholds to the lover . . . she conquered Paris and brought him to Greek cities to see your face, Spartan beauty. Venus taught Helen to yield to the Trojan lover and to silence her words with cautious signs.

If love makes Mars "soft," then surely the warrior should avoid it at all costs. Venus cannot be trusted. She ultimately caused the Trojan War by making Paris a slave to a woman. Basinio's Sigismondo also admits his dependence on love's whims for better or worse:

> Love has so much power . . . it can bring the dead back. . . . I was brought back from the waters of hell, when I remembered my lady in the middle of battle. If I recalled her face, it pleased me; if her locks came to mind, her hair is my great joy; if Isotta's waving arms moved me, these arms hold my courage; but if she looks down and modestly moves her decorous face, I am on fire—take away those grave flames, girl! Take those new torches away, Isotta! Put down those furies, Isotta! I beg you, girl, spare my soul![41]

A vision of the beautiful Isotta can save and encourage him in the heat of battle, but her disapproval can easily destroy him. Love can make the warrior both courageous by giving him something to fight for and weak by submitting him to the will of the beloved.[42] This long poem is a request from Sigismondo (though actually written by Basinio) for Basinio to write more poetry for him, the poetry about Isotta and the beautiful body that inspires him and gives him the will to survive the hell of war. Basinio asserts that his poetry has the power to imagine and make present the beloved to the lover.

The poems in Isotta's name similarly depict a woman who is much more than a beautiful object of affection. In Basinio's poetry, Isotta is an independent, intelligent, and thoughtful person. She is confused by the strong emotions of love. In a poem to Basinio, Isotta describes how she fell in love with Sigismondo, emphasizing in particular her extreme youth:

> Scarcely had I come out of the womb and brought on the death of my mother, when, as a little girl, I had little power to nurture that love, and it was always alone in my heart. Little by little as I grew and the years passed, so did love always grow with our time [together]. My sole care was to adorn my face and blond hair to be pleasing to him. Then suddenly my judgment was more mature than my years, and my flames were exposed. Our souls warmed, I burned in my whole heart, and was scalded by the blinding fires. He pleased me, as if he held golden reins bouncing upon his panting steed. That golden man met the opposing spears and excelled them all in my opinion. That face, I confess, destroyed me and held my eyes more often than was just.[43]

The seed of her passion was sown at birth. The inclusion of her mother's death in her own childbirth is odd, but perhaps Basinio liked juxtaposing the image of the fatal pains of her birth with Isotta's nascent passion for Sigismondo. The image of Isotta as a girl, making herself pretty to please him and lost in the stares of puppy love, tells the tale of a romance that remains innocent until, no longer able to contain her passion, she recklessly reveals it, and Sigismondo answers in kind. The loaded erotic image of Sigismondo "on his panting steed" outdoing the "spears" of rival suitors is jarring in the context of a girl's amorous longings. Isotta compares their love to a mutually felt intense "burning." Just as he had in an earlier poem about Sigismondo's love, Basinio has Isotta express welcome surprise that Sigismondo chose her: "Although there were many beautiful and spirited girls, who could indeed move the great gods, I alone have always pleased him and I alone have seemed worthy of his affections."[44] Basinio's story of their love shows no force or coercion on Sigismondo's side. Instead, Isotta nurtures the seed of her love until "her judgment" is mature enough for her to reveal it. Here, Isotta initiates the relationship. But it is not exactly equal as she is still a child loving a man.

In the first poem, Basinio's Sigismondo writes from Rome, where he is viewing the "monuments of our ancestors." But because Isotta is absent, he says, "these wonderful ruins cannot delight me." Sigismondo declares to Isotta that he fights wars to be worthy of her love, so that "I may appear famous in your judgment." He says: "If I sweat in famed arms, if I get trophies, I deservedly hope for long-lasting love making from you and because of this victory I believe our fidelity will be perpetual."[45] The plural of love (*amores*) signals the erotic nature of the deal: my sweat and victory on the battlefield earn passionate love from you. The three pillars of Sigismondo's life are on display here, and Isotta's love takes priority over classical antiquity and war.

Although love can inspire heroism in Basinio's poems, Isotta tells Sigismondo to avoid danger and be safe. Rumors of Sigismondo's death on the battlefield disturb her. She does not wear pretty clothes, or comb or perfume her hair: "Alone as I am, for whom do I style my blond hair and strive to be pleasing? The admirer of my beauty is far away. . . . Am I to stroll in the shade in my fancy clothes, while he suffers the dog days of summer? Am I to pass my time carefree in festive dancing, while he fights?" Isotta begs Sigismondo to stop fighting: "I confess that indeed you are doing great things, but the glory is not worth submitting your life to a thousand dangers."[46] To please Isotta, Sigismondo must stay far from the chaos of war. But virtue is made and glory is earned in battle amid danger and death. Isotta seems to resent Sigismondo's success and lashes out in a desperate plea:

> Not without me will you lead a triumph after routing the enemy, not without me will laurel wreaths crown you. I do not begrudge you nor stand in the way of such great honors, as long as you return victor to your homeland from the enemy. Only let your fidelity remain unblemished as it is now. Let that fidelity, I beg you, remain for the sake of our relationship, and do not let another love wound our vows.

Like a rock star's sudden success, Sigismondo's victories will lead to temptation and infidelity. Although Sigismondo is shown as a virile man, full of passion and attractive to women, Basinio maintains the fiction of the exclusivity of his romance with Isotta. He nevertheless intimates something of

Sigismondo's notorious uncontrollable libido in the tormented jealous imaginings of Isotta about other women ("naiads") lusting after her Sigismondo at his triumphs:

> For they say (may the report be false) that those girls could stop Odysseus' boat with their beauty. Alas, I imagine them touching your face. . . . What does love not imagine? A thousand naiads appear to hang out of open windows, as the whole city follows the sight of you. They admire your face and locks. . . . Woe, how I fear. What does a woman not dare in loving? I beg, may my imaginings be false, and let one or other girl not put her rash arms around your dear neck and seek your embraces.[47]

It took Odysseus ten years to return to Ithaca from Troy largely because of women, who saved, enticed, or imprisoned him.[48] The naiads swooning out of windows over Sigismondo are both classical water nymphs and clearly modern city women. Basinio imagines a potent irresistible Sigismondo, like Odysseus, overcoming sexual temptations and returning to his wife, Penelope, but with the potential for dalliance along the way.

Basinio also dwells on the jealousy theme in two other descriptions of the triumph. In one poem, Sigismondo is marching through Florence, enjoying the triumph, when all of a sudden he stops at the sight of a beautiful girl in a window, whom he mistakes for Isotta:

> Your face, goddess, appeared from a window, looking out and counting the triumphant commanders. She had the same appearance, the same face, and look in the same light, and a neck whiter than fresh snow, a mouth too pretty with purple lips, and true brilliance in a strong body. I was stunned and thought that she was going to be you, my life. Paleness came over both my cheeks. . . . The commanders accompanying me were shocked since at one moment I was cheering, at the next I was sad.[49]

Waxing long about the beauty of another girl is certainly an odd way to praise Isotta. As if to stave off her jealousy, Sigismondo says that he must have imagined her. He elaborates further on the reasons for his mistake:

"Two reasons made me desire you and believe that I could see your face: the first is that you were watching these great triumphs and the second is that you also, goddess, desire to follow me." After stating "you would have seen," Sigismondo proceeds to describe the fanfare given to him in triumph. "A choir of virgins sang a sacred paean," "everybody poked fun at the captive Spaniards," and "noble Etruscan youths sang thanks" to Sigismondo "carried high on gold bedazzled horses." None of these celebrations, however, pleased him:

> Uncertain and thinking over what I had seen, I wanted to know who that girl had been. When I found out that she was not Isotta, I wailed and hope and courage failed me. I desired to write you about these trifles so that you might know, my girl, in what state of mind I was.[50]

Isotta's image has confused him and made Sigismondo question his life in the limelight of victory. He bewails her absence and goes on to reiterate that triumphs mean nothing to him if Isotta cannot be present:

> Let him perish, whoever has deserted his lady to follow triumphs. Will fame please ashes and bones after death? How men desire many wicked things for themselves! Live while you can and love tender girls: this is the one greatest cause of the highest good. Who except a fool goes out to die in the midst of enemies? He is mad who becomes famous from his own blood. Live while the times of swift life make haste; live and do not let glory make you long for death. There is no pleasure in the infernal regions; all love in a dead body ceases. Not me, I do not crave the trophies of renowned triumphs nor to be able to flatten enemy commanders. It is enough for me to placate an angry girl with my advances and too often to bear the scoldings of my lady. Let me wage wars here: faraway, go faraway triumphs![51]

These are surprising sentiments to be placed in the mouth of a famous mercenary captain, who appears single-mindedly focused on military glory and triumph in the other art and literature of his court. Basinio's poetry in particular supplies some of the richest images of a contemporary epic hero, fearless Sigismondo on the battlefield. Of course, the letter's fiction is that Sigismondo wrote it for Isotta, and Sigismondo could hardly have found a better expression of his love than that he would give up all glory just to please her. (The wording here, however, again implies that the virile Sigismondo could have multiple sexual conquests.) The idea that pleasure (*voluptas*) and love die with the body is an epicurean idea. In this image, love is passionate and physical; it is part of the body, not some spiritual connection that survives death. When Sigismondo commands us to live and love, he echoes the Roman poet Horace's famous words: "seize the day and put no trust in tomorrow."[52] Glory and bravery in battle are nothing, only the love of Isotta. "She will give me honor and fame," he says. "If she praises me, I will certainly be famous. Cruel Odysseus lived because of Penelope . . . so shall I have the fame of loving you as long as the stars stay in the heavens."[53] Venus has submerged the ambition for virtue and glory that Mars offers.

Isotta's response to Sigismondo's mistaken identification is in the next letter-poem: "You say that when you entered the city, you saw with palpitating heart the ambrosial cheeks of a placid girl, who looked like me; a lone girl who held your attention. O prince, I would have liked to have been her and not have you deceived in these marvelous ways!" Isotta then recounts all the amazing celebrations that she would have seen in Florence, had she been there. After forty lines of her description of the triumphal display, Isotta expresses her jealousy:

> I fear one thing, that that new image which appeared to you might snatch you up. Woe to me, if some girl persuades you now willingly to desert my bosom. I would rather perish and be dragged down in Styx's Avernus or sooner be burned by Jupiter's lightning bolt than that you might love another girl and forget about your Isotta, while I am alive.

Isotta, however, quickly corrects herself and insists that Sigismondo would never be unfaithful, since his "virtue, prowess, and trust have taught" him to be true to their love. She blames the strength of her love for the jealousy and concludes her letter with advice on how to rid himself of the image of the girl: "If you leave Florence and immediately discard the image of her, that vision will not disturb you so often—although you write that she is elegant, she is nevertheless not equal to me."[54] Isotta urges her Odysseus to avoid temptresses and return home.

In other poems, Basinio presents Isotta as a headstrong woman. Fearlessly, she yearns to accompany Sigismondo on campaign:

> O most brave prince, I am sad and absent, left behind alone in Rimini. Would you be ashamed, if a woman came with you to camp and followed your orders? Camilla came with her bow to help Turnus, and Hercules' wife always followed him. . . . From her walls, Andromache often watched Hector fighting in the middle of the Greeks. His famous wife emboldened Hector, and she alone moved her husband: a girl gave purpose to such a great commander.[55]

Isotta compares herself to women from classical literature, who all crossed gender roles and were associated with war. Camilla was a warrior huntress, who fought at the side of Turnus against Aeneas and the Trojans in the *Aeneid*. Hercules's wife Deianeira is an odd comparison, since although she was known for her fighting skills, she accidentally caused the death of her husband. Struck by Hercules and dying, the centaur Nessus convinced Deianeira that if she soaked a cloak in his blood and gave it to Hercules to wear, the hero would not be unfaithful, but the cloak poisoned her beloved husband. Hector's wife, Andromache, is a more fitting exemplar. In the *Iliad* (VI.433–439), Homer describes Andromache standing on the ramparts of Troy and giving battle advice to Hector. After providing literary precedents for her desired action, however, Isotta corrects herself so as not to offend Sigismondo: "But I would certainly not be able to embolden you, o greatest man, since you alone are the bravest in great Italy. But, if savage wars tire you out, on your return I would be able to comfort you often in my sweet bosom."[56] Basinio's Isotta explores the role of the female lover warrior in this hyper-masculine war culture, ultimately deciding that, unlike her classical examples, Isotta does not dare to offer to fight or provide military advice. Instead, she resorts to the allure and comfort of her sexuality.

In another poem, Isotta goes further and speaks of wanting to fight. She compares herself to an amazon warrior:

> Since . . . you will eternally desire to pursue the wars of Mars, I will take up arms and imitate the amazons, and follow your standards with shielded breast, just like Penthesilea once raged in the midst of thousands and excelled brave men. Nor did Camilla fall in the Latin war without taking her vengeance, and many more whose names you read. Why should I not dare to do battle after such great examples? Why should I be afraid to endure battles with you as my commander? With you as my commander I will not dread the cold of a numbing winter nor will I flee the violent signs of an Icarian hound.[57]

Penthesilea, queen of the amazons, fought for the Trojans. Achilles vanquished her in battle, then upon removing her helmet, fell in love with her and cried over her death.[58] Humanists often compared noble Renaissance women to classical counterparts, but generally chose famous virgins and stoic matrons, not a gender-bending warrior queen.[59]

Only one letter survives that is actually from Isotta to Sigismondo. Just like her character in Basinio's poems, in Isotta's letter dated December 20, 1454, she is jealous and worried that Sigismondo might love another woman. She is angered by a report that Sigismondo betrayed her with a specific woman: "I have come to know about a certain betrayal that my Lord has committed with the daughter of Galeazzo Malatesta." Because Sigismondo, who was away on campaign, had told her that he would not write to her anymore, Isotta sadly declares: "I lack nothing else to make me entirely discontent! Please, if you love me entirely as you say, do not deny me this, which is my great joy, that is writing. . . . have compassion on poor little me." Isotta ends the letter with news of their children, who are all well, and of "our son" who "is well and received with the greatest pleasure the horse."[60] The letter reveals that Isotta's actual love for Sigismondo shared several of the themes that Basinio developed in his invented epistolary poems, including jealousy, passionate expressions of affection, and the pain of the absent lover. The gift horse provides an image of domestic happiness and a loving father, Sigismondo, who presumably sent the horse. The letter, which was written in Italian, also reveals that Isotta herself was literate, that she read Sigismondo's letters and wanted more, and that she herself could write. Another source provides further evidence for Isotta's literacy. In an effort to claim his succession to the rule of Rimini after Sigismondo's death, Roberto Malatesta showed a letter to Pope Paul II that his mother, Isotta, had written, stating that he had been named the heir. The pope "recognized the woman's hand, which he knew from several letters that he had received from her before."[61] Roberto emphasized her autograph (*literas chirographi sui*). Isotta could not only read but also write, and if she also knew some Latin, which is possible for a courtly woman, she may very well have been an attentive and enthusiastic audience to Basinio's poetry, as he claims.

The Dead and Divinized Isotta

Several of the poems in the *Isottaeus* center on Isotta's imagined mortal illness, death, and divinization, even though she was alive and, indeed, would outlive Sigismondo.[62] Sigismondo describes to Isotta his nightmare. "You appeared to me," he says, "standing close by with disheveled hair, sad, discolored, and barely raising black and blue eyes from the ground; no one should believe it you, Isotta. But although you were weak and pale, you were still pretty. You said: 'Oh prince, the greatest care of my life, help your dear girl.' I immediately woke, disturbed to the heart, for every lover easily believes whatever he fears." Sigismondo then opens a window but finds the sky dark. The omen, as he calls it, came true as a messenger announced Isotta was indeed sick: "your girl is in danger of her life, for a fever torments her dying body in bitter turns and enrages her entire heart in flame." Amid much wailing Sigismondo laments that he cannot leave the war against Alfonso and has to send a letter instead. In the theme of love versus war, war wins this time, even against the imagined death throes of his beloved. He tells her to do everything to get better and ends with a prayer: "Oh proud Apollo . . . help my girl, and apply your healing hands."[63]

In her reply, Isotta describes her joy at receiving Sigismondo's concerned letter, which is more salvific than any medicine:

> I gave the letter a thousand kisses and cherished it like your eyes. I seemed to hear your spoken words, see your face before me, and fall under your embraces. What am I saying? This sick mind of mine was revived just as a flame comes alive when wine is poured on it. . . . I said "If he is well, I will soon be safe." . . .

> There is no need for Apollo's medicine; come back to me and you will become my life and salvation.[64]

The thought of Sigismondo's love is enough to revive her, just as alcohol feeds a dying flame. Her love, Isotta says, is so strong that not even death can extinguish it:

> If some sensation exists among the shades deep under the earth, and my mind remains the same as it was before, neither death, ashes, nor stone will suppress my love, but my flame will survive after I am dead.[65]

Misery in the absence of the beloved is a common theme in literature, but Basinio pushes this tension further in the imagined illness of Isotta. The fictive device also serves as a segue to the theme of life and love after death and Isotta's divinization.

In several poems, Basinio has Isotta claim to be mortally ill and use her imminent death to try to persuade Sigismondo to return from the field:

> But if you come, o divine one, you alone will console your lover and perhaps bring about an ancient salvation. . . . So many times love alone called Castor back from the shades of Styx, saved by the love of his brother. . . . I am tormented and there is no medicine for such a great pain that can contain my tears. Love alone has not abandoned me, and it grows in immense evils. Frigid death rules over my sick limbs in my weak body, but love burns in my frozen chest.

Pollux begged Jupiter to bring his twin brother Castor back from dead and to make them both immortal. Jupiter assented and made them a constellation in the night sky. Only Sigismondo and the image of his face keep Isotta out of Tartarus:

> I feel completely lost and cannot remember any part of my dead self. Although I have forgotten myself, I remember my joys and hold you, o Sigismondo, always before my eyes. . . . If any part of

> me was sweet to you, look at my fate, o divine one, and take pity on my soul. Do not let another girl take your love from me . . . and take your face away. If I learn of this, then you will send me to sad Tartarus, and she will rejoice in my tears.

Isotta is jealous even in death. Besides keeping her alive, Sigismondo's devotion makes her into a goddess. Isotta explains to him how to make her divine:

> Come before my tomb, which is made of Parian marble and receives my body. Give your tears here, spread pious lilies, and place purple roses in order. If bodies have any sensation after death, I will receive these charming prayers, having already become a goddess. For if you love me, I will be a goddess and a deity after death, and my spirit will influence all times. Born under the hills of Rimini, the Moors will pray to me and the rich Arabs place incense. Every barbarian people and the land of Italy will approve of me, since I was a girl worthy of such a great man. But my tongue cannot speak nor my mouth utter more. I die and slip away before my time. Farewell and remember us for a long time; behold the darkness is covering my wretched head as the night rushes in.[66]

After starting the poem in a dying state and begging Sigismondo to save her, Isotta predicts that she will become a goddess after death and be celebrated. This is certainly not a Christian conception of death. A devout Christian would not talk of becoming a god, granting prayers, and being worshipped with incense by Muslims. Her worthiness to receive Sigismondo's love is her claim to sanctity.

In Basinio's poem, Sigismondo responds by comparing himself to Priam viewing the body of his son Hector and to Orpheus wailing over his dead Eurydice. "Life is not pleasing," he says, "nor will I enjoy having lived, if I lose her." Sigismondo tells Basinio to rush to her side:

> Tell her not to stop fighting the fates, that she was the only girl to rival all the goddesses. Tell her that so many thousands of

> Romans prayed to the eternal gods and the great deities that she not be consumed but rather saved for me and remain as hope, the cause of great good.

This encouragement leads Sigismondo to elaborate on the power of prayer:

> Indeed prayers could carry sailors from sharp shoals and guide their sails to a calm sea. Prayers recalled Hypolitus from death. Prayers made a goddess out of a cow, over whom her father Inachus had bewailed. . . . Terrified of wild beasts, the cow first went to the mountains, then after she learned to pray to you, o great Jupiter, she held the temples and hearths of Egypt. O Polyphemus, at your prayers, Galatea halted her white horses. With prayers Odysseus won over Neptune, Aeneas Juno, and the Trojans Athena.

After Theseus had Hypolitus killed for allegedly raping his stepmother, Phaedra, the goddess Artemis resurrected the boy because of a vow of chastity that he had taken to the chaste goddess. Jupiter tried to hide Io from his wife, Juno, by turning her into a cow, which was then venerated. The cyclops Polyphemus eventually seduced the sea nymph Galatea. After ten years and several shipwrecks and other dangers, Odysseus was finally able to placate Neptune and return to Ithaca. Aeneas similarly placated Juno and succeeded in founding the Trojan colony in Italy that became Rome. These "prayers" hardly serve pious Christian ends; the ethos is thoroughly pagan.

The word *preces* is ambiguous. Sometimes *preces* has religious import and means "prayers to a god"; other times *preces* refers to mere requests or entreaties. Basinio seems to play with these different senses of the word in what the character Sigismondo writes to the poet:

> If prayers overcame all the wills of the great gods, then let my prayers keep Isotta safe. I pray to you, [poet], comfort her and heal my lady in her pain, so that all grief might leave her body. Oh divine poet, the greatest hope of our fame, you who alone will be the glory of our name, I pray you to make haste on my behalf and fulfill this great trust and fly as soon as possible to

> her house. If you do this and encourage the suffering girl with words, she will perhaps be liberated by your words.

The abrupt shift from prayers to the gods to prayers or requests for the poet to take care of Isotta emphasizes the divine power of poetry. In Basinio's obviously self-serving work, the poet not only makes Sigismondo famous and promotes his glory, but he can also heal with his words and coax Isotta back to life.

Basinio's Sigismondo laments that nothing compares to the pain he would feel over Isotta's loss:

> Extreme cold has not in any way hurt me, nor have the sad winter of a finished year nor snow hurt me. . . . The ice on frozen ponds often pressed under my feet everywhere has not blocked me. Great commanders often stable their horses in the frost, as soon as icicles form on their manes. But I have always led brave men in arms in order to achieve the honor of immortal fame. . . . What great help will you northerners lose in a single Isotta, if she is laying down and about to die! For if I suffer, the troops will suffer along with the rest of the army.[67]

The image here is of Sigismondo as a strong warrior, able to withstand the harshest cold and push himself further than any general in pursuit of glory, but that strength is subverted by the power of his love for Isotta. Just as the living Isotta inspires Sigismondo to fight bravely for glory, so the dead Isotta would turn the tides of war.

Up until this point, the conceit could be plausible, in that it could be an exaggerated account of an actual illness. But Basinio's next response is the letter that Sigismondo had feared. The poet informs his master about the death of Isotta. Before she died, Basinio was able to see her:

> As soon as I began to console her with your words, she seemed eased of such great ills. She was not afraid of death in itself, but the idea that love might abandon her disturbed her. Ah how many times she poured out tears as I told her the words from

> your mouth. She asked: "Is heroic Sigismondo, my hope, well? If he is well, I must be entirely saved. I do not fear Persephone, not the iron omens of death, not the nearest kingdoms of Dis in Styx. As long as Sigismondo is safe and sound, no Isotta will perish. I will survive if he is saved."

Even though it would have demonstrated the divine power of his verse, Basinio's poetry did not save Isotta. She dies. Basinio's comforting words alleviate her pain but also free her to accept her inevitable demise in the knowledge that her beloved is safe and that their love will continue even after she dies:

> Although a great pallor came over her after she had scarcely spoken these words, she was still quite happy. Her head fell down and her lips spoke up no more, nor were they able to speak aloud . . . with trembling sobs she moved the air and said: ". . . O cruel gods . . . I beg you to take pity on that divine king [Sigismondo]; I am not asking for these gifts for myself. It is enough for wretched me to serve a powerful lord; it is enough for me to be present quite often at his feet. I beg you, gods, grant these just gifts; give them to such a great commander. You once gave Achilles power and arms; it is fitting that you not deny Sigismondo his life. Achilles was worthy to mount Hector's chariot and able to wage war."

Isotta's last prayer is for the gods to favor Sigismondo and provide him with the tools to achieve victory in battle. She is not the divine one here. Isotta acknowledges her beauty but insists on her role as a servant "at his feet," content to please and serve him. Her words, Basinio writes, "could have moved savage tigers," and no one could "hold back tears." Isotta finally dies: "Although her breath had come to its final hour, it gave forth ambrosial sounds. Then little by little her entire face grew pale, just as a sunny day becomes cloudy. She appeared neither dead nor alive." In the remainder of this poem, Basinio describes the "new tomb" for Isotta that Sigismondo had built to show her "glory":

> She rests high up in the temple of your titular deities [Genii] and stays in snow-white marble, a high goddess, whom twin distinguished elephants carry to the stars and marble brightens with eternal images. She rests in a sacred church, where the children of her dear body are: both men and women bewail her bones. Every street is full of wailing and miserable howling, and the earth and marble ground resound. All things roar with howling women; old matrons and married girls moan. Birds are pounding their lamenting chests with beaks and fish hiding in frozen waters. Why am I referring to the feelings of animals? The elements mourn in wonderful ways. For when the girl had to be taken away and carried to the grave, great Jupiter intoned and groaned; stormy rains rushed down from broken clouds, and the black ground was filled with water from the sky. Hollow clouds put the distraught sun away into darkness.[68]

Although elsewhere Basinio shows his rivalry with sculptors, here he praises the "snow-white" marble of Isotta's tomb, the twin elephants, and Agostino's marble reliefs (fig. 6.1). Basinio stresses how the material and the artistry of sculpture raise the "goddess" Isotta "to the stars" with "eternal images." In his hyperbole, all mourn Isotta, even birds and fish, and the stormy rain that Jupiter sends.

The news has the expected effect on Sigismondo. In a distraught letter to Basinio, he compares himself to Orpheus:

> Day is not pleasant; neither night nor the brave deeds of my right arm can please me . . . such an immense grief has conquered my will, and a thousand dangers threaten my mind. I purposely avoid human contact, since I do not want to know my own life. Rather, I wander dazed in the frozen mountains and force myself to go forth on uncertain roads. Often I go to the marble tomb with sweet piety; often I look upon the bright sculptures in the new temple. With beating heart I have often brought my sad foot to her altar so that I might hear her words. And after I sense that she hears no complaints, I force myself to go outside.

Confusion, loss of purpose, and inability to socialize characterize the widower, who is still grasping for his beloved and some sign that she still exists and longs for him. He turns to Cupid and Venus for help:

> Oh gods, I beg forgiveness for where my grief is leading me; oh holy child and you, nurturing mother Venus. You granted me a beginning of such a great love, now put an end to your divine wills. With you as my guides, let me go out into the entire world, rough beaches, and barbarian kingdoms, east and south, north and west.

But Sigismondo abruptly turns from pleading to forget his love to the opposite, longing to hold on and summon Isotta from the dead through black magic:

> Such great love is in my soul to address the ghost of Isotta and to believe in magic incantations. Let me use herbs and the strange power of stones. I am certain to disturb the dogs of hell. Hearing magical spells and often summoning the soul of my lady will please me. Drawn out of her tomb, she who is my life will perhaps hear my words. I myself will come alone to the nocturnal altars of Hecate and will recite spells known to the earth, just as the ever disheveled bacchante cultivates the Eleusinian mysteries with the torch of Bacchus. I will perform these ceremonies as long as life is left for me, and perhaps I will find my Isotta.

If he had read Basinio's poem, Pope Pius would have been shocked but not surprised at the images of Sigismondo eagerly performing the rites of black magic and necromancy and worshiping at the altar of Hecate, who was Diana, the goddess of magic and witchcraft. True Christian love would be comforted by the thought of heaven and not obsessed with a physical return to this life. Basinio's poetry certainly supports the pope's criticism of Sigismondo's ungodly passion for Isotta, whom, the pope contended, Sigismondo called a goddess and to whom he dedicated a church.

Basinio invents even more images of Sigismondo doing pagan rites that the Church would have condemned as demonic and akin to witchcraft.

Sigismondo, the confused lover, asks the poet about life after death, the divine secrets revealed only to poets: "Come now, Basinio, for Apollo confers his divine desires on the poet, advise me, while I am pressed by such great misfortunes, whether ghosts, who wonderfully live again, can touch and shades and souls be held." Sigismondo then returns to his attempts to contact Isotta using black magic:

> In my grief, I wander as a pilgrim through the whole world [collecting flowers and stones]. With all these and other herbs I will try to open her tomb and summon her pious ghost. Now let Medea give me her powerful herbs and potions, and with them I want a thousand poisons.

Sigismondo is shown invoking the greatest evil witch of antiquity, Medea, who murdered her own children and brother. But desperation and doubt over the efficacy of séances and magic to bring back Isotta plague Sigismondo. There is nevertheless no sense of Christian guilt over using the dark arts, only the fear that they will not work:

> Woe is me! Why am I arming myself in vain with the arts of magic? No incantations please my insane mind. I would have a good mind, if the life of my girl were summoned and came before my face. And let her come, as she once was, with her hair decked out, as artists sculpt her in bronze. And let her want to wear her pink tunic for me, or, if it pleased her, the snow-white or purple one. And let her not come pale with a sad or tough face, but let her be elegant and remain with her ambrosial cheeks.[69]

In the end, all Sigismondo needs is to see Isotta, happily clothed and dolled up to look her best. His fantasy centers on Isotta's physical beauty. She says no words nor does any actions. Sigismondo is describing a picture of Isotta—a portrait of his lover to make her present once again. The only portraits we have of Isotta are the profile medals of Matteo de' Pasti. Basinio may have been imagining this medal, since Isotta's pulled-back hair is meticulously shown in the bronze, though of course bronze could not show the pink of her tunic or of her cheeks (fig. 6.2).

Basinio's response to his invention of the mourning and desperate Sigismondo is a prophetic tour de force that finishes the entire book of poems with both the *deus ex machina* of Isotta's return to Sigismondo as a favor-giving goddess and the guarantee of Malatesta fame for posterity. Comfort takes the form of prophecy, as Basinio asserts the divine power of his poetry to uncover the secrets of the future and to immortalize Sigismondo and Isotta. As if in answer to Sigismondo's craving to see Isotta in her fully styled hairdo, Basinio declares:

> Isotta will come with ornate hair, as she was ornate in your kingdom. After she has become a goddess, she will lead you through the wild enemy, and, like a thunderbolt, she will guide eager horses. . . . Whatever she will be (for she will not be lost in the shadows of Styx), whether goddess or nourishing spirit of heaven, she will not bear your begging, your pleading; but she will come as a girl sent from the heavenly abodes. Do not cry; shower just prayers on pious spirits and win over the great gods with gifts. Ask her, and she will willingly assent to friendly prayers and grant you your great requests.[70]

Isotta will not lose her body to Styx but will have the same hair style as when she was living. When Isotta returns as a goddess, the new golden age will come:

> Then the entire human race will give you praise and worship you as equal to the stars in beauty. After you have climbed the starry sky of heaven and the great palace of heaven has summoned you, another golden people will be born to the world and there will be rivers of snow-white white milk again. . . . and the most celebrated fame of the ruler of Rimini will live on in monuments and the highest glory of the unconquered commander.[71]

Sigismondo will live on in the memorials that he leaves for later generations. As a god, he will ensure that another golden age returns. At the most basic level, however, Sigismondo's victories make him attractive to Isotta—so attractive as to conquer death itself.

The story is pure fiction as Isotta was not dead. Basinio used the supposed death to draw out pathos and to emphasize the lengths of Sigismondo's love, even at the risk of making Sigismondo into a demon-invoking, spell-casting witch. In playing with different themes, Basinio shows a multidimensional dynamic love that elicits strong emotions of jealousy, desperation, and longing—even beyond the grave. Petrarch explores the power and pain that he, the poet, feels in loving Laura. Basinio imagines love as a mutually destructive force that often centers on negatives, on the lover bewailing his or her absent or dead beloved. This love is jealous, desperate longing that is ultimately satisfied in a way that Petrarch's love for Laura could never be. Like Laura, Isotta dies, but, unlike Laura, Isotta becomes a goddess, who receives prayers and grants favors. This love is erotic and pagan. There is an afterlife but no evidence of a monotheistic all-powerful God, only the goddess Isotta who will answer prayers and come back to the living to start a new golden age with Sigismondo. The journey is melancholy, which gives their love remarkable human dimensions, but the ending is triumphal and celebratory.

Porcellio on Jupiter's Love for Isotta

The most beautiful girls in antiquity attracted the attention of the gods. Apollo chased down Daphne, and Jupiter had many human paramours. Malatesta poets praise Isotta's beauty for exciting the lust of the gods and causing discord in Olympus, as gods fought for her hand, and goddesses raged in anger. Basinio first described the turmoil that a beautiful woman could cause in Olympus. At the triumph in Florence, Sigismondo puts on a garment that Isotta wove with the loves of the gods:

> Sigismondo put on a stiff cloak, which Isotta, a goddess of girls, wove by hand in gold with wonderful figures. She began with the frequent loves of the gods and dressed Jupiter in the figure of a river swan, soft feathers sticking to his skin, whenever he played with open wings in the lap of Leda; how Apollo burned with great love for Daphne and leapt across the Peneus river in a swift run, as she let her hair fall down her snow-white neck behind her in the placid breeze. This ornament, this beauty the girl wrought through her art.[72]

Isotta's sexual allure is even more tantalizing in her association of the seductive Sigismondo with the playful swan in Leda's lap and Apollo lusting after Daphne. The sensuality is unabashed and inescapably pagan. In this context, *diva puellarum* is best rendered as "goddess of girls." The next lines elaborate on this divinity:

> Jupiter lusted after Isotta on account of her outstanding beauty, manners, and birth. Discord arose, disturbed the gods, and spread through all the heavens. But Isotta followed the advice of the gods: while her sweet life remained, she took Sigismondo as her first lover, but, when she died, she joined herself as a goddess to Jupiter in high heaven.[73]

Basinio's argument is certainly flattering: Isotta is so beautiful that at her death, Jupiter will make her a goddess and take her as his lover. The logic gets more complicated when we recall that Sigismondo is also destined to become a god. Basinio's image contrasts with the Christian ideal of chastity and its oft-perceived dangers of physical beauty. One extreme example is Saint Lucy, who gouged out her eyes because they had attracted the attention of a lover.

Porcellio developed the idea of Jupiter's lust for Isotta in his book *On the Love of Jupiter for Isotta* (1455).[74] Probably just before Porcellio and Basinio quarreled over the status of Greek, the Neapolitan poet imitated his more accomplished but much younger rival. This may have been one of the poems that Basinio criticized, provoking Porcellio's ire and igniting the controversy. Like Basinio's *Isottaeus,* this book is made up of poems in the form of letters and speeches, supposedly authored by Jupiter, Isotta, Sigismondo, Mars, Apollo, Saturn, the Moon, Mercury, Venus, Athena, and Earth. Porcellio's book (forty pages of Latin in the 1539 edition) treats many of the same themes as in Basinio's more developed and accomplished poetry. In the first letter Jupiter bewails to Isotta how Cupid has made him suffer, "that you would rather follow the rule of Sigismondo than the arms of Jupiter." He declares:

> Although [Sigismondo] is the pride of youth and outstanding in arms, his fate is mortal and the gods immortal. Although he rules over numerous peoples, administers justice, is a god of

> poets and music, the greatest commander in deeds, virtue, and faith, and an ornament and great glory of his age, how can he compare with me? I throw lightning bolts and am the greatest king of men and the father of the gods. Jupiter's rule turns heaven; Jupiter guides everything in his judgment and will. I breathe souls into bodies and allocate lifetimes.[75]

Such overblown praise of Sigismondo as preferred over the king of gods dominates the poem. The arguments that Porcellio has Jupiter use verge on being offensive to Sigismondo. Jupiter asks Isotta if Sigismondo can give her "greater honor and glory" than he can. He accuses Isotta of impiety: "What power does Malatesta have? In joining him, are you despising supreme Jupiter and the gods? You know not whom you despise. Sigismondo takes up arms at my will and serves at my command." In conclusion, Jupiter promises after her death to make her a "noble star at the feet of Jupiter."

In response, Porcellio's Isotta says that when she read Jupiter's letter, she "collapsed out of shame, and my heart became colder than marble. My servants ran to me, screamed, tearing their hair, and picked up the cold limbs of their lady." Isotta tells Jupiter that if Sigismondo discovers the letter, "he will no longer give sacrifices and pious incense to Jupiter." If, she says, Venus and Cupid have overcome you, the king of the gods, then "you have neither the highest honor nor glory, and the name 'all-powerful' is false." Once Jupiter starts acting like the god he is, Isotta says: "I will obey your wishes and commands." Isotta is specific about what the gods should give mortals: "I gain the laws of modesty, the examples of virtues, and faith preserved always with piety. These are the examples that the gods have given virgins, and this is what makes us equal to the gods." The image here is of an Isotta so strong and confident that she lectures Jupiter on morality. She is probably referring to the virgin goddess Diana, but she also might be criticizing the other gods for their lascivious behavior, often noted by early Christians. She tells Jupiter to "control his furies." Sigismondo, Isotta says, is "the god of my heart. I prefer to follow him through snow and horrid arms, than to follow you, although you yourself are a god. . . . If mortals earn heaven through virtue, then Sigismondo has especially earned it through his glory alone." Isotta then describes the signs of Sigismondo's divine virtues and generosity, including the architecture and sculptures in the Tempio: "Here, my Jupiter built for me a tomb resting on twin elephants." And she compares his exploits in battle to Alexander's and Caesar's. In conclusion, Isotta upbraids the god: "Shame on you for writing to me, O father of the gods and king of men, and shame on you for trying to seduce a modest girl."[76]

Jupiter does not give up but writes another letter to Isotta to convince her to leave Sigismondo. He says that Sigismondo is only a "leader of men, but I am the father of the earth and the heaven-dwellers . . . he gives his laws to his subjects, I give life and take it away . . . and I give my laws to men and gods." Although Porcellio is trying to praise Sigismondo, the drawn-out absurdity of the comparisons is not at all flattering. How could it be? Jupiter promises to father a divine child with Isotta, just like Hercules and Bacchus, who had human mothers. In frustration, he curses Isotta: "Let her die and then think about her Sigismondo. Let him wail, since he cannot help his lover, and let him ever cry over her death. Let him accuse me of sending thunderbolts, and think nothing sweet after this." Tormented love is one thing, but wishing your patron dead could hardly have been well-received praise. Like Basinio, Porcellio imagines Isotta's death and Sigismondo's misery in order to stress that this is not a Christian ideal of earthly chaste love. Jupiter nevertheless ends more positively: "Be mine, let me be yours: when you die, I will immerse you in Lethe, and you will become a goddess, equal to Jupiter."[77]

Sigismondo now enters the debate and writes a letter to the god Mars, asking him to intercede on his behalf. Sigismondo protests that he has always followed Jupiter's commands. If Mars helps him, Sigismondo promises to offer incense on his altars, to place garlands on the god, and to have two statues made of him.[78] In the next verse epistle, Mars enlists the help of Apollo. "In Rimini," he says, "there is a goddess with an outstanding body, a goddess worthy of her Caesar, Sigismondo . . . no female is equal to her, no goddess. . . . He equally burns in his hot marrow for her. He lives in love with her, she in love with him." Mars has a plan to distract Jupiter. He tells Apollo to tell Jupiter that he has seen a beautiful nymph that "you would put among the goddesses or demigoddesses." The danger of course will be keeping it from Juno's jealous ears. We must do this, Mars says, because Sigismondo is "born of divine origins, first among heroes, and a demigod." Mars refers to the sacrifices and devotional acts that Sigismondo has made for the god and insists that the gods owe him their help.[79] In a letter to his father, Saturn, Jupiter complains of the "gods conspiring against my wishes." Nothing, he says, will move Isotta. Jupiter describes how Apollo came to him in a golden chariot and begged him to stop trying to convince Isotta: "Remember that you are Jupiter, the most famous of the gods, and it is disgraceful for gods to be soft. If your lust is so great, you have your choice of a thousand girls to enjoy." Mars takes a harder approach and warns Jupiter that if he persists, "ancient chaos will return and mix the cold with the hot." Jupiter begs Saturn to "put an end to their traps" and help him to win Isotta.[80] Saturn in turn calls on Luna to intercede for his son. Jupiter, Saturn writes, "is melting like ice in the rays of the sun, and he suffers a thousand wounds from the blind god [Cupid]." Isotta, he says, "flees him, like a lamb flees a wolf" because she is devoted to Sigismondo: "She is the prince's goddess and he is the virgin's god." Porcellio calls Isotta a virgin and a lamb because he is perhaps imagining her before she accepted Sigismondo as her lover. Saturn tries to convince Luna to kidnap Isotta:

> Take the goddess while she sleeps at night, take her to the sacred shrine at Cynthus, and cover her chest with flowers and green leaves, so that when Jupiter sees her, he will be happy with his father. . . . After she is kidnapped to Cynthus and placed in a temple, he will hold the sleeping Isotta in his lap. Thus will Jupiter's anger fall and peace will return.[81]

The idea of a young woman getting kidnapped, stripped, and covered with leaves for the enjoyment of another male is hardly romantic; it is downright creepy. It is rape. As Luna is the chaste goddess Diana devoted to virgins, she refuses to deceive the "friendly modest nymph."[82] But Jupiter is relentless, and discord ensues in heaven.

War has broken out in Olympus over Jupiter's refusal to give up his infatuation with diva Isotta, and Mercury calls an assembly of the gods to make peace and resolve the problem. He describes the conflicts that have upset Olympus. Saturn ate his children but was deceived by his wife, who replaced a rock for Jupiter, who was then able to unseat his father as sole ruler. Jupiter in turn had to battle the giants. Now, however, the gods are fighting for a "squalid reason, and love moves arms . . . celestial spirits fight in a civil war, and the bloodied bodies of gods are falling." (It is not clear how immortal bodies "bleed" and fall, but the image is evocative of war.) This is not exactly a positive view of love: it is "squalid" and no justification for war. "Order has broken down, and even the stars are going to fight." However, Mercury argues, "[even though] Sigismondo was struck by the same arrow of Cupid, loves the same girl, and should rightly concede to Jupiter, Isotta favors Sigismondo, and the goddess has grown accustomed to living with this man. . . . Sigismondo is in her heart and always on her lips." The importance placed here on Isotta's choice gives her an independence not normally given to upper-class women in her time. She is the prize, but in this case the prize decides who is the winner. In mythology, Jupiter takes the women he desires without bothering to try to win them. In the end, Isotta's choice and her love for Sigismondo is the deciding argument: "That man, Isotta declares, is my Jupiter. May I die a blessed nymph in Sigismondo's lap."[83] This all leads to Mercury's proposed solution to the Olympian strife:

> As long as the fates stretch her thread whole, let the goddess Isotta live for Sigismondo, her commander. It is a worthy thing to place a mortal among mortal cares, and to join the endless to the eternal. But after fate has cut the girl's coil, let her be Jupiter's so that he may rejoice in his desire. Since she has lived modestly with her commander, let her become a new star in the sky.[84]

Although the plan works and is accepted, in terms of romance it nevertheless ends on an off note. Isotta and Sigismondo will be together in life, but at death Isotta will belong to Jupiter in such a way as to fulfill his wish or desire (*votum*). The eternal love of Isotta and Sigismondo will be broken and shared with another: "Let one death separate the two entangled [lovers]. Let mortal limbs belong to man, but after death let her shine among the stars before Jupiter."[85] Isotta becomes a star for her new lover Jupiter.

Porcellio left Rimini in 1456 and went to Milan, where he attempted to win the patronage of Francesco Sforza.[86] The humanist Francesco Filelfo, who at first welcomed Porcellio into his house, reported in a letter to Sigismondo that Porcellio had delivered an oration "before the prince [Sforza] and his entire court about your [Sigismondo's] divine virtues, which moved the listeners with its incredible kindness." Filelfo wrote that Porcellio "also showed some poems in twelve most pleasing epistles that were so full of your praise and glory that you should be judged the only prince of our time that the learned should venerate." The poetry, Filelfo continued, reignited "his love for Sigismondo so much that I could think of nothing more desirable or sweeter than you."[87] Filelfo's enthusiasm for Porcellio's mediocre verse is explained by an earlier attempt to win Sigismondo's patronage.[88] The opportunistic Filelfo, however, later revealed his true esteem for Porcellio. In a letter to another humanist in 1468, Filelfo called Porcellio "dirty and obscene" and laughed about Porcellio's habit of "blaming others for his own errors, like a most shameless monster." "The beast," Filelfo continues, "neither knows how to make an elephant care for a gnat, nor an eagle for a fly."[89] After Porcellio lost the patronage of the elephant (Sigismondo), he worked for a short period for the eagle (Federico da Montefeltro, the duke of Urbino).

The romance of Sigismondo and Isotta celebrated in the poetry of Basinio and Porcellio was a public and political ideal. Isotta's tomb, inscribed with the date of their adulterous affair, monumentalized this love and so was repeatedly celebrated by Malatesta poets and reviled by Sigismondo's enemies. The image of Isotta was propagated and diffused in both the poetry and the medals cast to be given as courtly gifts; like the tomb, the medals were dated 1446, when Sigismondo's wife, Polissena Sforza, was still very much alive. This erotic ideal of love has more in common with the pagan love poetry of antiquity than any Christian ideal of marriage, any medieval chivalric battle for unrequited love, Dante's ennobling Beatrice, or Petrarch's inspiring, emotionally vexing, yet unattained Laura. Basinio draws on Ovid's mythology and sensuality and Propertius's melancholy and magical remedies. The love that Basinio praises is not a chaste, unfulfilled desire but a fully consummated pleasure. Humanist wedding orators promoted a classically inspired marriage ideal that included mutual attraction and fulfillment of sexual desire.[90] Basinio similarly presents Sigismondo and Isotta's romance as love based on mutual longing and sexual enjoyment, but marriage is never even mentioned, and their consummated love is celebrated long before their official marriage. The classical poet Sextus Propertius (50–15 BCE) used similar images of love's torments, including his imagined mistress's death and entombed body, and magical incantations, but nothing as extensively described as in Basinio's poetry.[91] Both Basinio and Porcellio end their accounts in an earthly sensual triumph. Their poetry is both based in reality—as Sigismondo did marry and make an elaborate tomb for his lover—and a crafted fiction of a pagan erotic love that is central to Sigismondo's public image.

❖ 7 ❖

Questioning Virtue in Malatesta Literature

Heroes rarely find universal approbation. Hercules, Odysseus, and other classical heroes excited the envy of the gods and were punished with countless trials. Achilles and Aeneas angered rival heroes, who sought their destruction in fame and deed. Hannibal, Scipio, Pompey, and Caesar saw their reputations questioned. Sigismondo Malatesta was no different. Before his troubles with Pius II, Sigismondo had already had his detractors. Even his court humanists were not always the most positive publicists of Malatesta virtue. He had been a great patron to Guarino's students, but when he refused one employment, Sigismondo felt the sting of an irate humanist's pen. The Hungarian humanist Iannus Pannonius (1434–1472) wrote two damning epigrams against the patron who had refused him. Both question the sincerity of Sigismondo's literary circle: "When you read about the Malatesta triumphs and the splendid deeds of Sigismondo, you read nothing but the empty lies of frivolous poets, for whom hunger alone is their muse." The second epigram plays on the Malatesta emblem of an elephant: "Malatesta, the middling tyrant of Rimini, is sung throughout the world as greater than the highest Caesars. But poets are making an elephant out of an ant, and forcing flies to become Jupiter's thunderbolts."[1] Such invective was commonplace at a time when writers relied on patronage for their very survival. Basinio and to a lesser extent Valturio certainly fit the profile of humanists surviving off their pens by writing overblown flattery and presenting their patron as a classical hero and mythical commander. Despite their bombastic praise, however, Malatesta humanists also include criticisms of their patron. These problematic passages reveal the complex role that literature played in Sigismondo's court.

The Dangers of Classicism

Before and during Sigismondo's reign, patrons and writers questioned the use and morality of pagan poetry in Christian society. They raised issues about whether poetry was merely for pleasure or whether it could rise above puffery by providing examples to follow or avoid, and thus reform morals. Some of Sigismondo's Malatesta predecessors were interested in classical antiquity, whereas others were openly hostile, as they saw pagan literature as a serious threat to Christian morality. A distant relative, the lord of Pesaro, Malatesta dei Sonetti (1370–1429) earned some fame for his poetry, but his knowledge of antiquity was not remarkable. Another relation, Pandolfo II Malatesta (d. 1378), received a famous letter from Petrarch on the active and contemplative life, but again there was nothing unchristian in Petrarch's treatment of the theme. In fact, there was not the slightest whiff of paganism in Malatesta culture—quite the opposite. Sigismondo's learned but devout uncle and adopted father, Carlo Malatesta violently attacked pagan poetry and for a while was at the center of the debate over the value of pagan literature. Carlo had shocked humanists throughout Italy when in 1397 he had the famous statue of Virgil in Mantua torn down and cast into the Mincio River. Such an impulsive act of violence against culture was incomprehensible from a learned man.[2] Although devoted to Christian piety, Carlo had always shown respect for the fashionable interest in classical antiquity. For his brother's wedding in November 1395, Carlo put on a magnificent *ludus Troiae,* a re-creation of the Trojan War.[3] In 1409 Carlo hosted the Florentine humanist Leonardo Bruni for several months. He took Bruni hunting and enjoyed his company at banquets. In three letters, Bruni praised Carlo's erudition and debating skills. Bruni called Carlo the "most beautiful exemplar of great antiquity."[4] Carlo nevertheless condemned classical poetry and anything smacking of pagan religion. He had laws against blasphemy and idolatry passed and insisted that holy days be observed in Rimini.[5] At the news of the destruction of Virgil's statue, the humanists Pier Paolo Vergerio and Coluccio Salutati wrote letters in defense of pagan literature. Carlo had claimed that monuments should be reserved for saints, not pagan poets; and he compared poets to actors who peddle falsehoods. In his defense of poetry, Vergerio pointed out that Carlo himself paid for clowns to entertain his court and that he would be better off supporting poets, who could encourage virtue by celebrating the deeds of heroes. Vergerio acknowledged the value of statues of saints, but recalled how statues of heroes had encouraged great men, such as Scipio Africanus. Artists and poets should also be remembered for their gifts. Carlo nevertheless held fast to his beliefs. Fourteen years later Bruni recalled having shouting matches with Carlo over the value of pagan poetry.

Carlo's antagonism to poetry and general prudishness were voiced anew by a major figure in Sigismondo's court. In his treatise on the art of war, the otherwise humanistic Valturio restates the ancient arguments against poetry in Plato's *Republic* and Augustine's critique of theater in the *City of God* and *Confessions*. Unlike Carlo, who destroyed the statue of Virgil because he saw it as a locus of pagan idolatry, Valturio attacks poetry and theater for being detrimental to virtue and virility by promoting lust and effeminacy. He recalls how "ancient commanders used to make sacrifices to the muses before battle both so that they might remember their discipline and be ready for danger, and so that their deeds might be worthy of memory."[6] Valturio approves of this practice but only in a limited way: "Poets should be heard and read . . . especially when they offer great learning and wisdom."[7] Poetry must be didactic.

To stress the moral dangers of literature, Valturio appropriates whole sections of Augustine's critique of Roman theater. He repeats Augustine's example of the youth in Terence's play who is excited to wickedness by the shameful conduct of Jupiter with Danaë: "what will youths and maidens do when they see people watching this without any shame? Surely they will be told what they can do and be inflamed by lust, which is most excited by the eye."[8] Theater awakens Augustine's "lust of the eyes" and endangers morals. Valturio follows Augustine in arguing that the Roman gods wanted squalid plays put on for them, but at least the ancient Romans did not honor actors: "What except lust do the most shameful movements of actors teach and promote? Their bodies are weakened and softened into the gait and build of women, and with their immodest gestures they pretend to be shameless women."[9] Actors are dangerous to civic health and should be exiled: "when they pretend adultery, they teach it; and with their imagined rapes, they educate for real rapes." Poets, Valturio continues, also undermine civic and individual morality: "Plato saw all poets, except Homer, as adversaries in the ideal republic and judged that they should be ejected from the city lest their stories destroy the correct view of god. Plato did not tolerate injuries to the gods nor that the minds of citizens be hoodwinked and corrupted by reading such stories."

As his concern in the treatise is military, Valturio condemns love poetry or effeminizing verse as more appropriate for "Venus' army than the school of Mars." Such poetry "with its sweetness softens the spirits of the bravest men . . . and destroys all the nerves of virtue." The only poetry that Valturio approves is epic. In their descriptions of battles and heroes, Homer and Virgil promote an ideal of virility. Epic poets also provide good advice for leadership and strategy in war.[10] Valturio's critique is more of a caveat about certain kinds of lascivious verse than an outright condemnation. He praises Sigismondo's interest in Homer and the epic verse produced in Rimini. Valturio may have had some of the more erotic love poetry written for Sigismondo and Isotta in mind, but more likely he wanted to appropriate Plato and Augustine's argument to display his knowledge and because their arguments related to the overall purpose of his treatise. Both Carlo and Valturio's objections to pagan poetry acknowledged the power of words to affect the human condition, to influence behavior, and to tether the soul further to its sensual or celestial nature.

Although Sigismondo did not erect any statues to his court poets, he did bury them prominently on the side of a church and filled that church with numerous images of pagan gods, which would surely have been even more offensive to Carlo than a statue of Virgil in a town square. Carlo's criticism of pagan literature may have been echoed in Valturio's prudery, but these arguments otherwise fell on deaf ears, as Sigismondo was the patron of some of the most outrageously pagan verse in the Renaissance.

Sculpture and Poetry in Sigismondo's Court

Sigismondo was well aware of the power of literature and art. In obviously self-serving passages, Basinio and Valturio justify Sigismondo's cultural patronage by defending the role of letters and art in immortalizing their patron and his glorious deeds. In a chapter on triumphal commemorations and statues in antiquity, Valturio explains how the gods of Greek myths had once been men, who because of their accomplishments and great virtue were declared to be gods after their deaths.[11] Monuments and reverence easily turned into altars and full-out worship. Demigod heroes, such as Hercules, but also the Olympian gods including Jupiter, had their origins this way. By founding cities and building monuments in their names, Alexander and Caesar helped make themselves immortal and worthy of the worship due to gods. The pharaohs in Egypt built the pyramids, and the emperors Trajan, Hadrian, and Antoninus raised columns and obelisks in Rome for the same reason. Septimius Severus, Vespasian, and Titus erected triumphal arches that depicted their conquests. Valturio explains this process of divinization:

> The ancients made statues so that they might have some pleasure from viewing such images, and then a little later out of love they began to worship the memory of the dead kings, so that they might appear thankful to the well-deserving rulers and entice their successors to desire to rule well. As Cicero says, the life of man and common usage brings it about that fame and desire raise men excelling in good deeds to heaven. Because of their great virtue, Hercules, Castor, Pollux, Aesclepius, and Liber (Bacchus) were made divine, and the memory of brave men was made sacred in honor of the immortal gods.[12]

For this reason, Valturio continues, the Moors made their kings gods and the Romans made their Caesars gods. In Greece, three-time Olympic winners were deified. Valturio approvingly lists the extravagant statues raised for great commanders in ancient Rome. Effigies of Scipio Africanus, Pompey, Caesar, and Augustus in gold, silver, and bronze graced the forum.[13] Valturio's account of the commemorative role of monuments and sculptures in antiquity is largely lifted from the late antique Christian apologist Lactantius, who used these stories to dismiss pagan idolatry as false and manmade.[14] Although he plagiarizes Lactantius, Valturio eschews any moralizing about the false pagan gods and instead argues that triumphal commemorations and statues are important precisely because they lead to divinization and instill virtue.

Ecphrases of works of art were a trope in classical poetry, but Sigismondo's extensive patronage of sculpture was surely the reason Basinio included several ecphrases of sculptures in his poetry. There is a lengthy description of statues of heroes, poets, and philosophers in his early poem the *Diosymposis,* which is about a banquet hosted by Oceanus for the Olympian gods.[15] Apollo and the muses entertain the gods with song during their meal. The gods then go to the fields of the blessed and the temple of fame, where they see diamond statues of the heroes Odysseus and Achilles, followed by numerous poets. The divine poets (*vates*) are also sculpted out of diamond. The gods first see the Greek poets: Homer, Orpheus, Archilochus, Sophocles, and Aristophanes, among others; then the Latin poets: "the glory of the Roman tongue, who sang the fates and wars of Aeneas in the supreme poem" (Virgil), Horace, and Catullus. At the end of his description of the statues of the poets, which include lyric poets as well as playwrights, in addition to authors of epic, Basinio puts a statue of himself: "And I was no vain part of such a great labor."[16] Although he modifies the list, Basinio follows the precedent of Dante, who places himself among the great poets of antiquity in limbo (*Inferno,* canto IV). After the poets come statues of men "renowned for their fame and proud in their deeds." "Behold," Basinio writes, "two heroes with ivory scepters stand together: Augustus, by his fame the Caesar for all ages to come, then Sigismondo, shining in his family armor."[17] Next to them is a statue of Malatesta Novello, beloved patron of poets. Ecphrases of statues dominate this short poem, but likenesses of poets receive most of the praise, and this, along with Fame's lengthy address to divine poets, shows Basinio's preference for inspired verse over chiseled stone. He even makes the statues of artists ("artifices") out of mud and places them in the "shadows" outside the Temple of Fame to be forgotten in "eternal sleep."[18] Likewise, describing the statues of the poets as being made of diamond both exalts the poets and makes it clear that these are literary inventions, as such a sculpture was completely unfeasible. In her speech, Fame addresses the poets as "the priests of the goddesses." By calling poets *sacerdotes* (priests) of the *dearum* (goddesses or, here, muses), Basinio emphasizes the priestly role of poets, whose verse is able to penetrate divine mysteries.

The superiority of poetry to sculpture is a common theme in Basinio's poetry. In the *Hesperis,* Basinio recalls how after meeting Pope Eugenius IV, Sigismondo walked among the Roman ruins and contemplated the ancient statues of the great families of Rome:

> He focused on the temples and the altars of the gods, and, as he looked at the statues of ancient men, he ever bewailed that the fame of his ancestors had been lost on stones. He admired the statues of the Curii that were missing hands, and the Aemilians who completely lacked ears, the images of ancient tribes, and other Romans, whom it would take too long to recall. Sigismondo then said "what good is marble or faces like the living? Let a muse and her nine sisters remember me and all my deeds in a favorable song. None hid great-hearted Achilles in marble, a hard image in unrefined rock. . . . If such a poet arises in our time, I would like these signs for myself, not hard marble, but a tongue to convey my courage and declare my old triumphs."[19]

The passage recalls Horace's insistence that his poetry was "a more lasting monument than bronze" and Petrarch's contention that "human memory is fleeting, pictures fade, statues crumble, and in the mortal world nothing is more stable than letters."[20] Poetry lasts forever. Although Basinio portrays him spurning crumbling marble statues, of course Sigismondo was a major patron of sculpture. Basinio's passage reveals the artistic rivalry in Rimini in the early 1450s, a time when Basinio was composing his epic verse and Agostino di Duccio was carving marble for the Tempio. A part of the way Basinio competes is by drawing on models from a greater antiquity. Aeneas and Virgil would be the obvious models for epic verse in Rome, not Achilles and Homer. Basinio, however, saw himself as Homer and Sigismondo as Achilles. Here, Rome reminds Sigismondo of ancient Greece.

In the *Isottaeus,* Basinio explicitly argues for the superiority of poetry over art. He praises the bronze medals that Sigismondo had cast of Isotta but then asserts the superiority of poetry as a medium of praise. Basinio says that Isotta is the "most fortunate girl, worthy of father Jupiter and to have heaven as her home." Because of his poetry, he says, the fame of Isotta will never die:

> As long as the Malatesta reign and appreciate the Latin language, Isotta, you will read poems with me and Sigismondo, and after death you will live on, o goddess, with your commander.

> What good is it to cast your face in metal and produce your eyes in living bronze? Recently I saw likenesses of your face, which Sigismondo had had made with amazing artifice. Add the soul and they could equal your face in every respect; the human hand has dared to unveil such greatness. . . . Nevertheless, this image does not speak to your habits and spirit, and such a great face will be bereft of your charms. Dido, the lover, lives on, and famed Lucretia survives, but they both lack bronze. Poets do this, and their praise is splendid; they make your name eternal in the world. No centuries will silence your genius or your honest fidelity.[21]

The portrait medals of Sigismondo's beloved would be perfect likenesses if only they could capture Isotta's soul and habits. The rivalry between poetry and artistic representation is an ancient debate revived in the Renaissance. In several epigrams, for example, the Roman poet Martial (40–102 CE) describes how time destroys images but words are indestructible.[22] Artistic rivalry is no doubt at play here. Matteo de' Pasti's bronze medals were prized objects in collections throughout Italy. They were surely topics of conversation in Rimini, and Basinio describes himself admiring the medals.[23] Time will eventually destroy all sculpture because of its materiality, but is poetry any less ephemeral? Basinio purposely weakens his argument for poetic immortality in order to stress the need for the continued patronage of his poetry: you will be immortal as long as the Malatesta family continues to support poetry.

It is a testament to the power of poetry that in antiquity and the Middle Ages, Virgil's *Aeneid* was considered authoritative on philosophy and religion, so much so that church officials had to warn the laity not to practice the *sortes vergilianae*. This was a form of "Bible bingo" whereby people would seek advice in making life decisions by flipping to a random page in the *Aeneid*. Before becoming emperor, Hadrian consulted the *Aeneid* to discover how best to deal with the new emperor Trajan. Hadrian's finger landed on a prophetic passage about the future peaceful Roman king Numa Pompilius (*Aeneid* VI.808–812). Interpreting the passage as referring to his future reign and sanctioning his ambition, the young Hadrian married the daughter of Trajan's sister to solidify his succession.[24] Saint Augustine's conversion to

Christianity became a reality, when, upon hearing a child's voice, he opened a volume of Paul's letters at random and read the famous injunction to renounce fleshly desire and put on Jesus Christ (Romans 13:14–15). After climbing to the summit of Mont Ventoux, Petrarch played the same game with Augustine's *Confessions* and was similarly remonstrated.[25] Examples of this practice are plenty. There is a certain logic to using divine scripture or saintly writings as a guide to life, and of course for those with true faith, nothing is random. But why would Christians consult the *Aeneid*—a work full of pagan deities and religious doctrines at odds with Christian belief? Rhetoric, eloquent speech, and prose can persuade listeners and move them toward virtue or vice, but verse was considered more powerful; the music of its form can transport the meaning of its words to a higher realm. Even without its poetic form, the *Aeneid* was a compendium of pagan religious lore and sophisticated philosophical doctrines.[26] But in verse its content becomes prophetic. Lucretius tried to elevate epicurean arguments by putting them into verse and largely succeeded. Lucretius's truths were this worldly about banishing fear and living in the present. Virgil, however, was the mystic; he provided revelations about the other world.

In the fourteenth century, Boccaccio explored the divine role of poetry as the sum of cultural memory and the driving force animating life in history. He demonstrated the importance of poetry in his massive, multivolume *Genealogy of the Pagan Gods.* Poetry, Boccaccio stresses, originated in mythology and fulfills the need to give form to human life and make sense out of history. In recalling the origins of gods, heroes, and cities, mythology preserved civilization and served as an account of human creativity. Like mythology, poetry totalizes human experience and gives it meaning. In bringing back to life dead gods and heroes and long-destroyed cities, mythological tales and poems become antidotes to the destructive finality of time and death. In his *Life of Dante,* Boccaccio calls theology "God's poetry," and declares that only poets can penetrate into the divine and see the true relation of the changeable material world to the eternity of God.[27] In his *Divine Comedy* (1308–1321), Dante Alighieri makes the most influential argument for the poet-theologian and anchors the idea in Christianity. He interweaves Christian theology and pagan classical lore in his elaborate descriptions of hell, purgatory and paradise. Virgil is Dante's guide through hell and part of purgatory. As a pagan, Virgil cannot take Dante to the top of Mount

Purgatory and into Paradise. Another poet, Statius, whom Dante believed to be a secret Christian convert, meets Dante and Virgil in Purgatory and guides Dante after Virgil departs. In Canto 22, Statius declares: "Because of you I was a poet and because of you a Christian."[28] In the same way, Virgil had guided Dante. In limbo, Dante meets the unbaptized poets. Virgil joins Homer, Horace, Ovid, and Lucan, who, Dante writes, "[all] turned to me with a welcoming nod, and my master smiled, and they gave me an even greater honor, since they invited me to join their ranks, so that I became the sixth among such intellects."[29] In placing himself next to Homer and Horace, Dante showed himself to be a classical poet. But because of his Christian vision, Dante was superior to them all, even Virgil, who cannot pass into Purgatory, and Statius, who cannot reach Paradise. The pagan poets, however, have a special status.

Later writers continued to extoll the divine virtues of poetry. Before becoming Pope Pius II, Aeneas Piccolomini argued passionately that poetry was a far superior discipline to the study of law. "The poet," he says, "seeks honor and reputation by singing the praises of the gods and by extolling virtue and love; through these he makes a path to heaven while you remain earthbound with your precious gold and riches."[30] In Rimini writers extolled the humanist conviction of the power of words to move people and a quasi-religious belief in the divine nature of poetry. In his description of the Florentine triumph after Piombino, Basinio digresses to explain why both heroic commanders and poets were crowned with laurels:

> The archer Apollo sported perpetual laurels on his head, and the same prize was once given to poets and deserving commanders. They gave it to poets because of their eloquent tongues, and to commanders because of the fame they earned in battle. . . . Just as laurel leaves are eternally in bloom and below the ethereal sun shine high above the shadows, so do the fame of commanders and the indelible names of poets blossom.[31]

Basinio elevates poetry by equating it to military virtue and glory in battle. The implication is that just as Sigismondo is awarded an elaborate triumph for his victory on the battlefield, Basinio serves a vital function in Rimini and deserves reward. "Fame," he says, "is the god of men. It rolls through many mouths and great peoples, is carried to great cities through time, and is reborn in every age."[32] Poetry has divine power because it makes the inner man famous. Poetry can even replace a proper burial in a tomb and the presence of a mourning family. After describing the heroic death of a youth at the siege of Piombino, Basinio says: "You will lie covered in straw and decorated by no tomb. No father, no mother, no friends will gather your limbs; o tough rewards of raging war! Only our muses will remember you. Our consolation will be enough for you, since we offer poetry perhaps worthy of future fame."[33] Poetry serves as the greatest memorial of virtue since it records a narrative of heroic acts on the battlefield and proclaims the noble ends of warriors to the world.

In the presentation poem that he wrote to impress Sigismondo and request patronage, Basinio calls himself a second Virgil: "When I come to Rimini, a second divine poet after long centuries, I will bring the muses." Basinio promises to spread the fame of Sigismondo's glory, so that "every Arab," "the distant Moors, the Italians, and the Greek poets will sing your deeds," and when he dies Sigismondo will rightfully take his place among the gods, and everyone will worship him.[34] Such outlandish praise and prophecy from a poet is absurd. The flattery, however, worked, as Sigismondo hired Basinio as court poet and commissioned him to write his life as a classical epic.

In a verse letter that Basinio wrote in Sigismondo's voice to Basinio, the lord of Rimini praises the divine nature of poetry and urges Basinio to write more. He refers to Orpheus and the ancient poets who sang of heroes. After recalling some of the adventures of Jason and the Argonauts, Sigismondo declares:

> How often did Medea marvel at Jason reciting poetry, and the barbarian captive was stunned by his new verse! How often would she have preferred to give up her magical incantations and invoke the plucking of Orpheus' lyre! Whatever gifts poets had, I believe, were gifts of the gods; even barbarians cherish poets. Therefore, come, write willingly so that your sweet poems might soften for us the hard work of stiff Mars.[35]

Poetry is greater than magic: it entrances barbarians and comforts the exhausted. Basinio's verse, Sigismondo continues, recalls the beauty of

Rimini and reminds him of his love for Isotta on the battlefield, inspiring him to fight for glory.

Later, in the *Hesperis,* Basinio again emphasizes the importance of his poetry. When the character Sigismondo sees the poets in the Elysian Fields, he "looks up and restores their ancient honor." The economically precarious humanist poet is again asserting his worth before his patron. In Basinio's verse, Sigismondo duly shows his respect:

> O fortunate chorus of poets, who sing songs that please the gods, and fortunate heroes whom you sing about for posterity. It is no wonder that great Apollo considers you worthy of his wreath. Your poems are read above and below [Olympus], and your fame is no less on earth than it is among the gods. O chorus of divine poets be not concerned about death in either place. The bitter day of death comes with great gain, since another life awaits you and many honors. Go famous crowd of gods.[36]

Poets not only make heroes immortal with their verse; they themselves transcend the human condition. Poets are divine, as their songs connect the mortal with the divine.

Much of this was clearly self-serving, but Sigismondo hired Basinio after reading his letter, patronized other poets, and enshrined them in the Tempio. Poetry could raise the ordinary to the heavens and bestow immortal fame, but it could just as easily be used to criticize rulers, tarnish their image, and question their actions. Malatesta poetry is full of outlandish praise but also includes some negative images of Sigismondo. These passages suggest that poets in Rimini had some latitude and took their role as humanists seriously. They also reveal Sigismondo to be a tolerant, if not liberal-minded, patron. After all, Sigismondo sent copies of the *Hesperis* and Valturio's treatise on the art of war to other rulers.

Antiwar Rhetoric in the *Hesperis*

The *Hesperis* is the ultimate accolade for a ruler with classical interests. Just as the *Aeneid* became the paean of Augustan Rome, so was the *Hesperis* meant to be the call to unite Italy against a foreign invader under the single benevolent rule of Sigismondo. It may, therefore, be surprising that Basinio included extensive criticism of Sigismondo in the poem and ended the epic with a lengthy accolade of another hero. This was, however, a mark of classical epic. Even Virgil's virtuous Aeneas betrays flaws as, for example, when Aeneas is unable to control his anger in the last scenes of the *Aeneid* (X.537–541, 550–556). Basinio's contemporary Filelfo, in his mostly laudatory epic poem about Francesco Sforza, also includes criticism of his protagonist, even showing Sforza at times to be greedy, sadistic, and untrustworthy. There is nothing in Basinio's *Hesperis* as damning as Filelfo's description of the sack of Piacenza and the extensive laments over the city's raped and abused women.[37] The *Hesperis* is tamer and more in line with Virgilian epic than the *Sforziad*. By including subtler criticism of his hero, Basinio, like Virgil, eschewed any serious political critique and instead sought to capture the ambiguity of the human condition and thus make his poem more compelling and lifelike. The negative images that follow thus reveal more about Basinio the poet than about Sigismondo the ruler.

In the *Hesperis,* before the first big battle of the second Tuscan War, a large Italian army girded itself for war. Sigismondo had just inspired his men with an eloquent battlefield speech when an old man wearing an elaborate helmet depicting the sacrifice of Iphigenia at Aulis decided to speak out against the war and to question Sigismondo's motives:

> O ancient race of magnanimous men, noble Italians, what madness is commanding you to obey false Sigismondo? . . . what is this great fury you all have that at the command of one man you are leaving your ancestral lands and ancient homes to be prey for Alfonso? Hold back . . . if Sigismondo begins something great with his arms, this virtue does not come without wounding our homeland, and Italy is bent by the great burden of his deed. Therefore, come let us all leave him to go alone and wage a cruel war in vain, so that he may unhappily realize how much we do for him.

The sower of discord calls Sigismondo *vanus,* "false" or "a fake," a dictator who does not care about others and makes his subjects pay for his own glory and war-mongering:

> Indeed great men celebrate him as proud by our labor, but we commoners are given no honor, and as obscure souls, nobodies, and unknowns we lay hidden in the carnage. As often as fame reports him celebrating having routed great troops and enemy companies, so often have we protected him and snatched him from the greedy jaws of the enemy. These are the prizes that Sigismondo repays, the gifts for his great deeds. Besides, if honor were taken away and no glory given, Sigismondo the hero would still be outstanding in wealth and [could] reward his men with riches; [instead] he uses the gold everywhere in his castle and the silver, which he guards for the fatherland, to enrich his nobles and Latin allies. This is not liberty for the Italians; these are not the prizes of our labor!

The common soldiers do the commander's dirty work and protect him with their own lives in battle. In the end Sigismondo takes all the credit for their bravery, and the common soldiers are left with nothing. Greedy Sigismondo even steals from the patrimony of the city to enrich his friends and allies. The old man offers surrender and the single monarchy of Alfonso as the best chance at peace:

> Surely it would have been better to serve the Spanish tyrant or to suffer extreme hardship than to destroy ourselves among ourselves? If the fates command foreign tyrants to rule, let them rule. Let the Italians live under one king and let us not have so many kings, so many Sigismondos called to rule. Let us take away his arms and make him equal to the others. . . . Obey as commander the king, whom the fates of the gods have brought. Do not lose your bodies to the sword! Do not waste the wealth of your fatherland! Alfonso will see who were the guilty ones, he who once forgave all the citizens of Naples, and the Italians will finally have an end to their woes.[38]

The old man advocates appeasement to a single foreign ruler, who is sanctioned by divine fate. He presents Sigismondo as an upstart petty tyrant, one of many who prevent a united Italy. Far from making Sigismondo divine, he wants to strip the proud ruler and drag him down as an "equal" to the average soldier.

Basinio calls the old man Seneucus and says that he was "depraved, known for his biting tongue, and hideous in every respect. He was bald, with rotten teeth, and missing his right eye. His head sat upon a twisted necked and revealed wicked shoulders. He was a lame man and left curved tracks from a bent foot." Although it would be hard to describe a more menacingly ugly villain by Renaissance standards, Seneucus's speech would surely have been offensive in any context. His accusations are perhaps unremarkable if compared to the venomous attacks in Pius's invective, but they strike a discordant note in a laudatory and often sycophantic work dedicated to his patron.

The character Sigismondo's reaction to these criticisms of his leadership is anticlimactic. He seems to have heard the lengthy speech and allowed the old man to finish: "After he spoke, Seneucus wet his face with false tears and went quiet, as hatred rose in everyone. Sigismondo, whom he had scorned, ordered him thrown out of the camp and whipped with hard reeds."[39] Basinio first stresses the army's negative reaction to Seneucus's treason, then Sigismondo's punishment of the rebel with the equivalent of a spanking. No disavowals or justifications are given as responses to the accusations. Instead the old man is dismissed as the generic bitter sower of discord, who unsuccessfully tries to bring down the hero. This is also an example of the merciful commander, who forgives and does what he has to do without spite or vengeance.

Ferrante reacts differently to a similar situation in the same book of the *Hesperis*. When the Spanish hear that Sigismondo and the Italian army have come to expel them from Tuscany, they are shocked and disturbed by the news. A soldier named Tagus rises and addresses Ferrante and the Aragonese commanders:

> I fear Sigismondo (who is notorious to us) and his allies. I fear Sigismondo above all; with what great courage he puts himself in front of the Italians and denies the Spanish a place in Lazio. . . . Italy is unwearied by wars; a tough race, who rejoice in labor, are unconquered in courage and delight in their proud commander. If fortune has raised this man up, what land, what shores, and

> what seas will hold our commanders and the Spanish? . . . Will Sigismondo forgive Alfonso, if he begs? . . . Obey your Tagus' true warnings . . . and let us seek safe Naples, while the fates allow it, while Jupiter himself does not prevent it.[40]

For the character Tagus, Sigismondo's virtue and success in battle are the results of divine favor. The Spanish invasion had been successful before Sigismondo's arrival. His leadership unites the Italian people into an unbeatable fighting force. With fortune and the gods on his side, there is no way to defeat Sigismondo. The Spanish should give up, abandon Tuscany, and return to Naples.

Unlike Seneucus, Tagus is a powerful warrior, who usually fights alongside Ferrante. His words are therefore more dangerous to morale than the easily dismissed utterings of the old Seneucus. Ferrante feels the need to respond:

> O false Tagus, unlucky in courage and a coward of all men, renowned for your tongue! When we have need of a favorable Mars, and Pallas Athena calls us to battle, then your virtue is copious and the power of your tongue is more at hand than usual. But when there are no preparations for war and we are patiently enjoying a good peace, you are the first to demand war and make noise over everything with your eloquent words. . . . Allow me along with all my allies to confront the Italians and with our large force vanquish the few Tuscans and Sigismondo, whom you think the force of the gods and the entire force of man cannot beat. For Sigismondo is mortal, and, although he has hands like fire and passions like hot iron, I will prepare to fight against him. Mars belongs to no one, and fortune's arms are fickle. Since I have learned to be good at arms, do not think me fearful nor worry over my allies.[41]

Ferrante is surprisingly calm and logical. The silver-tongued trouble-maker has poor timing and always goes against the dominant winds: when war is necessary, he speaks against it; when peace reigns, he calls for war. Ferrante then counters Tagus's arguments.

Although he denies Sigismondo's divinity and questions his divine favor, Ferrante does not vilify his enemy. Basinio even has Ferrante praise Sigismondo—"hands like fire and passions like hot iron." Seneucus's attack is much more violent and cutting than Sigismondo's actual enemy, who does not talk of Sigismondo's tyranny or cowardice on the field of battle. Ferrante's response is practical. Tagus later falls at the hands of Sigismondo, and Ferrante prays to Jupiter to save Tagus, but to no avail.[42] Surprisingly, the cruel Ferrante is shown as being in some ways more accepting of criticism than Sigismondo; Basinio does not invent these episodes simply to showcase Sigismondo's greater clemency. Unlike Seneucus, Tagus is respected and a member of Ferrante's inner circle. The existence of these criticisms in the *Hesperis* raises potentially sensitive issues about Sigismondo garnering all the glory and his military conduct. By putting them in the mouth of a pathetic character, Basinio denudes them of their power. He also diffuses potential criticisms by addressing them.

Other Heroes in Sigismondo's Army

Sigismondo is certainly the central figure in the *Hesperis*. But several other warriors are praised and endure heroic deaths on the battlefield, sometimes at the expense of the main character. In the battle against the Aragonese, Sigismondo's beloved captain, Antonio da Narni, dies at Vada. As the Malatesta army is dodging arrows beneath the walls of Vada (fig. 4.1):

> A [Spaniard] seized a concave iron reed and with a sulfuric flame fired a leaden ball at Narni. Like a thunderbolt, the bullet fell through the air and split the fragile breeze. The unlucky man had hardly seen the sulfuric balls and the shadows of the dust [when] he caught the bullet in his chest; he fell over and black darkness covered his eyes, paleness discolored his bluish cheeks and his once purple nails, and the heat itself left his body. . . . Sigismondo especially cried, . . . sighing: "These were not my orders, o Narni, and I would never give you such commands; do not fight without me. . . . You fall on behalf of your occupied land, and rejoice to sleep in beautiful death. The Spanish leaders and the barbarian enemy will not go unpunished, Narni."[43]

In Basinio's rendering of the soliloquy, Sigismondo chastises Narni for disobeying him and fighting without him. Here courageous disobedience in the service of the state leads to a hero's death, one that the compassionate ruler must avenge, according to the laws of ancient honor.

A similar scenario is treated in a Latin oration in the Malatesta court. Pietro Parleo composed an oration on behalf of a captain who had committed a capital offense by disobeying a direct order from Sigismondo.[44] In his Ciceronian oration, which was probably a rhetorical exercise, Parleo draws on examples in Livy to justify the soldier's action and to argue that the authority of the state and tradition are superior to a dictator's commands. The classical values of honor, patriotism, and service to the state, which abound in Cicero's writings, are also exemplified in Parleo's main source, the ancient historian Livy. It was supposedly at the battle of Vada in 1453 when a captain in Sigismondo's army disobeyed a direct order from Sigismondo not to cross the battle line on pain of death. In Parleo's account, the captain saw a golden opportunity, broke formation, engaged the enemy, and achieved a stunning victory. Although he was victorious and saved many peoples' lives, according to Sigismondo's edict, the captain should be executed for disobedience. Like Basinio's epic, this oration also presents the 1453 campaign in classical language and form. But unlike Basinio, Parleo draws almost exclusively on examples from Roman republican history and presents war from the perspective of the entire army. Sigismondo's role is limited and criticized in favor of an unknown heroic captain in his army. In the oration, Parleo has the captain defend his actions by defining the nature of obedience and by arguing for the superior authority of ancient tradition over Sigismondo's command. True obedience, the captain argues, requires a man to think for himself: "Those are the best who both think by themselves and guide all things to their right end; they are in second place, who obey those correctly commanding; and those who neither think for themselves nor listen to good commanders are useless."[45] The captain claims to have been following the "will of the commander" and praises his initiative in taking advantage of an opportunity for victory: "If you, commander, had had the opportunity, place, and time, and the certain hope of accomplishing a doubtless victory, as I saw and understood with my long experience and knowledge of war; had you seen this yourself, surely you would have given the signal and commanded me to fight, and condemned my waiting and staying in place." Instead of following Sigismondo's orders to the letter, the captain uses his own "experience and knowledge of war" to support his actions. Finally, he warns (maybe even threatens) Sigismondo of the consequences of his condemnation: "I fear that you are seeking praise for severity, [but] will be accused of ingratitude, and that everyone will believe that you were envious of my bravery and denied the glory of kindness."[46] No ruler would want to appear ungrateful and envious of his subjects. In his defense, the captain claims that he was obedient to the larger purpose of victory over the enemy. He obeyed the will of the commander not the direct order. Obedience is only required when the command accords with the circumstances and reason. Baldassare Castiglione later addressed a similar problem of whether a courtier was required to act immorally at the command of his prince. The courtier's actions, Castiglione states, should guide the prince toward virtue and away from vice.[47] The courtier therefore must speak the truth even to an unwilling prince. In the same way, Parleo's captain insists that obedience is secondary to virtue and reason.

In addition to the claim that he was not disobedient to the commander's will, the captain calls on the authority of the soldier's oath—the *sacramentum*—against the commander's orders:

> That ancient oath (*sacramentum*), which we all swore before we entered the military, that we would always fight for your dignity, the safety of all, and victory, was before my eyes, and it occurred to me that our ancestors often swore to their consuls and generals that they would never flee, leave out of fear, nor break the line except to take an arrow, wound the enemy, or save a citizen. If I had scorned doing these this time, everyone would call me a perjurer, a hater of your rule, and a traitor of the army.[48]

The description of the *sacramentum* comes from Livy, who includes the same exceptions to the oath ("wound the enemy, or save a citizen").[49] The introduction of the *sacramentum* leads to the most radical critique of Sigismondo's rule. Parleo's captain asserts the superiority of precedent and ancient tradition to the authority of the prince: "For we are all bound more to that ancient oath than to the recent edict of a commander (*ducis*). For those things that come before in time are rightly superior, since they were not annulled." The captain then lists no less than seven inviolate eternal ideals that are superior to a commander's ephemeral orders: "We owe more to victory, more to welfare, more to trust, more to the oath, and more to our homeland, religion, and worship, which ought to be always firm and inviolate, than to the orders of commanders, which change according to place, subject, and time; especially if, while [we are] following the orders of our commanders, a manifest loss occurs to the state."[50] The soldier's ancient duty to his oath, religion, and patriotism, all trump Sigismondo's orders.[51] The captain explicitly states that Sigismondo's orders were faulty and would have led to a disaster, had he obeyed them. Unlike Basinio's image of heroic divinely inspired leadership, Parleo's oration emphasizes the transitory and fallible nature of rule.

When he wrote this oration and perhaps delivered it, Parleo was employed in Sigismondo's court as official historian and teacher of classics. The fact that he is openly critical of Sigismondo is an example of how much license humanists had in the Malatesta court. The oration, which I have discussed at length elsewhere, is full of descriptions of republican heroes and arguments for self-sacrifice, duty, and true virtue to preserve the state. Although dependent on Sigismondo's patronage, Parleo reminds the prince that his power rests on the popular will and the competence of his officers. Sigismondo, he warns, should avoid the accusation of envy and ingratitude and embrace the many heroes in his army. Even as a showpiece or a rhetorical exercise, Parleo's oration is a radical critique of Malatesta rule in Rimini. It raises issues and problems about the nature of military power, the conduct of war, and the limits of a prince's authority. Because it is a rhetorical exercise, Parleo can rely on the license of genre to include potentially subversive content.[52]

Basinio also raises questions about Sigismondo's preeminence by ending the *Hesperis* with an account of the unparalleled heroism of another of Sigismondo's soldiers, Tolonius, who may never have existed. The Spanish decide to abandon the fortified city of Vada and head to their ships in the harbor. The Italians realize their enemies are escaping but are initially cut off from the harbor by fire, which Vulcan has spread to aid the Spanish retreat. Sigismondo quickly redirects the fire against the Spanish ships leaving the harbor. The Italian hero, Tolonius, "outstanding in courage, distinguished in his ornate armor, and already superior to his age in virtue," jumps into the sea, swims out, and grabs onto the side of a departing Spanish ship, calling them cowards and holding the ship back. Three ships pass by as the Spanish captain Alcon struggles to control his ship:

> In shock and gripped with bitter fear, Alcon sees the Tuscan hanging onto his ship and holding it back with his hand. "O wretched Tuscan," he says, "are you trying to bring the Spanish back to this land?" He said no more, drew his sword, and cut your right arm off, o great Tolonius. The arm fell trembling, useless in the watery waves. But young Tolonius held onto the boat with his left hand and continuously whipped the winds with the bloody stump of his right arm, while shouting: "What, Spaniard, are you threatening? You cannot leave here; you have no power. The other Tuscans are setting fire to your ships." He had hardly spoken, when the enemy sword sliced his left arm. Like the stump of a tree shorn of its branches in winter. . . . Tolonius held firm before the boat, throwing over his entire chest and still directing the ship to the shore. Shocked by this, the brave Alcon struck him on the head and scattered Tolonius' brain everywhere, but fell headlong and crashed the boat.[53]

The violence is absurd and drawn out. Having lost both his arms, Tolonius still manages to take the ship down with the bloody stump of his remaining body. Basinio ends his account with this lengthy description of Tolonius's last heroic deed. The Spanish escape or die in the water. Sigismondo tears down the walls of Vada and buries the dead. Wailing over Tolonius fills the air. Basinio writes a twenty-five-line-long paean for the fallen Tolonius:

> Oh eternal honor of our people, Tolonius, a distinguished name for generations to come that will never die. Piety, love of praise, knowing virtue, and glory ordered you to scorn death. Chance did not take you to your fate, but on your own accord you willingly submitted to distinguished death. The iron enemy was shocked by this example of ancient virtue, blood, and courage. All shouted that the Tuscans had iron chests . . . and would not yield . . . with the great ship of your body, o Tuscan, you took down such great bodied men. O the shame, your right arm

> snatched by a cruel wound! O dead youth, worthy of king Nestor! O great honor, killed before your time, have you not decorated our triumphs with eternal praise? Mars of course envies you for daring such great honor in your youth and raising your soul over the stars.[54]

The sentiments in this eulogy sum up the warrior values of pagan antiquity. Love of praise, virtue, and the search for a glorious death are the mark of the pagan hero. But it is Tolonius who is "an example of ancient virtue," not Sigismondo.[55] Mars envies Tolonius for his heroic daring, which made him divine, not Sigismondo. In an epic about his patron, Basinio ends his poem with a lengthy description of another hero's dramatic death and then a panegyric for this other hero. Following the Tolonius episode, the last forty lines of the entire poem describe the history and beauty of Rimini and Sigismondo's building of the Tempio in fulfillment of his vow to the gods. For Sigismondo, this must have been an anticlimax. Basinio mentions Sigismondo only in passing. By including these other heroes, Basinio makes his panegyric more complex. Sigismondo is not so much the lone hero as the inspired leader of heroes. He is nevertheless still a god, and his great charisma inspires his men to heroic action.

Sigismondo's Prowess and the Debate over Ancients and Moderns

The debate about whether the moderns had surpassed the ancients was a favorite topic of the humanists. Basinio had no doubt that Sigismondo had equaled and in fact rivaled the ancients in his prowess:

> O Sigismondo, I will never be silent about your deeds, you who saved the pious kingdoms of your Italy. For who would have been silent about the greatest wars of great-hearted Achilles? (Even you, sweet Homer, would be insane to do so.) Who would not sing on his ivory lyre about Hannibal? Or who had great honor in Troy? What ungrateful [poet] would allow the tough Scipios to lie dead, their bodies in unknown soil? Should my muses then be silent about you, o most brave one, since your fame already surpasses the ancient commanders?[56]

In arguing for the need of epic poets to preserve the deeds of heroes, Basinio equates Sigismondo with Achilles, the Scipios, and, surprisingly, the ferocious yet brilliant Hannibal, who all but destroyed the Roman Republic. In the last line, Basinio unquestionably places Sigismondo before all the ancients. Such unadulterated praise for his patron, however, is not echoed by Valturio.

Valturio may have praised Sigismondo as "divine and sent from heaven," but he was well aware of Sigismondo's human limitations and supplied the necessary rhetorical spin to recast failure. As discussed previously, Valturio criticized the prevalent practices of astrology and augury in Sigismondo's court. In the chapter on triumphs, Valturio describes Sigismondo's defense of Venice against Francesco Sforza, an embarrassing episode, which a more laudatory writer would have skipped. Valturio highlights the fact that Sigismondo was put in charge of the entire Venetian army but blames the failures not on Sigismondo but on Sforza's deceit and the Venetians' inability to listen to Sigismondo: "and the success of the desired hope in you would not have been lacking, if they had followed your advice."[57] Valturio's interpretation is awkward and faintly desperate.

Who could honestly live up to the standard of Alexander or Caesar? Italian rulers were constantly told to model their behavior on the ancient commanders.[58] It was exactly this classical yardstick that prevented Valturio from portraying Sigismondo as the greatest commander ever. At first glance, Valturio's numerous snippets of praise for his patron in his treatise on the art of war suggest a humanist's greasing. But if this were indeed the goal—to present Sigismondo as the new Caesar or Alexander—Valturio would not have held back in the most important topic for praise in his work, whether Sigismondo has equaled the ancients in his prowess and the art of war. In a chapter on the classic question of which ancient commander was the greatest, Valturio copies out whole pages from Livy and Plutarch on the ancient debate with abbreviation but little paraphrase.[59] Valturio looks at each commander's virtue against the "divine will of Fortune." Achilles, for example, had greater bravery and virtue than Hector. Brennus, who united the Gauls against Rome, Hannibal, Pyrrhus, the two Scipios, and Pompey are all praised. Following his ancient sources, Valturio declares Alexander "the greatest" and then calls him inferior only to Caesar. Only at the end of the long chapter does he turn to the commanders of his own day. Valturio declares that no living commander can match the prowess of the ancients:

> Whoever thinks with insolent and bold determination that recent deeds should be compared to the accomplishments of these great commanders and emperors must not have any knowledge of antiquity or truth. For I would especially desire that the excellence of these commanders should be brought to our times and our commanders, but as I think over the crafty and clever advice of our ancestors, and their wondrous, incredible, and almost divine glory in the military arts, as a fair and unbiased judge, I find no one whose deeds should be in their own right compared.[60]

Only after explicitly arguing against the possibility of any Renaissance rivalry does Valturio finally say that Sigismondo comes closest to the unattainable splendor of the ancients:

> But for all that, o most energetic commander, Sigismondo Pandolfo, since among famous and illustrious men, there usually exists a rivalry, as to who are thought worthier in military skill, the use of arms, the number of battles, the variety of peoples and enemies [conquered], honesty, prudence, dignity, trust, constancy, magnanimity, speed, and the other outstanding signs and virtues of commanders, and as to who seem to approach closest to those ancients; some may place the others of our age in the same middling place, but with credible arguments and without controversy they always not only place you before the rest, but find agreement with the greatest men versed in such matters. This is not in the least doubted, but brighter than light to anyone recalling the greatness of your exploits, since you alone up to now have held upon your shoulders, like Atlas, an Italy, mangled and broken by the fires of so many wars and threatened with extreme ruin; you were summoned here to prevent Italy as a whole from totally collapsing upon herself. . . . In fighting, daring, and acting everywhere you endured all this with magnanimity, splendor, glory, virtue of mind, and the strength of your arm, so that not only to all of us, but to foreign countries and the most distant peoples, you easily appear the first among the most

> excellent and experienced commanders, who are the most warlike and learned in combat.[61]

The reader expects Sigismondo to rival the great commanders of antiquity. The very last line clearly refers to the earlier statement that Sigismondo is the greatest commander among his contemporaries, not as compared to the ancients.[62] Why does Valturio not praise Sigismondo as equal, if not superior, to the ancients? Such a failure on the part of a court humanist, a paid flatterer, is telling of how seriously Valturio and Sigismondo looked to the example of the ancients. Despite these reservations, Sigismondo is the only modern that Valturio includes in his massive treatise on war.

An even greater rebuff of Sigismondo occurs in the oration that Giannozzo Manetti delivered in front of Sigismondo and his men in the field before the siege of Vada in 1453.[63] Manetti was one of the Florentine ambassadors entrusted to hand over the baton to Sigismondo to command the Tuscan forces against the Aragonese invasion.[64] Although the purpose of the oration was formally to hire Sigismondo as military commander of Florence and its troops against the Aragonese incursions, Manetti also praises the Malatesta family and their numerous alliances over the years with Florence, discusses the nobility of the military arts, and argues that every city should have a *milizia* for its own protection. Manetti draws extensively on Leonardo Bruni's popular treatise *De militia* ("On Knighthood") (1422), for his discussion of *milizia,* Roman triumphal crowns, and ancient political ideas from Aristotle and Cicero.[65] In his life of Manetti, Vespasiano da Bisticci says that Manetti delivered the oration in the vernacular so that the entire army could understand it. He writes that the oration was "thought so worthy that no more could possibly be said about military science."[66] Vespasiano apparently thought that the encomiastic oration was an appropriate genre for military theory. By contrast, the humanist Naldo Naldi concentrates on Manetti's rhetorical form and delivery: "Everyone in the army attentively listened and were so stupefied by the elegance and dignity of his oration, that he obtained the highest praise and glory for it."[67] In a biography dedicated to Manetti and his eloquence, the subject matter of the oration, Sigismondo and the military arts, is not important.

Two recent Italian scholars have seen the oration as marking a shift toward the triumphal imagery of Sigismondo that was just then being fashioned in the art of the Tempio.[68] But in the oration, Sigismondo barely receives as much praise as his ancestors; in fact, Galeotto receives lengthier and more detailed praise for hiring John Hawkwood to fight for the Florentines against the Pisans in 1369. Sigismondo, Manetti says:

> . . . was born from such brave valiant commanders; and to this natural origin he added a continuous use and practice of military exercise from the time he was thirteen until today; one cannot nor should not doubt reasonably that he has the best intelligence and a singular skill at arms, especially since he is endowed with wondrous ingenuity and a profound memory.

Manetti makes this rather bland praise for Sigismondo even less impressive by giving the credit for Sigismondo's qualities to another mercenary captain. Manetti continues:

> [Sigismondo] served for ten years continuously under the command of the magnificent Francesco (Sforza), who was at that time a count but today by the excellence of his virtues the illustrious duke of Milan. [Sforza] is such an excellent master of the art and discipline of war in our times that he could deservedly compare and be equal to any of those famous and glorious captains of antiquity.[69]

Earlier in the short oration, Manetti had already praised Sforza after referring to the ancient debate over the best commander and Plutarch's comparison of Alexander and Caesar: "But why," Manetti says, "do we need to go back and recount more famous and celebrated examples of those brave and glorious ancients, when we have the notable and marvelous example of one before our eyes in Francesco Sforza, the duke of Milan."[70] Manetti's praise for Sforza continues for several lines, focusing on his conquest of Milan and great dominion in Lombardy. Why did Manetti praise Sforza so much and Sigismondo so little? Manetti was well aware that Sigismondo had already saved Tuscany once in 1448, when he himself persuaded Sigismondo to lead Florence; yet this is not even mentioned. The oration in fact appears to be a set piece in topic and examples, many taken from Leonardo Bruni's *On*

Knighthood. There are formulaic and legalistic parts about the baton and the nature of command in the midst of an antiquarian discussion with little or no detail about the specific occasion. Florence and Sforza were of course great allies at this time; the whole reason that the Aragonese invaded Tuscany was to get to Milan, where Alfonso and Ferrante had a claim. Perhaps Manetti had originally written the oration thinking that Sforza, not Sigismondo, would be given the command to defend Florence. As it is, Manetti's oration hardly reflects a turn to a more triumphal image of Sigismondo. At least Valturio had said that no modern could compare with the ancient commanders but that Sigismondo came closest to the ideal. In a well-received oration delivered in front of Sigismondo and supposedly in praise of Sigismondo, Manetti declares that another mercenary, Francesco Sforza, has equaled the ancients.

Ten years earlier, Manetti had written to another mercenary captain, Niccolò Piccinino, to request safe conduct and offer his laudatory pen. In the letter Manetti spends three pages on the great commanders, from the Assyrians, Medes, and Persians to the Trojans, Greeks, Macedonians, and Romans. Like them, he says, Piccinino has "waged war for no other reason than the desire for empire, fame, and glory."[71] Such flattering comparisons may not be surprising, but they show that Manetti could have easily praised the more successful Sigismondo with greater zeal. Piccinino's response to Manetti survives and provides a rare glimpse of a potential patron's reaction to humanist excess. "I do not have those praiseworthy qualities," Piccinino writes, "nor am I worthy to be compared to those great ancient commanders, as you do. I am rather a worm and a pirate (*saccomanno*) worth nothing compared to them."[72] Such candor and self-deprecation points to the awkward status of the mercenary as "pirate" or hero. Soon after this exchange, Piccinino perished at the hands of Francesco Sforza in 1444.

The debate over the superiority of the ancients or the moderns was a commonplace from antiquity (when it referred to an earlier age) that continued in the Renaissance. In his work *On Famous Men,* Petrarch had refused to include any men of his own time, since few if any could match the virtue of the ancients.[73] In the early fifteenth century, Leonardo Bruni had bewailed the impossibility of writing a biography for any of his contemporaries. The men of his own age could not compare with the giants of antiquity, whether in literature, statesmanship, or war.[74] Some humanists, however, took the modern side. Poggio Bracciolini called Alfonso of Aragon superior to Augustus, Trajan, Marcus Aurelius, and the Antonines. (Incidentally, the same author made no such claims in a dedication of a book he wrote for Sigismondo Malatesta.[75]) Benedetto Accolti and Gianantonio Campano praised the superiority of Renaissance military practice over that of the ancients in terms of discipline and the art of deception. Accolti also pointed out the invention of gunpowder, the use of cavalry, and advances in siege warfare and armor.[76] Valturio, in contrast, rarely goes much beyond his ancient sources and so misses the opportunity to extol actual military innovations in fifteenth-century Italy.

Valturio does repeatedly place Sigismondo among the ancients in specific categories.[77] Yet such praise is sometimes limited, especially where it is expected most. Basinio wrote an entire epic about Sigismondo's role in the two Tuscan Wars. In a treatise on the art of war, dedicated to Sigismondo Malatesta, Valturio barely mentions the victories at Piombino and Vada. Sigismondo's tactical genius and campaign victories receive only passing references and praise. The most detailed description, oddly, comes in a chapter on banquets. Valturio refers to the Piombino campaign. But it was not Sigismondo's skill and bravery on the battlefield that impressed Valturio the most. It was Sigismondo's conduct before the battle in camp. In a chapter on avoiding banquets in encampments, Valturio refers to numerous classical examples of commanders' eating habits: how Masinissa walked while eating, Hannibal ate once a day at sunset, Septimius Severus ate only vegetables in camp and made everyone drink vinegar instead of wine, etc. He then says:

> O Sigismondo, I cannot be silent about your great similarity and harmony with the best commanders and emperors. Nothing more similar could be imagined nor greater said, since in imitating them you have equaled and excelled every kind of man, commander, and emperor in your endurance of hardship, night vigils, thirst, hunger and every kind of anguish. For who does not know that you never spurn the most vile food? During the Piombino expedition you joined your men and ate not only the stale bread that they ate but bread that was black, hard as a rock, and green with mold and wooly fuzz, which dogs, low-lying animals, and pack animals loath. I ignore the acorns of cork, which

> you mix in like a condiment for flavor and seem like regal delicacies to you. I pass over the hot and sulphuric water from stagnant wells, and although you had no wine and the water brought sickness before quenching thirst, it seemed like nothing to you and your men to drink from those waters with great pleasure.[78]

It is certainly heroic in a way to eat rancid food and drink contaminated water with a smile. But this is not perhaps the most flattering praise for a patron in a book that Sigismondo himself would send to the Ottoman sultan and that would be copied in lavish editions for the libraries of Lorenzo de' Medici, Federico da Montefeltro, Louis XI, Matthias Corvinus, and other potentates.[79] Elsewhere in his treatise, Valturio insists on the value of lunch, citing the example of Leonidas, who encouraged the Spartans, saying: "Eat lunch as if you are going to eat dinner in hell."[80] The general who endures hardship as an example to his men is a theme in classical literature, but food heroism is not as common.[81] There are, however, similar accounts of food heroism in the lives of Caesar and Mark Antony.[82] For Caesar it serves as an example of his true nobility, as he willingly eats the rancid food a host gives him. Antony was probably Valturio's model, since Plutarch tells us that Antony was "an amazing example to his soldiers . . . drinking foul water contentedly and eating wild fruits and roots."[83] Plutarch's lives were translated into Latin in the fifteenth century and were very popular in Italian courts, as rulers found inspiration and models for their own conduct in the lives of the great ancient commanders.[84] It is faint praise to have Sigismondo equal the ancients only in his ability to eat gross food.

The early 1450s were the high point of Sigismondo's career. He had achieved two stunning victories against the Aragonese, and the art and literature in his court overflow with triumphal images of Sigismondo as a classical hero. Basinio went further than any other court humanists in immortalizing Sigismondo, even making him into a god destined to reside in Olympus. So why would Basinio include critical voices accusing Sigismondo of being a tyrant? Why would he end the grand epic with the heroic death of a minor character? The simple answer to both questions is that Basinio considered his poem to be more than panegyric. His ambition was to be a great poet, a new Homer and Virgil. In order to achieve this, his epic had to be literature; it had to have the complexity of the *Iliad* or the *Aeneid* and contain believable negative characters and contrary turns of fortune. Basinio refused Pope Nicholas V's offer to translate Homer because he wanted to produce enduring literature of his own. His poetry, as he asserted in the *Hesperis,* was meant to reach the ears of the gods on Olympus. The court historian Parleo showed the same devotion to literary form in his Ciceronian oration, supposedly delivered in front of Sigismondo. Like Basinio, Parleo reminds his patron and ruler that he is not the only man of virtue in his army. In his patronage and public image, Sigismondo consciously modeled his life on the ancients. The fact that both Valturio and Manetti refuse to declare Sigismondo superior or in some passages even equal to the ancients reveals how seriously humanists and their employers held the imitation of the ancients not only in words but also in deeds. Their refusal, especially on the part of Valturio, shows an element of sincerity in their praise and a remarkable tolerance in Pius's brutal ego-obsessed tyrant. Despite or perhaps because of the occasional blame and missing praise in their works, Sigismondo had his humanists entombed with full honor along with his family in the Tempio.

✣ 8 ✣

Sigismondo's Peril and Defiance

The bull that condemned Sigismondo to hell was widely distributed.[1] Pius made sure that all the rulers and clerics of Italy heard his warnings about engaging with Sigismondo. Sigismondo was also well aware of what had taken place. How did he respond to the spiritual and physical violence of Pius's decree? When a few months earlier, Pius excommunicated Sigismondo, Cicco Simonetta, the Milanese chancellor, reported:

> In these days His Holiness has pronounced a terrible sentence against Sigismondo in a public consistory of cardinals. He has decided to brand him a rebel against the holy Church, to confiscate all his possessions, [and] to excommunicate him. He has placed a straw man in Sigismondo's likeness in Campo de' Fiori, chopped off its head, burned it, and thrown the ashes to the wind. When Sigismondo learned of this, as far as we know, he lived in great fear and anguish.[2]

Whatever Sigismondo's inner state, he reportedly remained outwardly composed. According to Benzi in the invective: "even though excommunicated, Sigismondo fearlessly attended church services, not because he sought for anything holy in the church or was worshiping Christ in His house, but to prevent his subjects from learning that he had been judged a heretic, and to spite the Church's majesty by scorning her censures."[3] In the invective, the cool way in which Sigismondo took the news was further proof of his perfidy.

Others were uneasy at the pope's vindictive exercise of his spiritual authority. A Florentine present at the bonfire reportedly commented: "By

God this is ill done!" He was promptly arrested but later released "amid much laughter" since he claimed to have been criticizing not the pope's condemnation but merely the resemblance of the manikin to Sigismondo. But even Federico da Montefeltro, Sigismondo's great nemesis, found the whole performance "disgusting."[4]

Pius intended the reverse canonization to have a much more dramatic effect, to make Sigismondo feel the torments of hell while living. In the invective, Pius accordingly described hell and the eternal punishments of the damned in great detail. If Sigismondo thinks that he has lived a pleasant life and avoided the punishment of hell, Pius says:

> He knows not what stories are told about the afterlife, that those who did something impious and wicked are disturbed and tormented in hell by the burning torches of demons, and burned by a never extinguishing fire. But one day you will feel it; you will feel it, O Sigismondo; you will feel, sadly, that hell exists; you will feel Gehenna burning without end; you will feel that God's anger in no way lacks its executor; and you will feel the devil torturer. Do not think that you will avoid punishment by dying, [since] you will live in greater torment when you are dead, and you will understand that as a most wretched dead man you cannot die.[5]

Pius seems to take pleasure in describing the torments awaiting Sigismondo in the afterlife and also relishes the idea of Sigismondo's guilty conscience in this life. Because animals and demons feel no guilt, Pius has to backtrack and admit to there being some good in Sigismondo, but wholly for sadistic reasons: "Although you are wild, we do not believe that you are wholly lacking in humanity. That sense of moral order remains, some knowledge of reason remains, and a spirit and a mind remain conscious and mindful of a badly lived time, which prick you not only when you are awake but also when you are asleep."[6] Pius's evocative description of the inner torment of sin has an almost modern ring; it originates in a rational realization of a wicked act but descends to the irrational in the terrifying inability to stop or control these maddening regrets. Furies remain as obsessions.

The pope delves deeper into the workings of the human psyche in his description of the nightmares to come from Sigismondo's guilty conscience:

> Will you not be terrified, disturbed, and overwhelmed, when in your sleep come to you the images of the women you took from their husbands? What is the state of your mind, when the image appears to you of a brother, whom you cruelly murdered when you could not rape his sister? What will you answer the clerics, quietly rebuking you, whom you tortured to death for not revealing to you the confessions of honest married women? With what expression do you in your dreams look upon the image of that virgin, whose impregnable virtue you stormed and murdered?[7]

Pius uses vivid and varied rhetoric in his predictions of Sigismondo's tortured mind. Beyond *schadenfreude,* the pope seems positively gleeful in his endless litany of mental and physical woes.

If Sigismondo was tormented over his eternal damnation, he did not show it and was certainly not frightened into submission, as the pope must have hoped. Sigismondo's immediate reaction to Pius's invective and planned reverse canonization was defiance. He wrote a letter to his erstwhile father-in-law and powerful ally, Francesco Sforza, the Duke of Milan, on March, 26, 1462:

> I have just learned of the verses that His Holiness pronounced against me and in my dishonor, and which he sent to be read out in Florence. Since I am determined to do as that one who said: "I will surrender my honor to no one," I first wanted to inform you as my lord, that I do not intend to tolerate such things, even if His Holiness is my lord, and I his vicar and servant. When such accusations are spread around, however, I will try as far as I can: [but] when hurt by the pen, I will hurt others in the same way; if I am attacked with a sword, I will do my best to defend myself with a sword until death, since, although I am a poor

> man, I will remember that saying that "a beautiful death honors an entire life."[8]

The letter's logic is clear. It acts both as a request for help from a powerful patron—Sigismondo calls Sforza "my lord"—and as a warning to other rulers that Sigismondo will not back down in his fight against Pius II.

The importance of honor was paramount in fifteenth-century Italian society. The brutal vendettas that tore apart Italian cities often started from the slightest insults and acts of disrespect. Sigismondo cites the Bible (Proverbs 5:9) and classical ideals; a beautiful death honoring an entire life comes right out of the literature of pagan antiquity from Homer's heroes dying on the Trojan battlefield to Horace's sweet death on behalf of the fatherland. In the *Hesperis,* valor and heroic death as the crowning victory of life is a dominant theme. Here, under terrible pressure in the crisis of his life, Sigismondo turns to the same classical ideal to describe his own virtue. Sigismondo's defiance also underscores the Renaissance view of the pope as a secular ruler. The pope was of course the head of the Catholic Church and held special spiritual powers, but in matters of politics, the papacy was treated like any other state jockeying for power in the Italian peninsula. The Papal States indeed occupied much of central Italy in the fifteenth century. Cardinals led armies to expand papal territory or to defend papal strongholds. In addition to controlling a formidable military force, popes could and did on occasion use their spiritual authority to prevail over other rulers. In the eleventh century, Pope Gregory VII excommunicated King Henry IV and brought the monarch to his knees in repentance. One hundred years later, Pope Innocent III (1161–1216) confidently argued for the superiority of the papacy over secular rulers in all political as well as religious matters. But excommunication could backfire, as when Pope Boniface VIII (1235–1303) dramatically excommunicated King Philip IV of France, only to have the monarch send a group of mercenaries to teach the pope a lesson.[9]

Pius II had already excommunicated Sigismondo. He not only released Sigismondo's subjects from their bonds of fealty toward their lord but threatened that "if they did not cease to obey him, they could be captured and sold as slaves."[10] But when this failed to turn the tide in the territorial war, Pius invented the bizarre idea of a reverse canonization. Pius argued that if he had power to canonize saints to heaven, then he must surely have the power to condemn sinners to hell. Jesus did, after all, hand the first pope, Peter, the keys to Heaven and Hell. If Pius developed the theology to justify his reverse canonization, Sigismondo emphasized the legality of his claim to the disputed territory and his legitimate rejection of the pope's condemnation. Ever since the thirteenth century, the Malatesta had ruled Rimini as papal vicars. Popes Eugenius IV and Nicholas V had both renewed Sigismondo's rule. In his letter to Francesco Sforza, Sigismondo asserts this right, when he says: "His Holiness is my lord, and I his vicar and servant." Despite its apparent subservience, such language denotes a legalistic contract: Sigismondo was the pope's servant, but the papacy had appointed and confirmed Sigismondo as lord of Rimini and other cities in the Romagna. Pius therefore had no right to take away what had been officially given Sigismondo. Although the papal invectives against Sigismondo focus on his heretical beliefs and sexual improprieties, the political motives behind them were clear to all at the time. Several Italian rulers condemned the pope's use of such extreme spiritual warfare in a territorial dispute with one of his papal vicars. As Pius himself and other sources attest, ambassadors from Venice, Milan, and Florence implored Pius to be merciful toward Sigismondo.[11] All to no avail.

Sigismondo's Hell

In his response to Francesco Sforza, Sigismondo refers to a beautiful death but makes no mention of the afterlife, punishment of sin, or hell. After hearing of his canonization to hell, Sigismondo may have recalled the life and last night of his holy half-brother. On his deathbed, Galeotto reportedly fought off demons for two hours; he spat on them and scorned their torments, as he clutched and kissed a cross and screamed at the devils, "go away, you will not have anything here." Then the fight ended; his face brightened, and smiling he uttered his last words: "Now I see the heavens opening."[12] Would the warrior, Sigismondo, have felt as confident of victory in battling such infernal foes?

Upon hearing of Pius's reverse canonization, Sigismondo may also have thought about his namesake character's visit to the underworld in Basinio's epic. After describing the bliss of Olympus, the heaven that his brother Galeotto enjoyed, and the celestial abode that Sigismondo was destined to inhabit, the nymph Isotta turns from the vision of the great Thunderer to what awaits the damned:

> Opposite this heavenly abode, where Tartarus fades in the squalid depths, every evil, crimes, . . . hatreds, dire famine, mourning, wailing, sighing, pain, worries (the avengers of wicked deeds), death, toil, and savage robberies make an unspeakable bed. Here murders are stabled in spilled blood, and black wounds, blind love, the mad longing of youth, black envy devouring itself, ambition unaware of right, discord (the author of wicked deeds), and an endless arrogant faithlessness. You must flee far from such things—it is enough to hear the moaning and wailing of the wicked.[13]

Even in this very pagan text, a Christian sense of crime and eternal hellish punishment serves as contrast and warning. Sigismondo could find no comfort even in the writings of his most classical poet.

Later in the poem, after visiting the Elysian Fields, Sigismondo meets his father, who takes him on an extended tour of hell. Here Sigismondo sees:

> A black silent image of sad night, obscured in blind darkness, dense, and hovering in eternal horror. All impious people with wicked souls go through deep empty chaos to this place. Those guilty of madness and cruel love are imprisoned here; fraud and the various arts of deceit; fear and sorrow bring forced tears to faces; pallor, unrighteous envy, and cruel hatred, heavy in ambition, and discord disturbing different minds. This is the road that the gods call black.[14]

Such horror is reserved for those guilty of the crimes of which Pius later accused Sigismondo: impiety, cruel love, deceit, hatred, and ambition. Even though the *Hesperis* predates the invective by seven years and celebrates Sigismondo as a lover, clever deceiver, and proud warrior, Basinio adumbrates Pius's list of Sigismondo's crimes. In the *Hesperis,* Pandolfo explains the cause of such darkness to his son:

> Some never obeyed the great Thunderer and did not wish to follow the light. They hover in black darkness. They saw the right and the good but fell from true reason, abandoned justice, and had no faith. Their eternal punishment is to be without the serene face of God, never to approach the threshold of the highest father, and to return again here with the body to come. O what a miserable thought to understand that after many centuries such horrors are awaiting them! The infinite time is bitter for many. Just as the generous day and bright sun move happy and peaceful things for good people, so do the black abyss and infernal chaos become dark for the wretched in the midst of shadows.[15]

According to Christian theology, hell is by definition the lack of God, and God is light. The corporeal return here probably refers to the second coming, when even the damned will get their bodies anew, only to suffer in them for eternity.

After this fairly orthodox theological description, Basinio rehashes images and punishments from classical mythology and Dante's *Inferno*. Pandolfo shows Sigismondo the chained three-headed dog Cerberus and the fury Tisiphone, who guard the gates of the underworld in the *Aeneid* (book VI). The sinners that Sigismondo sees in this deepest part of hell all relate to particular vices that tempted Sigismondo or somehow relate to the accusations that Pius will later use to destroy his character. Destroyers of cities and the temples of the gods are punished here, as are blasphemers and treaty-breakers. Catiline appears, as do Cethegus and Lentulus, who plotted against Caligula, and "other citizens disturbed by a faithless heart" are in the depths of hell. Pius will accuse Sigismondo of sacking helpless towns, filling a church with demons, sacrilege, blasphemy, breaking treaties, and rebelling against papal rule. In the poem, Sigismondo then asks his father about the fate of the giants and the titans. These are the greatest examples of hubris against the gods: they challenged the gods and lost. Tantalus, who stole nectar and ambrosia from the gods to give to mortals, is tormented by thirst, unable to drink though immersed in sweet water, and by hunger, a branch with sweet fruit hanging above him just out of reach. Tantalus explains their fates to Sigismondo:

> Why do you wonder why those who desired to enter heaven with a proud step are here in the deep depths of hell? Whoever seeks the highest places, holds the lowest. No one, no human could ascend to heaven without being thrown down from its great height to wash his head in the waters of Styx. Do you see the giants Aloeus, Otus, and tough Ephialtes, who dared to stack high mountains on mountains?[16]

Hubris and boldly entering Olympus will only lead to destruction and eternal damnation. Tantalus then shows Sigismondo Tityos, whom Apollo killed for attempting to rape Latona. Like Prometheus, Tityos is splayed out on his back, with a vulture eternally eating his regenerating liver. Tantalus concludes his speech with a warning: "The Titans ever dwell in the black darkness, for a great weight presses them down, since they went against the gods and Jupiter and tried to besiege Olympus. How far are these wretches now from Jupiter!" Elsewhere in the same poem, Galeotto told Sigismondo that his great virtue and warrior pride have assured him a place in Olympus, as discussed in Chapter 5. Hardly a saint like his brother, Sigismondo walked a fine line between the example of the classical heroes, beloved by the gods and divinized, and the titans, struck down for their hubris and eternally suffering.

Basinio includes only some of the seven deadly sins that frame the architecture of Dante's hell. Lust, envy, and anger appear, but gluttony and sloth are missing. The active Sigismondo who scorned rich food hardly needed a warning about these. Although the *Hesperis* precedes Pius's invective, Basinio focused on the fates of particular sinners, who were damned for the crimes for which the pope will accuse Sigismondo. Did Basinio believe that Sigismondo was guilty of these sins and needed to be remonstrated? Dante, after all, saw and focused on many of the sins with which he himself was struggling: lust, pride, and fame. The simplest explanation for why Basinio placed these sinners in the deepest part of hell and described them and not others is that these were the most common, dangerous, and tempting vices of any ruler, but especially such a youthful, passionate, confident, and powerful lord as Sigismondo.

Sigismondo is brought back to the world of the living by the nymph: "Why, Sigismondo, immortal glory of the Italians, are you not fleeing this place, while you can?"[17] Had Pius read Basinio's poem, he might have thought these words prophetic. This is, after all, where he condemned Sigismondo to be in the reverse canonization of 1462. As a traitor to God and his pope, Sigismondo was condemned to spend eternity "spewing boiling foam out of his stomach" or "entombed naked in icy sands."[18] In Basinio's 1455 poem, Sigismondo's guide showed him the way out; seven years later, the pope made him no longer a safe observer but a victim of the torture without escape. Now in the lowest point of his life, the lofty verse that made him into a god would have appeared even more fantastic, as hubris, the arrogance of a mortal not knowing his limits. And Basinio's images of the dark void of hell, filled with the wailing and misery of the damned, may have appeared less as literary imaginings and more as the frightening reality that awaited him.

Like Basinio's poetry, Giovanni Cocchi's treatise on the immortality of the soul contained abundant images of pagan hell and Christian damnation that Sigismondo may have recalled at the news of the reverse canonization. Thirteen years before Pius enlisted him among the damned, Sigismondo had hosted a debate on the nature of the soul, which the Franciscan friar Cocchi led, recorded, and later turned into a treatise on the immortality of the soul, as discussed in Chapter 5.[19] Cocchi drew on both the Christian theology of Saint Augustine (354–430 CE) and the astrological and neoplatonic religious ideas of the pagan Macrobius (fifth century CE). For Augustine, who helped codify Christian theology, hell was where the damned experience a second death; the worm of conscience gnaws at them and because the soul was so attached to the body in life, it feels bodily pain from the torments of eternal flames. Physical pain in this world can therefore act as premonitions of the horrors of hell, except that in hell the pain will be continuous, eternal, and more extreme, as there is no hope of relief. Far from escaping the prison of the body in death, the damned are trapped in the tormented flesh.[20]

Cocchi refers often to Augustine and the second death of the damned soul.[21] He describes Augustine's argument about how the damned, including demons, are able to suffer physical pain without having bodies.[22] But Cocchi then turns away from the afterlife to the consequences of sin for the living. He sees the pain of hell as a psychological state that traps the living, as shown in his use of Macrobius's allegorizing of Virgil's underworld in the

Aeneid. "Phlegethon," Cocchi writes, "represents the fires of anger and desire; Acheron whatever ill things we did or said to others; Cocytus whatever made men weep and cry; Styx whatever ingorged human souls in hatred." The vulture devouring the liver of the immortal Prometheus, Cocchi continues, represents the "torments of the conscience, our inner selves enslaved to disgrace."[23] Hell is not only after death but also the guilt that the living experience. Cocchi argues that bad things happen to sinners, but most of his examples are pagan and involve punishments in this life. They include the tyrant Dionysius drowned for his sacrilege of Proserpina's temple, the madness that Hercules suffered for impiety, and the lightning that struck Hercules's son Aristodemus for his impiety toward Apollo's oracle.[24] There has to be some punishment for sin, Cocchi concludes, as otherwise there is no reason to be good:

> What use would there be in cultivating piety, justice, generosity, and all the other virtues, if there were no difference between good and evil? What good would great men have gained from renouncing all pleasures, scorning any kind of home, wearing themselves out in divine studies, and tolerating all kinds of bitter and harsh conditions, if rapists, assassins, profligates, and hedonists met the same death as the innocent and just?[25]

For virtue to be rewarded, vice must be punished. Although he borrows liberally from Augustine, Cocchi's other sources and examples are predominantly pagan. If he only briefly mentions the hope given to the Jews in Egypt, Joseph, Jacob, the Apocalypse of John, and Saint Paul, Cocchi uses whole sections of Homer, Virgil, Lucan, and Statius to map the geography of hell and Macrobius to explain its deeper meaning.[26] Rather than refer to Jesus and the Christian harrowing of hell, Cocchi repeatedly cites as evidence Orpheus's trip to hell to retrieve his deceased spouse.

Cocchi exhibits a pagan-Christian eclecticism, as do many Renaissance intellectuals immersed in antiquity. His theology was contaminated by his reading pagan literature and absorbing the doctrines of ancient pagan philosophy. Even though Augustine had painstakingly distinguished Christian from pagan, his adoption of pagan ideas and culture was seen as approval by Renaissance ears that were unable or uninterested in picking out the subtle and major religious differences. If, as Cocchi emphasizes in his dedication, Sigismondo was an active participant in the debate over the immortality of the soul, which formed the nucleus of his treatise, then we can assume that Sigismondo was exposed to pagan and Christian notions of the soul and the nature of hell. Despite these pagan examples and terms, Cocchi's hell is essentially the same place of eternal torment that Christians envisioned and therefore did not offer a more pleasant alternative to Sigismondo's imagination.

If the culture of Sigismondo's court praised pagan values that were antithetical to Christian morality, the same writers described hell and eternal damnation in terms that were as unremittingly grim as those of any Christian preacher. Virtue and the path to heaven were radically different, but vice and the path to hell more or less followed Christian norms. The pagan values that Basinio celebrates as taking one to heaven are the same qualities and behaviors that cause people to be tortured in his depiction of hell. This tension in Basinio's text suggests the dissonance between these ancient ideals and the Christian ethos.

The War before Hell

The years leading up to the reverse canonization had been a downward spiral for Sigismondo. He had chosen the wrong side, the losing side in the succession crisis of Naples. When King Alfonso died in 1458, the Frenchman Jean d'Anjou (1424–1470) tried to assert his family's claim to the throne. Sigismondo supported Jean's claim, which further enflamed Aragonese wrath. Pope Pius backed Alfonso's son, Ferrante, who easily succeeded his father, and Jean returned to France, leaving his allies to deal with the wreckage of their support. Sigismondo's defiance against the pope was also falling apart. He was still refusing to pay the tribute from Rimini that he owed the pope. On Christmas day in 1460, Pius formally excommunicated Sigismondo and released his subjects from their oaths of fealty.[27] Then, when campaign season reopened, the pope sent his mercenaries to reclaim the Malatesta lands in the Marches. Sigismondo met them with a small army in July 1461 near Nidastore. They were surrounded and vastly outnumbered. The pope's army had three thousand cavalry and two thousand infantry against Sigismondo's one thousand three hundred cavalry and five hundred infantry. It looked bleak, and his men were disheartened, but Sigismondo found a weakness and persevered. Rather than surrender or await the enemy, he decided to attack. In a stirring battlefield speech at dawn, Sigismondo reportedly told his men that victory would be theirs because of their superior "virtues": "In this day reawaken your proud spirits by beating the enemy." The enemy's great weakness, he said, was that they underestimated the Malatesta army, which was abundantly clear in their negligent and haphazard encampments:

> Their low opinion of us will make our victory all the better, since with your virtues you will knock down their arrogance. If we lose, I have been informed, the pope wants to imprison all of us in the Campidoglio as rebels of the Holy Church—it would be better to die than to let ourselves be reduced to such extermination. If you were to say, "Sigismondo, there are a lot more of them, how can we win?" I would answer the following: It is true that there are a lot more of them than us, but we are more manly and you have done more famed deeds than they have. They have been thrown together without thought of each other, while we all are of one will and have been brought up together; we recognize each other's work and would never abandon each other. I only want one thing from you: stick to the plan and show true obedience, and I promise you great reward for your efforts. Besides the great reputation that will follow you, since your fame will always be alive . . . you will all become rich.[28]

In an eloquent classicizing oration, Sigismondo praises his men for their superior martial virtues, uses the enemy's disdain to anger and excite them, scares them with the consequences of failure (declaring death better than loss of liberty), refers to his men's superior manliness against the more numerous enemy, reminds them of their common background and vows of obedience, and promises rewards in fame and wealth. As proof of the victory at hand, Sigismondo proudly recalled his blood descent from Scipio Africanus and pointed to the landing of an eagle in the camp, "which the ancient and brave Romans believed to be a sign, called an augury." Sigismondo's speech is recorded in the vernacular (presumably the original language) in Broglio's chronicle, a medium far removed from the hyperclassicizing Latin epic verse of the *Hesperis*. Four years after Basinio's death, in much less triumphant times, Broglio presents Sigismondo still calling upon antiquity and classical values in a moment of crisis.

Sigismondo outsmarts the numerically superior enemy by launching several simultaneous attacks on the weak points of their camps. He inspires his men to heroism by throwing himself into the thick of battle "like an enraged lion," shouting "Either I will die or we will have our victory!" Despite being twice wounded, Sigismondo continued to fight "inflamed like a ferocious bear, personally performing amazing deeds."[29] The battle lasted all day and into the evening, and in the end Sigismondo was triumphant. But instead of pushing further, he tried to use the victory to barter for a more favorable peace settlement with the pope. The victory, however, proved pyrrhic as it merely enraged Pius and made him even more determined to crush Malatesta rule. The pope took advantage of the temporary ceasefire and spent the winter devising his infernal canonization and putting together a much bigger army to be led by Federico da Montefeltro.

Courting the Turk: Sigismondo and Mehmet II

Sigismondo was still defiant, but with few allies, men, and resources he could not hold out for long. It was after the excommunication and before the reverse canonization, when in 1461 he tried to form an alliance with the Ottoman Sultan Mehmet II (1432–1481).[30] To facilitate the Ottoman advance into Italy, Sigismondo sent to the sultan Valturio's treatise on the art of war and a map of the Italian coast. Mehmet was interested in Italian art and had asked Sigismondo to send an artist to work in his court. In September, Matteo de' Pasti left Rimini for Constantinople, but he did not get very far. The Venetians intercepted the artist in Crete, confiscated the map and treatise, and held him under arrest. The geographic map of Italy had obvious strategic importance, but Valturio's treatise with its antiquarian focus would have hardly supplied practical information for planning an invasion of Italy. The colorful illustrations of siege engines in the treatise would have perhaps appealed to the sultan, known for his use of creative mobile fortresses against walled cities and castles. In the dedication, Valturio praises the Ottoman sultan in a much more explicit and grandiose way than he does even his own patron, Sigismondo. "In military matters," he declares to

Mehmet, "you surpass all commanders not only of our age but of earlier times." Valturio calls Mehmet "the wondrous glory of the world's princes" and "most invincible." He compares the sultan to Alexander the Great in his love of art—"just as Alexander had Apelles, so does Mehmet now have Matteo de' Pasti."[31] The Venetians eventually released Matteo, but Sigismondo's reputation took another blow. Now he was a traitor not only to Naples and the pope but to Italy and Christianity. There is tremendous irony here: a mercenary, extensively celebrated as the savior of Italy against barbarians, seeking an alliance with the ruler who was deemed by Italians the "most barbaric" foreigner of the time and helping him invade Italy.

The episode is wholly inconsistent with the image of Sigismondo in the *Hesperis* (1455), where the mercenary is shown ready to embark on a crusade to retake Constantinople. During the second Tuscan War (1453), Basinio presents Alfonso of Aragon attempting to bribe Sigismondo into peace. He promises to send Sigismondo to battle the Turks and regain Byzantium, and then, as a reward, to give him part of his Italian kingdom. In his response, Sigismondo says, "I will go to battle the Turks on my own accord as soon as winter has frozen the waters."[32] Later, in the *Hesperis,* the goddess Juno tries to convince Jupiter to support the Aragonese cause in Tuscany. At a certain point, she concedes and tells Jupiter to let Sigismondo beat the Spanish, since she has:

> . . . no greater joy than that he might leave the Tuscan cities in peace and defend the Greeks from the invading Turks. O father of the gods, what murders, what great slaughter have the Greeks now suffered! So many thousands of Greek men have been unspeakably put to death! Let them [Sigismondo and Ferrante] hurry to Samos with three hundred ships, and the long Sea of Marmara will boil with bloody water. Now Priam's Troy rises again for me.[33]

Basinio must have been composing the *Hesperis* when news arrived of the siege and fall of Constantinople in May 1453. It must have been difficult for him to continue the theme of the epic poem, that the Tuscan War was greater and more violent than the Trojan War, when such a real catastrophe had just occurred.[34] These snippets about the Turks in the *Hesperis* are later additions in the face of the tragedy.

There is no mention of Sigismondo's attempted alliance with the Turk in the papal invective or in Pius's *Commentaries.* Why was this not one of the pope's accusations? The reverse canonization took place and the invective was read out on April 27, 1462. Sigismondo's episode with the sultan was common knowledge by December 1461, as ambassadorial reports reveal that the Curia was well aware of the situation.[35] Soon after the reverse canonization Pius warned Borso d'Este in a letter dated June 5, 1462, not to help Sigismondo, since he "was zealously supporting the impious Turks' invasion of Italy."[36] The pope included all kinds of hearsay about Sigismondo's misdeeds in the invective and would not have scrupled at the need for further evidence. In the *Commentaries,* Pius indirectly connects Sigismondo to the Ottoman threat in a speech to the Venetian ambassador in November 1462. In a lengthy oration justifying his actions, Pius declares: "What if Sigismondo invited the Turks to invade Italy? His mind is so evil. The voyage from Aulona (commonly called Valona and held by the Turks) is not far to Rimini. Sigismondo will do anything not to lose his dominion." Later in the speech, the pope says: "As far as the Turks are concerned, they have no other way to reach Rimini, except by the Adriatic, over which you [Venetians] claim supreme guardianship."[37] Pius seems to refer to Sigismondo's attempt to enlist the Sultan. But it is odd that there is nothing more explicit in the *Commentaries,* since they were constantly revised by the pope and later his editor, Gianantonio Campano. Even after the failed attempt with Matteo de' Pasti, there is evidence that Sigismondo was planning to send another ambassador to the sultan with a copy of Valturio's treatise, which may have included an illustration of the Adriatic Sea. Sigismondo's faithful servant Enrico Aquadelli was supposed to leave for Constantinople on April 28. The reverse canonization on April 27 must have forced Sigismondo to abandon his second attempt to ally himself with the Turks.[38] This second attempt underscores Sigismondo's defiant attitude toward the pope. Maybe it was such a sensitive issue that Pius worried that publicizing it might somehow encourage such alliances.

Sigismondo's attempted alliances with the Turk in 1461 and 1462 show the extent of his desperation. He had won a few victories on the battlefield, but

Pius hired Sigismondo's archenemy Federico da Montefeltro, who had more money and men than the lord of Rimini, whose resources were badly depleted. It was when the war was at its most intense in 1461 that Sigismondo tried to make the alliance with the Ottoman sultan. Sigismondo's failed attempt to join the Turk must have sorely angered Pius, who spent his papacy pursuing a crusade against the Ottoman Turks to take back Constantinople. In the end, the sultan did not come, and Sigismondo's war with Pius II and the papacy was hopeless.

After Hell

Soon after the reverse canonization and the burning of Sigismondo in effigy in Rome, Federico da Montefeltro destroyed Malatesta forces in Senigallia on August 12, 1462.[39] After suffering further losses in Puglia, Sigismondo headed home, but a "horrendous storm" sunk his ship: "Observers on the coast saw him disappear and everyone assumed he had drowned. But," Pius regretfully intoned in his *Commentaries,* "the wind and the sea could not destroy a man worthy to be burnt at the stake and threw him up onto the Dalmatian coast, shaken and shocked. Then, in disguise as was his habit, Sigismondo with a few companions walked over rough mountain passes to Friuli, and from there to Venice to plead for help."[40] Few allies remained. His French allies had suffered an unrecoverable defeat in Troia and left Italy. Venice was his last hope.

Venice tried to placate the pope, but he would not budge. Sigismondo was surely despondent, and the next campaign season, in 1463, was even worse. Despite help from Venetian galleys, the Malatesta city of Fano fell in September 1463, and Senigallia, which had still been holding out, finally capitulated.[41] The papal forces now surrounded Rimini. "Broken in spirit," Sigismondo declared to Pius: "I am beaten and ask for peace, ready to submit to your conditions. The conqueror's honor is to spare the conquered. I confess, I have gravely sinned against you but I have also paid a heavy penalty. If I am saved, I will take care not to hurt the Church in the future."[42] The pope wanted Rimini, but Venice, fearing a threat to its Adriatic supremacy, prevented its occupation by papal troops. Pius was anxious to start his crusade against the Turks, and Venice refused to help unless the pope made peace with Sigismondo. Acceptable terms were finally negotiated. Sigismondo paid the tribute to Rome that he could and, after meeting other conditions, was allowed to continue as lord of Rimini at least in name. He had to confess to being a heretic and "abjure in particular his beliefs concerning the resurrection of the dead and the immortality of the soul." After a three-day fast, his subjects had to confess and express remorse for their sins. Only then were they allowed to receive the sacraments and follow their prince again. To cure his heresy and paganism, Sigismondo had to recite once a day the basic teachings of the Catholic Church (in the form of the Creed) and fast every Friday for the rest of his life. He had to agree to go on pilgrimage to the seven churches in Rome and the Holy Sepulcher in Jerusalem.[43] On December 2, 1463, Sigismondo was formally given back Rimini to rule. He had lost all the neighboring cities that had traditionally been under Malatesta rule, including Senigallia and Fano, and he was bankrupt. Sigismondo was a broken man but not completely hopeless. Although he was now poor and had "few possessions," Sigismondo reportedly declared, he still had "enough thoughts."[44] He was perhaps referring to the sustaining power of his cultural and humanistic interests, but more likely he was thinking about the possibility of regaining his position in the political arena of Italy.

Pius could now focus on planning the crusade to retake Constantinople. Having gained the necessary allies in the venture, he set out for Ancona to lead the Christian fleet against the infidels. The crusaders, however, waited in vain for the Venetian galleys to carry them to their destination. By the time the fleet finally arrived weeks later, many of the crusaders had given up and gone home, and the pope lay dying of fever. On August 14, 1464, Pius died in Ancona, and the crusade ended before it could even leave Italian shores.[45] Ironically, the one man whom Pius had hated the most ended up leading the crusade that the pope had spent his papacy trying to organize.

Without Pius's consent, Venice hired Sigismondo to lead a crusade against the Turks in the Morea in March 1464. No other reputable captain would take on the difficult commission. Sigismondo might have seen it as a way to regain a foothold in Italian politics and to refinance his bankrupt city. Initially, he had a strong force and received reinforcements, but conditions in the Peloponnese were harsh. The whole area suffered from starvation, and the number of men and their supplies dwindled with every Ottoman incursion. Sigismondo had some successes and managed to retake lower Mistra in August 1464, where he was able to recover the body of Plethon before being forced to retreat when an Ottoman contingent was sent to crush the Italians in the fall. He failed, however, to retake the palace in Mistra because Venetian naval support was called away to alleviate an attack on Rhodes. Lacking men and provisions, Sigismondo was released from Venetian service after eighteen months in the Morea and returned to Rimini in April 1466. Pius's successor, Pope Paul II (1417–1471), acknowledged Sigismondo's moderate success and summoned him to Rome to be honored for his service with a golden rose.[46] Isotta and Sigismondo's two sons, Sallustio and Roberto, had been left in charge of Rimini while Sigismondo was away. As a condition of the contract, Venice had guaranteed the protection of Rimini. When a rumor of Sigismondo's death endangered Isotta's control, the Serenissima accordingly sent the necessary support. Isotta showed her strong leadership by torturing and putting death a trusted Malatesta councilor who had tried to stop the Venetians and circumvent Isotta by putting Roberto in power.[47]

In November 1465, Malatesta Novello, Sigismondo's brother and the ruler of Cesena, died, and a succession crisis ensued.[48] Pope Paul II sent papal troops, but Novello had appointed Roberto Malatesta to succeed him, and the Venetians were also trying to take control. In the end, the pope won, and Cesena was transferred to papal control in December 1465. Pope Paul II bought off Roberto and gave him some minor towns to rule. With Cesena under papal rule, Paul had his eyes set on Rimini. When he was in Rome in April 1466, Sigismondo tried to negotiate for a return of some of the Malatesta territories as a reward for his crusading, but Paul would not budge. Frustrated with only empty promises, Sigismondo left Rome in June and returned to Rimini, where he tried to organize the other Romagna lords, cement his ties with the mercenary captain Bartolomeo Colleone, and assure the support of Venice. Paul tried to appease Sigismondo by appointing him governor of the town of Santarcangelo and the vicariate of Mondavio. Thinking that the pope was becoming more conciliatory, Sigismondo returned to Rome for more talks in the fall.

Paul, however, had no intention of yielding. Instead, he bribed Sigismondo with a pension and kept him waiting in Rome, while papal troops were sent to surround Rimini and isolate him from his allies. When Sigismondo realized the deception, he became enraged and, according to Broglio's chronicle, thought of nothing but "how to kill the pope." He decided to do it with a dagger. He would ask for an audience, get close to the pope, and, with the concealed weapon, stab him to death. "This," he reportedly said, "was the honor owed the descendent of the Scipios for the treachery of the popes." "The unfortunate lord," Broglio recounts, "roared . . . like a savage lion with a ravenous appetite desiring food."[49] Sigismondo probably would have carried out his plan and murdered the pope, but Paul was suspicious or forewarned and postponed the agreed audience for the following day and in the presence of seven cardinals. By that time, Sigismondo had calmed down and perhaps did not have an opportunity with the cardinals present. Paul denied any wrongdoing and assured Sigismondo that Rimini was his, at least until his death. In order to placate, isolate, and keep an eye on Sigismondo, Paul hired him to fight on behalf of the papacy. This meant that Sigismondo was often in Rome during the last year of his life.

Paul never fully trusted Sigismondo, and when revelations emerged in February 1468 of a so-called humanist conspiracy to murder the pope, the pope immediately suspected Sigismondo's involvement.[50] His failed assassination attempt alone would have made him a viable suspect, but Sigismondo's checkered past with the Turks must have also been on the pope's mind, as the Sultan Mehmet II was also believed to have a role in the plot. The purported ringleader of the conspiracy, Filippo Buonaccorsi "Callimaco" (1437–1496), in 1466 had written an ode to Sigismondo in which he praised his triumph in the Morea and said that Sigismondo "gave hope to the man shipwrecked in a storm." In 1468, after being arrested and imprisoned in Castel Sant'Angelo, the disgruntled former papal abbreviator, Platina (1421–1481) was questioned under torture on a recent meeting he had had with Sigismondo. The humanist insisted that their conversations were about literature, arms, and the great minds of the past and present rather than any secret nefarious plans.[51] Platina was surely being defensive, but his argument must have been accepted, since, as far as we know, Sigismondo himself was not questioned on his role in the conspiracy and continued to work for the pope. If Platina's account is accurate, even at this low point of his life, far removed from the boundless potential in Basinio's verse, Sigismondo was still obsessed with classical antiquity. Perhaps he saw an escape from his sad predicament or wanted desperately to believe himself still the equal of Alexander and Caesar. Soon after the excitement over the conspiracy in the spring of 1468, while fighting for the papacy against Norcia, Sigismondo became sick.[52] On October 9, 1468, Sigismondo Malatesta died in Rimini at the age of fifty-one.

Sigismondo's premature death, according to the contemporary Byzantine philosopher George of Trebizond (1395–1486), was a direct result of his pagan blasphemy. While in Rome in 1466, Sigismondo had met the philosopher, who was shocked and disgusted to find out that Sigismondo had brought the body of the pagan Plethon back to Italy and planned to entomb it in a Christian church. George warned Sigismondo that "unless he threw out of his city the Apollo, who lives in the corpse of Gemistus [Plethon], something bad would befall him." Sigismondo promised but never disposed of the body and, thus, according to George, God punished him with a severe illness that almost killed him. After recuperating, Sigismondo promised to throw Plethon's body in the sea, but again he did not do it. Once more he became sick, and this time it killed him. George said that he immediately wrote to Isotta and her children to warn them and urge them to dispose of Plethon's body.[53] Plethon's tomb still stands with an honorific inscription on the exterior of the Tempio. It rests next to Basinio's and Valturio's tombs. As far as we know, the pagan philosopher's body is still in the tomb. The only source for the story is George of Trebizond, who hated with passion Plethon and Platonism. Even if an invention, the anecdote shows how at least one prominent intellectual in Rome saw paganism as scandalous, dangerous, and indeed fatal. Sigismondo's recovery and reburial of Plethon's corpse in Rimini in 1466 demonstrates that he had not lost interest in Greek philosophy and ancient paganism, even after Pius had forced him to confess his heresy and every day recite the exclusive Christian Creed of faith. At the end of his life and in the most miserable state of his affairs, Sigismondo was still inspired by the beliefs and values of pagan antiquity.

Over a decade earlier, in 1455, the same year in which Basinio finished the *Hesperis,* and years before the reverse canonization, an elderly Florentine humanist, Poggio Bracciolini, dedicated an ominous work to Sigismondo Malatesta, *On the Misery of the Human Condition*. This little dialogue on human folly and how vice and fortune ultimately destroy all human hope of happiness serves as a stark contrast to Basinio's image of Sigismondo as a superman made into a god by his outstanding virtue and prowess. One of Poggio's interlocutors in the dialogue declares:

> [Fortune and vice] throw our lives into turmoil with all sorts of ailments and passions. We have neglected reason . . . and enslaved ourselves to a host of passions wholly contrary to it. The consequence is that we have lost the right path and found no haven of peace—we are anxious and harassed wanderers, restlessly driven hither and thither by lust, with no end laid down to our desires. So it is that we ourselves cause our afflictions . . . we have become fortune's slaves, when we could be free.[54]

Such a warning, so inconsonant with the springtime hope in the Malatesta literature of the time, reads in retrospect as prescient of the blows of fortune that Sigismondo would soon receive from the papacy. Six years later, Poggio's description of the travails of fortune and vice could easily have characterized the reprobate overambitious Sigismondo in Pius's invectives: a slave to lust and passion.

Sigismondo did what he had to do to survive against the papacy. But his attempted assassination of Paul II and his possible involvement in the conspiracy to murder the pope in 1468 show him defiant, uncontrite, and essentially unyielding before the expanding Papal States. Sigismondo also never abandoned his interest in classical antiquity, as the reported conversation with Platina suggests, nor his fascination with the sophisticated philosophical paganism of antiquity, so vividly demonstrated in his reverential reburial of Plethon's corpse in the Tempio Malatestiano. He continued to live a publicly pagan life, even as he was forced into Christian observance.

Conclusion

The Pagan Renaissance

In the letter offering his services as court poet, Basinio demonstrates his skill by describing Sigismondo praying to the pagan gods:

> Waving your spear, you prayed to the gods and encouraged your men. Looking upon the threshold of ethereal Olympus, you began to summon the gods and make vows: "I pray to you, o gods, guardians of Italy, ever the greatest spirits, you who have favored Romulus' city and people, and you, Vesta, protector of the robed Roman, banish this madness from your lands. I, Sigismondo, will adorn your altars with great gifts and hold long parades."[1]

It is unlikely that Sigismondo considered himself a pagan. But the image of him in the literature that he patronized was extremely pagan. It was so in Basinio's first petition request, which evidently pleased Sigismondo so much that Basinio was paid to continue his portrait of the pagan in a Christian world.

Basinio's magnum opus, the *Hesperis,* paints an even more extensive pagan image of Sigismondo, but a few passages demonstrate the tensions between such paganism and Christian piety. Basinio presents Sigismondo praying to all the gods for the walls of Gradara to withstand siege. Shortly before the first Tuscan War, Alessandro Sforza and Sigismondo's long-time enemy Federico da Montefeltro invaded Malatesta lands and succeeded in taking several towns in the Romagna. Observing the enemy's attack, Sigismondo stood up, called upon the gods for help, and rallied the defenders:

> O high Jupiter, father of the gods, who wield s lightning and excites terrifying flames from stormy clouds, whom the sea and land feel; and you, mother of the gods, who build towers on mountaintops and whom Phrygian lions carry; you also holy Venus, who gave birth to gods and men, and nymphs of the rivers, spirits most pleasing to our souls; and you gods and goddesses who justly see mortal affairs, both you who inhabit the halls of great heaven and you who live in pleasing lands far from heaven; and the ruler of the nereids of the deep sea, streams, and rivers, and you powerful Diana, nourisher of the woods. Indeed, having prayed to all the great spirits, I believe that one Jupiter alone exists; nor indeed can the power of the spirit be divided. One and the same spirit necessarily rules from heaven. This God is the author of just equality. Since we think him mindful of right and pleasing, we ask for his help with our just arms.[2]

The abrupt change from all the gods to the one true god in Basinio's rendering of Sigismondo's invocation reveals the tension and perhaps trouble that such pagan imagery and prayers to pagan gods could cause in fifteenth-century Christendom. These last lines protest and correct the outlandish paganism of the previous lines and therefore suggest that all the pagan invocations were not harmless classicism.

Later in the speech, Sigismondo returns to the gods: "Because he has been wearing down the walls of Gradara in vain for many days over much time, Sforza surely calls the gods wicked. Do the powerful gods and goddesses of Italy, by Jupiter, favor the one who is devastating the cities of Hesperis?" Sigismondo accuses Sforza of blasphemy in calling the gods wicked and of sacrilege in attacking the divine cities of Italy. He then calls on Juno, Iris, and the other gods to bring down violent rain from Olympus to stop the siege.[3] Basinio writes that these prayers were effective because after forty days of intense siege, Federico and Alessandro were forced to abandon their attack, and the fortress of Gradara survived intact.[4] Couched between overtly pagan prayers, Sigismondo's assertion of monotheism is awkward and out of place. There are several reasons Basinio might have felt a need to insert this Christian correction. Perhaps he wanted to quell religious censors or felt that Sigismondo would have protested at having such a strong image of pagan worship ascribed to him. Basinio himself might also have felt a need to reassert his own Christian belief. Whatever the reason, these lines emphasize the danger in classical imitation.

At the end of the *Hesperis,* Basinio makes another revealing distinction. After the Tuscan Wars, Sigismondo returned to Rimini and "fulfilled his vow to the gods. He gave honor to the highest god and built a wondrous temple of parian marble in the middle of the city, which Jupiter's hard lightning bolts, which he used to topple the savage giants, would not move."[5] *Templum* is not so much the issue as the plural gods (*superis*).[6] But in the next line Basinio makes god singular and adds *summo,* the highest, which presumably means the Christian God. The reference to Jupiter's lightning bolts could be interpreted as an assertion of Christian superiority, that even the most powerful pagan god could not hurt the Christian church. This would, however, probably be reading too much into the phrase, which merely serves to emphasize the sturdiness of the marble structure.

Basinio's only explicitly Christian poem is one that he dedicated to the Virgin Mary in his youth. He was guilt-stricken by his interest in pagan poetry and mythology:

> Do not cultivate ambiguity: now let all fables be far away. Our ship is sailing a greater sea. Mother of Christ, you are present, and greetings to you, o famed son, accept the first fruits from my poetry. . . . Please take back your tears, o divine woman, and the great evils into which our ship has sunk. Take pity on my shipwreck. We are ever tossed on a high sea and the prow of our ship goes far afield in the incessant waters.

Basinio starts the poem by urging boys, girls, and priests to sing the Virgin's praises. He then begins his prayer. *Ambages,* or "ambiguity," refers to pagan mythology, full of half-truths and lies. Basinio's obsession with pagan poetry threatens his Christian faith with "shipwreck." He begs for mercy and offers to change his life:

> The omnipotent father has put you in charge of famed Olympus, and piety has brought you to the sky. . . . Would that I could compose worthy praise for you and that my tongue could reveal what my mind feels! If you favor me, Homer will no longer dominate me, nor will all of Greece with her poetry. Then I would not compose verses to the empty spirits of the gods, nor would Apollo speak through my mouth. . . . I will not compose poems for peaceful slumber, nor will sweet Homer always be my guide. But I would only care for what is done in Olympus, what your high son is doing in heaven.[7]

Although he promises to dismiss pagan literature and mythology and the empty pagan gods, Basinio's prayer framework is still pagan, and he refers to heaven as Olympus. He offers to switch divine allegiances, if the Virgin Mary shows him favor. What could this favor be? And how would Basinio recognize it as coming from Mary? "Peaceful slumber" refers to secular poetry that pleases and delights but has no Christian purpose.

The poem is undated but was probably written in the 1440s, during Basinio's extensive Greek studies in Ferrara. It shows that Basinio was aware of the differences and conflicts between pagan and Christian religious doctrines. He uses pagan terminology but also sees the impiety in following so closely Homer's descriptions of the pagan gods, setting out a stark distinction between Homer and Jesus. Despite his youthful guilt and promise to turn his genius toward Christian truths and praise for the Virgin and Christ, Basinio wrote some of the most outlandishly pagan poetry of the Renaissance; he chose Homer.

Twentieth-century scholarship largely demolished the idea that the Renaissance was a revival of paganism against medieval Christianity. Scholars showed that most humanists were actually practicing Christians, some took holy orders, and a few even became popes, notably Pope Pius II. In fact, far from rejecting Christianity in favor of paganism, humanists, they argued, developed a new kind of Christian spirituality, built on a Franciscan engagement with the world.[8] Other scholars have argued that humanists appropriated the forms of ancient literature not to challenge the dominant Christianity but to reform the Church through eloquence. Hagiography and church sermons were thus classicized but still Christian. Even the great humanist critic of the Church, Lorenzo Valla (1407–1457), who exposed the forgery of the Donation of Constantine in a diatribe against the papacy, has been seen as a devout Christian committed to Church reform.[9] In contrast, however, some scholars have argued that several humanists adopted not only the forms but also the pagan ethos of the culture they so revered.[10] The Florentine Platonist Marsilio Ficino (1433–1499) and other Renaissance philosophers promoted a number of pagan ideas that were incompatible with Christian beliefs, including the preexistence of the soul, astrological magic, Neoplatonic mysticism, and natural religion.[11] The prevalence of astrology and learned magic in the Renaissance, moreover, betrays a belief in a pagan deterministic view of human nature.[12] Alternatively, some humanists were receptive to Platonic ideas of monotheism and the tolerance that perforce followed polytheism and the plurality of ancient pagan beliefs. The political historian Quentin Skinner has essentially defined the Renaissance as the humanist adoption of pagan conceptions of virtue, honor, praise, fortune, and free will. Pagan notions of time, virtue, fortune, nature, the soul, and fate can be detected in many humanist works.[13] The idea of a pagan Renaissance has certainly returned to scholarly debate.

An extreme example of this is Machiavelli. Although Machiavelli is inconsistent on religion, and there is much scholarly debate, few other Renaissance writers took such explicit potshots at Christianity.[14] Machiavelli was responding to the tragedy of recent events, when Italian armies collapsed before the better-trained, better-armed, and ferocious military machines of France and the Habsburg princes. Italians, he believed, had lost the warrior spirit of antiquity. If they wanted to succeed against foreigners, Italians had to return to their roots and reclaim ancient Roman virtue.[15] The Christian church was corrupt and destined to be ever weak because it lacked an efficient mode of succession: papal policy could never be consistent, given that popes did not live long, and successors despised their predecessors.[16] Machiavelli's attack on church corruption was not new. But his criticism of Christian ideals was positively revolutionary. Even if a perfect Christian community were possible, it would still be bad. Christian ideals and virtues, with their focus on humility and the afterlife, had sapped humanity of life. The Christian ethos had made men weak by condemning glory as vanity and praising inactivity and cowardice over bravery and assertive action. If they wanted to succeed in the world, Machiavelli argued, Italians should replace the emasculating doctrines of Christianity with the life-affirming power of pagan virtues: fame, power, ambition, magnificence, glory, wealth, and that intangible *virtù,* which Machiavelli defined as a particularly manly ability to win; these pagan values were more conducive to success than Christian humility, meekness, and poverty.[17] The *Discourses on the First Decade of Livy* (1517) was Machiavelli's attempt to define pagan virtue from the history of the most successful empire to date. How did Rome achieve its greatness? The liberty of its citizens and its efficient government were duly noted factors. But most of all, the Roman religion inspired heroes to fight for the honors that they and their families would receive in this life. Religion provided the authority to shape society and guide the army to victory. Roman religion included the afterlife, but it was fundamentally about this life: augurs, omens, lots, the stars, and horoscopes were used to control the here-and-now, not to provide a comfortable afterlife. The Elysian Fields were entered not by abstention and monastic contemplation but by public virtue and heroic actions.[18] The real Renaissance was to be had in Roman religion and pagan morality.

Machiavelli was advocating a pagan ethos that previously had not been enunciated so forcefully and brilliantly, but it was nonetheless something that had already been voiced in quattrocento Italy. Intellectuals in Rimini and elsewhere in Italy were obsessed with ancient literature and culture: they read Latin and Greek closely and intensively; they imitated its language and copied its thought structures; and they appropriated the forms of pagan literature and adapted pagan ideas and concepts to their own lives. Even if they did not literally worship pagan gods, pagan values were an intrinsic part of the literary inheritance from antiquity that humanists conveyed in their imitations and appropriations of pagan literature. They may still have maintained the forms of Christian worship, but their Christianity was contaminated by pagan ideas. Pico della Mirandola (1463–1494) advocated a syncretic ancient theology and found concordances among the pagan Orphic mysteries, the Hebrew Cabala, and Christian theology, but much humanist literature, especially in Sigismondo's court, contained pagan concepts that were totally incompatible with Christian doctrine.[19] Machiavelli was writing a good fifty years after Sigismondo Malatesta was dead. But he expressed and made explicit ideas about paganism, war, glory, and masculine virtue that had already permeated the writings of the fifteenth-century humanists at the Malatesta court in Rimini. There is no evidence that Machiavelli read the works of these writers, but he reacted to the same classical texts that they absorbed and to similar cultural tensions and shifts.

The fact that pagan gods and mythology were omnipresent at the Malatesta court does not necessarily mean that there was a full revival of pagan religion, that the Malatesta family invoked prayers or sacrificed animals to Mars and Apollo. The ancient gods were essential poetic devices in Malatesta literature, but ones that carried with them a whole set of cultural and moral values. It is of course possible to appreciate a different religious culture without believing in it. But this is a modern attitude. After all, the dominant Church view about elite pagan religion was not that it was pure make-believe and therefore ineffective. In Christianity, pagan deities either became saints, such as Mercury to Saint Christopher, or demons, such as Diana linked to the female servants of Satan. What Christianity, therefore, did not adopt, it condemned as linked with the devil.[20] Like pagan gods, demons could be enticed to grant favors through sacrifice, invocation, and vows.

It is no coincidence that the Church cracked down on magic and witchcraft just when thousands of previously unknown classical texts became available in the fifteenth century. The witches themselves tended to be illiterate women who would not have even heard of, let alone read, Apuleius, the Sibylline books, or the occult texts of Neoplatonism, but the Dominican censors who composed the *Hammer of Witches,* the popular Church-sanctioned manual for witch-hunting, were reacting in part to a pagan religious revival. When people prayed to gods or demons, they were making pacts with the devil. They entered a world in which they had little control; they opened the door to evil, which could lead to quick gain, wealth, and power, but made the recipient a slave to the demon. This is why the Church condemned the occult arts and pagan worship. The Church demanded to have the monopoly on magical practice and controlled the only safe way to the divine, to the singular all-powerful Christian God.[21]

The pagan religious ideas and practices so ubiquitous in Malatesta literature went beyond mere literary conceit, as pagan content inescapably affected and reflected the religious culture that produced it.[22] Sigismondo Malatesta and the intellectuals in his court may have seen themselves as Christians, who built churches and received the sacraments, but their Christianity was contaminated: Macrobius, Virgil, and Plato shaped debates about the soul; Homer, Cicero, Livy, Plutarch, and Caesar guided notions of heroism and civic virtue; and Catullus, Propertius, and Ovid provided the vocabulary and ideals for passionate romance and sexuality.

Literature always holds something of the context in which it was written.[23] Classical literature provided Renaissance intellectuals with models to imitate but also solid information about religion, philosophy, and the spiritual world. Specialization was uncommon in the premodern world, and literature often contained deep philosophical and religious beliefs, and so Virgil's *Aeneid* was used to access divine truths, just as the Bible was. In an argumentative and serious work of theology, the *City of God,* Saint Augustine quite often uses the *Aeneid* as a source for Platonic ideas about the soul and the afterlife, and a basis for his own theological meditations.[24] Basinio's epic poem imitates and repeats many of the pagan religious ideas that are essential to Homer's and Virgil's poems.

More than any other humanist poet, Basinio was competing with Virgil and Homer. He refused to translate Homer not because he lacked the ability but because he saw himself as a vatic, inspired poet, channeling the divine truths of the spirit. To be a modern-day Homer or Virgil, Basinio had to be a prophet, inspired by the muses to reveal a world in which the divine was immanent, a world in which heroic individuals, such as Sigismondo, could transcend the limits of the human condition through prowess in battle, true pagan virtue, and philosophical contemplation. This inventive and laudatory poetry is a testament to the resurgence of Platonic-Macrobian ideas about the universe, the nature of the soul, and the afterlife, ideas and values that are ubiquitous in Malatesta court literature and art and that informed Sigismondo's public image and actions both in the triumphant 1450s and in his desperate last years.

The heart of religion is morality. Behavior brings one closer to or further from the divine. When pagan antiquity returned through its powerful literary culture, it brought with it a morality different from Christianity, a pagan morality that focused more on heroism in this world, action, and strength than contemplative prayer and humility. Fame and glory in this life led to a blessed afterlife; the Elysian Fields, in particular, were reserved for men who had been politically active and had sacrificed themselves for the common good. Whereas Christian martyrs accepted their torments for God and their own salvation, the heroes of pagan antiquity died to save their comrades and their homeland. Such comparisons may simplify the situation, but different religions reward and punish sometimes radically different behaviors. In the classical and Christian traditions, morality starts in religion; laws worked because they had otherworldly authority, whether it came from Numa Pompilius's wise nymph or Moses's burning bush. The God of the Hebrew Scriptures might have been a jealous god, but his transformation in the New Testament into a singular, all-powerful, loving, good, and perfect being, had little resonance in the brutal, conniving, jealous, and destructive world of pagan polytheism. What does it mean when in Porcellio's epic poem, Jupiter is enraged by frustrated love and starts a war in Olympus over Isotta degli Atti? Or angry gods both help and plot against Sigismondo in battle in Basinio's epic? In Malatesta poetry, Sigismondo is repeatedly presented as sacrificing bulls to Mars and the gods. The point is not that Sigismondo actually sacrificed—that would be a naïve reading—but that these images were acceptable to the ruler and found an audience all over Italy, as copies of the works were given to other rulers.

Sigismondo promoted an image of himself as a pagan. Such a construction may not have been in opposition to Christianity; the Tempio was, of course, a Franciscan church. But it certainly nuanced and even submerged Christian truths in an assertive pagan way, just as the Christian church was encased in pagan imagery, and a pagan philosopher and a classicizing poet were enshrined in tombs on its outer walls. The pronounced paganism of Sigismondo's court may also have had a political motive. In the fifteenth century, the Papal States were consolidated and expanded. Popes and cardinals led armies into battle and perpetrated brutal acts of violence in subjecting peoples to Church rule. But they were always holy men with special exclusive access to the divine. Their swords were all the more unstoppable as they controlled the only way to heaven. Rimini was part of the Papal States that stretched from just above Naples to Bologna and all the way across to the Adriatic. The Malatesta court had governed Rimini for the popes since the thirteenth century, but relations inevitably became tense when the popes returned to Rome in the fifteenth century, sought greater control, and expanded their domains in Italy. It is no coincidence that the pagan content of Malatesta culture grew significantly as the papacy started reasserting its hold on the Romagna in the 1450s. A stronger papacy meant a weaker Malatesta government. In the *Discipula* invective, Pius accused Sigismondo of "affirming in many places . . . that clerics should not be allowed to have civil dominion."[25] Before the disastrous war with Pope Pius II (1458–1464), Sigismondo was already trying to check the expanding Church by political, military, and cultural means. Alfonso of Aragon had been Sigismondo's mortal enemy since 1447 and continually tried to turn Pope Nicholas V against the lord of Rimini. Relations were further exacerbated after Sigismondo soundly beat Ferrante, Alfonso's son, in 1453. When a Spaniard became Pope Calixtus III in 1455, the Aragonese had a powerful ally in their anti-Malatesta quest. Sigismondo responded to the pressure by supporting the Angevin claim to the throne of Naples. Jean d'Anjou came down with a small army but was forced to retreat and return to France in failure. Sigismondo's cultural patronage with its pagan focus could be read as part of his ultimately futile efforts to consolidate and assert his own empire against the hierarchical Christianity of an ever-expanding papacy.

In his highly sophisticated use of verbal and visual classical rhetoric, Sigismondo emerges as the epitome of Burckhardt's ruler, the self-asserting Renaissance individual who crafts his state as a work of art.[26] In Rimini, paganism becomes the ultimate rhetorical device to bolster and assert the political presence of one of Italy's minor yet outspoken city-states. Malatesta humanists saw their patron as a reborn classical hero, a warrior in the mold of Alexander, Caesar, and the ancient commanders, who embodied the ideals of pagan virtue, imbibed pagan wisdom, and lived the principles of the Greek *paideia;* Sigismondo was a Homeric hero who had undergone the Spartan training of his body and exhibited ancient Roman valor on the battlefield. This portrait of Sigismondo was an assertion of power and a bulwark against an imperialistic papacy in fifteenth-century Italy.

War, sexuality, and religion are all subjects on which Christianity and paganism conflict. Sigismondo was notorious for his libido, his military aggression, and his disrespect for Christianity. This reputation came from a hostile smear campaign against Sigismondo in his later life, and for this reason, some scholars have tried to deny its accuracy. In Malatesta court literature, however, many of these same qualities were not denied but were transformed into positive praise. Humanists praised Sigismondo's passionate devotion to one woman rather than violent insatiable lust; they celebrated Sigismondo's craftiness and glory rather than treachery in war and hubris; and they extolled his extreme piety to the pagan gods rather than his hostility to Christianity. All these ideals expressed in the art and literature of the Malatesta court show that the culture was pagan, and this culture was directly connected to morality and religion. The vehemence and success of Pius's attack demonstrates the dangerous power of the pagan culture Sigismondo created in Rimini. If this Homeric Renaissance in Rimini was a short-lived, isolated phenomenon, a limit case in the embrace of pagan values, the image of pagan heroism celebrated in Sigismondo's court would resurface again in Machiavelli's writings. The ways in which Sigismondo's legacy, as a demon or a hero, has resonated over the centuries, even into the terrible ideologies of modern times, suggest how much was at stake in this cultural war over Sigismondo's soul.

NOTES

ACKNOWLEDGMENTS

INDEX

Notes

All translations are my own unless otherwise noted.

1. The Pope's Wrath and the Black Legend

1. Latin in Enea Silvio Piccolomini Papa Pio II, *I commentarii,* ed. Luigi Totaro, second edition (Milan: Adelphi, 2004), 1448–1449 (bk. VII, ch. 11), 1558–1559 (bk. VII, ch. 3); Francesco G. Battaglini, *Della vita e de'fatti di Sigismondo Pandolfo Malatesta* (Rimini: ex typographica Albertiniana, 1794), 510; Ludwig von Pastor, *The History of the Popes from the Close of the Middle Ages,* ed. Frederick Ignatius Antrobus (St. Louis: Herder, 1906), vol. 3: 125–126; Giovanni Soranzo, "La tragica sorte dello stato di Sigismondo Pandolfo Malatesta," in *Studi Malatestiani* (Faenza: Società di Studi Romagnoli, 1952), 197–212, esp. 205–207; Andre Vauchez, "Pio II e la canonizzazione infernale di Sigismondo Pandolfo" in *La signoria di Sigismondo Pandolfo Malatesti,* vol. 2: *La politica e le imprese militari,* ed. Anna Falcioni (Rimini: B. Ghigi, 2006), 557–571; and Costanza Gislon Dopfel, "Reshaping Rome's Narrative: The Curious Case of Sigismondo Malatesta's Execution" in *Early Modern Rome, 1341–1667,* ed. Portia Prebys (Rome: SATE, 2011), 682–690, who reads the placement of the bonfires in three different squares as Pius's attempt to assert papal power over Rome.
2. "Una festa da mascare" in Bartolomeo Bonatto, "Letter to Ludovico Gonzaga, Marquis of Mantua," described in *Sigismondo Pandolfo Malatesta e il suo Tempo,* ed. Franca Arduini (Rimini: Neri Pozza, 1970), 29.
3. Andrea Benzi-Pius II, *Discipula veritatis,* in *Pii secundi epistolae* (Milan: Antonius Zarothus, 1487), n.p., 77 in scan of this edition, available at http://fondosdigitales.us.es/fondos/libros/204/67/epistola-siue-oratio-pii-in-conuentu-mantuano/. Henceforth pages refer to this scanned edition. See also Pastor, *History of the Popes,* vol. 3: 117. See the official letter (dated 23 February 1461) that Pius sent to

Sigismondo's vassals, relieving them of their oath of fealty, in Luigi Tonini, *Rimini nella signoria de' Malatesti, parte seconda al volume quinto: Appendice di documenti* (Rimini: Albertini, 1882), 222–223.

4. Pio II, *I commentarii*, 908–913 (bk. V, ch. 12). The longest version of the invective is available only in the 1487 edition of Pius's works (Milan). Shorter versions are found in other editions. On the problematic relations between the invective and the bull, see Franco Gaeta, "La 'leggenda' di Sigismondo Malatesta," in *Studi malatestiani,* ed. Philip James Jones (Rome: Istituto Storico Italiano per il Medievo, 1978), 164–169; and Piero Craveri, "Benzi, Andrea," *Dizionario biografico degli italiani,* vol.8 (Rome: Istituto della Enciclopedia italiana, 1966), 712–714.
5. Benzi-Pius II, *Discipula,* 98.
6. Ibid., 95.
7. Ibid., 92.
8. Pius II, *Commentaries,* ed. Margaret Meserve and Marcello Simonetta and trans. Margaret Meserve (Cambridge: Harvard University Press, 2003), 327 (bk. II, ch. 32).
9. Ibid., 332–335 (bk. II, ch. 32). I have paraphrased the Latin. For the other accusations, see *Discipula veritatis* and Giovanni Soranzo, "Un'invettiva della curia romana contro Sigismondo Pandolfo Malatesta" part 1, *La Romagna* 7 (1910): 462–489; part 2, *La Romagna* 8 (1911): 150–175; part 3, *La Romagna* 8 (1911): 241–288.
10. Battaglini, *Della vita,* 300–301.
11. Reginald Gregoire, "Tra leggenda agiografica e religiosita' francescana: Galeotto Roberto Malatesta (1432)," in *Templum Mirabile: Atti del convegno sul Tempio Malatestiano* (Rimini: Fondazione Cassa di Risparmio di Rimini, 2003), 123–137; Anna Falcioni, "Malatesta, Galeotto Roberto," *Dizionario biografico degli italiani* 68 (Rome: Istituto della Enciclopedia italiana, 2007).
12. Pio II, *I commentarii,* 1906–1909 (bk. X, ch. 13). On Galeotto, see also Jones, *Malatesta,* 175.
13. Helen Ettlinger, "The Sepulchre on the Facade: A Re-evaluation of Sigismondo Malatesta's Rebuilding of San Francesco in Rimini," *Journal of the Warburg and Courtauld Institutes,* 53 (1990): 133–143; Gaspare Broglio Tartaglia, *Cronaca malatestiana del secolo XV,* ed. Antonio G. Luciani (Rimini: Bruno Ghigi, 1982), 43. His body appears to have been left where Galeotto had wished it, humbly buried in the ground in front of the church, as noted in Falcioni, ""Malatesta, Galeotto Roberto."
14. Pius II, *Commentaries,* 328–329 (bk. II, ch. 32). I translate *daemones* as "demons" (plural) instead of "the devil." See succinct discussion in Marco Folin, "Sigismondo Pandolfo Malatesta, Pio II e il Tempio Malatestiano: La chiesa di

san Francesco come manifesto politico," in *Il Tempio Malatestiano a Rimini,* ed. Antonio Paolucci (Modena: Franco Cosimo Panini, 2010), vol. 2: 29–31.

15. *Der Briefwechsel des Eneas Silvius Piccolomini,* ed. Rudolf Wolkan, Fontes Rerum Austriacarum, vol. 61 (Vienna: A. Holder, 1909), 214, *Ep.* 94, to *Gaspari Sligk, imperiali cancellario, November 1443.* I wish to thank Emily O'Brien for giving me the reference for this and the following Piccolomini letter.
16. Ibid., 190, *Ep.* 78, *genitori suo Silvio,* September 1443, ". . . vicit cupido, incalui, mulierem arsi multisque blandimentis adorsus sum."
17. Ibid., 191, *Ep.* 78.
18. Emily O'Brien, "Aeneas Silvius Piccolomini's *Chrysis:* Prurient Pastime or Something More?" *Modern Language Notes* 124 (2009): 119–120. For Pius's views on clerical celibacy, see Anthony D'Elia, *The Renaissance of Marriage in Fifteenth-Century Italy* (Cambridge: Harvard University Press, 2004), 123.
19. On Pius's views on conciliarism, see Emily O'Brien, "The Conciliar Histories of Aeneas Silvius Piccolomini," in *Councils and Reform: A Fifteenth-Century Legacy Revisited,* ed. Gerald Christianson, Thomas M. Izbicki, and Christopher Bellitto (Washington, D.C.: Catholic University Press, 2008), 60–81.
20. Philip James Jones, *The Malatesta of Rimini and the Papal State: A Political History* (Cambridge: Cambridge University Press, 1974), 33–34. See the somewhat biased history of the family in Pio II, *I commentarii,* 1867–1913 (bk. X, ch. 13).
21. The best account of Sigismondo's political life is Jones, *Malatesta,* 176–239.
22. Pius II, *Commentaries,* 332–335 (bk. II, ch. 32). I have paraphrased the Latin.
23. Pastor, *History of the Popes,* vol. 3: 123–125.
24. Benzi-Pius II, *Discipula,* 69.
25. Erich Meuthen, *Nicholas of Cusa: A Sketch for a Biography,* trans. David Crowner and Gerald Christianson (Washington, D.C.: The Catholic University of America Press, 2010 (orig. 1964)), 58–68, 130; Edgar Wind, *Pagan Mysteries of the Renaissance: An Exploration of Philosophical and Mystical Sources of Iconography in Renaissance Art* (New York: Norton, 1968 (orig. 1958)), 218–221, 248.
26. Pius had a difficult relationship with the cardinal, who once broke down in tears and offered his resignation because, he said, the pope refused to consult with the cardinals, as noted in Pio II, *I commentarii,* 1445 (bk. VII, ch. 9).
27. Pio II, *I commentarii,* 910–913 (bk. V, ch. 12).
28. Benzi-Pius II, *Discipula,* 69.
29. Ibid., 70.
30. Ibid., 90.
31. Ibid., 63.
32. Ibid., 64.
33. Ibid., 65.
34. Ibid.

35. Ibid., 68.
36. Ibid., 67.
37. Ibid., 89.
38. Dante Alighieri, *Inferno,* XXXIII.146–147; Niccolò Machiavelli, "Belfagor, the Devil Who Took a Wife" (1515–1520), in *The Portable Machiavelli,* ed. and trans. Peter Bondanella and Mark Musa (New York: Viking-Penguin, 1979), 419–429.
39. Benzi-Pius II, *Discipula,* 78.
40. Ibid., 90; Pio II, *I commentarii,* 910–911 (bk. V, ch. 12).
41. Bernardino, *On the Torments of Hell; De Christ. Rel.,* 14; *De Evang. Aet.,* 12, 22; *Extraordinarii,* 18; *Opera,* III, 383 (1745). Also discussed in Franco Mormando, *The Preacher's Demons: Bernardino of Siena and the Social Underworld of Early Renaissance Italy* (Chicago: University of Chicago Press, 1999), 14–15.
42. *Reject Aeneas, Accept Pius: Selected Letters of Aeneas Sylvius Piccolomini (Pope Pius II),* intro. and trans. Thomas M. Izbicki, Gerald Christianson, and Philip Krey (Washington, D.C.; Catholic University Press, 2006), 13; Aeneas Sylvius Piccolomini, *De viris illustribus,* ed. Adrianus Van Heck (Vatican City: BAV, 1991), 37–41. On Bernardino's popularity, see Mormando, *Preacher's Demons,* 1–4. The bull for Bernardino is in Laerzio Cherubini, ed., *Magnum bullarium Romanum* (Lyons: Arnaud, 1692), vol. 1: 275–277.
43. Aeneas Sylvius Piccolomini, *Europe (c. 1400–1458),* trans. Robert Brown, ed. Nancy Bishaha (Washington, D.C.; Catholic University Press, 2013), 287–288; Dionisio Pacetti, "Gli scritti di S. Bernardino da Siena" in *S. Bernardino da Siena: Saggi e ricerche pubblicate nel quinto centenario della morte (1444–1944)* (Milan: Vita e Pensiero, 1945), 134, n. 2; Celestino Piana, "S. Bernardino da Siena teologo," in *S. Bernardino da Siena: Saggi e ricerche pubblicate nel quinto centenario della morte (1444–1944)* (Milan: Vita e Pensiero, 1945), 195.
44. *De viris illustribus,* 37; Mormando, *Preacher's Demons,* 241, n. 4.
45. The 1461 bull for Catherine of Siena is in Cherubini, *Magnum bullarium,* vol. I: 386–389.
46. For the shift in focus from medieval magus to Renaissance witch, see Brian P. Levack, *The Witch-hunt in Early Modern Europe,* second edition (New York: Longman, 1995).
47. Mormando, *Preacher's Demons,* 54–66.
48. Ibid., 59.
49. These examples are translated and quoted in ibid., 91.
50. Bernardino da Siena, *Prediche volgari sul Campo di Siena, 1427* (Rusconi: Milan, 1989), vol. II: 894–895.
51. Piana, "S. Bernardino," 186–187. See, for example, Thomas Aquinas, *Summa theologica,* II.1.Question 87.4, and Augustine, *City of God,* xxi.11.

52. Dionisio Pacetti, "Cronologia bernardiniana," in *S. Bernardino da Siena: Saggi e ricerche pubblicate nel quinto centenario della morte* (1444–1944) (Milan: Vita e Pensiero, 1945), 454.
53. Pio II, *I commentarii,* 910–913 (bk. V, ch. 12).
54. Craveri, "Benzi," 713.
55. Cherubini, *Magnum bullarium,* vol. 1: 388.
56. Ibid., 389.
57. Caroline Walker Bynum, *Holy Feast and Holy Fast: The Religious Significance of Food to Medieval Women* (Berkeley: University of California Press, 1987), 167.
58. Cherubini, *Magnum bullarium,* vol. I: 388.
59. Bynum, *Holy Feast,* 168; Bull for Catherine of Siena (1461), 388–389.
60. Cherubini, *Magnum bullarium,* vol. I: 387.
61. Ibid., 389.
62. Bynum, *Holy Feast,* 169.
63. Quoted in ibid., 179.
64. Ibid., 175.
65. Catherine of Siena, *The Dialogue,* trans. and intro. Suzanne Noffke (New York: Paulist Press, 1980), 4.
66. Ibid., 71, 73.
67. Ibid., 251–255.
68. Ibid., 74–75.
69. Ibid., 77.
70. Ibid., 75.
71. Introduction to ibid., 6–7.
72. Ibid., 214–215, 249, 328.
73. Cherubini, *Magnum bullarium,* vol. I: 387.
74. Ibid., 387.
75. Ibid., 387.
76. Catherine of Siena, *Dialogue,* 91, 99, 158, 161, 268.
77. Giovanni Simonetta, *Rerum gestarum Francisci Sfortiae mediolanensium ducis commentarii,* ed. Giovanni Soranzo (Bologna: Zanichelli, 1932–1943), 335; Fra Jacopo Filippo Foresti, *Supplementum chronicarum* (Brescia: Boninus de Boninis, 1485), fol. 342. On this, see Lawrence S. Rainey, *Ezra Pound and the Monument of Culture: Text, History, and the Malatesta Cantos* (Chicago: University of Chicago Press, 1991), 89–93.
78. Giovanni Gioviano Pontano, *De immanitate liber,* ed. Liliana Monti Sabia (Naples: Loffredo, 1970), 33 (ch. 17), says that Roberto had to use a dagger to escape his father's advances. Pio II, *I commentarii,* 908–911 (bk. V, ch. 12), suggests these crimes in his rhetorical complaint that the invective did not include how Sigismondo raped his daughters and sons-in-law.

79. Cesare Clementini, *Raccolto istorico della fondatione di Rimini* (Bologna: Forni, 1969) (facsimile of the 1617/1627 edition); Battaglini, *Della vita.* On Francesco and his brother Angelo Battaglini, see Antonio Piromalli, *La cultura letteraria nelle corti dei Malatesti* (Rimini: Ghigi, 2002), 85–89. On the nineteenth and early twentieth century historiography on the accusations of Sigismondo's wife murders, see the overview by Rainey, *Ezra Pound,* 91–117, and his summary, available at http://www.english.illinois.edu/maps/poets/m_r/pound/poundandmalatesta.htm.
80. Luigi Passerini, "I Malatesta di Rimini," *Tavola XIII* in *Dispensa,* 161 (Milan: Tipografia delle Famiglie Italiane, 1869) of Pompeo Litta, *Famiglie celebri italiane* (Milan: Tipografia delle Famiglie Italiane, 1819–1874, *Dispense,* 1–176, as discussed in Rainey, *Ezra Pound,* 99–101.
81. Soranzo, "Un'invettiva." On the immediate context of Soranzo's writings, see Rainey, *Ezra Pound,* 113–115.
82. Burckhardt, *Civilization,* 39, 151, 288. On this, see Rainey, *Ezra Pound,* 101–102, and Piromalli, *La cultura letteraria,* 107–111.
83. Friedrich Nietzsche, *All too Human: A Book for Free Spirits* (1878); as discussed and quoted in Rainey, *Ezra Pound,* 158.
84. J. A. Symonds, *Renaissance in Italy,* vol. 2: *Age of the Despots* (London: Smith Elder and Co., 1897), 135.
85. Charles Yriarte, *Un condottiere au XVe siècle: Rimini: Études sur les lettres et les arts à la cour des Malatesta* (Paris: J. Rothschild, 1882). On Yriarte's importance for the modern image of Sigismondo, see Rainey, *Ezra Pound,* 109–112.
86. Yriarte, *Un condottiere,* 103, 146, 191, 198; Giovanni Soranzo, "La sigla 'SI' di Sigismondo Pandolfo Malatesta," *La Romagna* 6 (1909): 306–324.
87. Corrado Ricci, *Il Tempio Malatestiano* (Rome: Bettstetti & Tuminelli, 1924), 315–319.
88. Gabriel D'Annunzio, *Francesca da Rimini* (Rimini: Raffaelli, 2003), 161–162, reprint of 1903 ed. Dante, *Inferno,* V.31 "the infernal storm that never stops." On D'Annunzio, see Piromalli, *La cultura letteraria,* 112–135.
89. Edward Hutton, *Sigismondo Pandolfo Malatesta: The Lord of Rimini: A Study of a Fifteenth Century Italian Despot* (New York: E. P. Dutton, 1906), 27.
90. Antonio Beltramelli, *Un tempio d'amore* (Rimini: Raffaelli, 2004 (orig. 1912)).
91. Ibid., 30, 48. On Beltramelli, see Rainey, *Ezra Pound,* 72–73.
92. Antonio Beltramelli, *L'uomo nuovo* (Rome: Mondadori, 1923), 56–57. On the violent Romagna of the Middle Ages, see John Larner, *The Lords of the Romagna: Romagnol Society and the Origins of the Signorie* (New York: St. Martin's Press, 1965).
93. Rainey, *Ezra Pound,* 4–5, 27, reads the Cantos in direct relation to the rise of Fascism in Italy.
94. Ezra Pound, Draft A, lines 39–51, quoted in ibid., 30.

95. Quoted and discussed in detail in Rainey, *Ezra Pound*, 30–37; Pius II, *Commentaries*, 328 (bk. II, ch. 32).
96. Henri de Montherlant, *Malatesta* (1946) act IV, scene 9.
97. Soranzo; Jones; Anna Falcioni, *La signoria di Sigismondo Malatesta. L'economia* (Rimini: Bruno Ghigi, 1998); *La signoria di Sigismondo Malatesta. La politica e le imprese militari*, ed. Anna Falcioni (Rimini: Ghigi, 2006). On Sigismondo's artistic patronage and the Tempio, see Ricci, *Tempio;* Marilyn Aronberg Lavin, "Piero della Francesca's Fresco of Sigismondo Pandolfò Malatesta before St. Sigismund: ΘΕΩΙΑΘΑΝΑΤΩΙ ΚΑΙ ΤΗΙ ΠΟΛΕΙ," *The Art Bulletin* 56.3 (1974): 345–374; Angelo Turchini, *Il Tempio Malatestiano, Sigismondo Pandolfo Malatesta e Leon Battista Alberti* (Cesena: "Il Ponte Vecchio," 2000); Stanko Kokole, "Agostino di Duccio in the Tempio Malatestiano, 1449–1457: Challenges of Poetic Invention and Fantasies of Personal Style," 2 vols. (Ph.D. diss., The Johns Hopkins University, 1997); Ettlinger, "The Sepulchre on the Facade," 133–143; Charles Hope, "The Early History of the Tempio Malatestiano," *Journal of the Warburg and Courtauld Institutes* 55 (1992), 51–154; Maria Grazia Pernis and Laurie Adams, *Federico da Montefeltro & Sigismondo Malatesta: The Eagle and the Elephant* (New York: Peter Lang, 1996).
98. Jean Seznec, *The Survival of the Pagan Gods: The Mythological Tradition and Its Place in Renaissance Humanism and Art* (Princeton: Princeton University Press, 1995), 136.
99. Among others, see the previously cited studies of Ettlinger and Lavin.
100. Roberto Valturio, *De re militari* (Paris: Apud Christianum Wechelum, 1534). The best life of Valturio is still Aldo Francesco Massera, "Roberto Valturio: 'Omnium scientiarum doctor et monarcha' (1405–1475)," 1925–1927, reprinted in *Roberto Valturio: Saggi critici*, ed. Paola Delbianco (Rimini: Y Press, 2006), 27–42.
101. Basinio da Parma, "Hesperis," in *Basinii parmensis poetae opera praestantiora* (Rimini: Albertiniana, 1794), vol. 1: 1–288. A. Campana, "Basinio da Parma," *Dizionario biografico degli italiani* 7 (Rome: Istituto della Enciclopedia italiana, 1965): 89–98; Kristen Lippincott, "The Neo-Latin Historical Epics of North Italian Courts: An Examination of 'Courtly Culture' in the Fifteenth Century," *Renaissance Studies* 3.4 (1989): 415–420.
102. On the classical sources of the *Hesperis*, see Vladimiro Zabughin, *Vergilio nel Rinascimento italiano da Dante a Torquato Tasso*, ed. Stefano Carrai and Alberto Cavarzere, 2 vols. (Trent: Università degli Studi di Trento, 2000), vol. 1: 287–293; Antonio Belloni, *Storia dei generi letterari italiani: Il poema epico e mitologico* (Milan: F. Vallardi, 1912), 92–100; and Christoph Pieper, "In Search of the Marginal Author: The Working Copy of Basinio of Parma's *Hesperis*," in *Neo-Latin Philology: Old Tradition, New Approaches*, ed. Marc van der Poel (Leuven University Press, 2014), 49–70. The latter was too recent for proper use.

103. Massera, "Roberto Valturio," 241; Giovanni Soranzo, "Una missione di Sigismondo Pandolfo Malatesta a Maometto II nel 1461," *La Romagna* 3.6 (1909), 7. Although the *Hesperis* was "incomplete" at Basinio's death, Sigismondo's distribution or intention to distribute the poem is clear, as he had at least three manuscript copies of it made and paid the artist Giovanni da Fano to illustrate each with about twenty sumptuous images in color. On this, see Otto Pächt, "Giovanni da Fano's Illustrations for Basinio's Epos Hesperis" in *Studi malatestiani,* ed. Augusto Campana (Faenza: Lega, 1952), 91–111, and Campana, "Basinio," 95–96.

104. In the Sistine Chapel there are five sibyls and seven Hebrew prophets. Images of the sibyls in Italian churches start appearing in the later fifteenth century, decades after the Tempio. On this, see Charles L. Stinger, *The Renaissance in Rome* (Bloomington: Indiana University Press, 1985), 309–314.

2. Court Culture and the Renaissance in Rimini

1. Philip James Jones, *The Malatesta of Rimini and the Papal State: A Political History* (Cambridge: Cambridge University Press, 1974), 123–125, 154–158, 165; Robert Tavernor, *On Alberti and the Art of Building* (New Haven: Yale University Press, 1998), 216. Pandolfo's impotence is noted in Giovanni di M. Pedrino, *Cronica del suo tempo,* ed. A. Pasini (Rome: Biblioteca Apostolica Vaticana, 1929), vol. 1: 161–162. Pius questions Pandolfo's paternity of Sigismondo, in Enea Silvio Piccolomini Papa Pio II, *I Commentarii,* ed. Luigi Totaro, second edition (Milan: Adelphi, 2004), 1904–1907 (bk. X, ch. 13).

2. The chief rebel was Giovanni di Ramberto. On this, see Francesco Gaetano Battaglini, *Della vita e de'fatti di Sigismondo Pandolfo Malatesta* (Rimini: Albertiniana, 1794), 286–292; Luigi Tonini, *Rimini nella signoria de' Malatesti, parte seconda al volume quinto* (Rimini: Albertini, 1882), 84–88; Jones, *Malatesta,* 171–175.

3. Battaglini, *Della vita,* 306–307; Tonini, *Rimini nella signoria de' Malatesti,* 97–98.

4. Gaspare Broglio Tartaglia, *Cronaca malatestiana del secolo XV,* ed. Antonio G. Luciani (Rimini: Bruno Ghigi, 1982), 47–48; Cesare Clementini, *Raccolto istorico della fondatione di Rimini* (Bologna: Forni, 1969), 303–304 (facsimile of the 1617/1627 edition); Jones, *Malatesta,* 180; Tavernor, *On Alberti,* 50; Marilyn Aronberg Lavin, "Piero della Francesca's Fresco of Sigismondo Pandolfò Malatesta before St. Sigismund: ΘΕΩΙΑΘΑΝΑΤΩΙ ΚΑΙ ΤΗΙ ΠΟΛΕΙ," *The Art Bulletin* 56.3 (1974): 356.

5. Lavin, "Piero," 354–356, 368–373. Although she acknowledges it, Lavin downplays the historical connection to the imperial knighthood and argues that the painting is an expression of Sigismondo's devotion to God and the city of Rimini.

6. Pedrino, *Cronica,* 47; Biondo (*Roma Triumphans,* bk. II) says that Carlo staged a "ludus Troiae" in Biondo Flavio, *Scritti inediti e rari di Biondo Flavio,* ed. Bartolomeo Nogara (Rome: Tipografia Poliglotta Vaticana, 1927), xxiv.
7. Battaglini, *Vita,* 310–311; Clementini, *Raccolto,* 305–306, 312–313.
8. Battaglini, *Vita,* 328; Broglio, *Cronaca,* in Tonini, *Rimini nella signoria,* 111, 128–129.
9. Minou Schraven, "Out of Sight, Yet Still in Place: On the Use of Italian Renaissance Portrait Medals as Building Deposits," *Res: Anthropology and Aesthetics* (2009) *55/56: Absconding,* 186; Clementini, *Raccolto,* 309. Artillery was used in Italian warfare from the late fourteenth century, as noted in Robert Douglas Smith, "Artillery," in *The Oxford Encyclopedia of Medieval Warfare and Military Technology,* ed. Clifford Rogers (New York: Oxford University Press, 2010), vol. 1: 84.
10. Roberto Valturio, *De re militari* (Paris: Apud Christianum Wechelum, 1534), 10–11 (bk. I, ch. 2); Battaglini, *Della vita,* 326.
11. Joanna Woods-Marsden, "Images of Castles in the Renaissance: Symbols of "Signoria"/Symbols of Tyranny," *Art Journal* 48.2 (1989): 130–137, esp. 131–133, 135.
12. Basinio da Parma, "Hesperis," in *Basinii Parmensis Poetae opera praestantiora* (Rimini: Albertiniana, 1794), vol. 1, *Hesperis,* 81 (IV.172–174); Carla Tomasini Pietramellara, "La Rocca Malatestiana: Da case fortificate a prigione," in *Castel sismondo e Sigismondo Pandolfo Malatesta,* ed. Carla Tomasini Pietramellara and Angelo Turchini (Rimini: Ghigi, 1985), 40–45.
13. Battaglini, *Della vita,* 131, published the six-line poem. On this and other humanist works in praise of Malatesta castles, see Piergiorgio Parroni, "I castelli nella letteratura umanistica e cortigiana," in *Castel Sismondo, Sigismondo Pandolfo Malatesta e l'arte militare del primo rinascimento,* ed. Angelo Turchini (Cesena: "Il Ponte Vecchio," 2003), 325–336, esp. 331–334.
14. Anne Dunlop, *Painted Palaces: The Rise of Secular Art in Early Renaissance Italy* (University Park: Pennsylvania State University Press, 2009), 114–122.
15. Joanna Woods-Marsden, "How Quattrocento Princes Used Art: Sigismondo Pandolfo Malatesta of Rimini and *cose militari,*" *Renaissance Studies* 3.4 (1989), 391–393.
16. Dunlop, *Painted Palaces,* 165–166.
17. Battaglini, *Della vita,* 263; Broglio, *Cronaca,* 3.
18. Woods-Marsden, "How Quattrocento Princes," 392.
19. Jones, *Malatesta,* 129, 175.
20. For the intimate connections between the two families, see Enrico Angiolini, "I Malatesti e gli Estensi," in *Malatesta Novello nell'Italia delle signorie: Fonti e interpretazioni,* ed. Marino Mengozzi and Claudio Riva (Cesena: Stilgraf, 2005), 107–139; Jones, *Malatesta,* 179.

21. Marco Viroli, *Signore di Romagna: Le altre leonesse, dame, amanti e guerriere nelle corti romagnole* (Cesena: "Il Ponte Vecchio," 2010), 71–87; Pedrino, *Cronica,* 128.
22. In 1435, for example, Sigismondo and Ginevra were in Ferrara for an extended period to celebrate Leonello's marriage to Margherita Gonzaga, as noted in Battaglini, *Della vita,* 316.
23. Anthony Grafton, *Commerce with the Classics: Ancient Books and Renaissance Readers* (Ann Arbor: University of Michigan Press, 1997), 19–35.
24. Valturio, *De re militari,* 5, 9 (bk. I, ch. 2); Giuseppe Mazzatinti, "La Biblioteca di San Francesco (Tempio Malatestiano) in Rimini" in *Scritti vari di filologia in onore di Ernesto Monaci* (Rome: Forzani, 1901), 345–352.
25. Valturio, *De re militari,* 12.
26. Woods-Marsden, "How Quattrocento Princes," 388–390.
27. Woods-Marsden, "Images of Castles," 130–137, esp. 131–133, 135; Woods-Marsden, "How Quattrocento Princes," 400–402.
28. As discussed above in chapter 1.
29. Michael Baxandall translates and discusses the letter in "Guarino, Pisanello, and Manuel Chrysoloras," *Journal of the Warburg and Courtauld Institute* 28 (1965): 186–187, 201–202. On Guarino's letter and Basinio, see Stanko Kokole, "Agostino di Duccio in the Tempio Malatestiano, 1449–1457: Challenges of Poetic Invention and Fantasies of Personal Style," 2 vols. (Ph.D. diss., The Johns Hopkins University, 1997), 244–253.
30. This was chiefly known from two popular texts from late antiquity: The Neoplatonic commentary of Macrobius on *Cicero's Dream of Scipio Africanus* (fifth century CE) and Martianus Capella's *Marriage of Mercury and Philology* (fifth century CE).
31. Kokole, "Agostino di Duccio," 248–253. On the Stoic and Neoplatonic meanings of the three graces in Renaissance art, see Edgar Wind, *Pagan Mysteries in the Renaissance: An Exploration of Philosophical and Mystical Sources of iconography in Renaissance Art* (New York: Norton, 1968), 26–35, 265.
32. Basinio, *Hesperis,* 183–184 (IX.36–41).
33. Ibid., 188 (IX.148–155).
34. Charles Mitchell emphasized the sun imagery in the Tempio and argued that the iconography centered on identifying Sigismondo with Apollo, in "Il Tempio Malatestiano" in *Studi Malatestiani,* ed. Philip James Jones (Rome: Istituto Storico Italiano per il Medievo, 1978), 71–103.
35. Marsilio Ficino, *de sole* (1494), available at http://www.users.globalnet.co.uk/~alfar2/ficino.htm; A. Keller, "Two Byzantine Scholars and Their Reception in Italy," *Journal of the Warburg and Courtauld Institutes* 20.3/4 (1957): 363–370, esp. 366–370.

36. Basinio, *Hesperis,* 243 (XI.419–425). Cf. Basinio, *Hesperis,* 13 (I.300–304), where Basinio compares Sigismondo to Orion's golden dog, shimmering, shining, and radiating.
37. Ibid., 234 (XI.200–207). Given the association of Sigismondo with Apollo in the *Hesperis,* it is odd that it is Apollo who comforts Alfonso after his defeat and Apollo who saves Ferrante from the raging Sigismondo in ibid., 74–75, 257 (IV.1–37, XII.264–265).
38. Christopher M. Woodhouse, *George Gemistos Plethon: The Last of the Hellenes* (Oxford: Clarendon, 1986), 147, 160; John Monfasani, *George of Trebizond: A Biography and a Study of His Logic and Rhetoric* (Leiden: Brill, 1976), 214. On Plethon's paganism, see Niketas Siniossoglou, *Radical Platonism in Byzantium: Illumination and Utopia in Gemistos Plethon* (Cambridge: Cambridge University Press, 2011).
39. Anthony Grafton, "Girolamo Cardano and the Classical Tradition of Astrology," *Proceedings of the American Philosophical Society* 142.3 (1998): 327.
40. Monica Azzolini, *The Duke and the Stars: Astrology and Politics in Renaissance Milan* (Cambridge: Harvard University Press, 2013), 100–134; Ferdinando Gabotto, "L'astrologia nel quattrocento in rapporto colla civiltà," *Rivista di filosofia scientifica* (1889): 377–413.
41. For praise of Sigismondo as a serious student of astrology, see Basinio, *Astronomicon,* facsimile of the manuscript, trans. Marinella De Luca, and ed. Donatella Frioli and Giordana Mariani Canova (Rimini: Cassa di Risparmio di Rimini, 1994), 8–9 (I.10–13); and Valturio, *De re militari,* 47 (bk. III). On this, see Benedetto Soldati, *La poesia astrologica nel quattrocento: Ricerche e studi* (Florence: Sansoni, 1906), 83. Azzolini, *Duke,* 248, cites a letter from 1452, in which a Mantuan astrologer begs to leave the service of Francesco Sforza because, he says, Sigismondo Malatesta had asked him to do astrological calculations.
42. Paul F. Grendler, *The Universities of the Italian Renaissance* (Baltimore: The Johns Hopkins University Press, 2002), 99–101.
43. Marco Bertozzi, "Il convito di Ferrara. Giorgio Gemisto Pletone e il mito del paganesimo antico ai tempi del concilio," in *Atti del convegno di studi nel 550° anniversario del concilio dell'unione delle due chiese d'oriente e d'occidente* (Ferrara: Università degli Studi di Ferrara, 1989), 133–141.
44. Biblioteca Casanatense cod. 103, *De immortalitate animae.* On this, see Angelo Turchini, *Il Tempio Malatestiano, Sigismondo Malatesta e Leon Battista Alberti* (Cesena: "Il Ponte Vecchio," 2000), 343–349. On Giovanni da Ferrara, or Cocchi, see Julius Kirschner, "Cocchi, Giovanni," *Dizionario biografico degli italiani* 26 (Rome: Istituto della Enciclopedia italiana, 1982), 472–473; and A. Rotondo, "Pellegrino Prisciani (1435–1518)," *Rinascimento* 11 (1960): 69–110, 75–78.

45. Basinio, *Astronomicon,* 104–109, 134–141 (II.143–180, 457–487); Soldati, *La poesia,* 88–89.

46. Stanko Kokole, "*Cognitio formarum* and Agostino di Duccio's Reliefs for the Chapel of the Planets in the Tempio Malatestiano," in *Quattrocento Adriatico: Fifteenth-Century Art of the Adriatic Rim,* ed. Charles Dempsey (Bologna: Nuova Alfa, 1996), 182; Turchini, *Il Tempio,* 453–454.

47. Macrobius, *Commentary on the Dream of Scipio,* trans. William Harris Stahl (New York: Columbia University Press, 1990) reprint of 1952, 136 (bk. XII, ch. 13). On the importance of Macrobius for decorative themes in the Tempio, see Charles Mitchell, "The Imagery of the Tempio Malatestiano," *Studi Romagnoli* 2 (1951): 77–90, and Mitchell, "Il Tempio," 71–103; Marco Bertozzi, "Segni, simboli, visioni: il Tempio Malatestiano e i suoi enigmi," in *Templum Mirabile: Atti del convegno sul Tempio Malatestiano,* edited by Marco Musmeci (Rimini: Cassa di Risparmio di Rimini, 2003), 156–161. Basinio, Valturio, and Cocchi all refer often to Macrobius.

48. Livy, *Histories,* 1.31–60.

49. Valturio, *De re militari,* 382–383 (bk. XII, ch. 13). On the complex but essential humanist context and classical sources for the mythological content, purpose, and meaning of Agostino's reliefs, see Kokole, "*Cognitio formarum,*" 177–206.

50. Tommaso Kaeppeli, "Le traduzioni umanistiche di Isocrate e una lettera dedicatoria di Carlo Marsuppini a Galeotto Roberto Malatesta (1430)," *Studi Romagnoli* 2 (1951): 63.

51. Transcribed in ibid., 63–65.

52. Vespasiano da Bisticci, *Commentario della vita di Messer Giannozzo Manetti* (Torino: 1882), vol. 2: 42–45, 85–86; Piero Scapecchi, "Victoris imago: problemi relativi al Tempio Malatestiano," *Arte cristiana* 74 (1986): 155–164.

53. On Eugenius IV's flight from Rome, see Anthony F. D'Elia, *A Sudden Terror: The Plot to Murder the Pope in Renaissance Rome* (Cambridge: Harvard University Press, 2009), 40–53.

54. Battaglini, *Della vita,* 317–318.

55. Ibid., 322; Tavernor, *On Alberti,* 50.

56. Leon Battista Alberti, *On Painting: A New Translation and Critical Edition,* ed. and trans. Rocco Sinisgalli (Cambridge: Cambridge University Press, 2011), 18.

57. Matteo de' Pasti, "Medal for Sigismondo Malatesta" (reverse), in *Il potere, le arti, la guerra: Lo splendore dei Malatesta* (Milan: Electa, 2001), 286, n. 111. Basinio refers to the dome at the end of the *Hesperis,* 288 (XIII.357–358). On Sigismondo and Brunelleschi, see Scapecchi, "Victoris imago."

58. Isabelle Hyman, "Brunelleschi, Filippo" DBI 14 (1972): 542; Giovanni Rimondini, "Frammenti di cultura prospettica brunelleschiana nel castello e nella Rimini di Sigismondo Pandolfo Malatesta," in *Castel Sismondo, Sigismondo Pandolfo*

Malatesta e l'arte militare del primo rinascimento, ed. Angelo Turchini (Cesena: "Il Ponte Vecchio," 2003), 263–280. The issue is problematic since Malatesta sources present Sigismondo as sole "auctor" of the Castello.

59. On Cosimo's cultural patronage, see Alison M. Brown, "The Humanist Portrait of Cosimo de' Medici, Pater Patriae," *Journal of the Warburg and Courtauld Institutes* 24.3/4 (1961): 186–221; and Dale V. Kent, *Cosimo de' Medici and the Florentine Renaissance: The Patron's Oeuvre* (New Haven: Yale University Press, 2000).
60. Cinzia Cardinali and Andrea Maiarelli, "Rassegna di lettere malatestiane dagli archive di stato di Firenze e di Siena," in *Malatesta Novello nell'Italia delle signorie: Fonti e interpretazioni,* ed. Marino Mengozzi and Claudio Riva (Cesena: Stilgraf, 2005), 169–205.
61. On the use of classical republican examples in Malatesta court literature, see Anthony F. D'Elia, "Heroic Insubordination in the Army of Sigismondo Malatesta: Petrus Parleo's *pro milite,* Machiavelli, and the Uses of Cicero and Livy," in *Humanism and Creativity in the Italian Renaissance: Essays in Honor of Ronald G. Witt,* ed. Christopher Celenza and Kenneth Gouwens (Leiden: Brill, 2006), 31–60.
62. Biondo Flavio, *Italy Illuminated,* ed. and trans. Jeffrey A. White (Cambridge: Harvard University Press, 2005), 283–287 (ch. 6.7–10), who surprisingly does not mention the arch. Turchini, *Il Tempio,* 289–300, includes fifteenth-century descriptions. On the arch, see *L'Arco d'Augusto: Significati e vicende di un grande segno urbano,* ed. Pier Luigi Foschi and Pier Giorgio Pasini (Rimini: Musei comunali, 1998), and Tavernor, *On Alberti,* 52, 221.
63. Basinio, *Hesperis,* 97 (IV.567–582). On this passage and the rivalry between sculpture and poetry in Rimini, see Chapter 7.
64. Ibid., 228 (XI.42–47).
65. Letter published in Biondo Flavio, *Scritti inediti e rari di Biondo Flavio,* with intro. By Bartolomeo Nogara (Rome: Tipografia Poliglotta Vaticana, 1927), 159–160.
66. Anthony Grafton, *Leon Battista Alberti: Master Builder of the Italian Renaissance* (Cambridge: Harvard University Press, 2002), 248–249; Girolamo Mancini, *Vita di Leon Battista Alberti,* second edition (Florence: G. Carnesecchi e Figli, 1911), 277–280.
67. On Alberti, see Mancini, *Vita;* Grafton, *Alberti;* Cecil Grayson, "Alberti, Leon Battista," *Dizionario biografico degli italiani* 1 (Rome: Istituto della Enciclopedia italiana, 1960): 702–709; and Tavernor, *On Alberti.*
68. Grafton, *Alberti,* 280–281.
69. On this, see Alberto Giorgio Cassani, "Alberti a Rimini: Il Tempio della buona e della cattiva fortuna" in *Leon Battista Alberti Architetto,* ed. Giorgio Grassi and

Luciano Patetta (Florence: Scala, 2005), 160. Mancini, 310, states that Sigismondo "probably met him [Alberti] in the papal curia," which may have included Cardinal Colonna. In the first edition of his work (Florence: Sansoni, 1882), 348, Mancini simply says that he has "no idea where they met."

70. The evidence and different theories are discussed in Cassani, "Alberti a Rimini," 159–164; Turchini, *Il Tempio,* 256–261; Mancini, 318–322; and Massimo Bulgarelli, "L'Architettura," in *Il Tempio Malatestiano a Rimini,* edited by Antonio Paolucci, (Modena: Franco Cosimo Panini, 2010), vol. 2: 79, who thinks it probable that Alberti visited San Francesco in 1450.

71. Giorgio Vasari, *Le vite de' piu eccellenti architetti, pittori, e scultori italiani,* first edition (Florence: Giunti, 1550), 378, quoted and translated by Charles Hope, "The Early History of the Tempio Malatestiano" *Journal of the Warburg and Courtauld Institutes* 55 (1992): 51.

72. Alessandro Volpe, "Giotto a Rimini," in *Il Tempio Malatestiano a Rimini,* ed. Antonio Paolucci (Modena: Franco Cosimo Panini, 2010), 145.

73. Translated in Lavin, "Piero," 345. In *Hesperis,* 131–132 (VI.266–284), Basinio has Sigismondo call for a feast day and annual games to remember his victory and the deeds of the fallen "for dear liberty." Sigismondo probably made the vow in 1451, as noted by Cassani, "Alberti a Rimini," 186.

74. Lavin, "Piero," 345–347; Hope, "Early History," 52–53. The triumphal theme in the exterior architecture is discussed in Massimo Bulgarelli, "L'architettura," in *Il Tempio Malatestiano a Rimini,* ed. Antonio Paolucci (Modena: Franco Cosimo Panini, 2010), 93–96.

75. Palms are also attributes of martyrs, but this association is unlikely, since the church is not dedicated to a martyr.

76. Corrado Ricci, *Il Tempio Malatestiano* (Rome: Bettstetti & Tuminelli, 1924), 257–259; Helen Ettlinger, "The Sepulchre on the Facade: A Re-evaluation of Sigismondo Malatesta's Rebuilding of San Francesco in Rimini," *Journal of the Warburg and Courtauld Institutes* 53 (1990): 133–143; Hope, "Early History," 96, 116–118; Rudolf Wittkower, *Architectural Principles in the Age of Humanism* (London: Warburg Institute, 1949), 33. Medals reveal that there was supposed to be a large window in this spot, and sources contain plans to cut away a pier in order to create a space of seven meters, which would have been much too big for a tomb.

77. John Pope-Hennessy, *Italian Renaissance Sculpture* (London: Phaidon, 1996), 146–149.

78. Valerius Maximus, *Factorum et dictorum memorabilium libri IX* (bk. VIII, ch. 14). Valturio draws extensively on Valerius in the *De re militari.* On classical precedents, see Jessie Poesch, "Ennius and Basinio of Parma," *Journal of the Warburg and Courtauld Institutes* 25.1/2 (1962): 116–118.

79. On the literary sources and identification of the figures in Agostino's triumphal reliefs, see Stanko Kokole, "The Tomb of the Ancestors in the Tempio Malatestiano," in *Drawing Relationships in Northern Italian Renaissance Art: Patronage and Theories of Invention,* ed. Giancarla Periti (Aldershot: Ashgate, 2004), 11–34, 16–23.
80. Petrarch, *Africa,* IX.290–403.
81. Lactantius, *On the False Worship of the Gods,* ch. 6. Lactantius's source on the sibyls was the Roman antiquarian Marcus Terentius Varro (116–27 BCE). See also Augustine, *City of God,* ch. 23.
82. Turchini, *Il Tempio,* 422–432, and for Poggio's letter, 618. On the importance of the sibyls in medieval and Renaissance Rome, see Charles L. Stinger, *The Renaissance in Rome* (Bloomington: Indiana University Press, 1985 (repub. 1998)), 309–312.
83. Anna Falcioni, "Malatesta, Sigismondo," *Dizionario biografico degli italiani* 68 (Rome: Istituto della Enciclopedia italiana, 2007), available at http://www.treccani.it/enciclopedia/sigismondo-pandolfo-malatesta_%28Dizionario-Biografico%29/.
84. Basinio, *Hesperis,* 86–87 (IV.308–329).
85. John Pope-Hennessy, *Italian Renaissance Sculpture: An Introduction to Italian Sculpture* (New York: Vintage, 1958), 69; Turchini, *Il Tempio,* 494, puts the date at 1449, which is the earliest official document.
86. The eccentric British art critic Adrian Stokes saw water as the overriding theme: "The Tempio Malatestiano at Rimini is an ideal quarry whose original organic substances were renewed by the hand of the carver to express the abundant sea collected into solid stone," *The Stones of Rimini* (University Park: Pennsylvania State University Press, 2002 (orig. 1934)), 43. On the astrological significance of the crab, see Piero Meldini, "Il Signore e il granchio: Cultura e iconografia astrologiche," in *La Cappella dei Pianeti del Tempio Malatestiano,* ed. Piero Meldini and Pier Giorgio Pasini (Rimini: Comune di Rimini, 1983), 14–18; Turchini, *Il Tempio,* 461–465; and Bertozzi, "Segni, simboli," 156–159, who reads the lone oarsman as the Neoplatonic descent of the soul.
87. See the perceptive essay by Cesare Vasoli, "Dalle armi alle lettere ed alla 'prisca sapientia': I due Malatesta," in *Il dono di Malatesta Novello,* ed. Loretta Righetti and Daniela Savoia (Cesena: "Il Ponte Vecchio," 2006), 29–44.
88. Francesco Uberti, funeral oration, quoted in Giovanni Soranzo, "Malatesta Novello, Signore di Cesena (1429–1465)," in *Malatesta Novello nell'Italia delle signorie: Fonti e interpretazioni,* ed. Marino Mengozzi and Claudio Riva (Cesena: Stilgraf, 2005), 369.
89. Ibid., 375.

90. Matteo Bosso, *Recuperationes fesulanae* (Bologna: P. de Benedictis, 1493), bk. II, and Francesco Uberti, both quoted in Soranzo, "Malatesta Novello," 380, 381.
91. Bosso, bk. II, quoted in ibid., 395.
92. Bosso, bk. II, quoted in ibid., 395.
93. Letter to Galeazzo Sforza, Count of Pavia (22 November 1458), in Biondo, *Scritti inediti,* 176.
94. Pier Giovanni Fabbri, "Dentro il dominio e la cultura dei Malatesti: Giovanni di Marco a Cesena," in *La biblioteca di un medico del quattrocento: I codici di Giovanni di Marco da Rimini nella Biblioteca Malatestiana,* ed. Anna Manfron (Cesena: Allemandi, 1998), 18.
95. Sebastiano Gentile, "Il sogno incompiuto di Malatesta Novello," in *Malatesta Novello Magnifico Signore: Arte e cultura di un principe nel Rinascimento,* ed. Pier Giorgio Pasini (San Giorgio di Piano: Minerva, 2002), 49–57.
96. Rinaldo Rinaldi, "Malatesta Novello e gli umanisti," in *Il dono di Malatesta Novello,* ed. Loretta Righetti and Daniela Savoia (Cesena: "Il Ponte Vecchio," 2006), 72–73; Marianne Pade, *The Reception of Plutarch's Lives in Fifteenth Century Italy* (Copenhagen: Museum Tusculanum Press, 2007), vol. 2: 171.
97. Novello's library contained fourteen Greek manuscripts, including works by Demosthenes and Xenophon, as discussed in Anna Pontani, "Per il catalogo dei manoscritti greci della malatestiana," in *Il dono di Malatesta Novello,* 503–512.
98. Fabbri, "Dentro il dominio," 26–29.
99. Ibid., 23.
100. Francesco Filelfo, *Odes,* ed. and trans. Diana Robin (Cambridge: Harvard University Press, 2009), 195–201, 346–355 (bk. V, ch. 10; bk. III, ch. 8).
101. Fabbri, "Dentro il dominio," 26, argues against a rift.

3. The Greek Renaissance and the Return of the *Paideia*

1. Lorenzo Valla, "The Glory of the Latin Language," in *The Portable Renaissance Reader,* ed. James Bruce Ross and Mary Martin McLaughlin (New York: Viking, 1953), 131–135; Leonardo Bruni, "The Lives of Dante and Petrarch," in *The Humanism of Leonardo Bruni,* ed. and trans. Gordon Griffiths, James Hankins, and David Thompson (Binghamton: Medieval and Renaissance Texts and Studies and the Renaissance Society of America, 1987), 96–97. On the use of the *Aeneid* as a model for epics about New World empires, see Craig Kallendorf, *The Other Virgil: "Pessimistic" Readings of the Aeneid in Early Modern Culture* (Oxford: Oxford University Press, 2007), 67–102.
2. On this, see Simone Marchesi, "Petrarch's Philological Epic: *Africa,*" in *Petrarch: A Critical Guide to the Complete Works,* ed. Victoria Kirkham and Armando Maggi (Chicago: University of Chicago Press, 2009), 113–140.

3. Hans Baron, "The Memory of Cicero's Roman Civic Spirit in the Medieval Centuries and in the Florentine Renaissance," in *In Search of Florentine Civic Humanism* (Princeton: Princeton University Press, 1988), vol. 1: 94–133.
4. See Cicero's comparison of Greece and Rome in *Tusculan Disputations,* I–IV.
5. The best discussion of humanist rhetoric and wisdom is still, Hanna Gray, "Renaissance Humanism: The Pursuit of Eloquence," *Journal of the History of Ideas* 24.4 (1963): 497–514, esp. 498–499, 504. See also Robert Black, "Humanism," *The New Cambridge Medieval History,* vol. 7 (Cambridge: Cambridge University Press, 1998), 255–257, 260–261.
6. Aldo A. Settia, "'De re militari': Cultura bellica nelle corti emiliane prima di Leonardo e di Machiavelli," in *Le sedi della cultura nell'Emilia Romagna: Epoca delle signorie, le corti,* ed. Giorgio Chittolini (Milan: Silvana, 1985), 65–66.
7. On Vergerio's revival of Ciceronian rhetoric, see Ronald G. Witt, *'In the Footsteps of the Ancients': The Origins of Humanism from Lovato to Bruni* (Leiden: Brill, 2000), 370–391.
8. Black, "Humanism," 247–248.
9. James Hankins, "The Study of Greek in the Latin West," in *Humanism and Platonism in the Italian Renaissance* (Rome: Storia e Letteratura, 2003), 273–292; Ian Thomson, "Manuel Chrysoloras and the Early Italian Renaissance," *Greek, Roman, and Byzantine Studies* 7 (1966): 63–82. See also Timothy Kircher, "Wrestling with Ulysses: Humanist Translations of Homeric Epic Around 1440," in *Neo-Latin and the Humanities: Essays in Honour of Charles E. Fantazzi,* ed. Luc Deitz, Timothy Kircher, and Jonathan Reid (Toronto: Centre for Reformation and Renaissance Studies, 2014), 61–91.
10. Black, "Humanism," 266.
11. James Hankins, "Humanism, Scholasticism, and Renaissance Philosophy," in *The Cambridge Companion to Renaissance Philosophy,* ed. James Hankins (Cambridge: Cambridge University Press, 2007), 36–38; Paul Oskar Kristeller, "The Aristotelian Tradition," in *Renaissance Thought: The Classic, Scholastic, and Humanist Strains* (New York: Harper & Row, 1955), 30–33. For medieval Latin translations of Aristotle, see Bernard G. Dod, "Aristoteles Latinus," *The Cambridge History of Later Medieval Philosophy: From the Rediscovery of Aristotle to the Disintegration of Scholasticism 1100–1600* (Cambridge: Cambridge University Press, 1982), 45–79.
12. Dod, "Aristoteles," 71; Hankins, "Humanism, Scholasticism," 32–35.
13. Dod, "Aristoteles," 64–68. See especially Dod's chart and catalogue of medieval translations of Aristotle, 74–79; Luca Bianchi, "Continuity and Change in the Aristotelian Tradition," in *The Cambridge Companion to Renaissance Philosophy,* 51–54; Charles Schmitt, "Towards a Reassessment of Renaissance Aristotelianism," *History of Science* 11 (1973): 159–193.

14. Francesco Petrarca, *Le familiari*, ed. Vittorio Rossi (Florence: Sansoni, 1937), vol. 3: 277 (XVIII.2). For Boccaccio's Greek, see Jon Solomon, "Gods, Greeks, and Poetry (*Geneologia deorum gentilium*)," in *Boccaccio: A Critical Guide to the Works*, ed. Victoria Kirkham, Michael Sherberg, and Janet Levarie Smarr (Chicago: University of Chicago Press, 2013), 236.
15. Guarino, in particular, as discussed in Thomson, "Chrysoloras." For Chrysoloras's teaching and influence, see James Hankins, "Manuel Chrysoloras and the Greek Studies of Leonardo Bruni," in *Humanism and Platonism in the Italian Renaissance* (Rome: Storia e Letteratura, 2003), 243–271.
16. Paul Botley, *Latin Translation in the Renaissance: The Theory and Practice of Leonardo Bruni, Giannozzo Manetti and Desiderius Erasmus* (Cambridge: Cambridge University Press, 2004), 5–62; James Hankins, *Plato in the Italian Renaissance* (Leiden: Brill, 1990), vol. 1: 41–46; Bianchi, "Continuity and Change," 51–52.
17. Silvia Ronchey, *L'enigma di Piero: L'ultimo bizantino e la crociata fantasma nella rivelazione di un grande quadro* (Milan: Rizzoli, 2006), 49, 60, 93–97, 201, and Anna Falcioni, "Cleofe Malatesti nelle fonti epistolari mantovane," in *Le donne di casa malatesti*, ed. Anna Falcioni (Rimini: Ghigi, 2005), 957–968.
18. Ferruccio Ferri, *Una contesa di tre umanisti: Basinio, Porcellio e Seneca. Contributo alla storia degli studi greci nel quattrocento in Italia* (Pavia: Fusi, 1920). On the social context of humanist poets, see Lauro Martines, "A Neighborhood of the Mind: Latin Poets of the Quattrocento," in *From Florence to the Mediterranean and Beyond: Essays in Honour of Anthony Molho*, ed. Diogo Ramada Curto, et al. (Florence: Olschki, 2009), 211–234.
19. Basinio, "1455 Letter to Roberto Orsi," in Ferri, *Una contesa*, 58–59. See also, Felice Vismara, *L'invettiva: L'arma preferita degli umanisti nelle lotte private, nelle polemiche letterarie, politiche o religiose* (Milan: Allegretti, 1900), 67–71.
20. Basinio, "Invective Against Porcellio and Seneca," lines 82–83; Ferri, *Una contesa*, 47. The argument that Latin eloquence depended on Greek was popular in the fifteenth century, as discussed by Hankins, "Study of Greek," 280–281.
21. Basinio, "Invective Against Porcellio and Seneca," lines 107–108.
22. Seneca, "Invective Against Basinio," lines 74–75, 99–100, 201–205. On Bruni's translation, see Marianne Pade, *The Reception of Plutarch's Lives in Fifteenth-Century Italy* (Copenhagen: Museum Tusculanum, 2007), vol. 1: 127–132; Botley, *Latin Translation*, 22; Hankins, "Chrysoloras," 256–257.
23. Porcellio, "Invective Against Basinio," lines 159, 185–196; Ferri, *Una contesa*, 58.
24. Basinio, "1455 Letter to Roberto Orsi," in Ferri, *Una contesa*, 58–61.
25. On Sigismondo's knowledge of Greek, see Francesco Gaetano Battaglini, *Della vita e de'fatti di Sigismondo Pandolfo Malatesta* (Rimini: 1794), 57; and Cesare Clementini, *Raccolto istorico della fondatione di Rimini* (Bologna: Forni, 1969), 282 (facsimile of the 1617/1627 edition).

26. On Basinio's authorship of the inscription, see Federicomaria Muccioli, "Le epigrafie gemelle in lingua greca del Tempio Malatestiano," in *Templum Mirabile: Atti del convegno sul Tempio Malatestiano,* ed. Marco Musmeci (Rimini: Cassa di Risparmio di Rimini, 2003), 73–85.
27. Botley, *Latin Translation,* 9.
28. Tommaso Kaeppeli, "Le traduzioni umanistiche di Isocrate e una lettera dedicatoria di Carlo Marsuppini a Galeotto Roberto Malatesta (1430)," *Studi Romagnoli* 2 (1951): 57–65, 64; *Iliad,* II.371.
29. On Broglio, see Alfred A. Strnad, "Broglio, Gaspare," *Dizionario biografico degli italiani* (Rome: Istituto della Enciclopedia italiana, 1972), vol. 14: 437–439.
30. Roberto Valturio, *De re militari* (Paris: Apud Christianum Wechelum, 1534), preface, 25, 24 (bk. II, ch. 2). Valturio, 359 (bk. XII, ch. 7), quotes Homeric words in Greek.
31. Leonardo Bruni, "The Study of Literature to Lady Battista Malatesta of Montefeltro," in *Humanist Educational Treatises,* ed. and trans. Craig W. Kallendorf (Cambridge: Harvard University Press, 2002), 113; Botley, *Latin Translation,* 9.
32. Bruni, "Study of Literature," 113.
33. Valturio, *De re militari,* 25 (bk. II, ch. 2). Valturio, 21 (bk. II, ch. 1), refers to Nestor's eloquence in *Iliad,* 1.247–52.
34. Ferruccio Ferri, *La giovinezza di un poeta: Basinii Parmensis Carmina* (Rimini: Artigianelli, 1914), XVIII, poem to Nicholas V, 1450, appendix XXVI.
35. Ferri, *Una contesa,* 24–37; Ferri, *La giovinezza,* xxxii–xxxviii; Donatella Coppini, "Un epillio umanistico fra Omero e Virgilio: Il *Diosymposeos liber* di Basinio da Parma," in *Confini dell'umanesimo letterario. Studi in onore di Francesco Tateo,* ed. Mauro de Nichilo, Grazia Distaso, and Antonio Iurilli (Rome: Roma nel Rinascimento, 2003), vol. 1: 313–322; G. Resta, "Vegio, Basinio, e l'*Argonautica* di Apollonio Rodio," in *Miscellanea Augusto Campana* (Padua: Antenore, 1981), vol. 2: 639–669.
36. Basinio da Parma, "Hesperis," in *Basinii parmensis poetae opera praestantiora* (Rimini: Albertiniana, 1794), vol. 1: *Hesperis,* 241 (XI.380–386).
37. Basinio, *Hesperis,* 56 (XII.227–230). See also Basinio, *Hesperis,* 260 (XII.331–340), where Juno refers to the Trojan War in relation to the Ottoman invasion.
38. Basinio, *Liber Isottaeus,* ed. Ferruccio Ferri (Città di Castello: Società Anonima Tipografica "Leonardo da Vinci," 1922), II.9.4; II.5.19–20; II.2.8; III.3.87.
39. Basinio, *Hesperis,* 84–86 (IV.265–293); Guglielmo Bottari, "L'Ulisse di casa Malatesta. A proposito dell'Hesperis di Basinio Basini," in *Ulisse da Omero a Pascal Quignard: Convegno internazionale, Verona, 25–27 Maggio 2000: Atti,* ed. Anna Maria Babbi and Francesca Zardini (Verona: Fiorini, 2000), 257–258, 260–261.

40. Valturio, 70 (bk. V, ch. 1); Basinio, *Hesperis,* 31, 50 (II.36–7, 513–14); Bottari, "L'Ulisse," 265.

41. Basinio, *Hesperis,* 208–209 (X.190–192), 150–153 (VII.250–335), 161–162 (VII.530–551), 165–168 (VIII.1–85), 173–174 (VIII.215–217); *Odyssey* V:382–464; Basinio, *Isottaeus,* III.3.25–28,81–82; Ferri, *La giovinezza,* 29; Bottari, "L'Ulisse," 256, 268–270.

42. For examples, see Ferri, *La giovinezza,* 33–34.

43. *Diosymposeos,* line 357, in Coppini, "Un epillio," 332; Basinio, Poem to Nicholas V, 1450, in Ferri, *Una contesa,* appendix 26, lines 59–64. Resta, "Vegio," 653, refers to Basinio's use of Homer through a Virgilian "filter."

44. Basinio, Poem to Nicholas V, 1450, in Ferri *Una contesa,* appendix 26, lines 54–57.

45. Sowerby's contention that Italian humanists failed to translate Homer because of their love for Virgil is clever but ultimately unsustainable since humanists cannot be said to have failed at something they never tried nor intended to do; their interest lay in creative reworkings of Homer in their own Latin poetry rather than direct translation. See Robin Sowerby, "Early Humanist Failure with Homer," *International Journal of the Classical Tradition* 4 (1997): 37–63, 165–194. For a similar critique of Sowerby, see Kircher, "Wrestling," 68–69.

46. *Hesperis,* XI.106–110; *Iliad,* bks. IV–V.

47. Pietro Parleo, *Vita Homeri,* in *Florence, Biblioteca Laurenziana,* MS LXIII, 30, fol. 180v.

48. Parleo, *Vita Homeri,* fols. 181r–187v. Pietro Perleone (Parleo) studied under Filelfo, then worked in his native Rimini as court historiographer, and later taught rhetoric and classical literature in Venice from 1457 to 1463. On him, see Margaret L. King, *Venetian Humanism in an Age of Patrician Dominance* (Princeton: Princeton University Press, 1986), 416–417.

49. "Plutarch," *Essay on the Life and Poetry of Homer,* ed. and trans. J. J. Keaney and Robert Lamberton (Oxford: The American Philological Association, 1996).

50. Bottari, "L'Ulisse," 255. A manuscript of Homer's Odyssey in Greek in the hand of Cyriac of Ancona also survives in the Malatestiana library in Cesena, as discussed in Gianfranco Fiaccadori, "Omerio fra I 'greci' di Malatesta Novello: Sul codice Malatestiano dell'Odissea," in *Il dono di Malatesta Novello,* ed. Loretta Righetti and Daniela Savoia (Cesena: "Il Ponte Vecchio," 2006), 324.

51. On the importance of Homer in Greek society and the cult of the poet, see Christopher P. Jones, *New Heroes in Antiquity: From Achilles to Antinoos* (Cambridge: Harvard University Press, 2010), Kindle edition, ch. 4; Gregory Nagy, *The Ancient Greek Hero in 24 hours* (Cambridge: Harvard University Press, 2013), Kindle edition, part I.

52. *Iliad,* IX.443; VI.208. Cicero explores this interpretation of Odysseus and Ajax in *On the Orator,* III.57.

53. Werner Jaeger, *Paideia: The Ideals of Greek Culture,* trans. G. Highet (New York: Oxford University Press, 1965 (orig. 1939)), vol. 1: 5–11.
54. On fame and the public nature of virtue in Homer and later literature, "kleos," see Nagy, *Ancient Greek Hero,* 26–31.
55. Valturio, *De re militari,* 25 (bk. II, ch. 2).
56. Ibid., 25 (bk. II, ch. 2).
57. Ibid., 70 (bk. V, ch. 1)).
58. Ibid., 72 (bk. V, ch. 1).
59. *Nicomachean Ethics* III.6–9, On courage, 70–72.
60. Lucian, "Anacharsis," 21, in A. M. Harmon, *Lucian with an English Translation,* Loeb Classical Library (New York: G. P. Putnam's Sons, 1925), vol. IV, trans. adapted from p. 35.
61. On Sigismondo's interest in Homer, see Pietro Parleo, *Vita Homeri,* in *Florence, Biblioteca Laurenziana,* MS LXIII, 30, fol. 180v, discussed above.
62. Pade, *Reception;* Botley, *Latin Translation.*
63. William Harrison Woodward, *Vittorino da Feltre and Other Humanist Educators: Essays and Versions, An Introduction to the History of Classical Education* (Cambridge: Cambridge University Press, 1905), 25; Kallendorf, *Humanist Education Treatises,* ix, xiv.
64. Plutarch, "The Education of Children" in *Plutarch's Moralia,* ed. and trans. Frank Cole Babbitt (London: William Heinemann, 1927), vol. 1: 36–39, 40–41, 56–59 (chs. 11, 12, 16).
65. S. C. R. Swain, "Hellenic Culture and the Roman Heroes of Plutarch," *The Journal of Hellenic Studies* 110 (1990): 129, 131–136.
66. James Hankins, "Life and Works," in *Humanism and Platonism in the Italian Renaissance* (Rome: Storia e Letteratura, 2003), 11; Hankins, "The Case of Leonardo Bruni," in *Humanism and Platonism,* 192.
67. St. Basil, "Address to Young Men on the Right Use of Literature," IV–V, trans. Frederick Morgan Padelford (1902), available at http://www.ccel.org/ccel/pearse/morefathers/files/basil_litterature01.htm#37.
68. Hankins, "Life and Works," 11; Hankins, "Chrysoloras," 255.
69. St. Basil, VIII, trans. Padelford.
70. Roman Garrison, *The Graeco-Roman Context of Early Christian Literature* (Sheffield: Sheffield Academic Press, 1997), 97–104.
71. Valturio, *De re militari,* 72 (bk. V, ch. 1).
72. Pier Paolo Vergerio, "The Character and Studies Befitting a Free-Born Youth," in Kallendorf, *Educational Treatises,* ix, 1–91, esp. 46–51.
73. Ibid., 20–21, 28–29, 32–37.
74. Ibid., 66–83.

75. Bartolomeo Platina, "De vita Victorini Feltrensis commentariolus," in Eugenio Garin, ed., *Il pensiero pedagogico dello umanesimo* (Florence: Giuntine-Sansoni, 1958), 668–699, 678, 682. Cf. Woodward, *Vittorino,* 65.
76. Aeneas Piccolomini, *The Education of Boys,* in Kallendorf, *Educational Treatises,* 126–259 (sections 13–14).
77. Alberti, in Garin, *Il pensiero,* 78 (bk. I); Leon Battista Alberti, *The Family in Renaissance Florence,* trans. Renee Neu Watkins (Columbia: University of South Carolina Press, 1969), 83–84.
78. Aristotle, *Politics,* 1337a–1339a.
79. Melinda K. Blade, *Education of Italian Renaissance Women* (Mesquite: Ide House, 1983), 44, 48.
80. Plutarch, "Life of Lycurgus" in *Plutarch's Lives,* ed. and trans. Bernadotte Perrin (Cambridge: Harvard University Press, 1967), vol. I: 244–255 (chs. 14–15); Sarah B. Pomeroy, *Spartan Women* (Oxford: Oxford University Press, 2002), 26–27.
81. Giovanni Dominici, *Regula di governo e cura familiare,* in ed. Garin, *Il pensiero,* 77.
82. Elsewhere, Galen allows for exercise with a small ball. On the ancient debate, see Jason König, "Training Athletes and Interpreting the Past in Philostratus' Gymnasticus," in *Philostratus,* ed. Ewen Bowie and Jas Elsner (Cambridge: Cambridge University Press, 2009), 258–259; Michael B. Poliakoff, *Combat Sports in the Ancient world: Competition, Violence, and Culture* (New Haven: Yale University Press, 1987), 93–94.
83. Giovanni Dominici, *Regula di governo e cura familiare,* in ed. Garin, *Il pensiero,* 77.
84. Nancy G. Siraisi, *Medieval and Early Renaissance Medicine: An Introduction to Knowledge and Practice* (Chicago: University of Chicago Press, 1990), 104–106.
85. Paolo Pino, *Dialogo della pitura* (Venice: P.Gherardo, 1548), fol. 31.
86. Alessandro Arcangeli, "Dance and Health: The Renaissance Physicians' View," *Dance Research: The Journal of the Society for Dance Research* 18.1 (2000): 5–6.
87. Patricia Simons, "Hercules in Italian Renaissance Art: Masculine Labour and Homoerotic Libido," *Art History* 31.5 (November 2008): 632–664; Anne Dunlop, "Parading David," *Art History* 35.4 (September 2012): 682–701, esp. 688–692. In the *Hesperis,* 213 (X.297–300), Basinio has Sigismondo describe the "large statue of Hercules" that he saw on his trip to the underworld.
88. Dunlop, "Parading David," 687–688.
89. Homer, *The Odyssey,* XIX.390–601. On this, see the famous essay by Erich Auerbach, "Odysseus' scar" in *Mimesis: The Representation of Reality in Western Literature* (Princeton: Princeton University Press, 1953), 3–23. For hunting descriptions in chivalric literature, see John Cummins, *The Hound and the Hawk: The Art of Medieval Hunting* (London: Weidenfeld and Nicolson, 1988).

90. Basinio, *Hesperis,* 76–77 (IV.53–60, 61–71). Basinio also describes Sigismondo hunting to relax after the Piombino victory in *Hesperis,* 122 (VI.34–38).
91. Basinio, *Hesperis,* 6 (I.124–132).
92. Einhard, *Life of Charlemagne,* XIX, XXII, XXX; John J. Butt, *Daily Life in the Age of Charlemagne* (Westport: Greenwood Press, 2002), 149–150. On hunting and combat sport in early modern Europe, see Edward Muir, *Mad Blood Stirring: Vendetta in Renaissance Italy* (Baltimore: The Johns Hopkins University Press, 1993), 151–154; Elisabeth S. Cohen and Thomas V. Cohen, *Daily Life in Renaissance Italy* (Westport: Greenwood Press, 2001), 285–288.
93. Alberti, *The Family in Renaissance Florence,* 257–258.
94. Valturio, *De re militari,* 64 (bk. IV, ch. 3).
95. Xenophon, *Cyropaedeia,* I.10, VIII.1.34–38; David Marsh, "Xenophon," *Catalogus translationum et commentariorum: Mediaeval and Renaissance Latin Translations and Commentaries, Annotated Lists and Guides,* ed. Virginia Brown (Washington, D.C.: The Catholic University of America Press, 1992), VII: 80–81, 116–121; Gary Ianziti, *Writing History in Renaissance Italy: Leonardo Bruni and the Uses of the Past* (Cambridge: Harvard University Press, 2012), 244–245; Botley, *Latin Translation,* 10, 71. On the Cyropaedea, see Jaeger, *Paideia,* vol. 3: 165.
96. On Plethon's ideas about reviving ancient Sparta, see Niketas Siniossoglou, *Radical Platonism in Byzantium: Illumination and Utopia in Gemistos Plethon* (Cambridge: Cambridge University Press, 2011), 350–351, 374–380; John Monfasani, "Platonic Paganism in the Fifteenth Century" in *Reconsidering the Renaissance,* ed. M. A. di Cesare (Binghamton: Center for Medieval and Early Renaissance Studies, 1992), 59–61.
97. Cyriac of Ancona, *Later Travels,* ed. and trans. Edward D. Bodnar (Cambridge: Harvard University Press, 2003), 328.
98. Letter to Roberto Valturio, 24 June 1449, in ibid., 360–362. Sigismondo's invitation to Plethon is mentioned in a 1475 epithalamium, as discussed in Christopher M. Woodhouse, *George Gemistos Plethon: The Last of the Hellenes* (Oxford: Clarendon, 1986), 147, 159–160, 227–228.
99. Vergerio, "Character," 68–71; Cicero, *Tusculan,* XXXIII.
100. Valturio, *De re militari,* 60 (bk. IV, ch. 3); Plutarch, "Life of Lycurgus," 256–257 (ch. 16). Valturio, *De re militari,* 82–3 (bk. V, ch. 2), mentions the Spartan whipping custom for making boys tough.
101. Valturio, *De re militari,* 60 (bk. IV, ch. 3).
102. Ibid., 61 (bk. IV, ch. 3).
103. Broglio, *Cronaca,* in Luigi Tonini, *Rimini nella signoria de' Malatesti, parte seconda al volume quinto* (Rimini: Albertini, 1882), 171–173.
104. Valturio, *De re militari,* 62 (bk. IV, ch. 3). For Valturio's sources, see Plutarch, "Life of Marius," in *Plutarch's Lives,* ed. and trans. Bernadotte Perrin (Cambridge:

Harvard University Press, 1959), vol. 9: 496–497 (ch. 13); Plutarch, "Life of Cato," in *Plutarch's Lives,* ed. and trans. Bernadotte Perrin (Cambridge: Harvard University Press, 1959), vol. 8: 248–249 (ch. 4).

105. Valturio, *De re militari,* 64 (bk. IV, ch. 3).

106. Ibid., 64 (bk. IV, ch. 3). Cf. Seneca, *De tranquilitate animi,* 17.4.

107. Plato, *Laws,* 794d–796d. Translation is from *Plato in Twelve Volumes,* vols. 10 and 11, trans. R. G. Bury (Cambridge: Harvard University Press, 1967, 1968).

108. Plato, *Laws,* 7.815–816A.

109. *Isottaeus,* I.1.19–26.

110. In Thermopylae the Persians are puzzled by the Spartan practice of combing each other's long hair before battle, Herodotus, *Histories,* VII.209.

111. Vergerio, "Character," 20–21, 86–87; Jennifer Neville, *The Eloquent Body: Dance and Humanist Culture in Fifteenth Century Italy* (Bloomington: Indiana University Press, 2004), 58–74.

112. Mario Filelfo, *Canzone morale di Mario Philelfo ad honore et laude di Maestro Guilielmo Hebreo,* lines 2253–2264, in *Fifteenth-Century Dance and Music: Twelve Transcribed Italian Treatises and Collection in the Tradition of Domenico da Piacenza,* ed. and trans. A. William Smith (Stuyvesant: Pendragon Press, 1995), vol. 1: 191.

113. Hesiod, *Theogony,* in Hesiod, *Theogony, Works and Days, Testimonia,* ed. and trans. Glenn W. Most (Cambridge: Harvard University Press, 2006), 79 (lines 1–8); *Homeric Hymns,* "To Pythian Apollo," in Hesiod, *The Homeric Hymns and Homerica,* ed. and trans. Hugh G. Evelyn-White (London: Macmillan, 1914), 338 (lines 201–203); Pindar, *Partheneia,* in Pindar, *Nemean Odes, Isthmian Odes, Fragments,* ed. and trans. William H. Race (Cambridge: Harvard University Press, 1997), 330 (Fr. 94c).

114. Margaret M. McGowan, *Dance in the Renaissance* (New Haven: Yale University Press, 2008), 209–228.

115. Clementini, *Raccolto,* 312. There was also a tournament, horse racing, and a fake battle, which included a besieged castle.

116. Plato, *Laws,* 794d–796d; Aristotle, *Politics,* 1337a–1339a.

117. Vergerio, "Character," 52–53, 84–87.

118. Valturio, *De re militari,* 29–30 (bk. II, ch. 4). In *Hesperis,* 139 (VI.450–455), Basinio shows Sigismondo enjoying music at a banquet.

119. Broglio, *Cronaca,* in Tonini, *Rimini nella signoria de' Malatesti,* 286–287.

120. Valturio, *De re militari,* 30 (bk. II, ch. 4).

121. Ibid., 30 (bk. II, ch. 4). Achilles and music is a common reference. See, for example, Plutarch, "On Music" in *Plutarch's Moralia,* ed. and trans. Benedict Einarson and Phillip H. De Lacy (Cambridge: Harvard University Press, 1967), vol. 14: 444–447 (ch. 40), and Vergerio, "Character," 85–87.

122. Valturio, *De re militari,* 61 (bk. IV, ch. 3).

123. Ibid., 62 (bk. IV, ch. 3). See Basinio, *Hesperis,* 24–26 (I.589–631), for a description of Sigismondo's hand-to-hand combat with Alfonso of Aragon, which is quoted in Chapter 4.
124. Basinio, *Hesperis,* 76 (IV.49–53).
125. On the manuscript illuminations, see Otto Pächt, "Giovanni da Fano's Illustrations for Basinio's Epos Hesperis" in *Studi malatestiani,* ed. Augusto Campana (Faenza: Lega, 1952), 91–111, esp. 95.
126. Valturio, *De re militari,* 62 (bk. IV, ch. 3); Vergerio, 76–79.
127. Plato, *Laws,* VII; Valturio, *De re militari,* 61 (bk. IV, ch. 3), stresses how the Romans trained boys in battle.
128. Vergerio, 68–71, 78–83.
129. Ibid., 66–69; Cicero, *de re publica,* IV.7; *de officiis,* I.7.23–4, I.12.38
130. Plato, *Gorgias,* 456d–457c.
131. Baldasar Castiglione, *Il Cortegiano,* XXI, trans. George Bull (Harmondsworth: Penguin, 1967), 62.
132. Leonardo Bruni, "Panegyric of Florence," in *The Humanism of Leonardo Bruni,* 143–144. Cicero, *de senectute,* 3.10.33; Pliny, *Historia Naturalis,* 7.28.83; Valerius Maximus, *Memorabilia,* 9.12.10.
133. Cicero, *Tusculan Disputations,* XXXIII; Plato, *Republic,* 458d. On the Greek naked athletic ideal, see Thomas F. Scanlon, *Eros and Greek Athletics* (Oxford: Oxford University Press, 2002), 220–221
134. Plutarch, "The Roman Questions," in *Plutarch's Moralia,* ed. and trans. Frank Cole Babbitt (Cambridge: Harvard University Press, 1936), 68–71 (ch. 40). My translation is adapted from Babbitt's and Poliakoff, *Combat Sports,* 103, who also quotes this. For further negative views of the Romans, see Pliny, *Natural History,* 35.13, and Tacitus, *Annals,* 14.20.
135. *Petrarch's Remedies for Fortune Fair and Foul,* trans. Conrad H. Rawski (Bloomington: Indiana University Press, 1991), vol. 1: 85–90 (bk. I, ch. 29). On Augustine's idea of exercising the mind, see ibid., vol. 2: 219–220, n. 17.
136. *Republic,* 403e–404b; *Laws* VII.795d–796b; 814c–814d. Diogenes Laertius, *Life of Plato,* 3.1.4, reports a tradition that as a boy Plato had wrestled at the Isthmian Games.
137. Jaeger, *Paideia,* vol. 3:144.
138. Sydney Anglo, *The Martial Arts of Renaissance Europe* (New Haven: Yale University Press, 2000), 172–201. On wrestling, boxing, and pankration in ancient Greece, see Poliakoff, *Combat Sports,* 68–88; E. Norman Gardiner, *Athletics of the Ancient World* (Chicago: Ares, 1987 (orig. 1930)), 181–221.
139. *Odyssey,* XVIII; *Iliad,* XXIII; Gardiner, *Athletics,* 23–24.
140. See, for example, Lucian, "Anacharsis."
141. Statius, *Thebaid,* VI.764–772; 876–904.

142. *Aeneid,* VI.643–44.
143. Paul F. Grendler, *The Universities of the Italian Renaissance* (Baltimore: The Johns Hopkins University Press, 2002), 15; Vladimiro Zabughin, *Vergilio nel Rinascimento Italiano da Dante a Torquato Tasso,* ed. Stefano Carrai and Alberto Cavarzere, 2 vols. (Trent: Università Degli Studi di Trento, 2000).
144. Valturio, *De re militari,* 61–2 (bk. IV, ch. 3).
145. Plutarch, "Life of Caesar" in *Plutarch's Lives,* ed. and trans. Bernadotte Perrin (London: William Heinemann, 1919), vol. 7: 484–485 (ch. 17). Alberti also uses Plutarch's description of Caesar's riding, in Alberti, *Family,* 84.
146. Valturio, *De re militari,* 62 (bk. IV, ch. 3).
147. Vergerio, "Character," 78–79.
148. On Federico and Vittorino, see Pierantonio Paltroni, *Commentari della vita et gesti dell'illustrissimo Federico Duca d'Urbino,* ed. Walter Tommasoli (Urbino: Accademia Raffaello, 1966), 45–46; Walter Tommasoli, *La Vita di Federico da Montefeltro (1422–1482)* (Urbino: Argalìa, 1978), 12–13. Settia, "'De re militari,'" 66, sees "echoes of Vergerio's treatise" in Sigismondo's education.

4. An Ancient Hero on Renaissance Battlefields

1. Roberto Valturio, *De re militari* (Paris: Apud Christianum Wechelum, 1534), 13–14 (bk. I, ch. 2); 362 (bk. XII, ch. 7).
2. The best survey is still Vladimiro Zabughin, *Vergilio nel Rinascimento italiano da Dante a Torquato Tasso,* ed. Stefano Carrai and Alberto Cavarzere, 2 vols. (Trent: Università degli Studi di Trento, 2000 (orig. 1921)), vol. 1: 289–302. See also Kristen Lippincott, "The Neo-Latin Historical Epics of North Italian Courts: An Examination of 'Courtly Culture' in the Fifteenth Century" *Renaissance Studies* 3.4 (1989): 415–428. Lippincott, 417, notes the similarities of the epic poems but stresses their different courtly milieux.
3. Guglielmo Bottari, "La 'Sphortias,'" in *Francesco Filelfo nel quinto centenario della morte,* ed. Rino Avesani, Giuseppe Billanovich, Mirella Ferrari, and Giovanni Pozzi (Padua: Antenore, 1986), 464; Diana Robin, *Filelfo in Milan: Writings 1451–1477* (Princeton: Princeton University Press, 1991), 56–81; and Craig Kallendorf, *The Other Virgil: "Pessimistic" Readings of the Aeneid in Early Modern Culture* (Oxford: Oxford University Press, 2007), 17–30.
4. Zabughin, 293–296. On the *Porcaria* and the conspiracy, see Anthony F. D'Elia, "Stefano Porcari's Conspiracy Against Pope Nicholas V in 1453 and Republican Culture in Papal Rome," *The Journal of the History of Ideas* 68.2 (April 2007): 207–231.
5. Zabughin, 296–297, 299–301; Guido Cappelli, "Pandone, Porcelio," *Dizionario biografico degli italiani* 80 (Rome: Istituto della Enciclopedia italiana, 2014);

Franco Pignatti, "Filelfo, Giovanni Mario," *Dizionario biografico degli italiani* 47 (Rome: Istituto della Enciclopedia italiana, 1997); G. M. Filelfo, *Amyris,* ed. Aldo Manetti (Bologna: Patron, 1978).

6. Kallendorf, *The Other Virgil,* 23; Robin, *Filelfo in Milan,* 56–81.
7. Gaspare Broglio [Tartaglia], *Cronaca malatestiana del secolo xv,* ed. Antonio G. Luciani (Rimini: Bruno Chigi, 1982), 3; Francesco G. Battaglini, *Della vita e de'fatti di Sigismondo Pandolfo Malatesta* (Rimini: Albertiniana, 1794), 263.
8. See, for example, Alison Brown, "The Humanist Portrait of Cosimo de' Medici" *Journal of the Warburg and Courtauld Institute* 24 (1961): 186–221; and Gary Ianziti, *Humanist Historiography Under the Sforzas: Politics and Propaganda in Fifteenth-Century Milan* (Oxford: Clarendon Press, 1988).
9. Basinio da Parma, "Hesperis," in *Basinii parmensis poetae opera praestantiora* (Rimini: Albertiniana, 1794), vol. 1: *Hesperis,* 75–76 (IV.32–34, 37–41).
10. Basinio, *Hesperis,* 76 (IV.42–45).
11. Roberto Valturio, *De re militari* (Paris: Apud Christianum Wechelum, 1534), 13 (bk. I, ch. 2).
12. Livy, XXI; Valerius Maximus, 3.1.1. Valturio probably got the examples from Pier Paolo Vergerio, "The Character and Studies Befitting a Free-born Youth," in *Humanist Educational Treatises,* ed. and trans. Craig W. Kallendorf (Cambridge: Harvard University Press, 2002), 73 (ch. 59).
13. Valturio, *De re militari,* 61 (bk. IV, ch. 3). Cf. Francesco Filelfo's praise for Sigismondo: "While still a tender lad, spirited and brave, he crushed an ambush which he skillfully uncovered—a frightening sight to terrible men," translation from Francesco Filelfo, *Odes,* ed. and trans. Diana Robin (Cambridge: Harvard University Press, 2009), 197 (III.8.29–31).
14. Basinio, *Hesperis,* 78–79 (IV.111–127, 128–137).
15. Ibid., 79–81 (IV.138–160, 167–171).
16. For a less sensational account of the rebellion, see Philip James Jones, *The Malatesta of Rimini and the Papal State: A Political History* (Cambridge: Cambridge University Press, 1974), 171–172; and the more colorful Broglio, *Cronaca,* in Luigi Tonini, *Rimini nella signoria de' Malatesti, parte seconda al volume quinto* (Rimini: Albertini, 1882), 84–88.
17. Jacob Burckhardt, *The Civilization of the Renaissance in Italy,* trans. S. G. C. Middlemore (Harmondsworth: Penguin, 1990), 32–33.
18. Petrarch, "Italia Mia," *Canzoniere (Rerum Vulgarium Fragmenta)* CXXVIII (1344). Machiavelli quotes four lines from Petrarch's "Italia Mia" in his concluding call for Italy to unite against the foreign invaders, Niccolò Machiavelli, *Il principe,* ed. Mario Martelli (Rome: Salerno Editrice, 2006), 321 (ch. 26).
19. Basinio, *Hesperis,* 95 (IV.530–532). Lippincott, "Neo-Latin Historical Epics," 419, calls the poem "an Italian national epic."

20. "Basinii Parmensis Epistola ad divum Sigismundum Pandulphum Malatestam dominum Arimini illustrem: Laudes et preconia eius continens et suorum," in Ferruccio Ferri, *La giovinezza di un poeta: Basinii parmensis carmina* (Rimini: Artigianelli, 1914), appendix 24, 41–44, lines 68–74.
21. Basinio, *Liber Isottaeus,* ed. Ferruccio Ferri (Città di Castello: Società Anonima Tipografica "Leonardo da Vinci," 1922), III.2.51–64.
22. Basnio, *Hesperis,* 249 (XII.41–42, 48–50, 52–55).
23. Livy, *History of Rome,* 30.1–45; Machiavelli, *Il principe,* 231–234 (ch. 17); Valturio, *De re militari,* 347.
24. Basinio, *Hesperis,* 232 (XI.152–162).
25. For Florentine fears of Sigismondo in the initial exchanges, see Luigi Rossi, *La guerra in Toscana del 1447–8* (Florence: 1903); Giovanni Soranzo, *Pio II e la politica italiana nella lotta contro i Malatesti (1457–1463)* (Padua: Fratelli Drucker, 1911), 30. On the war, see Jones, *Malatesta,* 198–200, who does not mention the details of the initial rejection.
26. Naldo Naldi, "In vitam Jannotii Manetti," in *Rerum italicarum scriptores,* ed. Ludovico Muratori (Milan: Palatine, 1731), vol. 20: 560–561.
27. Naldi, "In vitam," 559; Vespasiano da Bisticci, *Commentario della vita di Messer Giannozzo Manetti* (Torino: Unione Tipografico, 1882), vol. 2: 123–5; Broglio, *Cronaca,* in Tonini, *Rimini nella signoria de' Malatesti,* 182–185; Jones, *Malatesta,* 198–199.
28. Manetti's role is decidedly downplayed in other sources, which give more credit to the other Florentine ambassadors, Agnolo della Stuffa, Bernardo de' Medici, and Neri Capponi. See, for example, Machiavelli, *Florentine Histories,* IV.6; Pierantonio Paltroni, *Commentari della vita et gesti dell'illustrissimo Federico Duca d'Urbino,* ed. W. Tommasoli (Urbino: Accademia Raffaello, 1966), 84–86; and Neri Capponi, *Commentario, Rerum italicarum scriptores* (1917), vol. 18: 1204–1205. On this, see also Soranzo, *Pio II,* 34.
29. Vespasiano, *Commentario,* vol. 2: 125; Jones, *Malatesta,* 211, 214; Pius II, *Commentaries,* ed. Margaret Meserve and Marcello Simonetta, trans. Margaret Meserve (Cambridge: Harvard University Press, 2003), 327 (bk. II, ch. 32).
30. Basinio, *Hesperis,* 4 (I.69–70). Although he does not discuss the *Hesperis,* Thomas Greene used the motif of Mercury's descent and divine intervention with human affairs to explore the epic tradition, in *The Descent from Heaven: A Study in Epic Continuity* (New Haven: Yale University Press, 1963).
31. Basinio, *Hesperis,* 5 (I.100).
32. Ibid., 7–8 (I.154–180). Basinio uses the same simile of the surging roaring sea in ibid., 14 (I.326–332).
33. Ibid., 8–10 (I.187–195, 221–230).
34. Ibid., 10–11 (I.239–245).

35. Ibid., 11–12 (I.264–288).
36. Ibid., 13 (I.300–315).
37. Xenophon, *Constitution of the Lacedaimonians,* 6–10. Although not known for their cavalry, the Spartans did have a cavalry division in the Peloponnesian War. For the fox and the lion, see Machiavelli, *Il principe,* 234–242 (ch. 18). On lion imagery and masculinity, see Timothy J. Lukes, "Lionizing Machiavelli," *The American Political Science Review* 95.3 (2001): 561–575.
38. Basinio, *Hesperis,* IV.290–293. On this, see Chapter 2.
39. Dante, *Inferno,* Canto XXVI: lines 55–63. For Dante's treatment of Odysseus and the limits of heroic myth, see Giuseppe Mazzotta, "Ulysses: Persuasion versus Prophecy," in *Lectura Dantis: Inferno,* ed. Allen Mandelbaum, Anthony Oldcorn, and Charles Ross (Berkeley: University of California Press, 1998), 348–356.
40. Andrea Benzi-Pius II, "Discipula veritatis," in *Pii secundi epistolae* (Milan: Antonius Zarothus, 1487), n.p., 73 in scan of this edition, available at http://fondosdigitales.us.es/fondos/libros/204/67/epistola-siue-oratio-pii-in-conuentu-mantuano/. Henceforth pages refer to this scanned edition. At the battle of Senegallia in 1462, Pius elsewhere writes, "like a cowardly and most vile commander, Sigismondo ordered his men to fight, while he dumped his arms and fled on horseback," Pius II, *Commentarii,* in Enea Silvio Piccolomini Papa Pio II, *I Commentarii,* second edition, ed. Luigi Totaro (Milan: Adelphi, 2004), 1918–1921 (10.14). Other sources, however, report him fighting courageously at Senegallia. On this, see Giovanni Soranzo, "Un'invettiva della curia romana contro Sigismondo Pandolfo Malatesta," *La Romagna* 7 (1910): 470.
41. Basinio, *Hesperis,* 14–16 (I.333–366). For pagan sacrifices in Malatesta literature, see Chapter 5.
42. Ibid., 18 (I.421–425).
43. Ibid., 20 (I.475–478). Jupiter says the same thing to Juno, while admiring a statue of Sigismondo; Basinio, *Diosymposis,* ed. Donatella Coppini, in Donatella Coppini, "Un epillio umanistico fra Omero e Virgilio: Il *Diosymposeos liber* di Basinio da Parma," in *Confini dell'umanesimo letterario. Studi in onore di Francesco Tateo,* ed. Mauro de Nichilo, Grazia Distaso, and Antonio Iurilli (Rome: Roma nel Rinascimento, 2003), vol. 1: 323–336, 333 (lines 380–386).
44. Basinio, *Hesperis,* 24–26 (I.589–631).
45. Ibid., 26 (I.634–639).
46. Machiavelli, *Il principe,* ch. 25.
47. Basinio, *Hesperis,* 34 (II.91–99).
48. Ibid., 36 (II.161–165).
49. Ibid., 41 (II.283–287).
50. Ibid., 42 (II.300–306). Cf. same simile, "Basinii Parmensis Epistola ad divum Sigismundum Pandulphum Malatestam," lines 81–90.

51. Basinio, *Hesperis,* 44–45 (II.361–382).
52. This is also noted by Zabughin, *Vergilio nel rinascimento,* vol. 1: 293, 323. John Hawkwood was the first to use artillery on the battlefield in Italy in 1387, as noted in Michael Mallett, *Mercenaries and Their Masters: Warfare in Renaissance Italy* (London: Bodley Head, 1974), 160.
53. See Charlton T. Lewis and Charles Short, *A New Latin Dictionary* (New York: Harper & Brothers Publishers, 1879), *ad vocem;* Christina Shuttleworth Kraus and Anthony John Woodman, *Latin Historians* (Oxford: Oxford University Press, 1997), 68.
54. Vegetius, *Epitoma rei militaris,* IV.12–30. Vegetius (fifth century CE) was popular in the Renaissance. In addition to vernacular translations, more than seventy fourteenth- and fifteenth-century manuscripts survive, as noted in Josette A. Wisman, "Flavius Renatus Vegetius," in *Catalogus translationum et commentariorum: Mediaeval and Renaissance Latin Translations and Commentaries,* ed. F. Edward Cranz, Virginia Brown, and Paul Oskar Kristeller (Washington, D. C.: Catholic University of America Press, 1986), vol. 6: 177.
55. Basinio, *Hesperis,* 46 (II.404–407). For the echo in Olympus, see Basinio, *Hesperis,* 48 (II.462).
56. Machiavelli, *Discourses,* II.17. See the analysis of this in Harvey C. Mansfield, *Machiavelli's New Modes and Orders: A Study of the Discourses on Livy* (Ithaca: Cornell University Press, 1979), 238–243.
57. Basinio, *Hesperis,* 52–53 (III.8–22).
58. Ibid., 53 (III.26–29).
59. Ibid., 55–56 (III.90–103). For another of Sigismondo's prebattle speeches, see ibid., 92 (IV.448–458). Broglio, *Cronaca,* also reports a rousing battlefield speech by Sigismondo in 1461, in Luigi Tonini, *Rimini nella signoria de' Malatesti, parte seconda al volume quinto* (Rimini: Albertini, 1882), 282–287.
60. Benzi-Pius II, *Discipula,* 81.
61. Valturio, *De re militari,* 21 (bk. II, ch. 1). Cf. Valerius Maximus, *Memorabilia,* 9.1–2.
62. Basinio, *Hesperis,* 56–57 (III.103–118). Melanippus was one of Odysseus' men at Troy. As Sigismondo is cast as a new Odysseus, Melanippus is Sigismondo's man.
63. Ibid., 60 (III.196–200).
64. For Priam begging Achilles, see Homer, *Iliad,* XXIV.468–551. For Palinurus, see Virgil, *Aeneid,* V.835–871, VI.337–383.
65. Basinio, *Hesperis,* 66–67 (III.349–367).
66. Ibid., 67–69 (III.376–439).
67. Ibid., 70 (III.453–461).

68. For the negative association of the wolf in Florentine republican discourse, see Fabrizio Ricciardelli, "Lupi e agnelli nel discorso politico dell'Italia comunale," in *The Languages of Political Society. Western Europe, 14th–17th Centuries,* ed. Andrea Gamberini, Jean-Philippe Genet, and Andrea Zorzi (Rome: Viella, 2011), 269–285.
69. Basinio, *Hesperis,* 72 (III.513–515).
70. Valturio, *De re militari,* 360–1(bk. XII, ch. 7).
71. Basinio, *Hesperis,* 123, 125 (VI.42–47, 102–104, 113–115).
72. Ibid., 126–129 (VI.121–125, 151–156, 170–191). Cf. the description of the triumph in Basinio, *Liber Isottaeus,* ed. Ferruccio Ferri (Città di Castello: Società Anonima Tipografica "Leonardo da Vinci," 1922), III.4.39–52.
73. Jones, *Malatesta,* 202; Valturio, *De re militari,* 361 (bk. XII, ch. 7).
74. Paltroni, *Commentari,* 86–87.
75. Broglio, *Cronaca,* 156–157, 160.
76. Antonio Agostini, *L'assedio di Piombino,* in *Rerum italicarum scriptores,* ed. Ludovico Muratori (Milan: Palatine, 1731), vol. 25: 319.
77. Ibid., 340–350. Poggio Bracciolini also ascribes the victory to Rinaldo Orsini, who defended Piombino and refused Alfonso's bribes, *Poggii Historia florentina* (Venice: Hertz, 1715), 363–365.
78. Ibid., 364.
79. Tonini, *Rimini nella signoria de' Malatesti,* 192; Battaglini, *Della vita,* 415.
80. "Mars Phoebo S.D.P.," in Porcellio Pandone, "De amore Iovis in Isottam," in *Trium poetarm elegantissimorum, Porcelii, Basinii, et Trebani opuscula* (Paris: Simonem Colimeum, 1539), fol. 17r–17v.
81. Niccolò Machiavelli, *Florentine Histories,* VI.16.
82. Ibid., IV.6; V.33.
83. Machiavelli, *Florentine Histories,* trans. Laura F. Banfield and Harvey C. Mansfield, Jr. (Princeton: Princeton University Press, 1988), 151, n. 4; Mallett, *Mercenaries,* 197.
84. Alan Ryder, *Alfonso the Magnanimous, King of Aragon, Naples, and Sicily, 1396–1458* (Oxford: Clarendon, 1990), 302; Mallett, *Mercenaries,* 196; Jones, *Malatesta,* 200; Luigi Rossi, "Sull'abbandono di Piombino da parte del Re di Aragona nel 1448," *Archivio storico italiano* 3 (1903): 180.
85. Mario Tabanelli, *Sigismondo Pandolfo Malatesta: Signore del medioevo e del rinascimento* (Faenza: F. Lli Lega, 1977), 73–74; Gino Franceschini, *I Malatesta* (Milan: Dall'Oglio, 1973), 353; Rossi, "Sull'abbandono," 147–148.
86. Anna Falcioni, "Malatesta, Sigismondo," *Dizionario biografico degli italiani* 68 (Rome: Istituto della Enciclopedia italiana, 2007): 109; Jones, *Malatesta,* 190–197.
87. Basinio, *Hesperis,* 107–108 (V.206–221).

88. Ibid., 109 (V.250–255).
89. Ibid., 109–110 (V.264–276).
90. Benzi-Pius II, *Discipula,* 76–77.
91. Broglio, *Cronaca,* 137–138; Tonini, *Rimini nella signoria de' Malatesti,* 167–168.
92. Ludovico A. Muratori, *Annali d'Italia dal principio dell'era volgare sino all'anno 1750* (Venice: Giuseppe Antonelli, 1833), vol. 45: 232. Jones, *Malatesta,* 195–196, does not elaborate on the details of the siege.
93. For archival documentation on this campaign, see Luigi Rossi, "I prodromi della guerra in Italia del 1452–53: I tiranni di Romagna e Federico da Montefeltro," *Atti e Memorie della r. deputazione di storia patria per le provincie delle Marche* III. 1, N.S. (1906): 63–101, 103–124, 189–224, 279–305.
94. *Florentine Histories,* VI.28; translation in Machiavelli, *Florentine Histories,* trans. Banfield and Mansfield, 262.
95. Bracciolini, *Poggii Historia florentina,* 373–376; Jones, *Malatesta,* 209.
96. Mallett, *Mercenaries,* 104.
97. The oration is published in Vespasiano, *Commentario,* vol. 2: 203–228. For the details about this brief campaign, see Carlo Tonini, *Compendio della storia di Rimini* (Bologna: Forni, 1895–1896), vol. 1: 534–535; and Jones, *Malatesta,* 209.
98. Basinio, *Hesperis,* 133 (VI.307–308).
99. Ibid., 201, 202, 204 (X.5–9, 25–26, 28–30, 82–88).
100. Ibid., 218–219 (X.435–445).
101. J. R. Hale, "Gunpowder and the Renaissance: An Essay in the History of Ideas," in *Renaissance War Studies* (London: Hambledon, 1983), 389–420.
102. Basinio, *Hesperis,* 219 (X.448–454).
103. Ibid., 219–220 (X.458–466).
104. Machiavelli, *Il principe,* 136–139 (ch. 7).
105. Burckhardt, 41; David Abulafia, "Ferrante of Naples: The Statecraft of a Renaissance Prince," *History Today,* available at http://www.andallthat.co.uk/uploads/2/3/8/9/2389220/ferrante_of_naples_the_statecraft_of_a_renaissance_prince.pdf.
106. Basinio, *Hesperis,* 233 (XI.174–177). Machiavelli raises the issue of true glory, or *virtù,* in the example of the Sicilian tyrant Agathocles, who rose to power by murdering all the leading citizens in Syracuse. See Machiavelli, *Il principe,* 150–154 (ch. 8), and Victoria Kahn, "Virtù and the Example of Agathocles in Machiavelli's Prince," *Representations,* 13 (1986): 63–83.
107. Valturio, *De re militari,* 361 (bk. XII, ch. 7).
108. Basinio, *Hesperis,* 220–221 (X.479–491). Machiavelli says that only two hundred men defended Foiano but that they were "fierce and faithful" and withstood Ferrante's siege for thirty-six days; translation in Machiavelli, *Florentine Histories* (bk. VI, ch. 28), trans. Banfield and Mansfield, 262. Poggio adds that

the "women demonstrated amazing virtue and showed themselves no less brave than the men," Bracciolini, *Poggii Historia florentina,* 374.

109. Basinio, *Hesperis,* 223 (X.547–551).
110. Ibid., 228–229 (XI.50–54, 57–61, 72–73).
111. Ibid., 230 (XI.105–106).
112. Ibid., 235–237 (XI.233–269).
113. Ibid., 243 (XI.434–436).
114. Ibid., 248 (XII.27–34).
115. Ibid., 249–252 (XII.58–80, 96–99, 123–134).
116. Ibid., 254, 256 (XII.186–189, 225–232). Basinio had already referred to Athena with her Gorgon shield helping Sigismondo in his metered letter requesting Sigismondo's patronage in 1450, "Basinii Parmensis Epistola ad divum Sigismundum Pandulphum Malatestam dominum Arimini illustrem: Laudes et preconia eius continens et suorum," in Ferri, *La giovinezza,* 41–44 (appendix 24, lines 33–38).
117. Basinio, *Hesperis,* 257 (XII.256–263).
118. Thomas Greene calls this the necessary ingredient of a successful epic, "heroic energy, the superabundant vitality, which charges character and image and action alike," in "The Norms of Epic," *Comparative Literature,* 13.3 (1961): 204–206.
119. Basinio, *Hesperis,* 258 (XII.266–270).
120. Ibid., 261–263 (XII.364–371, 391–395).
121. Ibid., 264 (XII.418–420); Herodotus, *Histories,* VII.226.
122. Basinio, *Hesperis,* 265–267 (XII.463–465, 473–476, 491–495).
123. Tonini, *Compendio,* 534–535; Cesare Clementini, *Raccolto istorico della fondatione di Rimini* (Bologna: Forni, 1969), 381–382 (facsimile of the 1617/1627 edition).
124. Basinio, *Hesperis,* 267–268 (XII: 514–520).
125. Ibid., 271–272 (XII.607–620). Starvation was a standard siege method, as discussed in Machiavelli, *Art of War,* VII.157, who draws on Vegetius, *Epitoma rei militari,* III.26. For Machiavelli's use of the Vegetius, see Christopher Allmand, *The "de re militari" of Vegetius: The Reception, Transmission, and Legacy of a Roman Text in the Middle Ages* (Cambridge: Cambridge University Press, 2011), 139–147.
126. Basinio, *Hesperis,* 274–276 (XIII.8–43).
127. Compare with Filelfo's description of the siege of Piacenza in book three of the *Sforziad,* as discussed in Diana Robin, *Filelfo in Milan: Writings, 1451–1477* (Princeton: Princeton University Press, 1991), 63–81.
128. Valturio, *De re militari,* 361–362 (bk. XII, ch. 7).
129. Mallett, *Mercenaries,* 172; Girolamo Mancini, *Vita di Leon Battista Alberti,* second edition (Florence: G. Carnesecchi e Figli, 1911), 308.

130. Jones, *Malatesta,* 209; Machiavelli, *Florentine Histories,* VI.28. Poggio says that the Aragonese raised the siege because of frustration and winter storms, Bracciolini, *Poggii Historia florentina,* 375.

5. Astrology, Plato, and Pagan Worship

1. Andrea Benzi-Pius II, "Discipula veritatis," in *Pii secundi epistolae* (Milan: Antonius Zarothus, 1487), n.p., 84 in scan of this edition, available at http://fondosdigitales.us.es/fondos/libros/204/67/epistola-siue-oratio-pii-in-conuentu-mantuano/. Henceforth pages refer to this scanned edition.
2. Alison Brown, *The Return of Lucretius to Renaissance Florence* (Cambridge: Harvard University Press, 2010); Stephen Greenblatt, *The Swerve: How the World Became Modern* (New York: Norton, 2011).
3. Benzi-Pius II, *Discipula,* 84–85.
4. Enea Silvio Piccolomini Papa Pio II, *I commentarii,* ed. Luigi Totaro, second edition (Milan: Adelphi, 2004), 876–877 (bk. V, ch. 5).
5. Benzi-Pius II, *Discipula,* 85–86.
6. Ibid., 84.
7. Ibid., 81. Broglio calls Sigismondo "another Cicero," and his seventeenth-century biographer compares him to Cicero and Caesar in eloquence: Broglio, "Cronaca," in Luigi Tonini, *Rimini nella signoria de' Malatesti, parte seconda al volume quinto* (Rimini: Albertini, 1882), 324; Cesare Clementini, *Raccolto istorico della fondatione di Rimini* (Bologna: Forni, 1969), 296 (facsimile of the 1617/1627 ed.).
8. Roberto Valturio, *De re militari* (Paris: Apud Christianum Wechelum, 1534), 9 (bk. I, ch. 2).
9. Benzi-Pius II, *Discipula,* 81.
10. Ibid., 80–81.
11. Valturio, *De re militari,* 382–383 (bk. XII, ch. 13). See Kokole's exploration of the classical meaning of Valturio's "forms" in Stanko Kokole, "*Cognitio formarum* and Agostino di Duccio's Reliefs for the Chapel of the Planets in the Tempio Malatestiano," in *Quattrocento Adriatico: Fifteenth-Century Art of the Adriatic Rim,* ed. Charles Dempsey (Bologna: Nuova Alfa, 1996), 177–206.
12. On the classical sources of the iconography, see Stanko Kokole, "Agostino di Duccio in the Tempio Malatestiano, 1449–1457: Challenges of Poetic Invention and Fantasies of Personal Style" (Ph.D. diss., The Johns Hopkins University, 1997), esp. 244–253; Marco Bertozzi, "La vita postuma degli antichi dei nel tempio di Alberti e Sigismondo," in *Il Tempio Malatestiano a Rimini,* ed. Antonio Paolucci (Modena: Franco Cosimo Panini, 2010), vol. 2: 137–144; Marco Bertozzi, "Segni, simboli, visioni: Il Tempio Malatestiano e i suoi enigmi," in *Templum*

Mirabile: Atti del convegno sul Tempio Malatestiano, ed. Marco Musmeci (Rimini: Cassa di Risparmio di Rimini, 2003), 156–161.

13. Valturio, *De re militari,* 33 (bk. III).
14. Ibid., 33–34 (bk. III).
15. Ibid., 36 (bk. III).
16. Ibid., 36 (bk. III).
17. Ibid., 304 (bk. XI, ch. 8): on nautical astrology; 298 (bk. XI, ch. 6), on the winds, zodiac names, and properties; and 93 (bk. XI, ch. 3), on the moon.
18. Ibid., 42 (bk. III).
19. Ibid., 38 (bk. III).
20. Ibid., 41 (bk. III).
21. Ibid., 43–44 (bk. III).
22. Ibid., 45 (bk. III).
23. Ibid., 47 (bk. III). See also Basinio, *Astronomicon,* ed. Marinella De Luca, Donatella Frioli, and Giordana Mariani Canova (Rimini: Cassa di Risparmio di Rimini, 1994), vol. 1: 10–13; and Chapter 2.
24. On the widespread belief in astrology, see Monica Azzolini, *The Duke and the Stars: Astrology and Politics in Renaissance Milan* (Cambridge: Harvard University Press, 2013), 100–134; Wolfgang Hübner, "The Culture of Astrology from Ancient to Renaissance," in *A Companion to Astrology in the Renaissance,* ed. Brendan Dooley (Leiden: Brill, 2014), 17–58; William Eamon, "Astrology and Society," in *A Companion to Astrology,* 141–191; Ferdinando Gabotto, "L'astrologia nel quattrocento in rapport colla civiltà," *Rivista di filosofia scientifica* (1889): 377–413.
25. Valturio, *De re militari,* 33 (bk. III); Lucan, *The Civil War,* ed. and trans. J. D. Duff (London: William Heinemann, 1928), 48–53 (I.642–672).
26. Valturio, *De re militari,* 35 (bk. III).
27. Livy, 1.19–20; Plutarch, "Life of Numa Pompilius," in *Plutarch's Lives,* ed. and trans. Bernadotte Perrin (Cambridge: Harvard University Press, 1967), vol. 1: 305–381. Machiavelli praises Numa for his instrumental use of religion in the *Discourses,* I.11–12.
28. Valturio, *De re militari,* 45 (bk. III).
29. Broglio, *Cronaca,* in Luigi Tonini, *Rimini nella signoria de' Malatesti, parte seconda al volume quinto* (Rimini: Albertini, 1882), 283–284; Francesco Gaetano Battaglini, *Della vita e de' fatti di Sigismondo Pandolfo* Malatesta (Rimini: Ex Typographia Albertiniana, 1794), 506.
30. Basinio, *Liber Isottaeus,* ed. Ferruccio Ferri (Città di Castello: Società Anonima Tiografica "Leonardo da Vinci," 1922), I.9.1–4.
31. Basinio da Parma, "Hesperis," in *Basinii parmensis poetae opera praestantiora* (Rimini: Albertiniana, 1794), vol. 1: *Hesperis,* 113–114 (V.359–381).

32. Ibid., 21 (I.502–508).

33. Ibid., 16–17 (I.385–412).

34. *Discourses on the First Decade of Livy,* I.14. On this, see John M. Najemy, "Papirius and the Chickens, or Machiavelli on the Necessity of Interpreting Religion" *Journal of the History of Ideas,* 60.4 (1999): 659–681.

35. Basinio, *Hesperis,* 229 (XI.76–82).

36. On the belief in omens in the Renaissance, see Ottavia Niccoli, *Prophecy and People in Renaissance Italy* (Princeton: Princeton UP, 1990).

37. Valturio, *De re militari,* 37–38 (bk. III).

38. Ibid., 39: *"Aio te, Æacide, Romanos vincere posse."* Cf. Augustine, *City of God,* III.17.

39. Valturio, *De re militari,* 39 (bk. III).

40. Ibid., 40 (bk. III).

41. Ibid., 38 (bk. III).

42. *Concerning Prohibited Books,* Rule IX, condemned books on astrology, oracles, and omens, as discussed in Ugo Baldini, "The Roman Inquisition's Condemnation of Astrology: Antecedents, Reasons, and Consequences," in *Church, Censorship, and Culture in Early Modern Italy,* ed. Gigliola Fragnito (Cambridge: Cambridge University Press, 2001), 79–110, esp. 89–90; Hübner, "The Culture of Astrology," 55–56. In general, see Michael David Bailey, *Magic and Superstition in Europe: A Concise History from Antiquity to the Present* (Lanham: Rowman & Littlefield, 2007), 179–214.

43. On Cleofe, see Battaglini, *Della vita,* 269–270; and Silvia Ronchey, *L'enigma di Piero: L'ultimo bizantino e la crociata fantasma nella rivelazione di un grande quadro* (Milan: Rizzoli, 2006), 49, 60, 93–97, 201, and Anna Falcioni, "Cleofe Malatesti nelle fonti epistolari mantovane," in *Le donne di casa malatesti,* ed. Anna Falcioni (Rimini: Ghigi, 2005), 957–968, who publishes correspondence in which Cleofe strongly asserts her Roman Catholicism. For Plethon's funeral oration, see "Georgi Gemistii in dominam Cleopen divinissimi principis nostri uxorem oratio funebris," original Greek and Latin trans. in *Patrologiae cursus completus: Series Graeca,* ed. Jacques Paul Migne (Paris: 1866), vol. 160: 939–952; also discussed in Christopher M. Woodhouse, *George Gemistos Plethon: The Last of the Hellenes* (Oxford: Clarendon, 1986), 113–115. Cf. John Monfasani, "Platonic Paganism in the Fifteenth Century," in *Reconsidering the Renaissance,* ed. Mario A. Di Cesare (Binghamton: Center for Medieval and Early Renaissance Studies, 1992), 49, who points out a reference to the Eucharist in Plethon's eulogy.

44. On Plethon's paganism and Platonic revival, see Niketas Siniossoglou, *Radical Platonism in Byzantium: Illumination and Utopia in Gemistos Plethon* (Cambridge: Cambridge University Press, 2011), 125–160, and specifically for Mistra, 119–124; Monfasani, "Platonic Paganism," 45–61, esp. 52. See also the perceptive essay by

Cesare Vasoli, "Dalle armi alle lettere ed alla 'prisca sapientia': I due Malatesta," in *Il Dono di Malatesta Novello,* ed. Loretta Righetti and Daniela Savoia (Cesena: "Il Ponte Vecchio," 2006), 29–44.

45. Cyriac of Ancona, *Later Travels,* ed. and trans. Edward D. Bodnar (Cambridge: Harvard University Press, 2003), 360–362; Woodhouse, *Plethon,* 147, 160, 228; Bertozzi, "Segni, simboli," 161–165; John Monfasani, *George of Trebizond: A Biography and a Study of His Logic and Rhetoric* (Leiden: Brill, 1976), 214; Siniossoglou, *Radical Platonism,* 132.

46. On this, see James Hankins, *Plato in the Italian Renaissance* (Leiden: E. J. Brill, 1990), 2 vols.

47. Giovanni Cocchi, *De immortalitate animae,* Biblioteca Casanatense MS cod. 103. On this, see also Angelo Turchini, *Il Tempio Malatestiano, Sigismondo Malatesta e Leon Battista Alberti* (Cesena: "Il Ponte Vecchio," 2000), 343–349. On Giovanni da Ferrara, or Cocchi, see Julius Kirschner, "Cocchi, Giovanni" DBI 26 (1982), 472–473; Domenico Fava, "Fra Giovanni e Sigismondo Malatesta," in *Scritti vari dedicati a Mario Armanni in occasione del suo sessantesimo compleanno* (Milan: Hoepli, 1938), 49–62.

48. Fava, "Fra Giovanni," 57–58, 62.

49. Cocchi, *De immortalitate,* fols. 89r–89v. Cocchi copies from Macrobius, *Commentary on the Dream of Scipio,* trans. William Harris Stahl (New York: Columbia University Press, 1990) reprint of 1952, 129–130 (bk. X, ch. 17). On Augustine's negative views of the body, see Peter Brown, *The Body and Society: Men, Women, and Sexual Renunciation in Early Christianity* (New York: Columbia University Press, 1988), 387–427.

50. On Macrobius's paganism, see Christopher P. Jones, *Between Pagan and Christian* (Cambridge: Harvard University Press, 2014), Kindle edition, appendix: "Was Macrobius a Christian?"

51. Cocchi, *De immortalitate,* fols. 123v–124r; Macrobius, *Commentary on the Dream of Scipio,* 130 (bk. XI, ch. 1).

52. See Augustine, *City of God,* 21.3 and 19.28; 21.2.

53. Ferruccio Ferri, *La giovinezza di un poeta: Basinii Parmensis Carmina* (Rimini: Artigianelli, 1914), poem to Nicholas V, 1450, appendix XXVI: lines 30–43, 165–167.

54. Augusto Campana, "Isotta degli Atti," *DBI* (1962) [online] argues that the first couple elegies in the *Isottaeus* were the work of Tobia Veronensis (at Sigismondo's court 1446–1449), and the remainder were by Basinio. Because of their stylistic consistency, I am attributing all the poems in the *Isottaeus* to Basinio. Ferri, *La giovinezza di un poeta,* also attributes the entire book to Basinio.

55. Basinio, *Isottaeus,* II.1.41–52.

56. Ibid., II.2.39–42.

57. Ibid., II.2.45–52.
58. Ibid., III.10.31–36; Ferri, *La giovinezza,* 37.
59. *Aeneid,* 2.792–4; Basinio, *Isottaeus,* III.10.47–52.
60. Basinio, *Hesperis,* 71–72 (III.471–2, 483–4, 491–494).
61. Ibid., 178–179 (VIII.336–348).
62. Ibid., 179 (VIII.352–356).
63. Ibid., 192 (IX.245–253).
64. Basinio, *Isottaeus,* II.6.21–32. In II.5, Isotta bewails the loss of their son to Sigismondo.
65. See Cocchi, *De immortalitate,* esp. fols. 77v–78r, for Pythagorean metempsychosis. Plethon was seen as the reincarnated soul of Plato by, among others, Cardinal Bessarion, as noted in Edgar Wind, *Pagan Mysteries in the Renaissance: an Exploration of Philosophical and Mystical Sources of Iconography in Renaissance Art* (New York: Norton, 1958 (repub. 1968)), 256–258. The Florentine philosopher Marsilio Ficino also adopted Platonic and Pythagorean views of the soul, as discussed in James Hankins, "Marsilio Ficino on Reminiscentia and the Transmigration of Souls," *Rinascimento,* 45 (2005): 3–17
66. Basinio, *Hesperis,* 223–224 (X.559–571).
67. Ibid., 234 (XI.197–198).
68. Ibid., 236 (XI.249–255).
69. Ibid., 259 (XII.294–303).
70. "Sigismundus Pandulfus Malatesta Marti Pacis Bellique Deo," in Porcellio Pandone, "De amore Iovis in Isottam," in *Trium poetarm elegantissimorum, Porcelii, Basinii, et Trebani opuscula* (Paris: Simonem Colineum, 1539 (orig. 1456)), fols. 13v–15r.
71. "Mars Phoebo S.D.P.," in ibid., fols. 15v–18r.
72. "Iuppiter Saturno Patri S.P.D.," in ibid., fols. 18r–20r.
73. "Saturnus Lunae S.D.P.," in ibid., fols. 20v–22v.
74. "Mercurius in concione apud Deos sic loquitur," in ibid., fol. 23r.
75. Ibid., fol. 24v.
76. Porcellio probably would not have known this distinction. See Jones, *Between Pagan,* ch. 6.
77. Basinio, *Hesperis,* 19 (I.456–461).
78. Ibid., 19 (I.442–450).
79. Ibid., 23 (I.545–554).
80. Ibid., 23–24 (I.556–572).
81. On the differences between pagan and Christian prayer, see Jones, *Between Pagan,* ch. 6.
82. Basinio, *Hesperis,* 104 (V.119–130).
83. Cicero discusses immortality through letters in the *Tusculan Disputations* (bk. I).

84. Cocchi, *De immortalitate,* fols. 81r–82v.
85. On heroic divinization in Homer and ancient Greek religion, see Gregory Nagy, *The Ancient Greek Hero in 24 Hours* (Cambridge: Harvard University Press, 2013), Kindle edition, part 1. Hero worship was still popular well into the third century CE, as discussed in Christopher P. Jones, "Philostratus' *Heroikos* and Its Setting in Reality," *The Journal of Hellenic Studies,* 121 (2001): 146–149, and Christopher P. Jones, *New Heroes in Antiquity: From Achilles to Antinoos* (Cambridge: Harvard University Press, 2010), Kindle edition, chs. 1 and 3.
86. Cocchi, *De immortalitate,* fols. 88v–89r, is following Cicero, *Tusculan Disputations,* I.15.
87. Cocchi, *De immortalitate,* fols. 81r–82v.
88. Ibid., fols. 82v–83r.
89. Ibid., fol. 89r.
90. Cicero, *Tusculan Disputations,* I.15.
91. Most of Cicero's *On the Republic* did not survive, but Scipio's dream was well known through Macrobius's popular commentary. On Macrobius and the pagan notion of heaven, see Sabine MacCormack, *Shadows of Poetry: Vergil in the Mind of Augustine* (Berkeley: University of California Press, 1998), 109–111.
92. Basinio, *Hesperis,* 178 (VIII.318–320, 329–335)
93. Ibid., 177–178 (VIII.303–314, 321–328).
94. Ibid., 179–180 (VIII.363–383).
95. Ibid., 188 (IX.156–162).
96. Ibid., 190–192 (IX.215–244).
97. Ibid., 211 (X.255–256).
98. Ibid., 211 (X.264–265).
99. "Mercurius in concione apud Deos sic loquitur," in Porcellio Pandone, "De amore Iovis in Isottam," fol. 25r.

6. Pagan Sex and Heroic Virtue

1. See, for example, Seneca, *Hercules furens,* I.465–478: "Are we to call [Hercules] brave for giving away the lion skin on his shoulders and his club as a gift to a girl, and for having his chest shine forth, colorfully decked out in Tyrian cloth? Are we to call him brave for drenching his bristling locks in nard oil, for strumming an unmanly rhythm on the tambourine with his famous hands, and for wearing a barbarian's headdress on his ferocious forehead?"
2. Propertius, *Elegies,* II.22, translated by A. S. Kline (Liber Publications, 2001), available at. http://www.yorku.ca/pswarney/3110/Propertius.htm#_Toc500249318
3. As regent to her son, Sallustio, Isotta ruled Rimini when Sigismondo was fighting the Turks from 1464 to 1466 and for a year after Sigismondo's death in 1468,

as noted in Augusto Campana, "Isotta degli Atti," in *Dizionario biografico degli italiani,* vol. 4 (Rome: Istituto della Enciclopedia italiana, 1962), 551.

4. Helen S. Ettlinger, "Visibilis et Invisibilis: The Mistress in Italian Renaissance Court Society," *Renaissance Quarterly,* 47.4 (1994): 776.
5. Augusto Campana, "Poema antiMalatestiano di un umanista spagnolo per Pio II," *Atti del convegno storico piccoliminiano* (Ancona: Il Lavoro Editoriale, 1965), 193.
6. Andrea-Pius II, "Discipula veritatis," in *Pii secundi Epistolae* (Milan: Antonius Zarothus, 1487), n.p., 84 in scan of this edition, available at http://fondosdigitales.us.es/fondos/libros/204/67/epistola-siue-oratio-pii-in-conuentu-mantuano/. Henceforth pages refer to this scanned edition.
7. Dante, *Inferno,* V.73–142; Marco Viroli, *Signore di Romagna: Le altre leonesse, dame, amanti e guerriere nelle corti romagnole* (Cesena: "Il Ponte Vecchio," 2010), 29–50.
8. Viroli, *Signore,* 71–87. See also Silvia Pari, "Francesca da Rimini nei commentatori danteschi del trecento," and Roberta Iotti, "Parisina Malatesti d'Este," in *Le donne di casa malatesti,* ed. Anna Falcioni (Rimini: Ghigi, 2005), 95–119, 433–469. Pius himself refers to the lust of Francesca and Parisina in his condemnation of the Malatesta family, in Pius, *Commentarii,* in Enea Silvio Piccolomini Papa Pio II, *I commentarii,* ed. Luigi Totaro, second edition (Milan: Adelphi, 2004), 1912–1913 (10.13).
9. Francesco Gaetano Battaglini, *Della vita e de' fatti di Sigismondo Pandolfo Malatesta* (Rimini: Albertiniana, 1794), 300.
10. On Sigismondo's first two wives, see Roberta Iotti, "Ginevra d'Este Malatesti," and Bianca Orlandi, "Polissena Sforza: Seconda moglie di Sigismondo Pandolfo Malatesti," in *Le donne di casa malatesti,* 545–566, 569–579.
11. Gaspare Broglio Tartaglia, *Cronaca malatestiana del secolo XV,* ed. Antonio G. Luciani (Rimini: Bruno Ghigi, 1982), 49, 74–75; Philip James Jones, *The Malatesta of Rimini and the Papal State: A Political History* (Cambridge: Cambridge University Press, 1974), 186, 172–173, 191–193.
12. The letter is discussed and quoted in Franco Gaeta, "La leggenda di Sigismondo Malatesta," in *Studi malatestiani,* ed. Philip James Jones (Rome: Istituto Storico Italiano per il Medioevo, 1978), 173–175.
13. Benzi-Pius II, *Discipula,* 74–76.
14. Ibid., 75–76; *I Diurnali del duca di Monteleone,* ed. Michele Manfredi, Rerum italicarum scriptores, vol. 21.5 (Bologna: Zanichelli, 1958), 197; Giovanni Soranzo, "Un'invettiva della curia romana contro Sigismondo Pandolfo Malatesta," *La Romagna* 8 (1911): 241–256.
15. Benzi-Pius II, *Discipula,* 77.

16. Giovanni Soranzo questioned the accusation of Ginevra's poisoning because of Sigismondo's continued good relations with the Este family, "Un'invettiva," 157–159.
17. Benzi-Pius II, *Discipula,* 77–78.
18. See the excellent discussion about the sources related to this charge, the later historiography on this issue, and Ezra Pound's use of Polissena in the Malatesta Cantos, in Lawrence Rainey, *Ezra Pound and the Monument of Culture* (Chicago: University of Chicago Press, 1991), 82–154.
19. Basinio, *Liber Isottaeus,* ed. Ferruccio Ferri (Città di Castello: Società Anonima Tipografica "Leonardo da Vinci," 1922), III.1.81–82, in which Isotta refers to Niccolò Piccinino's invasion of the Marche in 1443. The Malatesta chancellor Carlo Valturi composed a love poem in Sigismondo's name to Isotta dated 1445, as noted in Campana, "Atti," 547.
20. Using archaeological evidence from Sigismondo's custom of burying medals in foundations, Rainey, *Ezra Pound,* 161, argues that the medals and the "public exaltation of Isotta began only after 1452."
21. Ettlinger, "Visibilis," 773–778.
22. "Isote Ariminensi forma et virtute Italie decori. M. CCCC.XLVI." Basinio and Porcellio praise the marble tomb as a fitting resting place for Isotta's earthly remains, Basinio, *Isottaeus,* I.6.52; 8.75–80; Porcellio Pandone, "De amore Iovis in Isottam," in *Trium poetarm elegantissimorum, Porcelii, Basinii, et Trebani opuscula* (Paris: Simonem Colineum, 1539 (orig. 1456)), fol. 9v.
23. On these issues, see Angelo Turchini, *Il Tempio Malatestiano, Sigismondo Malatesta e Leon Battista Alberti* (Cesena: "Il Ponte Vecchio," 2000), 163–179, and Campana, "Atti," 548.
24. Pius II, *Commentaries,* ed. Margaret Meserve and Marcello Simonetta and trans. Margaret Meserve (Cambridge: Harvard University Press, 2003), 328 (bk. II, ch. 32), my translation. See discussion in Campana, "Atti," 548. Mancini thought that Pius had misread the inscription and that the *D* merely stood for *Dominae* ("lady"), not *Divae,* Girolamo Mancini, *Vita di Leon Battista Alberti,* second edition (Florence: G. Carnesecchi e Figli, 1911), 306. Isotta, however, is frequently called "diva" in Malatesta poetry.
25. Christopher P. Jones, *New Heroes in Antiquity: From Achilles to Antinoos* (Cambridge: Harvard University Press, 2010), Kindle edition, ch. 1, loc. 75–82.
26. Basinio, *Isottaeus,* II.7.29–54.
27. Basinio da Parma, "Hesperis," in *Basinii parmensis poetae opera praestantiora* (Rimini: Albertiniana, 1794), vol. 1: *Hesperis,* 168 (VIII.81–85): ". . . sed ipsum ut vidit talem, se se inflammavit amore, candidaque implicuit sublato brachia collo. Ille Deae taedis, tantoque potitus amore laetus adit densos felici ex arbore lucos."

28. Ibid., 187–188 (IX.137–142).
29. Dante, *Inferno,* V.142: "E caddi come corpo morto cade."
30. For attribution, see Campana, "Atti," 552–553, and Ferruccio Ferri, *La giovinezza di un poeta: Basinii Parmensis Carmina* (Rimini: Artigianelli, 1914).
31. Basinio, *Isottaeus,* I.7.9–26.
32. *Petri Parleonis epithalamium in nuptiis Antonii Atti incipit foeliciter,* MS Venice, Biblioteca Nazionale Marciana Marc. lat. XI 80 (3057), fol. 346r–346v. On this, see Anthony F. D'Elia, *The Renaissance of Marriage in Fifteenth-Century Italy* (Cambridge: Harvard University Press, 2004), 104–105, 171. For Latin text, see Anthony F. D'Elia, "Marriage, Sexual Pleasure, and Learned Brides in the Wedding Orations of Fifteenth-Century Italy," *Renaissance Quarterly,* 55 (2002): 413.
33. For Amazons in literature and as decorations on wedding chests, see Cristelle L. Baskins, *Cassone Painting, Humanism, and Gender in Early Modern Italy* (Cambridge: Cambridge University Press, 1998), 26–49.
34. Basinio, *Isottaeus,* I.7.33–38, 41–57.
35. Boccaccio, *Decameron,* VI.1. On this, see D'Elia, *Renaissance of Marriage,* 97.
36. Roberto Valturio, *De re militari* (Paris: Apud Christianum Wechelum, 1534), 9 (bk. I, ch. 3).
37. Basinio, *Isottaeus,* I.6.43–54.
38. Ibid., III.10.9–17.
39. See Charles Yriarte, *Un condottiere au XVe siecle: Rimini: Études sur les lettres et les arts a la cour des Malatesta* (Paris: Rothschild, 1882), 389–392, and Aldo Francesco Massèra, "I poeti isottei," *Giornale storico della letteratura italiana,* 57 (1911): 1–32. On this episode, see also Rainey, *Ezra Pound,* 178–186.
40. Viroli, *Signore,* 139–147, transcribes fourteen poems in Sigismondo's name from a manuscript in Florence, MS Biblioteca Riccardiana 1154. A manuscript of Roberto Orsi's poems in Florence (Biblioteca Nazionale Centrale ms. Magl. VII 1200) contains several vernacular poems with Sigismondo's name, and the vernacular court poet Francesco Palmario di Ancona penned three poems about "Isotta mia," and others that imply Sigismondo's authorship in *Rime,* ed. Nelia Cacace Saxby (Bologna: Casa Carducci, 1997), 78, 79, 96. On Sigismondo's poetry see also Battaglini, *Della vita,* 59.
41. Basinio, *Isottaeus,* III.3.59–66, 89–102.
42. Another court poet, Palmario, describes love's power in Sigismondo's declaration: "[Isotta] is Medusa and I am her stone," in *Rime,* 94.
43. Basinio, *Isottaeus,* I.6.17–34.
44. Ibid., I.6.39, 47–50.
45. Ibid., I.1.32, 41–44.
46. Ibid., I.2.41–43, 81–82.
47. Ibid., I.4.27–34, 35–54.

48. These include Nausika, Calypso, Circe, and the sirens.
49. Basinio, *Isottaeus,* III.4.13–24.
50. Ibid., III.4.31–54 (summarized), 55–60.
51. Ibid., III.4.65–81.
52. Horace, *Odes,* I.11.
53. Basinio, *Isottaeus,* III.4.85–92.
54. Ibid., III.5.11–16, 49–56, 73–76.
55. Ibid., II.10.61–76.
56. Ibid., II.10.77–80.
57. Ibid., III.1.119–130.
58. On Penthesilea and Achilles, see the fourth century BCE account in Quintus of Smyrna, *The Trojan Epic,*I.476–674, esp. 656–674.
59. Female scholars and rulers were sometimes compared to Amazons, as discussed in Margaret L. King, *Women of the Renaissance* (Chicago: University of Chicago Press, 1991), 159, 188–191. In the *City of Ladies* (1405), Christine de Pizan praises the heroic exploits of Amazons in antiquity, including Penthesilea, and lauds the young Joan of Arc as a modern Amazon, as discussed in King, *Women,* 224–227.
60. Isotta, Letter to Sigismondo Malatesta (20 December 1454), published in Aldo Francesco Massera, *Amori e gelosie in una corte romagnola del Rinascimento (per la biografia d'Isotta da Rimini)* (Forli: L. Bordandini, 1917), 61–72; Campana, "Atti," 550.
61. Iacopo Ammannatti Piccolomini, *Pii secondi pont. Max. Commentarii rerum memorabilium* (Frankfurt, 1614), 404, as quoted in Massera, 1917, 72.
62. For the idea of a sick and dying lover, see Propertius, *Elegies,* II.28:1–46. The Urbino poet Angelo Galli wrote two short poems and two longer ones in the vernacular about a dead Isotta who returns and converses with Sigismondo, *Canzoniere,* ed. Giorgio Nonni (Urbino: Accademia Raffaello, 1987), 337–359 (poems 261–264). Although Galli makes classical references, he also refers to Christ, the Blessed Roberto, and God in the singular.
63. Basinio, *Isottaeus,* I.9.9–16, 26–28, 49–52.
64. Ibid., I.10.11–16, 22, 41–42.
65. Ibid., I.10.35–38.
66. Ibid., III.6.49–70, 73–88, 89–104.
67. Ibid., III.7.9–10, 19–24, 25–40, 41–50, 79–96.
68. Ibid., III.8.11–22, 23–46, 62–69, 75–94.
69. Ibid., III.9.9–24, 25–31, 37–50, 51–61, 81–84, 91–100. Cf. Basinio, *Hesperis,* 190 (IX.213), where Sigismondo's father tells him that "it is forbidden [*nefas*] for the living to manipulate [*tractare*] buried souls."
70. Basinio, *Isottaeus,* III.10.57–70.

71. Ibid., III.10.81–94.
72. Basinio, *Hesperis,* 130 (VI.223–233).
73. Ibid., 130–131 (VI.234–241).
74. Porcellio arrived in Rimini in 1454, as noted in Battaglini, *Della vita,* 112–116.
75. Porcellio, "De amore," fol.8r.
76. Ibid., fols. 8v–11r.
77. "Iuppiter Divae Isottae ariminensi salutem plurimam dicit," in ibid., fols. 11r–13r.
78. "Sigismundus Pandulfus Malatesta Marti pacis bellique deo," in ibid., fols. 13v–15r.
79. "Mars Phoebo S.D.P.," in ibid., fols. 15v–18r.
80. "Iuppiter Saturno patri S.P.D.," in ibid., fols. 18r–20r.
81. "Saturnus Lunae S.D.P.," in ibid., fol. 21v. Cynthus is a hill in Delos, the sacred birthplace of Diana and Apollo.
82. Ibid., fol. 22r.
83. "Mercurius in concione apud deos sic loquitur," in ibid., fols. 22v–24v.
84. Ibid., fols. 24v–25r.
85. "Deorum consensus et Pallas legatae ad Iovem Maximum," in ibid., fols. 25v.
86. Guido Cappelli, "Pandone, Porcelio," in *Dizionario biografico degli italiani,* vol.80 (Rome: Istituto della Enciclopedia italiana, 2014).
87. "Franciscus Philelfus Sigismundo Pandulfo Malatestae Salutem," in Franciscus Philelfus, *Epistolae familiares* (Venice: Gregorii de Gregoriis, 1502), fol. 94. Although Filelfo does not specifically say that Porcellio showed his poetry to Sforza and his court, the fact that he writes *Ostendit praeterea* ("he also showed") implies that the poems were shown after the oration was delivered. It is, however, unclear what poetry Porcellio showed.
88. For Filelfo's encomium and request for patronage from Sigismondo, see Francesco Filelfo, *Odes,* ed. and trans. Diana Robin (Cambridge: Harvard University Press, 2009), 194–201 (III.8).
89. "Franciscus Philelfus Iacobo Antiquario Salutem," in Philelfus, *Epistolae familiares,* fol. 204r. On this, see also Ferruccio Ferri, *Una contesa di tre umanisti: Basinio, Porcellio e Seneca. Contributo alla storia degli studi greci nel quattrocento in Italia* (Fusi: Pavia, 1920), 20–22, 71–72, and Battaglini, *Della vita,* 156.
90. D'Elia, *Renaissance of Marriage,* 83–116.
91. See Propertius, *Elegies,* II.28:1–46; IV.7:1–96002E.

7. Questioning Virtue in Malatesta Literature

1. Latin epigrams in Francesco Gaetano Battaglini, *Della corte letteraria di Sigismondo Pandolfo Malatesta* (Rimini: Ex Typographica Albertiniana, 1794), 131.

2. Philip James Jones, *The Malatesta of Rimini and the Papal State: A Political History* (Cambridge: Cambridge University Press, 1974), 128–129; John M. McManamon, *Pierpaolo Vergerio the Elder: The Humanist as Orator* (Tempe: Medieval and Renaissance Texts and Studies, 1996), 72–81.
3. Biondo Flavio, *Roma Triumphans,* bk. II; Biondo Flavio, *Scritti inediti e rari di Biondo Flavio,* ed. Bartolomeo Nogara (Rome: Tipografia Poliglotta Vaticana, 1927), xxiv.
4. James Hankins, "Latin Poetry of Leonardo Bruni," in *Humanism and Platonism in the Italian Renaissance* (Rome: Storia e Letteratura, 2003), 170–171, 128.
5. P. Jones, *Malatesta,* 129; Robert Tavernor, *On Alberti and the Art of Building* (New Haven: Yale University Press, 1998), 50.
6. Roberto Valturio, *De re militari* (Paris: Apud Christianum Wechelum, 1534), 22 (bk. II, ch. 2).
7. Ibid., 22 (bk. II, ch. 2).
8. Ibid., 23 (bk. II, ch. 2); Terence, *The Eunuch,* III.6; Augustine, *City of God,* II.7, VIII.35; Augustine, *Confessions,* X.26. For Augustine on theater, see Sabine MacCormack, *Shadows of Poetry. Vergil in the Mind of Augustine* (Berkeley: University of California Press, 1998), 198–199. On this passage in the sixteenth century, see Carlo Ginzburg, "Titian, Ovid, and Sixteenth-Century Codes for Erotic Illustrations," in *Clues, Myths, and the Historical Method* (Baltimore: Johns Hopkins University Press, 1989), 77–94.
9. Valturio, *De re militari,* 24 (bk. II, ch.2). Cf. Valturio's discussion of dance in ch. 4.
10. Ibid., 24–25 (bk. II, ch.2).
11. Ibid., 372–375 (bk. XII, ch.11).
12. Ibid., 374 (bk. XII, ch.11). Valturio quotes Lactantius, *Divine Institutes,* XV.5, who is in turn quoting Cicero, *On the Nature of Gods,* II.24.
13. Valturio, *De re militari,* 375 (bk. XII, ch. 11).
14. Lactantius in turn copied Cicero and the ancient Greek mythographer Euhemerus (fourth century BCE), who both theorized about how poetic and artistic memorial led to divinization in antiquity. On this, see MacCormack, *Shadows,* 140; Christopher P. Jones, *New Heroes in Antiquity: From Achilles to Antinoos* (Cambridge: Harvard University Press, 2010), Kindle edition, ch. 4; Christopher P. Jones, *Between Pagan and Christian* (Cambridge: Harvard University Press, 2014), Kindle edition, ch. 4.
15. Basinio, *Diosymposeos liber,* available in modern edition in Donatella Coppini, "Un epillio umanistico fra Omero e Virgilio: Il Diosymposeos liber di Basinio da Parma," in *Confini dell'umanesimo letterario. Studi in onore di Francesco Tateo,* ed. Mauro de Nichilo, Grazia Distaso, and Antonio Iurilli (Rome: Roma nel Rinascimento, 2003), vol. 1: 323–336. On the ecphrases in the Temple of Fame in the *Diosymposis* and the *Hesperis,* see Stanko Kokole, "The Tomb of the

Ancestors in the Tempio Malatestiano," in *Drawing Relationships in Northern Italian Renaissance Art: Patronage and Theories of Invention,* ed. Giancarla Periti (Aldershot: Ashgate, 2004), 11–34.

16. Basinio, *Diosymposis,* 332 (lines 342–362, 363): "Atque ego non fueram tanti pars vana laboris," On this, see also Coppini, "Un epillio," 308.
17. Basinio, *Diosymposis,* 332 (lines 364–367), on which see also ibid., 306–307.
18. Basinio, *Diosymposis,* 335 (lines 464–472). Coppini, "Un epillio," 310, also notes this.
19. Basinio da Parma, "Hesperis," in *Basinii parmensis poetae opera praestantiora* (Rimini: 1794), vol. 1: *Hesperis,* 97 (IV.567–82).
20. Horace, *Odes,* 3.30.1; Petrarch, *Familiar Letters,* VII.15, also cited in Coppini, "Un epillio," 310.
21. Basinio, *Isottaeus,* I.8.14–34.
22. Discussed in John K. G. Shearman, *Only Connect . . . Art and the Spectator in the Italian Renaissance* (Princeton: Princeton University Press, 1992), 114–115.
23. The vernacular court poet Francesco Palmario also praises de Pasti's rendering of Isotta's image, *Rime,* ed. Nelia Cacace Saxby (Bologna: Casa Carducci, 1997), 78.
24. Peter W. van der Horst, "Sortes: Sacred Books as Instant Oracles in Late Antiquity," in *The Use of Sacred Books in the Ancient World,* ed. Leonard Victor Rutgers (Leuven: Peeters, 1998), 168.
25. Augustine, *Confessions,* VIII.12:27–28. Augustine criticizes this use of pagan poetry in *Confessions,* IV.3.5. See James Christopher Warner, *The Augustinian Epic: Petrarch to Milton* (Ann Arbor: University of Michigan Press, 2005), 140–141. For Petrarch, see his letter on his ascent of Mont Ventoux.
26. On the *Aeneid* as a religious text, see MacCormack, *Shadows,* 84–87.
27. Giuseppe F. Mazzotta, "Boccaccio: The Mythographer of the City," in *Interpretation and Allegory: Antiquity to the Modern Period,* ed. Jon Whitman (Leiden: Brill, 2000), 354–358, 363–364. For Boccaccio's defense of poetry, see *Genealogiae deorum gentilium libri,* bks. XIV–XV.
28. Dante, *Purgatorio,* XXII.73.
29. Dante, *Inferno,* IV.98–102.
30. Piccolomini, "Letter to Goro Lolli (1444)," in *Selected letters of Aeneas Silvius Piccolomini,* ed. and trans. Albert R. Baca (Northridge: San Fernando Valley State College, 1969), 34.
31. Basinio, *Hesperis,* 124–125 (VI.81–85, 89–91).
32. Ibid., 127 (VI.163–165).
33. Ibid., 36 (II.149–154).
34. "Basinii Parmensis Epistola ad divum Sigismundum Pandulphum Malatestam dominum Arimini illustrem: Laudes et preconia eius continens et suorum," in Ferruccio Ferri, *La giovinezza di un poeta: Basinii Parmensis Carmina* (Rimini:

Artigianelli, 1914), 41–45 (appendix XXIV, lines 115–118, 141–152). Mercury declares that Sigismondo's "fame has reached the Armenians and the Indians and is known throughout the heavenly sky," in Porcellio, "Mercurius in concione apud Deos sic loquitur," in Preudhomme, *Trium,* fol. 25r.

35. Basinio, *Isottaeus,* III.3.31–38.
36. Basinio, *Hesperis,* 188–189 (IX.164–176).
37. On epideictic readings of the *Aeneid* in the Renaissance that stressed Aeneas's weaknesses, and Filelfo's negative images of Sforza in the *Sforziad,* see Craig Kallendorf, *The Other Virgil: "Pessimistic" Readings of the Aeneid in Early Modern Culture* (Oxford: Oxford University Press, 2007), 29, 30–50, 58–60. On Filelfo's description of the sack of Piacenza, see Diana Robin, *Filelfo in Milan: Writings 1451–1477* (Princeton: Princeton University Press, 1991), 63–81.
38. Basinio, *Hesperis,* 239–241 (XI.316–369).
39. Ibid., 241 (XI.369–372).
40. Ibid., 244–245 (XI.450–475).
41. Ibid., 245–246 (XI.480–497).
42. Ibid., 253 (XII.146–151).
43. Ibid., 269–270 (XII: 556–580). Broglio, *Cronaca,* also stresses Antonello da Narni's bravery in his account of Vada but refers the reader to Basinio for details, in Luigi Tonini, *Rimini nella signoria de' Malatesti, parte seconda al volume quinto* (Rimini: Albertini, 1882), 235–237.
44. The oration is printed and studied in Anthony F. D'Elia, "Heroic Insubordination in the Army of Sigismondo Malatesta: Petrus Parleo's *pro milite,* Machiavelli, and the uses of Cicero and Livy," in *Humanism and Creativity in the Italian Renaissance: Essays in Honor of Ronald G. Witt,* ed. Christopher S. Celenza and Kenneth Gouwens (Leiden: Brill, 2006), 31–60. Carlo Tonini dates the oration in *La coltura letteraria e scientifica in Rimini dal secolo XIV ai primordi del XIX* (Rimini: Tipografia Danesi Già Albertini, 1884), vol. 1: 180.
45. Translated in D'Elia, "Heroic Insubordination," 43.
46. Ibid., 43.
47. Baldassare Castiglione, *Il cortegiano,* IV. 5–26.
48. Translated in D'Elia, "Heroic Insubordination," 44.
49. Livy, XXII.38.2.
50. Translated in D'Elia, "Heroic Insubordination," 44–45.
51. These are the three republican values enshrined in Cicero's writings, as noted in Ronald G. Witt, *"In the Footsteps of the Ancients:" The Origins of Humanism from Lovato to Bruni* (Leiden: Brill, 2000), 493.
52. Erasmus similarly uses a rhetorical exercise to criticize clerical celibacy. See Erasmus, "Encomium matrimonii," in "On the Writing of Letters," trans. Charles Fantazzi, in *Collected Works of Erasmus* 25 (Toronto: University of Toronto

Press, 1985), and discussion in Anthony F. D'Elia, *The Renaissance of Marriage in Fifteenth-Century Italy* (Cambridge: Harvard University Press, 2004), 131–132.

53. Basinio, *Hesperis,* 284–285 (XIII.245–270).
54. Ibid., 286–287 (XIII.294–316).
55. In his brief treatment of the siege, Poggio mentions Sigismondo's leadership but, like Basinio, highlights the bravery of another defender, Aquilanus Traviglianus, who pretended to defect to the enemy but then led a surprise attack and "raised the spirits of the defenders," Poggio Bracciolini, *Poggii Historia florentina* (Venice: Hertz, 1715), 375.
56. Basinio, *Isottaeus,* III.2.7–16.
57. Valturio, *De re militari,* 361 (bk. XII, ch. 7); P. Jones, *Malatesta,* 202, sees it as a failure.
58. Guarino, for example, tried to persuade the future ruler of Ferrara, Leonello d'Este, to learn to swim with the example of Caesar, as noted in Marianne Pade, *The Reception of Plutarch's Lives in Fifteenth-Century Italy* (Copenhagen: Museum Tusculanum Press, 2007), vol. 1: 235. Vergerio similarly refers to Augustus to encourage his dedicatee to learn to swim, Pier Paolo Vergerio, "The Character and Studies Befitting a Free-born Youth," in *Humanist Educational Treatises,* ed. and trans. Craig W. Kallendorf (Cambridge: Harvard University Press, 2002), 41 (ch. 68).
59. Valturio, *De re militari,* 328–344 (bk. XI, ch. 15): "Aemulatio gloriae et ducum comparatio atque praestantia." The debate over the greatest commander had been reignited with the reintroduction of Plutarch's biographies in the early fifteenth century, as discussed in Paul Botley, *Latin Translation in the Renaissance: The Theory and Practice of Leonardo Bruni, Giannozzo Manetti and Desiderius Erasmus* (Cambridge: Cambridge University Press, 2004), 16–17.
60. Valturio, *De re militari,* 343 (bk. XI, ch. 15).
61. Ibid., 343–344 (bk. XI, ch. 15).
62. See also, ibid., 13–14 (bk. I, ch. 2), where Valturio praises Sigismondo for being the greatest of his age in his emulation of the ancients but not as their equal.
63. Giannozzo Manetti, "Orazione quando fu dato il bastone a Gismondo Malatesta," published in Vespasiano da Bisticci, *Commentario della vita di Messer Giannozzo Manetti* (Turin: Unione Tipografico-Editrice, 1882), vol. 2: 203–228. On this brief campaign, see Vespasiano, *Commentario,* vol. 2: 42–45, 85–86; Carlo Tonini, *Compendio della storia di Rimini* (Bologna: Forni, 1895–1896), vol. 1: 534–535; P. Jones, *Malatesta,* 209. On the political and rhetorical context of the oration, see D'Elia, "Heroic Insubordination," 36–38.
64. Poggii Bracciolini, "Historia Florentina," in *Rerum italicarum scriptores,* ed. Lodovico Antonio Muratori (Milan: Ex Typographia Societatis Palatinae, 1731), vol. 20: 429.

65. Manetti, "Orazione," in Vespasiano, *Commentario,* vol. 2: 204–213. On the popularity of Bruni's treatise, see Charles Calvert Bayley, *War and Society in Renaissance Florence: The De Militia of Leonardo Bruni* (Toronto: University of Toronto, 1961), 227; trans. and intro. Gordon Griffiths, James Hankins, and David Thompson, *The Humanism of Leonardo Bruni: Selected Texts* (Binghamton: Medieval and Renaissance Texts and Studies, 1987), 110.
66. Vespasiano, *Commentario,* 86.
67. "In vitam Jannotii Manetti Naldi Naldii," in Muratori, *Rerum,* vol. 20: 591.
68. Piero Scapecchi, "Victoris imago, problemi relative al Tempio Malatestiano," *Arte Cristiana* 74 (1986): 155–164; Andrea Donati, "L'immagine vittoriosa di Sigismondo Pandolfo Malatesta e l'orazione di Giannozzo Manetti per la consegna del bastone di comando dell'esercito fiorentino (Vada, 30 settembre 1453)," *Studi romagnoli* 61 (2010): 774–822. See also Angelo Turchini, *Il Tempio Malatestiano, Sigismondo Malatesta e Leon Battista Alberti* (Cesena: "Il Ponte Vecchio," 2000), 357–362.
69. Manetti, "Orazione," in Vespasiano, *Commentari,* 224–225.
70. Ibid., 217–218.
71. "Epistola mandò Giannozzo Manetti a Niccolò Piccino capitano di Santa Chiesa quando era nella Marca," published in ibid., vol. 2: 184–189, esp. 187.
72. "Risposta del detto Nicolò Piccinino a Jannozzo Manetti," in ibid., 189–190.
73. For the debate in antiquity, see, for example, Lucian, *Dialogue of the Dead,* XXV. On Petrarch, see Ronald G. Witt, "The Rebirth of Romans as Models of Character *(De viris illustribus),*" in *Petrarch: A Critical Guide to the Complete Works,* ed. Victoria Kirkham and Armando Maggi (Chicago: University of Chicago Press, 2009), 108.
74. Gary Ianziti, *Writing History in Renaissance Italy: Leonardo Bruni and the Uses of the Past* (Cambridge: Harvard University Press, 2012), 35–41.
75. Robert Black, "Ancients and Moderns in the Renaissance: Rhetoric and History in Accolti's Dialogue on the Preeminence of Men of His Own Time," *Journal of the History of Ideas,* 43.1 (1982): 6; a translation of Poggio's dedication to Sigismondo of his *On the Misery of the Human Condition* is in *Cambridge Translations of Renaissance Philosophical Texts: vol. 1: Moral Philosophy,* ed. Jill Kraye (Cambridge: Cambridge University Press, 1997), 18–19.
76. Black, "Ancients," 18–19.
77. Valturio compares Sigismondo to Fabius Maximus in clemency, Caesar in eloquence, and to Marius, Alexander, and Caesar in temple building after victory and celebrating triumphs; Valturio, *De re militari,* 347 (bk. XI, ch. 16); 360 (bk. XII, ch. 7); 381 (bk. XII, ch. 13).
78. Ibid., 145 (bk. VII, ch. 17).
79. Aldo Francesco Massera, "Roberto Valturio: 'Omnium scientiarum doctor et monarcha' (1405–1475)," originally published in 1925–1927, reprinted in *Roberto*

Valturio, "De re militari." Saggi critici, ed. Paola Delbianco (Rimini: Guaraldi, 2006), 39.

80. Valturio, *De re militari,* 205 (bk. IX).
81. See, for example, Tacitus's description of Corbulo's endurance of cold in *Annals,* XIV.24; and Caesar's fearless conduct, Plutarch, "Life of Caesar," *Plutarch's Lives,* ed. and trans. Bernadotte Perrin (London: William Heinemann, 1919), vol. 7: 482–485 (ch. 17).
82. Suetonius, "Divus Iulius," 53; Plutarch, "Life of Caesar," 484–485 (ch. 17). On the classical sources for this example, see Anthony F. D'Elia, "Iron Stomach: The Heroism of Eating Rancid Food, a *locus classicus*?" in *Renaissance Studies in Honor of Joseph Connors,* ed. Machtelt Israëls, Louis A. Waldman, et al. (Florence: Villa I Tatti, 2013), 155–159.
83. Plutarch, "Life of Antony," *Plutarch's Lives,* ed. and trans. Bernadotte Perrin (London: William Heinemann, 1920), vol. 9: 174–175 (ch. 17).
84. The Malatesta chronicler, Broglio, refers specifically to Leonardo Bruni's translation of Plutarch's life of Mark Antony (1404–1405), in "Estratti della Cronaca universale di Broglia di Tartaglia da Lavello," in *Cronache Malatestiane dei secoli XIV e XV,* ed. Aldo Francesco Massèra (Bologna: N. Zanichelli, 1922–1924), 181–192 (XV.2). For the popularity of Plutarch, see Pade, *Reception,* esp. on Bruni's "Antonius," vol. 1: 127–132.

8. Sigismondo's Peril and Defiance

1. Giovanni Soranzo, *Pio II e la politica italiana nella lotta contro i Malatesti (1457–1463)* (Padua: Fratelli Drucker, 1911), 228–229; Giovanni Soranzo, "Un'invettiva della curia romana contro Sigismondo Pandolfo Malatesta," *La Romagna,* 7 (1910): 475–476; Franco Gaeta, "La 'leggenda' di Sigismondo Malatesta," *Studi malatestiani,* ed. Philip James Jones (Rome: Istituto Storico Italiano per il Medioevo, 1978), 165.
2. In Soranzo, *Pio II,* 483–484 (document no. 21). See also the Mantuan ambassador's description in ibid., 486–487 (document no. 24).
3. Andrea Benzi-Pius II, "Discipula veritatis," in *Pii secundi Epistolae* (Milan: Antonius Zarothus, 1487), n.p., 79 in scan of this edition, available at http://fondosdigitales.us.es/fondos/libros/204/67/epistola-siue-oratio-pii-in-conuentu-mantuano/. Henceforth pages refer to this scanned edition.
4. Bartolomeo Maraschi, letter to Barbara of Brandenburg, the Marquise of Mantua, (Rome, 27 April 1462), described in *Sigismondo Pandolfo Malatesta e il suo Tempo,* ed. Franca Arduini (Rimini: Neri Pozza, 1970), 28–29.
5. Benzi-Pius II, *Discipula,* 96. If Sigismondo was indeed an atheist, as Pius alleged, then the idea of hell had no deterrent value against immoral behavior.

6. Ibid., 96–97.
7. Ibid., 97.
8. Ludwig von Pastor, *The History of the Popes from the Close of the Middle Ages,* ed. Frederick Ignatius Antrobus (St. Louis: Herder, 1906), vol. 3: 125, 409 (appendix 56).
9. Brian Tierney, *The Crisis of Church and State, 1050–1300, with Selected Documents* (Toronto and Buffalo: University of Toronto and the Medieval Academy of America, 1988 (orig. 1964)); Anthony F. D'Elia, *A Sudden Terror: The Plot to Murder the Pope in Renaissance Rome* (Cambridge: Harvard University Press, 2009), 40–76.
10. Mantuan ambassador report, published in Soranzo, *Pio II,* 486 (appendix 24); Francesco Gaetano Battaglini, *Della vita e de' fatti di Sigismondo Pandolfo Malatesta* (Rimini: Albertiniana, 1794), 523.
11. Enea Silvio Piccolomini Papa Pio II, *I commentarii,* ed. Luigi Totaro, second edition (Milan: Adelphi, 2004), 1975–1995 (bk. X, ch. 26), 2008–2011 (bk. X, ch. 29). On this, see Philip James Jones, *The Malatesta of Rimini and the Papal State: A Political History* (Cambridge: Cambridge University Press, 1974), 229–231; Soranzo, *Pio II;* Pastor, *History of the Popes,* vol. 3: 125–126.
12. Reginald Gregoire, "Tra leggenda agiografica e religiosita' francescana: Galeotto Roberto Malatesta (1432)," in *Templum Mirabile: Atti del convegno sul Tempio Malatestiano* (Rimini: Fondazione Cassa di Risparmio di Rimini, 2003), 128.
13. Basinio da Parma, "Hesperis," in *Basinii parmensis poetae opera praestantiora* (Rimini: Albertiniana, 1794), vol. 1: 180–181 (VIII.384–395).
14. Ibid., 192 (IX.255–265).
15. Ibid., 193 (IX.271–284).
16. Ibid., 195 (IX.318–325).
17. Ibid., 197 (IX.380–381).
18. Ibid., 196–197 (IX.363–372).
19. Giovanni Cocchi, *De immortalitate animae,* MS, Biblioteca Casanatense cod. 103. On Giovanni da Ferrara, or Cocchi, see Julius Kirschner, "Cocchi, Giovanni," *Dizionario biografico degli italiani,* 26 (Rome: Istituto della Enciclopedia italiana,1982); Domenico Fava, "Fra Giovanni e Sigismondo Malatesta," in *Scritti vari dedicati a Mario Armanni in occasione del suo sessantesimo compleanno* (Milan: Hoepli, 1938), 49–62.
20. Augustine, *The City of God Against the Pagans,* ed. and trans. R. W. Dyson (Cambridge: Cambridge University Press, 1998–2010), bk. XIX, ch. 28; bk. XXI, chs. 2–3, 9.
21. Cocchi, *De immortalitate,* fols. 132r–133r (III.1).
22. Ibid., fols. 131v–132r (III.1); Augustine, *City of God,* XXI.10.
23. Cocchi, *De immortalitate,* fols. 123v–124r (III.1); Macrobius, *Commentary on the Dream of Scipio,* trans. William Harris Stahl (New York: Columbia University Press, 1990 (orig. 1952)), 128–129, (bk. X, chs. 9–17).

24. Cocchi, *De immortalitate,* fols. 115r–122v (III.1).
25. Ibid., fol. 113r–113v (III.1).
26. Ibid., fols. 122v–126v (III.2).
27. The official letter (dated 23 February 1461) that Pius sent to Sigismondo's vassals relieving them of their oath of fealty is in Luigi Tonini, *Rimini nella signoria de' Malatesti, parte seconda al volume quinto: Appendice di documenti* (Rimini: Albertini, 1882), 222–223.
28. Gaspare Broglio, *Cronaca,* in Luigi Tonini, *Rimini nella signoria de' Malatesti, parte seconda al volume quinto* (Rimini: Albertini, 1882), 282–283.
29. Ibid., 283, 286, 287.
30. Although surprising, Sigismondo's attempt was not unique: both Lorenzo de' Medici and Ferrante of Naples had alliances with the Turks against the Venetians in the 1460s and 1470s, as discussed in D'Elia, *Sudden Terror,* 108–117, 131.
31. MS, Venice, Biblioteca Marciana Lat. VIII 29 (2498), fols. 283v–284r. The same letter of dedication is in MS, Paris, Biblioteque Nationale cod. Lat. 7236, fols. 200–201, and transcribed in Giovanni Soranzo, "Una missione di Sigismondo Pandolfo Malatesta a Maometto II nel 1461," *La Romagna,* 3.6 (1909): 14–16.
32. Basinio, *Hesperis,* 232–233 (XI.144–148, 169–171). Clementini published a 1453 letter on behalf of Nicholas V, in which the author praises Sigismondo's military skill and tries to shame him into undertaking a crusade for Constantinople, in Cesare Clementini, *Raccolto istorico della fondatione di Rimini* (Bologna: Forni, 1969), 386–387 (facsimile of the 1617/1627 edition).
33. Basinio, *Hesperis,* 256 (XII.331–340). Basinio similarly calls for Sigismondo to liberate Constantinople and wage war on the Turks in Basinio, *Astronomicon,* facsimile of the manuscript, trans. Marinella De Luca, ed. Donatella Frioli and Giordana Mariani Canova (Rimini: Cassa di Risparmio di Rimini, 1994), 134–141 (II.457–487).
34. Although even quite late in the poem Basinio says the Tuscan War was greater than Troy, Basinio, *Hesperis,* 256 (XII.227–230).
35. Soranzo, "Una missione," 5–8; Stefania Bolognesi, "La Parabola discendente di Sigismondo Pandolfo: Dall'alleanza con gli Angioini alla guerra con Pio II," in *La signoria di Sigismondo Malatesta,* vol. 2: *La politica e le imprese militari,* ed. Anna Falcioni (Rimini: Bruno Ghigi, 2006), 134–138.
36. Soranzo, "Una missione," 8.
37. Pio II, *I commentarii,* 1980–1981, 1992–1993 (bk. X, ch. 26). At the council of Mantua, Pius reports Sigismondo's military advice on winning a crusade against the Turks, ibid., 580–581 (bk. III, ch. 34).
38. Soranzo, "Una missione," 4, 12. Soranzo points out that several early manuscripts of the *De re militari* contain an illustration of the Adriatic Sea in bk. XI.

39. Pio II, *I commentarii,* 1914–1923 (bk. X, ch. 14).
40. Ibid., 1972–1973 (bk. X, ch. 25).
41. Ibid., 2308–2315 (bk. XII, ch. 8), 2458–2463 (bk. XII, ch. 33). See also Pius's speech to the cardinals in which he summarizes the campaign and declares plague, famine, and war to be the divine retribution for Sigismondo's sacrilege, in ibid., 2428–2431 (bk. 12, ch. 31).
42. Ibid., 2488–2489 (bk. XII, ch. 40); Pastor, *History of the Popes,* vol. 3: 125–128.
43. Pio II, *I commentarii,* 2488–2493 (bk. XII, ch. 40); Pastor, *History of the Popes,* vol. 3: 125–128; P. Jones, *Malatesta,* 228–238; Soranzo, *Pio II,* 442–449.
44. 5 December 1463, letter to Pier Francesco de' Medici, as quoted in Italian by P. Jones, *Malatesta,* 239.
45. Kenneth M. Setton, *The Papacy and the Levant (1204–1571)* (Philadelphia: American Philosophical Society, 1978), 260–270.
46. See Broglio's account in Tonini, *Rimini nella signoria de' Malatesti,* 302–305; Setton, *The Papacy and the Levant,* 251–253; Anna Falcioni, "Le ultime imprese militari di Sigismondo (1464–1468)," in *La signoria di Sigismondo Malatesta,* 147–169; P. Jones, *Malatesta,* 240–241.
47. P. Jones, *Malatesta,* 241; Augusto Campana, "Atti, Isotta degli," in *Dizionario biografico degli italiani* vol. 4 (Rome: Istituto della Enciclopedia italiana, 1962), 551.
48. For what follows, see Jones, *Malatesta,* 242–245, and Falcioni, "Le ultime imprese," 169–175.
49. Broglio, in Tonini, *Rimini nella signoria de' Malatesti,* 313–314; Jones, *Malatesta,* 244, n.3; Clementini, *Raccolto istorico della fondatione di Rimini,* 463, provides further details.
50. D'Elia, *Sudden Terror,* 127–128.
51. Anna Zanoli, "Callimaco a Sigismondo Malatesti," in *Templum Mirabile: Atti del convegno sul Tempio Malatestiano* (Rimini: Cassa di Risparmio di Rimini, 2003), 289–301; Bartolomeo Platina, "Liber de vita Christi ac omnium ponitificum," in *Rerum Italicarum Scriptores,* ed. Giacinto Gaida, vol. 3.1 (Bologna: Zanichelli, 1913–1932), 384.
52. Tonini, *Rimini nella signoria de' Malatesti,* 320–324; P. Jones, *Malatesta,* 245.
53. Quoted and translated in John Monfasani, *George of Trebizond: A Biography and a Study of His Rhetoric and Logic* (Leiden: Brill, 1976), 214. On Plethon's tomb, see Niketas Siniossoglou, *Radical Platonism in Byzantium: Illumination and Utopia in Gemistos Plethon* (Cambridge: Cambridge University Press, 2011), 9.
54. Poggio Bracciolini, "On the Misery of the Human Condition," in *Cambridge Translations of Renaissance Philosophical Texts: vol. 1: Moral Philosophy,* ed. Jill Kraye, trans. Martin Davies (Cambridge: Cambridge University Press, 1997), 22.

Conclusion

1. "Basinii Parmensis Epistola ad divum Sigismundum Pandulphum Malatestam dominum Arimini illustrem: Laudes et preconia eius continens et suorum," in *La giovinezza di un poeta: Basinii Parmensis Carmina,* ed. Ferruccio Ferri (Rimini: Artigianelli, 1914), 41–45 (appendix XXIV, lines, 97–105).
2. Basinio da Parma, "Hesperis," in *Basinii parmensis poetae opera praestantiora* (Rimini: Albertiniana, 1794), vol. 1: *Hesperis,* 103 (V.97–115).
3. Ibid., 105 (V.146–157).
4. P. J. Jones, *The Malatesta of Rimini and the Papal State: A Political History* (Cambridge: Cambridge University Press, 1974), 95–96.
5. Basinio, *Hesperis,* 288 (XIII.343–348).
6. In the *Discipula,* Sigismondo is described attacking a German noblewoman "*superos implorantem foeminam arripuit,*" where *superos* must refer to the saints: "as she was invoking the saints." Andrea Benzi-Pius II, "Discipula veritatis," in *Pii secundi Epistolae* (Milan: Antonius Zarothus, 1487), n.p., 75 in scan of this edition, available at http://fondosdigitales.us.es/fondos/libros/204/67/epistola-siue-oratio-pii-in-conuentu-mantuano/. Henceforth pages refer to this scanned edition.
7. "Basinius in honorem gloriosae Virginis Mariae matris Iesu omnipotentis," in *La giovinezza di un poeta,* ed. Ferruccio Ferri (appendix III, lines 7–50).
8. Paul Oskar Kristeller, *Renaissance Thought: The Classic, Scholastic, and Humanist Strains* (New York: Harper, 1955); Charles Trinkaus, *In Our Image and Likeness: Humanity and Divinity in Italian Humanist Thought,* 2 vols. (London: Constable, 1970); Charles Trinkaus, *The Scope of Renaissance Humanism* (Ann Arbor: Michigan University Press, 1983). John Monfasani, "Platonic Paganism in the Fifteenth Century," in *Reconsidering the Renaissance,* ed. Mario A. Di Cesare (Binghamton: Center for Medieval and Early Renaissance Studies, 1992), 45–61, contains an excellent synopsis of the issue.
9. John O'Malley, *Praise and Blame in Renaissance Rome* (Durham: Duke University Press, 1979); Alison Frazier, *Possible Lives: Authors and Saints in Renaissance Italy* (New York: Columbia University Press, 2005); Salvatore Camporeale, *Lorenzo Valla: Umanesimo, riforma e controriforma: Studi e testi* (Rome: Edizioni di Storia e Letteratura, 2002).
10. See, for example, William J. Bouwsma, "The Two Faces of Humanism: Stoicism and Augustinianism in Renaissance Thought," in *Itinerarium Italicum: The Profile of the Italian Renaissance in the Mirror of its European Transformations,* ed. Heiko A. Oberman and Thomas A. Brady (Leiden: Brill, 1975), 3–60.
11. See Marsilio Ficino, *Platonic Theology,* ed. James Hankins with William Bowen, trans. Michael J. B. Allen and John Warden, 6 vols. (Cambridge: Harvard

University Press, 2001–2006); James Hankins, *Plato in the Italian Renaissance,* 2 vols. (Leiden: Brill, 1990); James Hankins, ed., *The Cambridge Companion to Renaissance Philosophy* (Cambridge: Cambridge University Press, 2007); James Hankins, "Marsilio Ficino on *Reminiscentia* and the transmigration of souls," *Rinascimento,* 45 (2005): 3–17; Brian Copenhaver, "Hermes Trismegistus, Proclus and the Question of a Philosophy of Magic in the Renaissance," in *Hermeticism and the Renaissance: Intellectual History and the Occult in Early Modern Europe,* ed. Ingrid Merkel and Allen G. Debus (Washington, D.C.: Folger Shakespeare Library, 1988), 79–93.

12. Anthony Grafton, *Cardano's Cosmos: The Worlds and Works of a Renaissance Astrologer* (Cambridge: Harvard University Press, 1999); Ottavia Niccoli, *Prophecy and People in Renaissance Italy* (Princeton: Princeton University Press, 1990).
13. Christopher S. Celenza, *The Lost Italian Renaissance: Humanists, Historians, and Latin's Legacy* (Baltimore: Johns Hopkins University Press, 2004); Christopher S. Celenza, "Lorenzo Valla, 'Paganism,' and Orthodoxy," *Modern Language Notes,* 119.1 (2004): 66–87; Quentin Skinner, *The Foundations of Modern Political Thought, vol. I: The Renaissance* (Cambridge: Cambridge University Press, 1978)
14. For the scholarly debate on Machiavelli's views on religion, see the synopsis in Niccolò Machiavelli, *Discourses on Livy,* trans. Harvey Mansfield and Nathan Tarcov (Chicago: Chicago University Press, 1996), introduction, xxxiii–xxxvi; and the essays dedicated to the subject in *Journal of the History of Ideas* 60.4 (1999).
15. In general, see Quentin Skinner, *Machiavelli* (Oxford: Oxford University Press, 1981); Quentin Skinner, *Visions of Politics: Volume II: Renaissance Virtues* (Cambridge: Cambridge University Press, 2002); Harvey C. Mansfield, *Machiavelli's Virtue* (Chicago: University of Chicago Press, 1996).
16. For Machiavelli's criticism of the popes and the church, see *Discourses on the First Decade of Livy* (1517), I.12 and I.27, where he suggests killing the pope and all the cardinals.
17. Most forcefully argued in *Discourses on the First Decade of Livy* (1517), II.2. On this, see Skinner, *Foundations,* 87–101. On manliness and violence, see Timothy J. Lukes, "Lionizing Machiavelli," *The American Political Science Review,* 95.3 (2001): 561–575.
18. *Discourses on the First Decade of Livy* (1517), I.11, I.14, II.1, passim. On pagan morality, see the classic essay by Isaiah Berlin, "The Originality of Machiavelli," in *Studies on Machiavelli,* ed. Myron P. Gilmore (Florence: Sansoni, 1972), 149–206; Paul A. Rahe, "In the Shadow of Lucretius: The Epicurean Foundations of Machiavelli's Political Thought," *History of Political Thought,* 28.1 (Spring 2007): 30–55.
19. See Pico's 900 theses, ed. and trans. in S. A. Farmer, *Syncretism in the West: Pico's 900 Theses (1486): The Evolution of Traditional Religious and Philosophical Systems*

(Tempe: Medieval and Renaissance Texts and Studies, 1998). On Pico and syncretism, see Edgar Wind, *Pagan Mysteries in the Renaissance: an Exploration of Philosophical and Mystical Sources of Iconography in Renaissance Art,* second edition (New York: Norton, 1968), 17–25; and *Pico della Mirandola: New Essays,* ed. M. V. Dougherty (Cambridge: Cambridge University Press, 2008).

20. Sabine MacCormack, *Shadows of Poetry. Vergil in the Mind of Augustine* (Berkeley: University of California Press, 1998), 140, 152; Jean Seznec, *The Survival of the Pagan Gods: The Mythological Tradition and Its Place in Renaissance Humanism and Art,* trans. Barbara F. Sessions (Princeton: Princeton University Press, 1953), 212–213; Luc Brisson, *How Philosophers Saved Myths: Allegorical Interpretation and Classical Mythology* (Chicago: Chicago University Press, 2008), 127; Peter Burke, *Popular Culture in Early Modern Europe* (London: Temple Smith, 1978), 289–334.

21. Brian P. Levack, *The Witchhunt in Early Modern Europe,* third edition (New York: Routledge, 2013), 30–73; Robert W. Scribner, "The Reformation, Popular Magic, and the 'Disenchantment of the World,'" *The Journal of Interdisciplinary History,* 23.3 (Winter 1993): 475–494.

22. Seznec, *Survival,* 132–137. Christopher P. Jones has recently argued that Christians in late antiquity largely constructed the idea of pagans by separating and defining them as others, even though the differences were not always so clear-cut, in *Between Pagan and Christian* (Cambridge: Harvard University Press, 2014).

23. On the use of literature as sources for social history, see Lauro Martines, *Strong Words: Writing and Social Strain in the Italian Renaissance* (Baltimore: The Johns Hopkins University Press, 2001); Lauro Martines, "The Italian Renaissance Tale as History," in *Language and Images of Renaissance Italy,* ed. Alison Brown (Oxford: Clarendon Press, 1995), 313–330; Lauro Martines, *An Italian Renaissance Sextet: Six Tales in Historical Context* (Toronto: University of Toronto Press, 2004); Robert Darnton, "Peasants Tell Tales: The Meaning of Mother Goose," in *The Great Cat Massacre and Other Episodes in French Cultural History* (New York: Basic Books, 1984), 9–72.

24. In his discussion of hell (*City of God,* XXI.3), for example, Augustine quotes the *Aeneid* (6.719–721) about how souls desire to return to bodies and, therefore, can feel pain. On Augustine's reverential use of Virgil, see MacCormack, *Shadows,* 80, 84–85, 89–91, 105–107, 132–174. Later in life, however, Augustine expressed regret at the numerous references to Virgil and the pagan poets in his early writings, as noted in MacCormack, *Shadows,* 73.

25. Benzi-Pius II, *Discipula,* 84.

26. Jacob Burckhardt, *The Civilization of the Renaissance in Italy,* trans. S. G. C. Middlemore (New York: Penguin, 1990), 39, 151, 288.

Acknowledgments

My interest in Sigismondo Malatesta began when I was doing research for my dissertation and first book on nuptial oratory (2004). A little-known humanist, Pietro Parleo, had composed two wedding orations for members of Sigismondo's court. The epithalamia were in a manuscript in the Marciana library in Venice, which also contained a set piece that Parleo had composed in defense of a captain who had disobeyed Sigismondo, engaged the enemy, and won a stunning victory in battle. The classical ideals, Ciceronian style, and examples from Livy in the oration intrigued me and led to the publication of an article in 2006. Research for my first book and this article introduced me to Basinio, Valturio, and the largely untapped humanist culture of Sigismondo's court. In my 2009 book, I had detected a revived pagan homosexual culture among the so-called humanist conspirators against the pope in 1468. Malatesta literature now offered me the opportunity to examine pagan notions of virtue, manliness, sexuality, and religion in the public image of the most notorious proponent of the Italian Renaissance, Sigismondo Malatesta.

Two foundations provided funds for the research of this book. A grant from the Social Sciences and Humanities Research Council of Canada paid for targeted research trips to Rimini, Rome, and London, and the tools necessary for a historical investigation. In 2009–2010 I was the Lila-Wallace Reader's Digest Fellow at Villa I Tatti, The Harvard University Center for the Italian Renaissance, Florence, Italy. This wonderful year of research and study in a beautiful Tuscan villa was especially fertile because of the other fellows and scholars, with whom I discussed and debated ideas at lunches, coffee, and drinks, and who spared no criticism at a presentation of my preliminary research. I thank the following Tattiani: Monica Azzolini, Amy Bloch, Claudia Bolgia, Daniel Bornstein, Abi Brundin, Lorenzo Calvelli, Chris Carlsmith, Claudia Chierichini, Françoise Connors, Joe Connors, Donal Cooper, Michael Cuthbert, Anne Dunlop, Serena Ferente, Francesca Fiorani, Allen Grieco, Bob La France, Kate Lowe, Ann Moyer, Deborah Parker, Michael Rocke, Marc

Schachter, Carlo Taviani, Louis Waldman, and Joanna Woods-Marsden. My friends and colleagues at Queen's University, especially Jeff Collins, Ana Siljak, Andrew Jainchill, Harold Mah, Rebecca Manley, Rosanne Currarino, Jeff McNairn, Richard Greenfield, Amitava Chowdhury, Jamey Carson, Laura Carlson, Donald Akenson, Nancy Van Deusen, Cathleen Hoeniger, Pierre du Prey, Chris Fanning, and Michael and Marie-Claire Vandenburg, make doing research at this university enjoyable and productive. I am grateful for the feedback from other colleagues at an invited lecture in the middle stages of the book, including Jim Stayer, Jim Pritchard, Jane Errington, David Parker, and Marguerite Van Die. The late David McTavish, who had been a great supporter of my work since the beginning of my Queen's employment in 2000, will be sorely missed.

My ideas and chapter topics were largely formed in composing six papers for the Renaissance Society of America Annual Conference (2004, 2009–2012, 2014). Friends and colleagues on panels included Timothy Kircher, David Marsh, Margaret Meserve, Emily O'Brien, and Scott Blanchard. Two talks at the University of Toronto were also helpful, the first in December 2010, and then in June 2014, at which Konrad Eisenbichler and Mark Jurdjevic made suggestions. This book has especially benefited from the support and criticisms of Christopher Celenza, Kenneth Gouwens, Anthony Grafton, James Hankins, Gary Ianziti, Margaret King, and the anonymous readers for Harvard University Press. My editor, Kathleen McDermott, has been a great advocate throughout the lengthy publication process.

The research and writing of this book benefited tremendously from my training in Brazilian Jiu-Jitsu since 2008. I cannot imagine having completed the book without the regular beatings, submissions, sweat, and camaraderie of four martial arts gyms on two continents. All of my partners have contributed to my growth, but especially my coaches Chris Wellstood (Nova Unaio) and Rob Wynne in Kingston, Ontario, and in Florence Mario Puccione (Centurion Jiu-Jitsu) and Francesco Braccini (RUA67/Tribe Jiu-Jitsu). Their continued guidance in this intense martial art opened up new ways of thinking about the life of Sigismondo Malatesta, who was a student of martial arts, wrestled, and cultivated the ancient Greek ideal of mind and body. Reading and often having to decipher the challenging Latin of Basinio and Valturio, writing, and thinking through historical argumentation during the day was refreshingly complemented by evening efforts to learn complex moves in jiu-jitsu.

My wife and colleague in arms (so to speak), Una Roman D'Elia, is a rock on whose foundation I have formed and worked out my ideas. Her support, criticisms, and suggested revisions were essential at every stage of this book: inception, research, argumentation, writing, editing, rewriting, and the countless additional revisions that have led to publication. Our two children, Lucy and Zoe, inspire us ever to continue the fight. I dedicate this book to them.

Index